BRINGING INTERIORS TO LIGHT

BRINGING INTERIORS TO LIGHT

The Principles and Practices of Lighting Design

FRAN KELLOGG SMITH, ASID/CSI

FRED J. BERTOLONE, MIES/IALD

EDITED BY DIANE CASELLA HINES

WHITNEY LIBRARY OF DESIGN
an imprint of Watson-Guptill Publications/New York

To the memory of
John E. Flynn, AIA/FIES

DISCLAIMER

Senior Editor: Julia Moore
Associate Editor: Victoria Craven
Designer: Bob Fillie
Production Manager: Hector Campbell
Set in 9 point Century Old Style

Copyright © 1986 by Fran Kellogg Smith and
Fred J. Bertolone

First published 1986 in New York by the Whitney Library of Design
an imprint of Watson-Guptill Publications,
a division of Billboard Publications, Inc.,
1515 Broadway, New York, NY 10036

Library of Congress Cataloging-in-Publication Data

Smith, Fran Kellogg.
  Bringing interiors to light.

  Bibliography: p.
  Includes index.
  1. Interior lighting—Design.   I. Bertolone, Fred J.
II. Title.
TH7703.S57   1986   621.32′2   86-1687
ISBN 0-8230-7080-8

Distributed in the United Kingdom by Phaidon Press Ltd.,
Littlegate House, St. Ebbe's St., Oxford

Manufactured in U.S.A.

First Printing, 1986
4 5 6 7 8 9 / 91 90 89

CREDITS

Figure 1-8: Interior Design, Karen Libbey, ASID Associate; Lighting Design, Jan Moyer, ASID, Luminae. Figure 2-1: Interior Design, Leslie Emlay, ASID; Lighting Design, Fran Kellogg Smith, ASID, Luminae. Figure 2-2: Interior Design, Charles Falls, ASID. Figure 6-6: Interior Design, Florence Chandler, ASID; Lighting Design, Fran Kellogg Smith, ASID, Luminae. Color Plate 9: Interior Design, Peg E. Gorson, ASID; Lighting Design, Fran Kellogg Smith, Luminae. Color Plate 10: Interior Design, K.S. Wilshire. Color Plate 15: Lighting Design, Tully Weiss, MIES. Figure C2-1: Interior Design, Trisha Wilson & Associates; Lighting Design, Candace Kling, IALD. Figure C4-1: Interior Design, Charles Pfister, ASID; Architecture, SOM; Lighting Design, Jules Horton, IALD. Figure C5-1: Interior Design, Ingrid Leister, AIA, ASID; Lighting Design, Michael D. Shanus, MIES. Figure C6-1: Interior Design, Philip Schwartz, IBD; Architecture, L.A. Design; Lighting Design, Dick Harms, MIES, Luminae. Figure C8-3: Architecture, Smith, Henchman & Grylls. Figure 8-10: Interior Design, Karen Libbey, ASID Associate. Figure 9-3: Fiber optics display modules by Mario Conti. Figure 9-5: Interior Design, Nancy Glenn, ASID; Lighting Design, Fran Kellogg Smith, ASID, Luminae.

ACKNOWLEDGMENTS

THE AUTHORS would like to thank the many individuals who wittingly and unwittingly contributed to any wisdom or folly within. The technical references of John E. Kaufman and the Illuminating Engineering Society of North America kept us from becoming too lightheaded. James Nuckolls, Bill Lam, Lou Erhardt, Peter Boyce, and the late John Flynn were influential in our continuing the "perception" school of lighting philosophy. The artistry of David Winfield Willson, Mary Nichols, Jan Moyer, and Jim Terrell gave inspiration and direction to all of us who practice environmental lighting design. The authors' early mentors—Frank LaGiusa, The Lighting Institute of the General Electric Company, and Charlie Buchanan—and the others of the "Over the Hill Gang" can never be fully repaid.

Many people generously contributed their time to improve particular chapters. Our deepest appreciation goes to Michael Wilde and Stephen Selkowitz of The Lawrence Berkeley Laboratory; Katherine Burke, IDC; Ron Strandberg, IDC; Jo Drummond, CSI; Jerry Orland, FCSI; Hans Meier, FCSI; Basil Callori, AIA; Stephen Kliment, FAIA; Russ Randall, IEEE; James Jewell, MIES; Dorothy Fowles, IDEC; Betty Ann Raschko, IDEC; Jan Moyer, ASID; Michael Souter, ASID; Allen Lucas, ASID; Pat Pinckney, IALD; Motoko Ishii, IALD; John Watson; and in particular, Dr. Walter Chase, O.D.

The authors' children made their own dinners, selected their own schools and colleges, made their own travel arrangements, and moved away during this book's development. We would like to thank Lisa, Scott, Carol, and Christy for their early sainthood. In the same vein, Luminae staff members were more than reasonable when they were put off with, "We can't work on that project now, we're thinking!" Thank you, Jan, Nancy, Joanne, Jim, Patty, and Dick, especially.

Last of all, we thank our associates in this enterprise, Diane Casella Hines and Reiko Hayashi. Their understanding and support made this book possible.

CONTENTS

Acknowledgments   5

Preface   8

PART ONE   CREATING YOUR DESIGN   **10**

Chapter One   **ANALYZING THE PROJECT**
                Client Motivation   12
                Client Vision   14
                Daylighting   14
                Color   19
                Activities   22
                Mood   25

Chapter Two   **USING COMPOSITIONAL LIGHTING TECHNIQUES**
                Lighting for Unity and Harmony   28
                Compositional Working Methods   28
                Specific Lighting Techniques   30
                Decorative Fixtures   37
                Comparing Compositional Lighting Techniques   37

Chapter Three **WORKING WITH CONSTRAINTS**
                Design and Construction Schedules   40
                Complexity of Construction   43
                Code Compliance   46
                Budget   49

Chapter Four **SELECTING A LIGHT SOURCE**
                Incandescent and Gaseous-Discharge Lamps   52
                Optical Characteristics   52
                Electrical Efficiency   52
                Lamp Life/Dimming   57
                Color Rendering   58
                Invisible Light   59

Chapter Five **SELECTING FIXTURES**
                Beam Shapes   62
                Mountings   62
                Fixture Costs   72
                Appearance   73
                Safety   73
                Reading Fixture Catalogs   76

Chapter Six   **COMMUNICATING YOUR DESIGN**
                Drawings   78
                Project Manual Documents   95

PART TWO   LIGHTING SPECIFIC INTERIORS   **116**

Case Study One   **HIGHLIGHTING AN ENTRY:** La Entrada   118

Case Study Two   **INTERACTING IN PUBLIC:** Marriott Hotel Lobby   124

Case Study Three **CREATING A MOOD:** Willson Dining Room   130

Case Study Four	**MULTIPLYING PRODUCTIVITY:** California First Bank	134
Case Study Five	**DAYLIGHTING AN OPEN OFFICE:** Lockheed Missiles and Space Company	142
Case Study Six	**ENHANCING MERCHANDISE:** The Boutique ICE	148
Case Study Seven	**DISPLAYING FOR POSTERITY:** The Vatican Pavilion of the Louisiana World Exposition	154
Case Study Eight	**LIGHTING WITH CARE:** The Charter House Retirement Center	160
Case Study Nine	**DINING IN STYLE:** Anthony's Restaurant	168

	PART THREE	**SPECIAL LIGHTING NEEDS**	**174**
Chapter Seven	**LIGHTING FOR THE AGED AND INFIRM**		
	Barrier-Free Design Codes		176
	The Aging Eye		176
	The Ambulatory		178
	The Nonambulatory		179
Chapter Eight	**LIGHTING PLANTS—INDOORS AND OUTDOORS**		
	Indoors		182
	Outdoors		186
Chapter Nine	**LIGHT AS ART**		
	Hardware		192
	Kinetic Effects		194
	Illusions		196

	APPENDIXES	**200**
Appendix A	**LIGHTING CHARTS**	
	1. Structural Lighting Charts	201
	2. Beam Spread Charts	204
Appendix B	**LIGHTING DOCUMENTS**	
	1. Specifications for Construction Schedules	206
	2. Common Code Provisions	207
	3. Special Code Conditions	208
	4. Specific Language Regarding Substituted Items	208
	5. Application of Electrical Requirements in Typical Houses	209
	6. Submittals	210
	7. Sample Lighting Specifications	211
	8. Sample Additional Work Clause	212
	9. Sample Worksheet for Projecting Designers' Hours	212
	10. Sample Agreement for Lighting Consulting Services	213
Appendix C	**READY REFERENCE**	
	1. Line Types and Weights	214
	2. Lighting-Related Abbreviations	215
	3. Light and Light-Related Requirements for Popular Species of Indoor Plants	216
Appendix D	**DIRECTORY**	
	1. Lighting Manufacturers	218
	2. Lighting Organizations	218
Selected Bibliography		219
Index		221

PREFACE

There have always been two philosophies of interior lighting design. As early as 1912, Dr. Louis Bell laid out the choices:

> . . .two courses are open to the designer. In the first place, he can have the whole space lighted uniformly, more or less approximating the effect of a room receiving daylight through its windows. Or, throwing aside any purpose to simulate daylight in intensity or distribution . . . he can put artificial light simply where it is needed to serve the ends of art and convenience . . .[1]

Designers who subscribe to the first philosophy mentioned by Dr. Bell typically use recommended levels of illumination, glare-free fixtures, and energy-efficient light sources in an attempt to imitate the overcast skies idealized in the architectural engineering programs of the 1950s. But spaces lighted in this manner are, we believe, neither attractive and exciting, nor human. By adhering to the latter philosophy—one based on utility and aesthetics—designers can illuminate interiors so that they possess humanity, and also conserve energy.

Our book is intended as a guide to the art of lighting design. We offer a simple, secure procedure that will enable professionals to weave lighting into the fabric of design concept and decisions. This procedure derives from a two-fold thesis: (1) the proper person to coordinate lighting decisions is the interior designer or interior architect, and (2) lighting and finishes should be selected simultaneously. This thesis is based on studies that have proven that human behavior and impressions of a space are "cued" by surface brightnesses.[2] Unconsciously our movements and minds seek out the light. In the mind, brightness is a phenomenon of contrasts; these contrasts result from the physics occurring between interior finishes and reflected light. Establishing these contrasts is a matter of manipulating the finishes as well as the lighting.

Although this book is written especially for interior designers and architects, it is also of value to all persons involved in design and construction. Electrical engineers and contractors, building owners and managers, and those supplying fixtures and lamps are often asked for lighting recommendations. To produce more than a dutiful lighting layout, each should understand how to evaluate the lighting strategies offered by various surface finishes, daylighting conditions, and visibility requirements. In this book, these considerations are assembled in the logical sequence of the design process itself so that decisions can be made without confusion.

Bringing Interiors to Light is divided into three parts: (1) Creating and Communicating Your Design; (2) Lighting Specific Interiors; and (3) Special Lighting Needs. In Part One, a chapter is devoted to each of the six components vital to creating the design—assessment of the client's needs and the site, use of compositional lighting techniques, evaluation of construction constraints, selection of a light source, selection of fixtures, and communication of the design through drawings and the project manual. Also included in this last section are bidding instructions, specifications, and the fixture list.

Part Two presents nine case studies of specific interiors and the lighting designs created for them by a variety of distinguished designers whose artistry has brought new insights into this field; here the old rules have been broken and new paths forged. From the evocative display of sacred Vatican artifacts to the mechanical intricacies of custom light fixtures, these case studies present a wide spectrum of lighting designs.

Finally, Part Three addresses a variety of contemporary design issues requiring unique lighting solutions such as environments for the aged and infirm, and environments for plants and landscapes. Part Three also contains an important chapter on light as art, where contemporary artists and their innovative lighting techniques are presented. Their investigations into perceptual psychology foreshadow the day when designers will use optical illusions to shrink or expand spaces at will. Lighting experts have long been able to manipulate visual perception so that certain physical planes of an interior space disappear. Even now, visual artists are creating surfaces with only light. Who will be the first designer to lengthen corridors, push out walls, and raise ceilings with reflected light? This is the excitement of lighting today—and well into the next century. We hope that this book will be your guide on that creative journey.

Fran Kellogg Smith
Fred J. Bertolone
San Gabriel, California

NOTES

[1] L. Bell, *The Art of Illumination*, 2nd ed. (New York: Praeger, 1912) 208.

[2] John E. Flynn, "Interim Study of Procedures for Investigating the Effect of Light on Behavior and Impressions," *Journal of the Illuminating Engineering Society*, 3, No. 83 (1973): 87-94.

CREATING YOUR DESIGN

Part One

EVERY DESIGNER is commissioned to create an intuitive and practical design solution for a particular client—a solution devised to meet the needs of a unique program. When light is the designer's medium, the procedure changes only slightly.

As a medium of design, light is similar to other basic design elements: form, color, and texture. It orchestrates our perception of all these elements. Moreover, light guides our seeing, speeds our visual tasks, cues our behavior, and affects our attitudes.

The designer is a problem solver. He/she engages in a considerable amount of analysis before writing specifications. To select the right lighting, the designer analyzes all the components that influence the design. Part One deals with these components:

>Assessment of client and site
>
>Use of compositional techniques
>
>Evaluation of construction constraints
>
>Selection of light sources
>
>Selection of fixtures
>
>Communication of design

Completion of the first two items allows the designer to rough out a lighting concept that meets the client's needs. Throughout the third step that concept is tested for feasibility and modified accordingly. The next two components refine the concept into a concrete lighting design that is ready for execution. The final step communicates that design through drawings and documents.

By exploring these factors of analysis that affect lighting design decisions in sequence, their interaction will become apparent.

Chapter One

ANALYZING THE PROJECT

IN THIS CHAPTER, six factors by which the lighting designer can analyze a project are presented: client motivation; client vision; daylighting; color; activities; and mood. The designer can use these factors to analyze every project—regardless of the particular emphases of the clients' programs.

The first two factors—client motivation and vision—involve sensitivity. If you don't understand what motivates the client, you'll never deliver an answer for which he/she will pay. Even the vision of different clients varies widely; according to their visual age, people perceive spaces differently in terms of color, brightness, and satisfaction.

The third factor is daylight and its effects. Here the orientation of the building on the site plays an important role because it governs heat, glare, penetration, and even the colors of daylighting.

Color is the fourth factor. But because the intensity and direction of daylighting at the site can affect the perception of colors, the designer may be well advised to delay the selection of both lighting and color palette until the building's site is final.

The activities to be undertaken in the given space provide the fifth factor in our analysis. Particularly important are such task parameters as accuracy, speed, and familiarity. Because bright vertical surfaces also guide users' expectations of how to circulate through a space, setting cues to these activities is also part of the designer's assignment.

The mood of the space—the excitement or peace it communicates to its users, and its attraction for certain personalities—is influenced by lighting and is the sixth factor.

CLIENT MOTIVATION

Every client has motivations and values drawn from his/her own experience. These psychological factors, coupled with the activities that will be performed in the space, influence the image the client wishes the space to project.

Client image differs from mood in that the former is an active condition. It concerns the initial impact of the space on the visitor. Mood is more passive. It has to do with feelings about the space while experiencing it over a period of time.

Understanding a client's motivation is essential to producing a successful lighting design. One vehicle that ensures an adequate correspondence between the designer's goals and those of the client is the initial interview.

The Initial Interview

Unlike most design meetings, the initial lighting interview should take place at the client's home or business, and should be scheduled toward the end of the day. In this familiar setting, a client is less inhibited in discussing personal responses to the lighting effects at hand. Because light is intangible, it is easier to communicate about it by using examples that exist in the space where the interview takes place.

The interview is more productive at the end of the day for two reasons: (1) the designer can accurately assess nighttime viewing conditions, and (2) the client's eyes are likely to be tired. Since both views and eyes are under consideration, they are less likely to be misrepresented if the discussion takes place at twilight.

With reticent clients, the designer can begin by asking factual questions, but eventually such clients should be drawn out so that they talk about themselves and their preferences. For example, the client might be asked to designate special objects or areas to be well lighted. Can he/she describe what "well" means to him/her? On the other hand, the client should also be asked to discuss an example of lighting he/she does not like and why. A discussion of lighting the client finds irksome normally leads into a discussion of his/her vision and visual needs. Figure 1-1 suggests some useful questions for the lighting part of an initial design interview.

PROFILE QUESTIONNAIRE

JONES & JONES ATTYS AT LAW _____   **MARCH 25, 1988** _____
Client   Date

Scope of services   (✓) concept   (✓) installation administration

                           (✓) drawings/specs   (✓) corrections & focusing

Spaces to be designed	JLJ OFFICE	JCJ OFFICE	BOARD RM.	
ceiling ht.	8'-6"	8'-6"	9'-0"	
ceiling type	SUSPENDED	SUSPENDED	SHEET ROCK	
joist direction (N/S or E/W)	—	—	N/S	
alternate clgs.	(2'X2' TILES)	(2'X2' TILES)	—	
joist on-centers	Ø	Ø	16"	
Traffic patterns	TERMINUS	TERMINUS	TERMINUS	

Safety hazards

   (steps, etc.)   Ø   Ø   Ø   _____

Daily activities	NIGHT WORK	NO NIGHT WORK	MORNING/EVES	
	READING	READING	READING	
	RESEARCH	MEETINGS	MEETINGS	

Flexibility needs   SOFT EFFECT

   (switches, etc.)   DAYLT. GLARE   FOR MEETINGS   Ø

General light level preferred

   (demonstration by client)   JLJ - 100 F.C. / JCJ - 50 F.C.

Client incandescent vs. fluorescent preferences   INCANDESCENT

Lighting client does not like (example)   JLJ - GLARE / JCJ - HARSH SHADOWS

Attention-getting patterns and objects   ANTIQUE LEATHER BKS. / BDRM.

Client motivation   NEW GENERATION OF PARTNERS

Colors to predominate   YELLOW / GREEN

Impressions that visitors should have   NO-NONSENSE CONSERVATIVE EFFICIENT

Special areas   RECEPTION : 1ST IMPRESSIONS

Life cycle anticipated   20 YEARS

Maintenance   who **CLEANING CREW**   how often **INFREQUENTLY**   how complex **SIMPLE**

Expenditure preference

   inexpensive _____   moderate ___✓___   expensive _____

Deadline dates   ALL CONSTRUCTION IN SEPT.

                                                   COMPLETE BY ANNUAL CHRISTMAS PARTY

RH. _____   _J M Jones_ _____
Interviewer   Client

FIGURE 1-1:   Sample Client Profile Questionnaire
A formal interview format focuses attention on the client's goals but also puts the designer in charge.

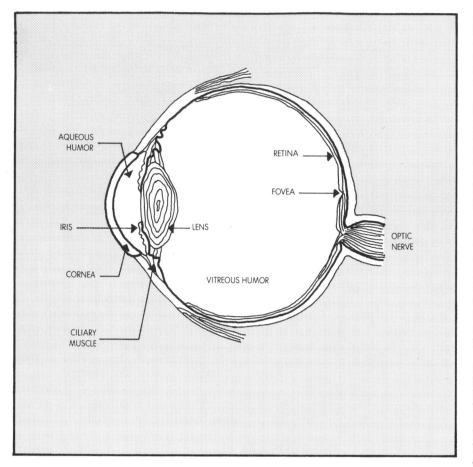

FIGURE 1-2: **Horizontal Cross Section of the Eye**
Like a camera, the eye admits light that registers on the retina, a sensitive plate at the back of the eye. The retina, acting as the brain's agent, presorts the information and transmits it. The iris contracts or enlarges its muscles to control the amount of admitted light so that the eye is able to see detail ranging from subtle moonlight to bright sunlight. The lens focuses on or "accommodates to" different distances; its muscles draw it into rounder or flatter shapes in order to resolve the detail. All the while the brain compares new information to other data in the same field of view or to information held in memory. This is how we see. (From John E. Kaufman, ed., *IES Lighting Handbook*, 1984.)

CLIENT VISION

Eyes can see an enormous range of brightness and still record fine detail. Visual targets may be colorless or colored, moving, flickering or steady, simple or complex, but the overall mental impression is still one of stability. Relying on constancies of size, color, shape, and brightness from memory, the eye and brain gather necessary information from the visual field.

Effects of Age and Experience

Eyes see differently depending on many factors, especially age and experience. Sensitivity to contrast is the major way that we "see," and this changes radically with age. At first, some of the decrease can be offset by task familiarity or eyeglasses, but eventually the changes are overwhelming.

Age affects visual acuity, peripheral vision, depth perception, glare and flicker tolerance, color vision, and the size of the visual field. The aged are protected against visual chaos in familiar environments because they remember. If the designer is changing a familiar environment, then he/she should gauge the age and visual behavior of the client's eyes.

Aging eyes can belong to anyone over 40. However, the client's or the user's vision may not wait for age 40. Many of the vision defects attributed to aging occur in some younger individuals. Even common eyeglass wearers are affected by the lighting; some refractive lenses cause people to experience increased glare. If the client interview reveals the likelihood of aging eyes, the designer can condition the redesigned space for the reduced visual performance of the occupants through lighting techniques (see Chapter Seven).

Experience also influences seeing. For instance, a designer's eyes are trained by years of studio exercises. It is unrealistic to believe that clients' eyes are trained to such a degree. However, even among individuals of the same age and experience, seeing differs widely. The point is that it is hard to know how your lighting design will look to your clients until you find out how they see.

The Science of Seeing

The designer sells visual satisfaction, not visual performance. But physiology (Figure 1-2) and psychology are so intertwined that the distinction is difficult. Today researchers in the field are discovering new methods and measures to study the visual and nonvisual cues that affect the seeing of people in an environmental context.

The most basic factor in ease of seeing is the degree to which detail stands out from background: larger detail is easier to see, but smaller detail can be made more visible by using more light. However, new research has shown that as the background becomes brighter with more light, the eyes become *less* sensitive to brightness differences (contrast); so still more light is needed.[1]

Visual information is also relative. When we see auto headlights on a rainy night, for example, they blind us. Isn't it strange that the same bright headlights do not even catch our attention on a dry, sunny day? Lights cannot be bright in a field of brightness, only in a field of dimness.

DAYLIGHTING

Daylight is the third of the six factors that should be evaluated and coordinated when planning a lighting design. This free light is often accompanied by excessive heat and glare, which the designer must control by methods discussed in this chapter.

Light

First, let us explore the "light" in daylight and its properties, which include:

How deeply it penetrates an interior

Its colors and their compatibility with the colors of the interior

Fading

Penetration. In some workspaces, the penetration of daylight can produce better visual contrasts on the task than many of today's overhead electrical lighting systems.[2] A higher contrast between printed matter and its background is achieved when daylight comes from side windows. Therefore, in offices or school rooms, deep daylight penetration is a design objective.

On the other hand, consideration of daylighting for the performance of tasks raises another aspect of penetration, that of excessive brightness. A radical imbalance of daylight can be costly for several reasons:

1. Perception. When occupants see high brightness, as they do through windows, their adaptation level is raised and their perception is that the interior is dim. Despite a measured abundance of footcandles on desk surfaces, this sensation of dimness will persist because the brain is evaluating light relatively.

2. Energy. If there is no apparent vertical brightness on the interior, the occupants will turn on the interior illumination in an attempt to make the interior seem equally bright and to correct the perceived darkness. This increases energy use.

3. Visual comfort. On particularly bright days, there is no overhead lighting system that can create equal brightnesses indoors and still be visually comfortable for the occupants.

Controlling Penetration. In the summer, the sun comes up in the northeast, arcs high and slowly in the sky, and then sets again almost northwest. This is very different from its pathway in winter, when the sun rises south-southeast and quickly sets south-southwest.

By using the solar geometry shown in Figure 1-3 designers can employ several tactics that promote the penetration of light and heat in winter, but constrict it in summer. They include planting deciduous trees, constructing window overhangs (Figure 1-4), reshaping window configurations, and using highly reflecting finishes on interior surfaces.

Window configurations, in particular, provide a permanent way to control interior penetration of light and heat. Codes often govern the ratio of windows to the square footage of the interior, but those windows can be any shape. Different window shapes serve different needs to admit light. Figure 1-5 illustrates some of these effects.

One of the simplest ways to manipulate the penetration of daylight deeply into an interior is to use light colors as reflectors. A high reflectance, matte white finish on ceiling and walls will diffusely reflect the window's light and distribute it more evenly and more deeply. If more light or heat is needed, a ground cover of white rock outside the windows can increase the penetration of daylight into the interior. On the other hand, if a building is in a hot climate and daylight penetration needs to be reduced, wide beds of turned earth directly outside the windows will absorb much of the light before it can be reflected inside. Table 1-1 shows the reflectances of some common ground cover materials that can be used to adjust the color and intensity of daylight reflected to the interior.

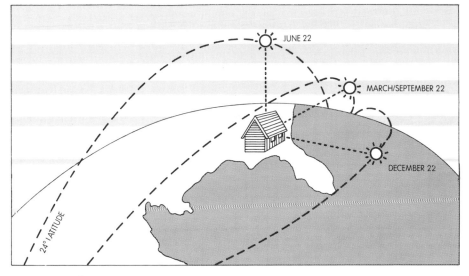

FIGURE 1-3: Solar Geometry
Keeping in mind that Florida lies at 24 degrees north latitude, it is obvious that most south-facing windows in North America will experience deeper penetration of beam sunlight than shown here. Maximum daylight penetration into an interior is taken as 15 feet on an average, but variance is wide from latitude to latitude as well as from season to season. (Illustration by Reiko Hayashi.)

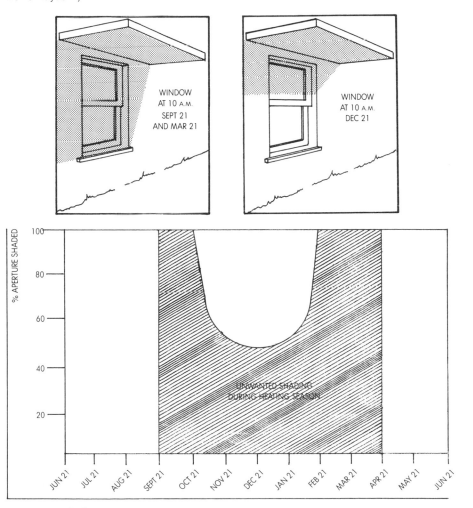

FIGURE 1-4: Shading
The peak heating and cooling seasons lag far behind the solar solstices. Therefore, if the summer shading requirement for south-facing windows is satisfied, then nearly half of the south windows must also be shaded some of the winter months. Awnings may provide a better solution because they are adjustable. (From *Solar Age*, November 1981; copyrighted 1981 Solar Vision, Inc.)

FIGURE 1-5: Windows Shaping Light
The diagrams below show how three different window shapes determine the shape of light entering an interior. But no matter what their shape, windows will appear less glaring when adjacent jambs are splayed, ceilings are chamfered, and finishes are light-colored.

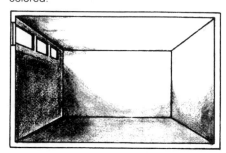

(a) Clerestories: The higher the window, the deeper the light will penetrate into the room. But because the ceiling is the primary reflector, the floor areas may seem dark by contrast.

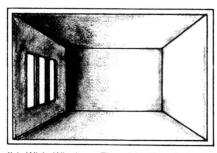

(b) Wide Windows: The wider the window, the more even the illumination, and the more cohesive the view and its information.

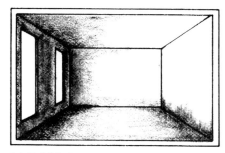

(c) Tall Windows: The information from the window's view is discontinuous, but the ceiling and floor surfaces are equally bright (for equal reflection factors). The inside wall shows the lack of uniformity typical of narrow windows. (Illustration by Reiko Hayashi and Fran Kellogg Smith.)

The Colors of Daylight. (See Color Plate 8.) Daylight changes its colors with the season, the latitude, and the time of day. Figure 1-6 explains how this change occurs. However, the colors of daylight can be modified. For example, if red-brick paving is used outside a window instead of white rock, the red brick will reduce the intensity of the daylight and add some pink to the light experienced within. Another way to change the colors of daylight is to use tinted glass which acts as a color filter. In an office that has blue-green tinted glazing, for instance, only the cool-colored finishes and fabrics will find color reinforcement from the filtered daylight; warm colors will be dulled, or grayed. (See Figure 1-7.)

Fading. Not only does light from the sun and sky contain visible daylight, it also contains wavelengths of invisible light. What is the effect of invisible infrared and ultraviolet wavelengths in daylight? Infrared makes some sensitive materials such as wood, rattan, and doré finishes dehydrate, crack, and peel. Ultraviolet causes fading. Certain pigment colors are more fugitive, that is, apt to fade (Color Plate 5.) Paint finishes, especially glossy ones, are not as susceptible as fabrics. Table 1-2 shows some fibers' fade susceptibility in descending order. For all surfaces, however, the degree of fading is regulated by the kind and intensity of the light and by the time of exposure.[3]

Heat
Daylighting's free heating potential can be a bonus. Although sunlight delivers only half the heat of a fluorescent lighting system (per unit of entering light), there is a distinct trend in certain types of North American architecture to add more glass to southern exposures—thereby increasing heat in winter—and to decrease glass on east, west, and northern ones—thereby reducing thermal losses. In some climates, however, air conditioning must be supplied in the summer, to remove heat gains, so the real costs must be calculated carefully.

What Happens at Night? When the sun sets, daylit interior spaces are affected. There are three major issues.

1. Privacy. At night passive solar homes look like fishbowls to the passerby. As with all visual perception, the compelling view is from the darkness (outside) into the light on the interior.

2. Windows as black mirrors. Seen from the inside in the light, a glass wall becomes a black mirror at night (Figure 1-8). Mercilessly, it reflects images of every brightness in the interior. Some good solutions for these unwanted reflections include: (1) balancing the illumination on both sides of the glass by recessing lights into the outside overhang where they will brighten vertical surfaces; (2) using louvers on the inside fixtures; (3) controlling the inside light so that it strikes only horizontal surfaces; (4) tilting the glass; and (5) covering the offending glass windows.

3. Thermal losses. Although in moderate to cold climates heat loss may be desirable in summer, winter heat loss is a major problem for spaces with large glazed areas. However, there are a multitude of clever solutions to this problem. (See also Langdon and Shurcliff in the Bibliography.[4])

Glare
This third factor of daylighting is concerned with its effect on the occupants' vision.

Direct Glare. In illuminating office environments especially, controlling glare is one of the greatest challenges with daylighting. Glare is an extreme-contrast relationship in which vistas seen through the windows are

TABLE 1-1 IESNA REFLECTANCES OF BUILDING MATERIALS AND OUTSIDE SURFACES

MATERIAL	REFLECTANCE AS A PERCENT	MATERIAL	REFLECTANCE AS A PERCENT
Bluestone, sandstone	18%	Asphalt	7%
Brick		Earth	7
light buff	48	Granolite	
dark buff	40	pavement	17
dark red, glazed	30	Grass	
Cement	27	(dark green)	6
Concrete	40	Gravel	13
Marble (white)	45	Macadam	18
Paint (white)		Slate	
new	75	(dark clay)	8
old	55	Snow	
Glass*		new	74
clear	7	old	64
reflective	20-30	Vegetation	25

*Depends on the angle between the glass surface and the light source.

Source: John E. Kaufman, ed., *IES Lighting Handbook Reference Volume 1981* (New York: Illuminating Engineering Society, 1981) 7-10.

FIGURE 1-6:   The Effects of Atmosphere on Daylight Colors
Early morning daylight tends to be cooler because the red wavelengths of light are absorbed in the moist morning air as they warm it. Noon daylight tends to be purer because it penetrates a relatively short distance through the atmosphere except in winter (see Color Plate 8). Early evening light is usually warm in color or even reddish. The exact color depends upon the density of the atmospheric pollution through which the light must travel to reach us. The importance of this phenomenon to designers is that the colors of the intruding daylight are flattering to interior surfaces of the same hue. (Illustration by Reiko Hayashi.)

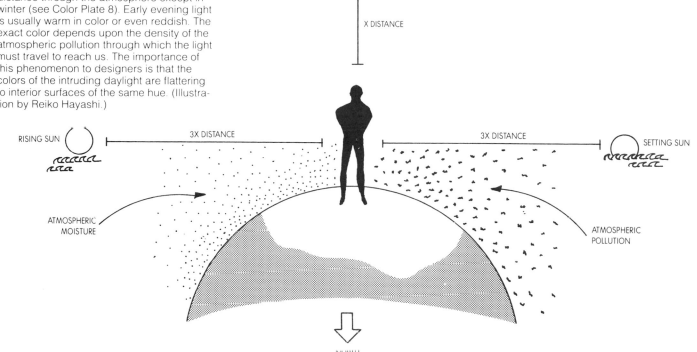

FIGURE 1-7:   The Effect of Green Window Glass on Color Transmissions
This absorption curve demonstrates that tinted glass absorbs almost all of the red frequencies of daylight and transmits no red to the interior of the building. A color palette of green carpet, teak woods, and fabrics in blue and green would mute the warmth of the woods for lack of color reinforcement. Different colors and thicknesses of glass transmit and absorb different portions of the color spectrum, but all act as filters, transmitting certain frequencies of light and not others. (Adapted from illustration by Raymond Perlman in *Light and Color*, copyrighted 1971 Western Publishing Co., Inc.)

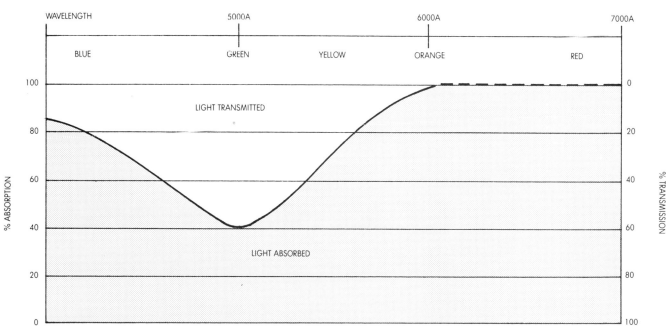

FIGURE 1-8: Black Mirror Effect
The "black mirror" effect of nighttime glass is seen at the top of the window where the decorative fixture is reflected as four dots of disturbing brightness. One easy way to counteract such visual clutter is to light a vertical object or surface outside the blackened windows and use this new brightness as a distraction. (Photograph by Mary E. Nichols.)

**TABLE 1-2   RESISTANCE TO DAMAGE CAUSED BY DAYLIGHT
OF SOME COMMON FIBERS**

EXCELLENT	GOOD	POOR	MAY DECOMPOSE IN DIRECT SUNLIGHT
Fiber glass	Nylon	Acetate	Olefin
Polyester	Antron, Caprolan,	Rayon	Patlin,
Dacron, Fortrel	Cordura Zefran	Natural fibers	Marquesa,
Acrylic		Cotton, Jute, Sisal,	Herculon
Acrilan, Creslan		Wool, Silk	
Modacrylic			
Verel			

Note: The fabric is more fade-resistant when (1) the fiber is thick; (2) the weave is tight; (3) the finish is shiny or bright; or (4) the color is highly reflectant.

Source: Debra A. Jose, "Photochemical Damage to Common Fabrics," an unpublished dissertation.

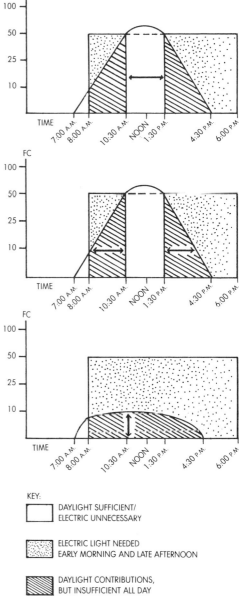

KEY:

☐ DAYLIGHT SUFFICIENT/
ELECTRIC UNNECESSARY

▨ ELECTRIC LIGHT NEEDED
EARLY MORNING AND LATE AFTERNOON

▨ DAYLIGHT CONTRIBUTIONS,
BUT INSUFFICIENT ALL DAY

FIGURE 1-9: Daylight Energy Savings Strategies
The energy savings that result from using daylighting in an office building can be determined by predicting the percentage of the year that the electric light system will not be in use. This percentage depends upon the particular control strategy chosen, the length of the work year, and the amount of daylight reaching a given area of the building. Having decided upon an appropriate lighting level for the office workers as a group, this level can then be compared to the hourly daylight contributions from nature. One of the three conditions pictured in the diagrams above can then occur. (From Solar Energy Research Institute (SERI) 1983.)

extremely bright and dark-colored adjacent surfaces, such as window jambs, are very black. When this occurs, the eye doesn't know whether to open up or shut down. Perforated shades, screens, grillwork, or blinds can be used to break up glare. Decreasing the daylight by as much as 50 percent with tinted glass will increase the evenness of the lighting and reduce glare.

Indirect Glare. Another problem that arises in office environments is that of brightness from windows being reflected on VDT screens. Such reflections obscure information on the screen. Positioning VDT screens and desks perpendicular to the window wall, with the windows to the operator's left, throws the shadow of his/her body and hand away from the work surface as well as eliminating window brightness from the screen.

Cost Considerations/Control Strategies
All buildings with windows are daylighted, but no electric energy is saved unless electric heating, air conditioning, or lighting is reduced (Figure 1-9). To limit lighting loads, three daylighting strategies are common: (1) light-level maintenance; (2) occupancy scheduling; and (3) individual control.

Light-Level Maintenance. This strategy depends on inexpensive photosensors. The electric lighting system is circuited so that the rows of lights next to the windows are automatically switched off by the photosensor when there is adequate daylighting to deliver task light to desks next to the windows. The middle rows of fixtures are dimmed in response to the daylight contribution to the midspace, while the inside rows at the core are almost always on.

Occupancy Scheduling. This is the best strategy for projecting cost savings and executing them, although it is initially expensive. Timers on the building's master computer are programmed with monthly, seasonal, or occupancy variations to cue lighting turnoffs or turndowns. Its success depends upon the accuracy of local weather data, because the daily, monthly, and seasonal cues de-

pend upon the "daylight factor" method of calculation and prediction.[5]

Individual Small-Site Controls. The lights are turned on manually, as needed. Electronic personnel detectors sample the immediate working area periodically and if no motion or body heat is detected by the sensors, the lights are turned off automatically. Studies suggest that 30 to 60 percent of a typical office complex is unoccupied at any given time.

Daylighting and Energy Conservation
The sun is dynamic and buildings are fixed, so the major problem in designing for a daylighted building is its inflexibility. Unexpected human and weather events mean that a daylighted building must offer back-up systems like adjustable perimeter lighting and heating systems. The designer must also equip the building with responsive window coverings to anticipate unwanted heat gains and losses as well as glare problems. The rating of window coverings by means of universally accepted metrics has just begun.[6]

Because the energy crisis has so profoundly affected our lifestyles, it is now vital that the designer incorporate energy-conscious elements into his/her design planning. Passive solar design and its accompanying daylight are the most important recent developments in lighting design. The admission of quantities of daylight to interior spaces affects the interior designer's choices of colors and finishes, fabric, space planning, furniture orientation and placement, and window coverings—as well as his/her choice of lighting systems and their controls. And it is becoming one of the most important of the six factors used to analyze a lighting project.

COLOR
Color is vital to the creation of a lighting design because it allows the designer to control brightness. Brightness is a relative evaluation made in the mind; an object appears as "bright," because the background next to it is "dim." The designer can use

pale colors to reflect the light and create brightness, but contrast must occur too—a pale object seen against a pale background will not seem bright. Pale surfaces appear to be brightest when they are seen against a background of darkness. (Color Plate 7.)

Therefore, the designer, by making astute color decisions about adjacent surface finishes, can establish the brightnesses with which to manipulate people's impressions and their use of the designed space. These design decisions are found in (1) the color palette and (2) the finish schedule. The finish schedule charts the distribution and proportions of the palette colors.

Color Perception

So color creates brightness; but what creates color? To paraphrase Edwin Land: We are forced to the astonishing conclusion that light waves are not in themselves color-making. Rather, they are bearers of information that the mind uses to assign appropriate colors to various objects. [7]

Color has both scientific and human aspects. Scientifically, the sensation of color results from the following:

Physics involved when surfaces absorb or reflect certain light rays

Physiology of the eyes' response to the reflected light rays

Psychology of drawing conclusions from these light rays

But it is the human aspect of color perception that influences these conclusions. Psychologists hold that the phenomena of memory, constancy, and adaption will lead the individual to see the colors he/she expects to see.

The Physics of Color

Every color has three properties—*hue, chroma,* and *value*—according to the Munsell Color System, the most widely used system for classifying colors. Hue refers to the name of a color family, like red. The purity of such a color can be altered by changing either its value or chroma. Value refers to the relative darkness or lightness of a color: additions of black or dark gray to a color produce tones of value; while additions of white produce tints of value. Chroma refers to the purity of a color. A high chroma color is almost totally undiluted but a low chroma color contains its complementary color—a low chroma red would contain a large amount of green.

Hue. Warm hues advance or seem to come closer to the viewer visually; cool hues seem to recede. To reinforce the hue, spaces having warm colors are lighted with incandescent or high pressure sodium bulbs or warm-colored fluorescents; cool colors are lighted with krypton, metal halide or cool-colored fluorescents. Many palettes contain both warm and cool colors. For these mixed palettes, the new "white" high pressure sodium light sources are good but they will emphasize the warm colors. Conversely, metal halide (multi-vapor II and metalarc C) light sources will emphasize cool colors in the mixed palette (Color Plates 2 and 3). With regard to brightness, most hues of the same value reflect the same amount of light, except for yellow and white which reflect a bit more.

Chroma. The more pure the color, the higher its chroma, and most important to the designer, the greater its visual impact. In lighting, the higher the chroma of color used on a particular surface, the more likely the light reflected off that surface will be similarly colored. For example, the light reflected off a very saturated Chinese red wall becomes almost visibly peach-pink and seems to turn nearby surfaces a bit pink too. If the entire room is Chinese red, the interreflected light will appear to turn the atmosphere pink by shifting all highly reflectant surfaces toward a pink coloration.

Value. This third physical property of color corresponds to its reflectancy (Table 1-3). Theory says that reflected light is composed of waves of visible energy. The shortest waves are blue; the longest ones are red (Figure 1-10). If light strikes a colored wall and the surface of this wall rejects waves of light that have a blue frequency, then a person passing would see the color of the reflected light and give the wall a familiar color name, blue. The proportion of

TABLE 1-3   IESNA EQUIVALENCY CHART: MUNSELL VALUE/ LUMINOUS REFLECTANCE

MUNSELL VALUE	PERCENT REFLECTANCE*
10.0	100.0%
9.5	87.8
9.0	76.7
8.5	66.7
8.0	57.6
7.5	49.4
7.0	42.0
6.5	35.3
6.0	29.3
5.5	24.0
5.0	19.3
4.5	15.2
4.0	11.7
3.5	8.8
3.0	6.4
2.5	4.5
2.0	3.0
1.5	2.0
1.0	1.2
0	0

*Relative to a perfect diffuser.

Source: John E. Kaufman, ed., *IES Lighting Handbook Reference Volume 1984* (New York: Illuminating Engineering Society, 1984).

light that this blue wall rejects is the wall's reflectancy. The proportion of light that was not rejected is sponged up into the wall—that is, absorbed. The amount of light that is reflected is measured in footlamberts (Figure 1-11). How to predict footcandles from a complete chart of colors and their reflectancies can be done with a key to color reflectancies, which at least one U.S. paint manufacturer has made available (Figure 1-12).

The Physiology of Color

The selection of colors by the designer is vital because these colors will determine the pattern of brightnesses in a given lighting plan. But not all colors are seen equally well by everyone. In assessing clients' color vision, there are several important considerations: (1) the age of eyes; (2) color constancy; and (3) color response.

Age. Aged eyes can't see colors well. Yellowing corneas can filter the entering light and make things appear more amber. As age increases, the eye scatters blue light before the blue sensation can reach the brain. Consequently, the ability to see blue and mixtures containing blue is reduced. Additionally, declining contrast sensitivity deprives the older person of the simultaneous contrast so important to color vibrancy. So the designer must be aware that older people need primary hues of high chroma in contexts of high contrast and should avoid using blues (see Case Study Eight).

Color Constancy. People see the colors they expect to see. We want that red apple to be red! This well-known phenomenon is called color constancy. Even if an isolated apple is not quite ripe, the eyes are still inclined to see it as "red." It is the mind, interpreting the visual messages of the eyes, that attempts to stabilize the world by imposing constancies. There are also constancies of size, brightness, and shape; through their use, we adapt or accommodate to the varied details of our environment.

Color Response. Also highly important for lighting design is the fact that people respond to color. Color makes us happy or sad, warm or cool, comfortable or uncomfortable. Therefore, the designer builds a color scheme around the client's color preference. The colors selected are usually a key to the mood. Warm colors are stimulating and cheerful; cool colors are quiet. But warm or cool, those colors should be supported by light sources that are rich in the same hues.

The Psychology of Color Contrasts

If purposefully patterning interior brightnesses is the designer's goal, then he/she should know how brightness can be intensified or weakened by contrasts of color. A designer must, therefore, know how to manipulate these contrasts to serve the design. The famous Bauhaus painter and

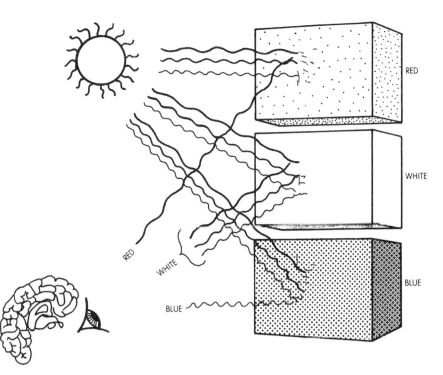

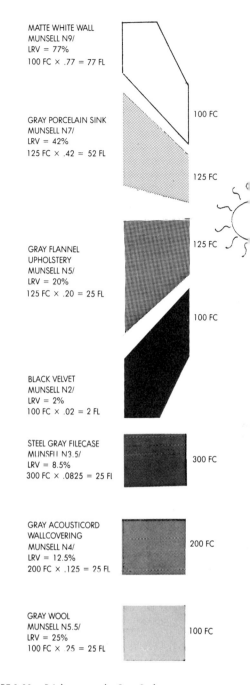

MATTE WHITE WALL
MUNSELL N9/
LRV = 77%
100 FC × .77 = 77 FL

100 FC

GRAY PORCELAIN SINK
MUNSELL N7/
LRV = 42%
125 FC × .42 = 52 FL

125 FC

GRAY FLANNEL
UPHOLSTERY
MUNSELL N5/
LRV = 20%
125 FC × .20 = 25 FL

125 FC

100 FC

BLACK VELVET
MUNSELL N2/
LRV = 2%
100 FC × .02 = 2 FL

STEEL GRAY FILECASE
MUNSELL N3.5/
LRV = 8.5%
300 FC × .0825 = 25 Fl

300 FC

GRAY ACOUSTICORD
WALLCOVERING
MUNSELL N4/
LRV = 12.5%
200 FC × .125 = 25 FL

200 FC

GRAY WOOL
MUNSELL N5.5/
LRV = 25%
100 FC × .25 = 25 FL

100 FC

FIGURE 1-10: Subtractive Color Theory
The color you see is a result of the light rays that reach your brain. The color "white" is the name used when more than two colors of rays reach the brain at the same time. (Illustration by Joanne Lim Stinson and Reiko Hayashi.)

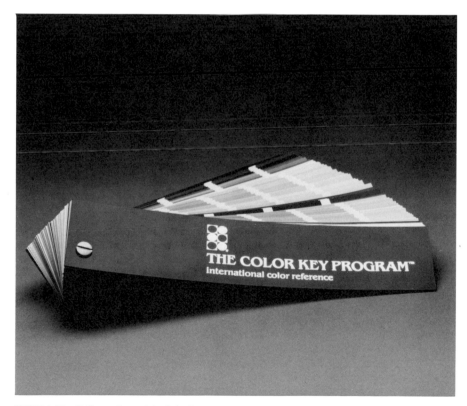

FIGURE 1-12: Reflectancies and the Color Key Program
The ongoing presence of the Grow Group Companies in the Inter-Society Color Council and its Color Marketing Group have long ensured that their paint colors correlate well with current fashions in furnishings, backgrounds, and floorcoverings. More recently, however, these manufacturers have enriched their Color Key Program by publishing the light reflectance value of each of their 800 colors in the fan deck pictured above. COLOR KEY PROGRAM® is an international color reference and is used exclusively by the Grow Group Companies, Ameritone and Devoe, as their specifications standard for architectural coatings and finishes. (Courtesy of Ameritone Paint Corporation.)

FIGURE 1-11: Brightness on the Gray Scale
When the same amount of light is shining upon a surface, the brightness of that surface is dependent upon the reflection or absorption characteristics of the surface itself. To find out how bright the surface will be, multiply the quantity of light arriving at the surface (footcandles) by the light reflectance value (LRV) typical of the color on the surface. The answer will be expressed in units of brightness, or footlamberts (fl):
fc X LRV = fl

Colors having more white in the mixture will reflect more light and create a brighter room by interreflecting light from wall to wall. Colors that are darker will absorb more light and rob the room of interreflected light. To make a light surface and a dark surface equally bright, the darker surface must be supplied with enough additional light to offset its lower light reflectance value. (Illustration by Joanne Lim Stinson.)

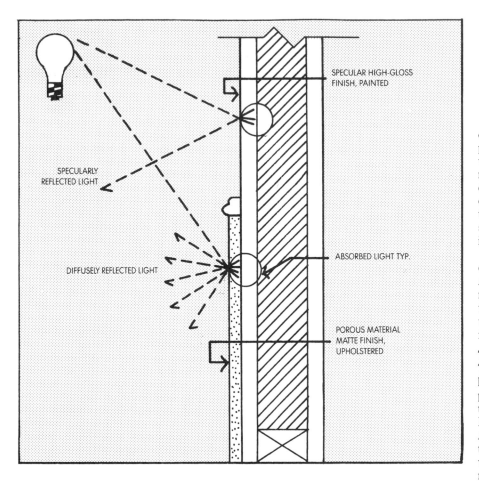

SPECULAR HIGH-GLOSS
FINISH, PAINTED

SPECULARLY
REFLECTED LIGHT

DIFFUSELY REFLECTED LIGHT

ABSORBED LIGHT TYP.

POROUS MATERIAL
MATTE FINISH,
UPHOLSTERED

FIGURE 1-13: Absorption and Reflection
The physical behavior of light shows why the color, texture, and finish of the room surfaces are so important to the designer. Only that light which is not absorbed will appear as brightness to the people in the room. (Illustration by Joanne Lim Stinson.)

colorist, Johannes Itten, devised seven principles of color contrasts that still serve the designer well (Color Plate 1).

Colorimetric Standards

Before the lighting is installed, it is important for the designer to know how the selected finish and fabric colors will appear (Figure 1-13). Measurements like Temperature Kelvin and Color Rendering Index have been devised by the lighting industry for the purpose of comparing the industry's sources of white light to one another. But neither measurement is useful to the designer because neither distinguishes which specific paint or finish colors will be reinforced by the color coming from the light source. The Spectral Distribution Chart profiles the exact colors that a light source emits and the relative intensity of each color emitted. It can be useful in matching room finishes with the colors of light that will come from that light source. Working samples of light sources are the one best way for the designer to know how colors will look with a specific light source. (See Chapter Four and Color Plates 2 and 3.)

ACTIVITIES

When formulating a lighting design, the fifth factor of analysis involves the activities that take place in the designed space. Several variables affect the appropriate amount of light for a given activity:

The color of that light

The angle of the light in relation to the task

The spatial distribution of light in the immediate environment—and even in the distant field of view

The variables that affect the performing of tasks in the work environment, for example, are many. First, most work tasks have visual and nonvisual components which must be properly separated. These visual components include size, contrast and color of details, the complexity and uniformity of the background against which the detail is seen, the extent to which form and texture is relevant, and the duration of movement.

Nonvisual, or human factors also are part of the relationship between light and work. Although only poorly understood, they must be considered. These include age of the workers' eyes, the workers' familiarity with the task, and how poor lighting affects fatigue, distraction, boredom, and stress.

Task Lighting

Today, *task lighting*—that is, the level of light necessary for the eyes and brain to perform a given task—is an area in which there is much contradictory research. The Illuminating Engineering Society of North America (IESNA) has recommended certain levels of light and also advised that within a given space these be kept within reasonable contrast limits in order to achieve optimum visual performance. But many unsolved problems exist. For example, there is still no definitive answer as to whether steadily increasing levels of light always provide greater ease of seeing. Visibility-level research suggests that they do, but research on apparent contrast perception suggests they do not—at least not for high-contrast tasks.

Meanwhile, the designer must closely analyze and evaluate the vision of the client or occupant and make a professional judgment about task lighting based on the information at hand. He/she must decide the amount and angle of light for a specific person to perform a specific task under given conditions of performance. If necessary, as the noted researcher John Flynn stated, "there is no substitute for a proper experimental investigation of the task itself . . . and no shame."[8]

At present there are four accepted techniques for task lighting:

1. Uniform ambient lighting

2. Local lighting

3. Specific task lighting

4. Task lighting at optimum angles

Which technique to use depends upon what tasks need to be illuminated and the vision of the people who'll be attempting them. This information is often gained in the client interview.

Uniform Ambient Lighting. Ambient lighting systems brighten the entire space. If the client or occupant is old, has low-contrast perception and vulnerability to glare, but needs lots of light, then ambient lighting will be best. By selecting a nonglaring, indirect, and attractive fixture and then calculating the number and locations of light sources needed to evenly fill an interior with the recommended level of light (Table 1-4), the designer can be sure that old eyes will be comfortable and able to function.

The problem is that contemporary energy conservation codes seldom allow the wattages required for such a system unless the enforcing agency can be convinced that such a high level of uniform light is needed. In response to restrictive energy codes, the IESNA has recommended a new procedure known as the Unit Power Density (UPD) method of calculation that salvages the useful remains of earlier calculation methods. It shows how to combine recommended lighting levels with restricted energy allotments.

Local Lighting. If the client or occupant has tasks to be performed that require very different levels of light within the same space, or if some tasks are performed only sporadically, then local lighting will be cost- and energy-efficient. For instance, the display floor of a home furniture store often has the decorators' desks arranged in pairs throughout the floor. The paperwork of a sale takes place at these desks and requires checking of small print on warehouse inventory lists, sales tax charts, etc. But the furniture displays would look washed out and bland if they were subjected to the same high levels of light as those needed for sales tasks. The obvious solution in this case is to deliver more light to the sales areas only. To keep task lighting within IESNA recommended contrast limits, some of the distant perimeter walls could be brightened with washes of light (appropriate to the furniture displays nearby). In a less complex setting, such as an executive office, the principle is more obvious, as seen in Figure 1-14.

Specific Task Lighting. For the space where bad visual conditions are inherent—one having occupants with weak eyes or one having excessive direct glare from uncontrolled daylighting—the designer can consider specific task lighting. It not only delivers the recommended footcandles to the task and its background, it also delivers light at angles that enrich the task's visual contrast. The best visual contrast relationship for many writing tasks is that created or reinforced by crosslighting at an angle approximating 27 degrees from vertical to the task. (See Figure 1-15.) Although this rule of thumb was abandoned by the IESNA as a lighting strategy for general illumination (equivalent sphere illumination) because it was not practical to calculate its

TABLE 1-4 IESNA RECOMMENDED LIGHT LEVELS

ACTIVITY	ILLUMINANCE CATEGORY
Banks	
Lobby	
General	C
Writing areas	D
Tellers' stations	E
Conference rooms	
Confering	D
Drafting	
Vellum	
High contrast	E
Low contrast	F
Light table	C
Food service facilities	
Dining areas	
Cashier	D
Cleaning	C
Dining	E
Kitchen	E
Hotels	
Bathrooms	D
Bedrooms	D
Corridors/stairs	C
Front desk	E
Lobby	
General	C
Reading	D
Merchandising areas	
Dressing areas	D
Fitting areas	F
Sales counters	E
Museums	
Nonsensitive art	D
Circulation spaces	C
Residences	
General	
Conversation	B
Passage	B
Specific tasks	
Dining	C
Grooming/shaving	D
Kitchen counters	
Critical seeing	E
Non critical	D
Reading	
Printed matter	D
Handwriting	E
Table games	D

ILLUMINANCE CATEGORY	TYPE OF ACTIVITY	RANGES OF ILLUMINANCES IN FOOTCANDLES
A	Public spaces with dark surroundings	2-3-5
B	Simple orientation for short temporary visits	5-7.5-10
C	Working spaces where visual tasks are only occasionally performed	10-15-20
D	Performance of visual tasks of high contrast or large size	20-30-50
E	Performance of visual tasks of medium contrast or small size	50-75-100
F	Performance of visual tasks of low contrast or very small size	100-150-200
G	Performance of visual tasks of low contrast and very small size over a prolonged period	200-300-500
H	Performance of very prolonged and exacting visual tasks	500-750-1000
I	Performance of very special visual tasks of extremely low contrast and small size	1000-1500-2000

Source: John E. Kaufman, ed., *IES Lighting Handbook Applications Volume 1981* (New York: Illuminating Engineering Society, 1981) 2.2-2.19.

effect on general office spaces, these angular principles are valuable for specific task lighting in many instances where visual blurring of miniscule written detail is a critical concern.

Task Lighting at Optimum Angles. The next way to handle task lighting with the utmost refinement is to use angular relationships on very specific tasks—a technique currently favored in Europe. For instance, reflected brightness that veils a specular surface will be minimal when light reflected from it does not coincide with the angle of view. Another example of a way to enhance the task is to adjust the lighting to it, for instance, viewing an object against an illuminated diffusion medium like opal glass. This can be a useful way to check its three-dimensionality (Figure 1-16).

The Traffic Pattern: A Nontask Activity

People are phototropic. Like their forebears they are fascinated by and drawn to light. This is one of the most powerful influences of light in designed space. Having identified the desired circulation patterns for a given space and assessed the safety hazards by means of the client interview, the designer should place the colors of highest reflectancy and focus the highest light level only on those surfaces toward which he/she wishes to have the occupants focus and move. To emphasize the apparent brightness of eyestopping surfaces, their highly reflectant color must be seen in contrast to adjoining colors whose reflectance is at least 40 percent lower. By creating these relative brightness contrasts, the designer can select that surface or feature that has the highest perceived priority.

But remember contrast. When a person enters a space he/she scans from left to right—first reading faces, then the relationship of planes and surfaces. It is the relative brightness of the surfaces in relation to one another that gives visual cues about how to use the space. By using light and color to manage those cues, the designer also manages behavior.

The principle of guiding the visitor's perception is to locate an eye-stoppingly bright, or light reflecting, surface so that it will be seen against a dark, or light absorbing, surface. When choosing the colors of these bright and dark surfaces, the light reflectance value (LRV) of the color is very important. To stop the eye, there must be at least four Munsell values, or a 40 percent difference between the reflectance of the bright color and that of the dark, background color. (On the other hand, to create less visual impact, these adjacent colors should differ by no more than 4 Munsell values or 40 percent reflectance.)

There are two factors that will vary the published reflectance of a color somewhat: the inherent texture or porosity of the surface to which the color is applied and the

FIGURE 1-14:   Recommended Brightness Balances

(Above) At the task (a), the recommended footcandles of light should be available, but the background surface, which is visually adjacent (b), should have no less than a third of the same level of light as the task. It is helpful if (a) and (b) are of similar color values. In the meantime, the surrounding vertical surfaces (c) should be no brighter than three times the task brightness, but no darker than one-fifth of the task brightness. For this reason, wallwashers are used on the far wall to build brightness and blinds are used at the windows to reduce brightness as needed. For prolonged work, these devices will maintain ratios of brightness that keep the eyes from continually adapting and re-adapting to varied levels of brightness. (Illustration by Joanne Lim Stinson.)

FIGURE 1-15:   Lighting at Optimum Angles

(Below) Just as you never position a worker with his/her back to a window, so you never position him/her with his back to a single light fixture; both positions will cause body shadows to cascade across the work surface. Conversely, you never want to place a light source in the ceiling directly over or in front of the task area. These locations are known as the "offending zone." Fixtures here are at a mirror angle to the task and their image will appear as indirect glare throwing a veil of shimmering brightness across the task when the worker looks down. In this case, the veil of brightness obscures writing. (Illustration by Joanne Lim Stinson.)

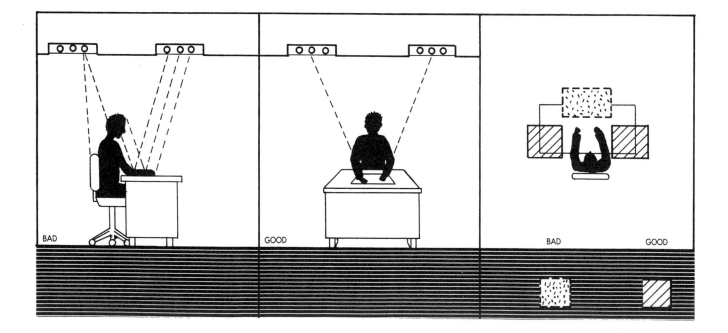

color capability of the light source. An example of the first variation is seen when an orange wall of painted sheet rock with a reflectance of 57 percent reflects more light than a wool, cut loop carpet dyed to an identical color of orange. The carpet may reflect up to 30 percent less light because of the characteristic absorption of wool and because of the tendency of the cut loop pile to trap light. The second cause of variation in the published LRV is less profound. Although more light is reflected from a cool-colored surface when it is lighted with a light source rich in cool, or bluish wavelengths, the variation is likely to be less than 9 percent from the published reflectance. (The Munsell company publishes both warm light source and cool light source reflectancies for a limited number of color samples.)

MOOD

The designer has always been involved in creating this sixth factor of our analysis, mood. It is the "sense of place" of architecture and the "ambience" of interior design. In an interview, the client can be asked to designate a desired mood by selecting three adjectives to describe how he/she wants people to feel about the given space, or how he/she wants people to characterize it. The designer can help define mood by drawing out of the client what moods or occupant impressions seem (1) to sell the most merchandise; or (2) draw the most visitors; or (3) bring the most diners back again, etcetera. It is not important whether it is the client or designer who defines the desired mood; it is only important that one of them do it, verbalize it, and put it in writing. Often the installed design fails to find client and/or user acceptance because mood and image were left unresolved at the outset of the project.

Psychological Effect of Lighting

Light and color provide the basis for visual mood. Much has been written on the sometimes miraculous psychology of color, but only in the 1970s did work on the psychology of lighting effects begin. Ambitious early work linked psychology to work productivity. The research of Taylor and Sucov noted that secretaries and clerks doing repeated and routine tasks preferred uniform light levels. Executives in the same study responded well to nonuniform lighting; their productivity was increased still further by colored light, and further yet by moving lights, but executive performance was retarded by uniform light levels.[9] The implications of this kind of early work were powerful and tantalizing.

The major investigations in the psychology of lighting, with the most influential and far-reaching effects, were the long, sophisticated studies of John Flynn, Terry Spencer, Osyp Martyniuck, and Clyde Hendrick. These investigators found that different people in different rooms do assess lighting

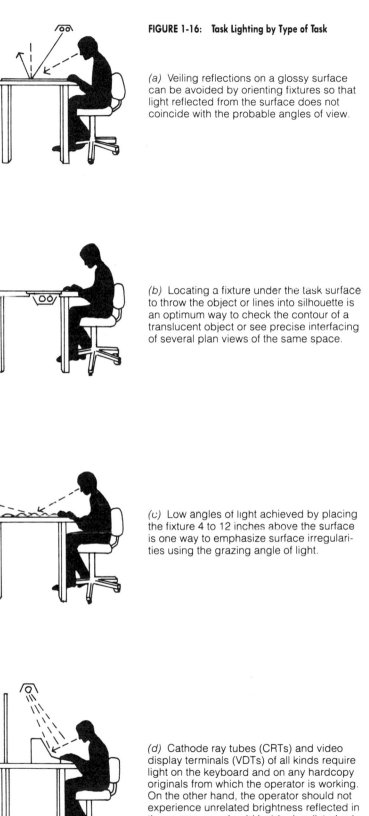

FIGURE 1-16:   Task Lighting by Type of Task

(a) Veiling reflections on a glossy surface can be avoided by orienting fixtures so that light reflected from the surface does not coincide with the probable angles of view.

(b) Locating a fixture under the task surface to throw the object or lines into silhouette is an optimum way to check the contour of a translucent object or see precise interfacing of several plan views of the same space.

(c) Low angles of light achieved by placing the fixture 4 to 12 inches above the surface is one way to emphasize surface irregularities using the grazing angle of light.

(d) Cathode ray tubes (CRTs) and video display terminals (VDTs) of all kinds require light on the keyboard and on any hardcopy originals from which the operator is working. On the other hand, the operator should not experience unrelated brightness reflected in the screen, nor should he/she be disturbed by high brightness in back of the screen. (Illustration by Joanne Lim Stinson.)

SUBJECTIVE IMPRESSION		LIGHT PATTERNS	LIGHTING TACTICS
Spacious		Uniform	Wall brightness useful, but not necessary
Intimate		Nonuniform	Low light levels near user and high brightness well beyond
Tense		Nonuniform	Intense direct light from overhead
Relaxed		Nonuniform	Wall brightness, but reduced overhead light
Pleasant		Nonuniform	Wall brightness necessary
Focused		Uniform	Bright horizontal task surfaces, some wall brightness

LIGHTING SYSTEM *(seen here)*

All fixtures on

All fixtures at one end on

Only overhead fluorescent fixtures on

Perimeter fixtures on

Combination of perimeter fixtures
and downlights on

Perimeter fixtures off

on a consistent basis. For instance, both old and young people will experience a room with only wallwashing as spacious and hushed. Regardless of the room's function, the impression of spaciousness and quietude will persist as long as the wallwashing light is present.

Lighting as a Behavioral Cue

Flynn's study clearly supports the notion that "lighting provides a number of cues which people use to interpret or make sense of space."[10] It also proves that these cues consistently relate to the type of lighting system and are at least partly independent of the room that is being experienced. (See Figure 1-17.) As early as 1974, Flynn suggested that for nonworking spaces, well-reasoned wallwashing (bathing a wall in light) would create interiors that seemed to be as well lit as spaces having uniform ambient lighting. An interior could, in fact, be pleasanter, more energy efficient, and better suited to its clients' needs when nonuniform lighting distributions were used. As the price of energy escalated, this energy-efficient aspect of Flynn's work became a major influence in lighting practice in North America. Flynn's timely research moved the so-called art side of lighting into parallel importance with the so-called science side of lighting.

LOOKING AHEAD

If the designer uses the six factors discussed in this chapter—client psychology, client vision, daylight, color, activities, and mood—as a means of both analyzing a project and organizing the preliminary data gathered on a project, he/she will be more

than three-quarters of the way toward producing an efficient, effective, and attractive lighting design. However, the needs of this lighting program must be satisfied with a design solution that composes the lighted space into a visual whole. The lighting techniques with which to do this are explored in the following chapter.

CHAPTER NOTES

[1]Gary Yonemura, "Light and Vision," *Development in Lighting 1*, ed. J.A. Lynes (Essex, England: Applied Science Publishers, 1978) 25-45.

[2]Robert E. Jennings and Eric Thrun, "Levels of Performance-Related Illumination from Daylight in Typical Office/School Interiors," *Journal of the Illuminating Engineering Society* 10, No. 1 (1980): 54.

[3]Robert L. Feller, "Control of Deteriorating Effects of Light Upon Museum Objects," *Museum* 18, No. 2 (1964): 57.

[4]William Langdon, *Moveable Insulation* (Emmaus: Rodale Press, 1980).

[5]The daylight factor is the average percentage of daylight outside the windows that will penetrate to the interior spaces on a particular date.

[6]Ongoing tests of the energy effectiveness of window-management devices have been started under the auspices of the Window Energy Systems Association and the Lawrence Berkeley Laboratories.

[7]G.R. Taylor, *The Natural History of the Mind* (New York: Elsevier, 1979) 206.

[8]John E. Flynn, "A Survey of Current Research in Light and Psychology," Designers Lighting Forum, Los Angeles, January 1975.

[9]E.W. Sucov and L.H. Taylor, "The Effect of Nonuniform Light Distributions on Behavior," Congress of the Commission Internationale de L'Eclairage, London, 1975; and W.W. Ramage, "Task Performance Under Stimulating Light," unpublished research (Pittsburgh: Westinghouse Research Laboratories, 1973).

[10]John E. Flynn, T.J. Spencer, O. Martyniuk, and C. Hendrick, *Interim Report: The Effect of Light on Human Judgment and Behavior* (New York: Illuminating Engineering Research Institute, 1975).

**FIGURE 1-17: The Effect of Light
on Impressions and Behavior**
Light controls how people experience a given place, how they use it, and whether they will return to it. Using Flynn's studies and those currently in progress by Craig Bernecker (Pennsylvania State University) and others, the designer will be able to create spaces of whatever mood the client desires and describes. (Photographs by Robert Fischer.)

USING COMPOSITIONAL LIGHTING TECHNIQUES

Chapter Two

IN LIGHTING DESIGN, composition refers to the organization of light and color to create brightnesses that pull the various parts of the design solution into a satisfying and visually logical whole. The pioneering research done by the late John Flynn has proven that both the behavior and the judgments of visitors to an interior are cued by the brightnesses they perceive. That is why the composition of brightnesses is such a potentially powerful instrument in design.

With brightness and shadow alone the designer can create a compelling visual experience that is not only affective but timely. As the cost of electricity has soared and the need to conserve energy has become imperative, using light selectively has delivered savings. Lighting compositions that depend on the juxtaposition of brightnesses—rather than on the uniformly high levels of illumination previously recommended—produce savings in energy costs so substantial that they can offset costs of labor, material, and design. Figure 2-1 illustrates these lighting alternatives.

LIGHTING FOR UNITY AND HARMONY

The ideal lighting composition harmonizes unity with variety; it is coherent and yet exciting. When composing a space with light, there are four elements to consider: (1) framing, (2) primary focus, (3) secondary focus, and (4) delight. Framing involves determining the most influential vista. Because first impressions are the most lasting, this is often the view from the entrance into the space. Next, the primary focus must be established. The following are some qualifications for a primary focus:

A vertical surface or object within the line of sight that provokes impact or appeal

A surface or object whose mass dominates the architecture or the interior

A particularly successful part of the interior design

Such a primary focus provides a unifying center around which the visitor's visual experience will be organized. He/she will move toward this center and sit facing it.

The secondary foci visually balance the primary one. One rule of thumb is to deal with bright vertical surfaces as if they had physical weight. Attention will be drawn to the broadest and brightest surface as if it were heavier, and will establish the direction of awareness and movement in the room. Figure 2-1c illustrates this primary and secondary foci.

Now comes the magic. In every lighting design there should be some kind of unexpected delight. It can be a special effect like the play of light and shadow; or it can be luminous art. Most importantly, it should give the project a uniqueness only the designer could conceive.

COMPOSITIONAL WORKING METHODS

One way to create the most efficient lighting design for a given project—that is, one that uses a minimum of electricity to deliver the maximum in meaningful brightness—is to begin by placing colors of high reflectance in those important places where the eye should stop. The greatest spread of the most highly reflecting color will be the primary focus if (1) color contrasts between object and background are proper and (2) the highly reflecting color is also lighted.

To insure that the proper contrast of adjacent colors has been developed, there should be at least 4 Munsell values or a 40 percent difference between the reflectancies of each pair of colors that will be seen together as object and background. There are several kinds of contrasts that involve hue and chroma as well as value (reflectancies). (Color Plate 1 illustrates some of these more classic contrasting relationships of object and background colors.) Additionally, backgrounds finished in the darker color would benefit from some texture. Conversely, objects with a pale, highly reflecting color should be smooth and shiny. Shiny surfaces are less porous and increase light reflectance; while matte or toothy textures sponge up additional light and decrease reflectance. By maximizing these

a

b

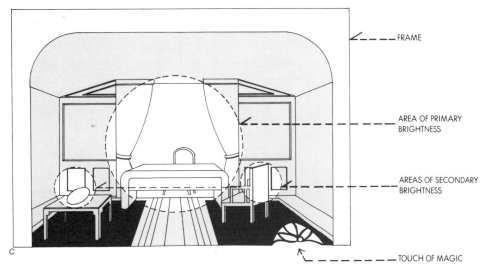

c

FIGURE 2-1: Lighting Composition
Before electricity became scarce and costly, ideal lighting consisted of evenly spreading a high level of footcandles across a space to illuminate any task to be done. Today, however, ownership budgets and energy codes will often allow designers to light only the critical parts of a space. The designer must use selective brightnesses to create spaces of equal appeal in designed appearance, user comfort, and function. (Photographs by Wen Roberts Photo, Inc.; Illustration by Reiko Hayashi.)

FRAME

AREA OF PRIMARY BRIGHTNESS

AREAS OF SECONDARY BRIGHTNESS

TOUCH OF MAGIC

FIGURE 2-2: Highlighting
(Above) Low-voltage lighting equipment has expanded the usefulness of highlighting immensely. Using the very precise optics of low-voltage light bulbs, brightness balances can be created which compose the space into a unified and interesting whole by highlighting only specific objects and surfaces in an otherwise dark environment. This technique is often used in museums, where sensitive artifacts benefit from dramatic effects like this that rely on contrast rather than an onslaught of raw footcandles. (Lighting by David Winfield Willson and Nancy Burns, Luminae; Photograph by Stone and Steccati Photographers.)

FIGURE 2-3: Wallwashing
(Opposite page, top) Some classic uses for wallwashing are (1) to feature the fireplace wall in a living room; (2) to unify a gallery wall while permitting changes of the art; (3) to light a staircase indirectly in order to avoid direct glare; and (4) to disguise the scars, bumps, or seams of an imperfect wall or ceiling surface.

FIGURE 2-4: Beam Play
(Opposite page, bottom) An example of an earlier use of beam play was the "pools of light" effect at the end of the "Jimmy Durante Show" which was seen on television in the early 1950s. More recently, shapes of light on walls or floors have developed from geometric to expressive. (Lighting by David Winfield Willson; Interiors by Baldwin/Clarke Associates; Photograph by Stephen Fridge © 1984.)

differences in the amount of reflected light, the designer will maximize brightness contrast and visual impact.

SPECIFIC LIGHTING TECHNIQUES
Once the reflectance characteristics of the space have been carefully planned, the designer can use one of the following lighting techniques to reinforce the areas of high contrast (see Figures 2-2 through 2-11).

Highlighting
Highlighting is a technique that creates more than five times the amount of brightness on a featured object than the brightness on the background. Its high contrast draws attention and determines how people will move and sit in a space (Figure 2-2). With this technique, the designer can plan a space that benefits the client. For example, a common device of store planners is to place the highest brightnesses on the displays within sight at the rear of the department so that curious pedestrians, walking between the store's escalators, will be drawn further into the department.

Low-voltage lighting has expanded the usefulness of this technique immensely. Using the precise beams of low-voltage light bulbs, brightness balances can be created that compose the space into a unified whole by highlighting specific objects and surfaces in an otherwise dark environment.

This type of low-voltage highlighting is energy conserving not only because of the electrical efficiency of the low-voltage lamp bulb and its transformer, but also because the user wastes no light on any surface other than the visual target—this is the so-called "efficiency in use." However, low-voltage highlighting is not without its problems. High amperages, voltage drops over long distances from transformer to bulb, and unsuccessful longterm dimming all present problems. (See Case Study Three, p. 130.)

Wallwashing
With this technique, the designer visually unifies a wall with a sheet of brightness (Figure 2-3). Four visual effects occur with wallwashing:

A directionality is created for the space.

Diverse objects on the wall are drawn together because the objects and the space between them are seen in the same light.

Large quantities of gentle, indirect light are bounced back into the space.

Texture of the wall seems flattened.

Incandescent, fluorescent, metal halide, and high-pressure sodium are among the many light sources used for wallwashing. However, the increasing cost of electricity makes the other sources more desirable than incandescents. When using fluorescents, the tubes should overlap by 2 inches

(5 cm) to prevent dark streams from appearing in the sheet of light (see Appendix A-1: Structural Lighting Charts). Remember when using HID (high-intensity discharge) lamp bulbs that they are extraordinarily powerful for their size. Consult with the fixture manufacturer for spacing recommendations.

Beam Play

If the designer can feature an object with an intentional beam of a highlight, then the beam itself can surely be used as a visual feature—that is, as a bright shape. Playful techniques with light beams and shadows can be used to enliven particularly bland space, such as a corridor (Figure 2-4).

Light sources that are in clear glass bulbs create the most distinct beam patterns and shadows. Sometimes the effect is created with *gobos*—stencils used to cut off all light not contributing to the desired light pattern. The critical concern is the optical relationship between the light source and the gobo in front of it. When selecting a fixture, the designer should look for one with as much flexibility in the socket's position as possible. In the final focusing phase, adjustment of the socket will determine the width of the light beam, as well as the crispness of the light pattern.

Another critical factor is the character of the surface onto which the pattern of light falls. The more textured or matte the surface, the softer the patterns. A reflectant surface with a Munsell value of between 5.5 and 8 is beneficial. Within these limits, the higher the color value or reflectance, the more visible the pattern and the more light reflected from the surface into the room. (See Table 1-3 for equivalencies.)

Shadow Play

This technique is the reverse of beam play. Here the pattern of light is the background, or negative space, while the shape of the shadow carries the visual message. For example, an interior can be softened by throwing the shadows of plants onto its ceiling. Shadows can also be used to expand the scale and impact of three-dimensional lettering and sculpture (Figure 2-5).

Fixtures used for shadow play are the same as those for beam play, but those having a wide and soft-edged beam are preferable to those having the more optically precise and hard-edged beam.

Silhouetting

This technique sandwiches an object between the viewer and a sheet of light. The object will be outlined by the light whose brightness acts as negative space. Its high contrast focuses attention on the outlined shape of the featured object. This technique can break up visual glare, or augment the importance of the featured object, but it obliterates detail on the front of the object (Figure 2-6). Wallwashing fixtures are often used to produce these silhouetting effects.

FIGURE 2-7:   Backlighting
An interesting application of backlighting is
its use behind draped fabrics in tented
ceilings, dining pavilions, and stretched-
fabric columns. Be sure that the fabrics are
chemically treated for flame retardancy and
noncombustion so as to resist the heat from
the light source. (Lighting/Interiors/Photo-
graph by Lloyd Bell, FASID.)

FIGURE 2-8:   Downlighting
The same downlighting technique that
designers successfully use for high-ceilinged
spaces may not be as successful in low-
ceilinged spaces where people may appear
ghastly with downlights directly above their
heads. If a designer insists on using
downlights in a space that has ceilings of 9
feet (270 cm) or less, then he/she must be
certain that the user will not be sitting directly
beneath the downlight. (Lighting by Nancy
Burns, Luminae; Interiors by Westin Services
and Supply; Photograph by Dick Busher ©
1983.)

rays of light showering down the wall to put flecks of brightness at the top of every textured bump in their path, and to put hard-edged shadows under each bump. This staccato pattern of brightness/shadow is the same as that found on rough textures in nature.

Like wallwashing, grazing is often used to define a space by featuring one wall over the others. By using a building material as if it was a sculptural panel, grazing light can create interest where there isn't any. It is this application that makes it especially suitable for corridors, and other areas where accessories would be inappropriate, too bulky, or too costly.

Some scalloping results when incandescent sources of light are used for grazing. Although they can create a rhythmic pattern of brightness on the wall, many people find them objectionable. The scallops of light can be visually obscured by raising the light source above the ceiling in a light slot, or by dropping a valance in front of them.

Uplighting
This technique is appropriate when what is up is interesting and should be emphasized. The varieties of uplight relate closely to fixture location (Figure 2-10). The following are some classic uses for uplighting:

Light a tall wall where maintenance of other hardware would be more difficult than the maintenance of fixtures buried conveniently in the sidewalk or lawn

Locate open top candlelamps at every table in a restaurant so that all the diners look romantic

Create movable pools of ambient light by using floor standing cylinders ("kiosks") to provide indirect, ambient light for clusters of workstations

Light a space entirely indirectly from uniformly spaced suspended uplights

The most common uplighting fixtures are called *indirect fixtures* (see Chapter Five). A wide variety of portable indirect fixtures are available, such as plug-in cylinders, pedestals, and kiosks. Wall bracket uplights are common. There are also direct burial uplights that can be mounted in floors, concrete, and earth, and often can be aimed, so that they function like upside-down accent lights.

Sparkle
In addition to the preceding classifications of lighting techniques, there is one that uses the light source itself instead of the object or surface that the light strikes. The technique of sparkle occurs when bits of pleasing brightness appear on a dark background. The brightness contrast with sparkle is higher than the other techniques, because the viewer is gazing at the light source itself.

However, sparkle is also glare. In work

FIGURE 2-9: Wallwashing and Grazing
(Left) For a wall that is 8 to 10 feet (240 to 300 cm) high, the common wallwasher is a recessed fixture that uses a 150-watt incandescent reflector flood bulb. Such fixtures are spaced 3 feet (90 cm) from the wall and are normally 3 feet apart in a row that parallels the wall. In using larger or smaller wallwashers, remember that for a smooth, even sheet of light, incandescent fixtures must be as close to one another (on center) as the distance from their row to the wall.

(Below) Factors to consider when selecting a downlight for use in the grazing technique include the height of the vertical surface, as well as the color and porosity of the textured surface off of which the light will reflect. Because the wall will absorb much of the light that cascades down it, the selection of the light source must be adjusted to suit the wall's reflectance characteristics. (General Electric Lighting Business Group.)

environments glare can add to visual discomfort and fatigue if experienced for long time periods. But for spaces where no tasks are performed and festivities will occur, sparkle can be welcome.

The following are some good uses of the sparkle technique:

Cue a mood of festivity

Attract the curious

Enliven conversation and interaction

Often sparkle is used to decorate, that is, to add a border around architectural planes or surfaces (Figure 2-11). Most of the light sources used for sparkle are assemblies of low-voltage incandescent bulbs formerly used as auto dashboard indicator lamps. They burn for 20,000 hours or more.

Light as Art
The fascination here lies with a product or effect that must be original and unique in both form and content. Artists today are creating works with a variety of light sources and forms. These works will be explored more fully and illustrated in Chapter Nine.

Works of art created from or with light can be used as the focal point of the designer's lighting plan with additional lighting balanced around its needs. This usually means a darkened space, because light-as-art shows best in a black, nontask environment where traffic and safety needs are not

FIGURE 2-10: Uplighting
Here, high-pressure sodium floodlights, usually found outdoors, have been used to turn a ceiling of khaki colored metallic plates into a beautiful gold color—a good use of uplighting. (Lighting by Fred J. Bertolone, MIES; Interiors by Hub McDaniels, ASID; Photograph by Dick Busher © 1976.)

FIGURE 2-11: Sparkle
Sparkle can be seen best in a dark environment. It is one of the lighting effects that is washed out by daylight. (Tivoli Industries.)

numerous. Flat, wide corridors are perfect for such artwork, as are some dining rooms, restaurants, and master bedrooms.

Luminous art can be visually fragile—that is, it can be washed away by daylighting. Such art usually tolerates competing attractions poorly; even the secondary brightness, normally used to balance the lighting composition, can easily overpower a piece of luminous art.

DECORATIVE FIXTURES

The proper use of decorative fixtures involves many considerations:

The task for which the light is needed

The suitable styling of a fixture

The attractiveness of nearby surfaces affected by the light from this fixture

How these bright surfaces will fit into the brightness balances of the space

Whether the brightness of the fixture fits into the intended brightness balances

Decorative fixtures can provide good task lighting because they are usually portable and can be positioned at an ideal angle and distance to the surface where the light is needed. Little light is wasted. However, it is often hard to locate a fixture with the right styling, finish, and scale to accessorize the interior. When the right one is found, the quality of its light beam is usually inadequate. A good combination of styling and usefulness is difficult to find (Figure 2-12).

In addition to traditional English, French, Chinese, and American colonial fixtures, there is a large variety of decorative architectural fixtures on the market. Eyeballs,

optical projectors, and low-voltage spotlights can be used for highlighting and beam or shadow play. Portable light boxes and luminous screens can be used for silhouetting and backlighting. Sparkle is achieved with rope and ribbon lights.

FIGURE 2-12: Decorative Portable
It is important to select a fixture for both its appearance and its effect on the brightness balances of a space. This incandescent fixture is not only beautifully configured, it also has a dimmer to adjust the light output. (Design by Georgina Aasen Casella; Manufactured by Casella Lighting.)

Most of these decorative portables, however, are available on a residential, rather than a commercial scale. For this reason, there are professional lighting design firms that design and build custom decorative fixtures, on a larger architectural scale. The designer can also try manufacturers specializing in church fixtures.

COMPARING COMPOSITIONAL LIGHTING TECHNIQUES
Four criteria can be used to evaluate the relative merits of the 12 compositional techniques discussed in this chapter: energy, expense, difficulty, and critical details. Table 2-1 presents a comparison of these 12 techniques.

LOOKING AHEAD
When the designer has assessed all the information about the project—client motivation, client vision, daylighting conditions, color palette, activities, and desired mood, he/she can compose the interior by allocating vertical brightnesses according to the priorities of the project. Then, a tentative lighting design can be planned.

By adding notes to the worksheets found in Figures 2-13 and 2-14, the designer can formulate a preliminary but thorough plan before testing its feasibility. An effective design must be able to withstand the rigors of budget, schedule, construction, and code restraints. These constraints will be discussed in the following chapter. Once these are evaluated and accommodated for by the preliminary plan, the designer can decide what sources of light to use and what fixtures to select, the topics of Chapters Four and Five.

Prioritize important areas	one WINDOW SEAT	two BED WALL	three VANITY/ DESK	four WING CHAIR (READING)	five	six
A. Decide on color rendition needed from the light source (cool/warm/both)	COOL	COOL	COOL	COOL		
B. Decide on the quality of light for mood (hard vs. soft)	HARD	SOFT	HARD BUT BLENDED	INVISIBLE		
C. Decide on the light intensity appropriate to the area (high/low/mid)	LOW	HIGH	HIGH	LOW		
D. Decide if the area should advance, recede, or remain (cool colors, low contrast, and dim light recede/ warm colors, high contrasts, and bright light advance)	RECEDE	REMAIN	REMAIN	REMAIN		
E. Decide on brightness contrast for each area in relation to the other areas	SECONDARY	BRIGHTEST	AUGMENTS SECONDARY	DON'T. FORGET		

FIGURE 2-13: Preliminary Lighting Design Decisions
This form of analysis will become second nature to the designer as he/she accumulates lighting successes.
(Concept by Peter Murphy, Design Lighting, Inc., Richmond, British Columbia, Canada. Adaptation by authors.)

TABLE 2-1   COMPARISON OF LIGHTING TECHNIQUES

TECHNIQUE	ENERGY EFFICIENCY	EXPENSE		DIFFICULTY	CRITICAL DETAILS
		First	Owning		
Front					
Highlighting					Highlighting: Short-lived lamp bulbs unless dimmed; may require hand-focusing with each lamp bulb change.
Low-voltage incandescent	3	9	1	10	
Beam Play					Beam Play: Hand focus first time. Be careful to match finish colors to light source colors.
Incandescent	8	2	8	7	
Metal halide	2	8	2	8	
Shadow Play					Shadow Play: Same as above.
Incandescent	8	2	8	7	
Metal halide	2	8	2	8	
Wallwashing					Remember to adjust set back distances (high-output fluorescents). Be wary of color distortions (low-wattage HID).
Incandescent	9	3	7	2	
Fluorescent*	5	4	2	9	
HID	1	9	1	5	
Rear					
Silhouetting					Silhouetting: Do not silhouette people.
Incandescent	9	3	7	2	
Fluorescent	6	4	2	5	
HID	1	9	1	4	
Backlighting					Backlighting: Do not cramp depth of lightbox.
Fluorescent	6	6	3	5	
Structural					(See Appendix A-1: Structural Lighting Charts.)
Fluorescent	6	4	2	6	
Down					
Downlighting					Downlighting: Never put downlights within 3 feet directly over seated persons.
Incandescent	11	4	9	3	
Fluorescent**	7	7	3	3	
HID	4	10	4	3	
Grazing					Grazing: Be flexible in adjusting for projection depth of textured finishes.
Incandescent	9	3	7	6	
Up					
Uplighting					Uplighting: Space may seem soupy & out-of-focus; uplight fixtures will silhouette against bright ceiling.
Incandescent	12	4	10	2	
Fluorescent	7	5	3	4	
HID	5	11	5	4	
Light as Object					
Sparkle					Sparkle: To be tested and installed by experienced contractor only.
Low-voltage incandescent	3	4	3	10	
Art					Art: Keep ambient light level low; very fragile.
Incandescent	3	6	10	11	
Fluorescent	6	6	9	11	
Decoratives					Decoratives: Balance effectiveness with appearance.
Incandescent	10	5	6	1	

*Low-energy ballast and matching lamps.

**Two-lamp downlight (compact "PL" lamps).

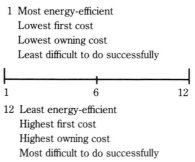

KEY

1 Most energy-efficient
    Lowest first cost
    Lowest owning cost
    Least difficult to do successfully

|———————|———————|
1   6   12

12 Least energy-efficient
     Highest first cost
     Highest owning cost
     Most difficult to do successfully

Column headings (left to right):

Light Sources: low-pressure sodium · high-pressure sodium · metal halide · fluorescent · mercury · incandescent · standard · quartz · low voltage
Controls: switches · dimmers
Fixtures: ballasts · standard · remote · energy · adjustable volts
mounting: recessed · semirecessed · surface mounted · track mounted · suspended · wall bracketed · burial · structural · portable
features: adjustable · accessory clips · sloped ceiling ring
accessories: louvers · lenses · shields · trims

ANALYSIS FACTORS	low-press. sodium	high-press. sodium	metal halide	fluorescent	mercury	incandescent	standard	quartz	low voltage	switches	dimmers	ballasts	standard	remote	energy	adj. volts	recessed	semirecessed	surface mtd	track mtd	suspended	wall brack.	burial	structural	portable	adjustable	access. clips	sloped ring	louvers	lenses	shields	trims
Client vision																																
needs extra light											●																					
glare sensitive							●										●				●	●				●	●			●		●
Daylight orientation																																
north				●	●																											
south		●									●																					
east				●	●																											
west					●	●																										
Climate																																
cold	●	●		●	●								●						●	●	●			●						●		
warm				●	●									●										●								
Color characteristics																																
warm			●	●	●		●				●															●				●		
cool		●	●	●						●																						
ultraviolet sensitivity	●	●					●	●	●																							
Reflectance																																
extra dark	●	●	●	●																												
extra light																										●						
Activities																																
precision tasks											●																		●	●		
traffic cues needed							●	●	●		●															●			●			
safety concerns							●	●			●															●			●		●	
CONSTRAINTS																																
Codes																																
building				●			●			●			●											●								
safety							●				●								●					●						●		●
energy	●	●	●												●						●			●								
Schedule																																
fast track				●			●				●									●	●			●								
Construction																																
limited plenum depth				●			●						●				●				●	●	●	●								
ceilings																																
attached							●												●	●	●					●				●		
suspended																																
high	●			●			●				●										●	●		●								
low				●			●						●								●	●	●	●								
Budget																																
first cost							●																									
installation cost							●														●											
owning and operating cost	●	●									●										●			●								

FIGURE 2-14: Planning Perception Chart
Because the lighting solution responds to parameters unique to each project, it is helpful to see that each parameter implies that certain lighting sources and lighting fixtures will be more successful than others. (Fran Kellogg Smith.)

WORKING WITH CONSTRAINTS

Chapter Three

THERE ARE FOUR major constraints the designer must work with when creating a lighting plan:

1. Schedule for design and construction

2. Scope and complexity of construction

3. Codes for public health and safety

4. Budgets for construction and operation

These parameters should be used to examine the basic concept of every lighting design for feasibility before the light sources and fixtures are selected.

DESIGN AND CONSTRUCTION SCHEDULES

An unrealistic design schedule—one that doesn't provide adequate time for the completion of all phases—causes failures in communication and oversights in planning. Ironically, such failures often guarantee that a project will run over schedule and over budget. For example, to save time, a designer sometimes delegates some of the design responsibilities to contractors by choosing the more rapidly written document of performance specifications. In such a case, an inadequate amount of design time may have been spent thinking about how a given product's performance will affect other products and systems. Often this inattention to detail necessitates changes in construction which causes delay. Although clear, thoughtful, and explicit plans and specifications may take more time initially, they always result in fewer problems and construction delays later (Appendix B-1: Specifications for Construction Schedules).

Because few schedules are ample, one frequent concern when specifying lighting fixtures is how quickly a manufacturer can ship under the worst of circumstances. The wise designer will often list as "equal" at least one manufacturer located in the vicinity of the project for each major fixture "type."

If delays in installing the lighting occur, one remedy is *liquidated damages*. These are sums of money paid by the general contractor to the owner in the event of a late project. To be enforceable, the amount of the damages must be fixed in the contract for construction, and must bear a reasonable relationship to the foreseeable losses if the project/facility is not opened on time. However, this remedy is more theoretical than practical. The difficulty in proving who originally caused a delay in construction often prevents damages from actually being paid.

The newest method of administering schedules and budgets is called *construction management*. Figure 3-1 compares this method to the previously preferred system based on the administration of the general contractor. Under this system, a manager is hired directly by an owner to play a dominant role throughout the design, bidding, and construction phases. Such a manager often furnishes the design team with a timeline that gives required percentages of completion and other "knock down" targets. Sometimes the manager goes on to the construction phase to act in lieu of the general contractor, furnishing a *critical path chart* (CPM) to the subcontractors during the construction phase.

Critical Path Method

The traditional scheduling method has been the use of a *bar chart,* but this lacks a systematic means of showing the effect of changes on affiliated trades. The CPM schedule is a network that graphically shows the relationships of the various trades and their activities. First, it shows the order of submittals, approvals, and fabrication activities as well as installation. Second, resources and time are estimated for each of these. Then, the interrelationships among the various activities are determined to be either critical or noncritical. The critical activities are linked to become the *critical path*. The CPM schedule provides the designer with an excellent way to check whether fixture orders and rough wiring and inspections are being performed as needed. This method also pinpoints precisely where and how delays in these activities will affect the total project.

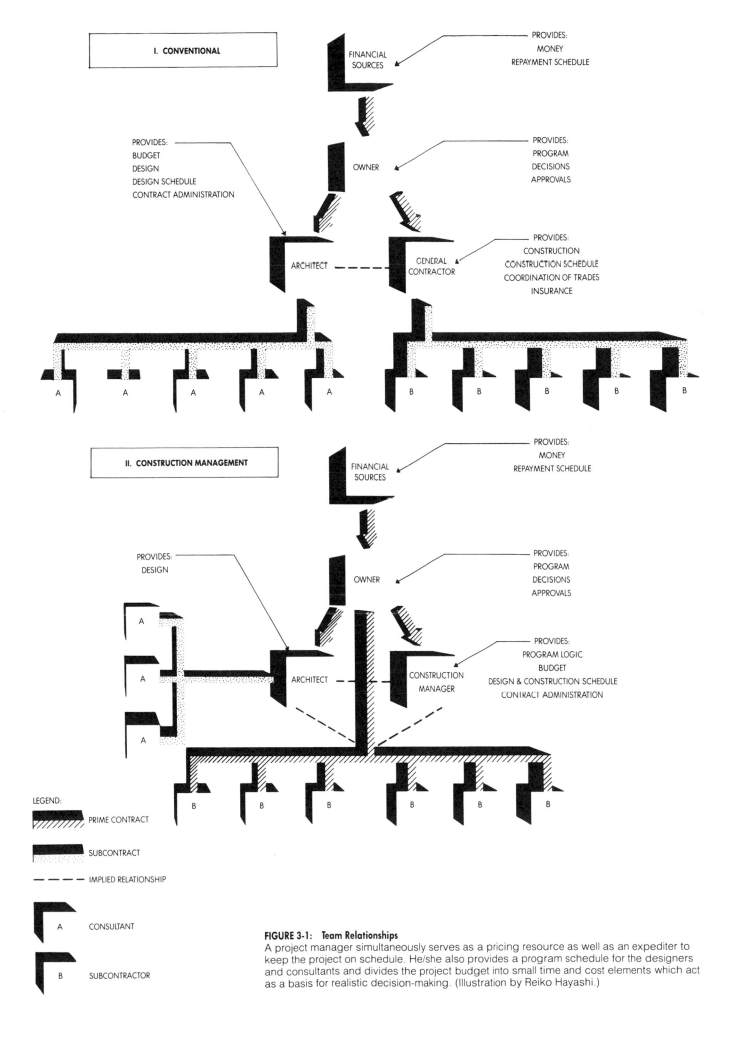

I. CONVENTIONAL

FINANCIAL SOURCES

PROVIDES:
MONEY
REPAYMENT SCHEDULE

OWNER

PROVIDES:
BUDGET
DESIGN
DESIGN SCHEDULE
CONTRACT ADMINISTRATION

PROVIDES:
PROGRAM
DECISIONS
APPROVALS

ARCHITECT

GENERAL CONTRACTOR

PROVIDES:
CONSTRUCTION
CONSTRUCTION SCHEDULE
COORDINATION OF TRADES
INSURANCE

A   A   A   A   A   B   B   B   B   B

II. CONSTRUCTION MANAGEMENT

FINANCIAL SOURCES

PROVIDES:
MONEY
REPAYMENT SCHEDULE

OWNER

PROVIDES:
DESIGN

A
A
A

PROVIDES:
PROGRAM
DECISIONS
APPROVALS

ARCHITECT

CONSTRUCTION MANAGER

PROVIDES:
PROGRAM LOGIC
BUDGET
DESIGN & CONSTRUCTION SCHEDULE
CONTRACT ADMINISTRATION

B   B   B   B   B   B

LEGEND:

PRIME CONTRACT

SUBCONTRACT

— — — IMPLIED RELATIONSHIP

A   CONSULTANT

B   SUBCONTRACTOR

FIGURE 3-1: Team Relationships
A project manager simultaneously serves as a pricing resource as well as an expediter to keep the project on schedule. He/she also provides a program schedule for the designers and consultants and divides the project budget into small time and cost elements which act as a basis for realistic decision-making. (Illustration by Reiko Hayashi.)

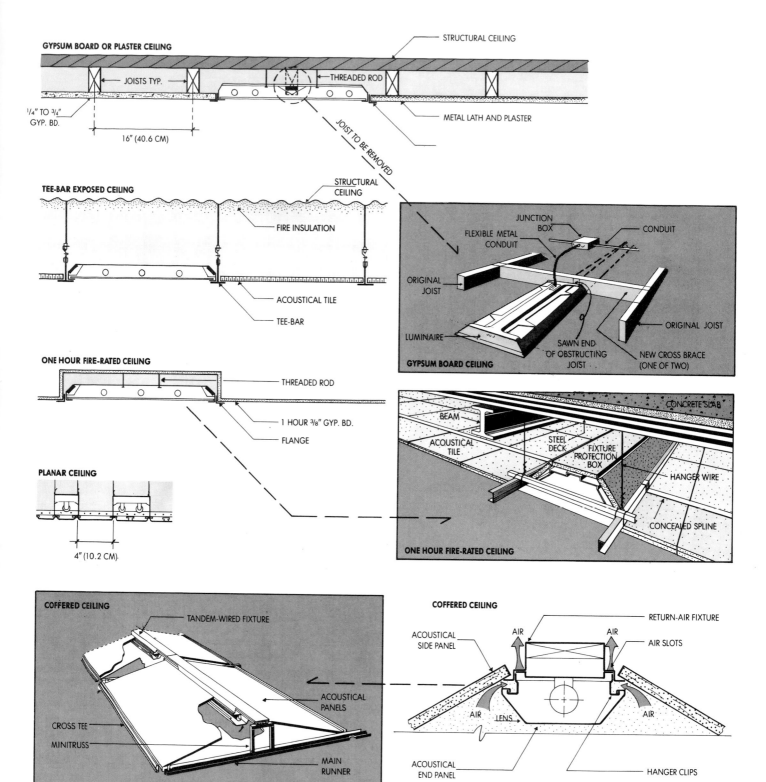

FIGURE 3-2:   Typical Ceilings with Recessed Fixtures
If the designer intends to use recessed fixtures in attached ceilings, care must be taken to orient the fixture pattern so that the recessed housings will lie between the ceiling joists or rafters. On an attached ceiling, the most easily installed fixtures are surface-mounted or suspended. (Illustration by Reiko Hayashi.)

COMPLEXITY OF CONSTRUCTION

The second constraint affecting lighting design is the size, scope, and complexity of the construction project. If the construction process is an extended one, a simple but bold lighting design will fare far better than one that relies on exact recessing locations or precision adjustments performed by hand. Experimental lighting equipment—and especially experimental lighting concepts—should be reserved for smaller projects where less misunderstanding is likely to occur and where such experimental equipment can be attentively "road tested."

Scale

There are two construction variables that can adversely affect the lighting concept: scale and time. The former can be divided into two aspects: the scale of individual spaces and the scope of the project as a whole. If the spaces are large, it often leads to the specification of a large number of custom fixtures. Although custom fixtures are costly, both in design time and purchase price, a designer can easily control their design, quality of manufacture, purchase, and delivery. This is partly because the design and manufacturing process are agreed upon by the designer and the fixtures' manufacturer. Additionally, they may decide that the purchase should be made directly by the owner in order to protect the fixtures from being knocked off. The illicit knock-off is usually manufactured with a low grade of materials and by a factory that has limited understanding of design objectives and criteria for fixtures.

As for the scope of the project as a whole, a large one will bring out every conceivable kind of lighting vendor. A design specifier needs to be very assertive about his/her specifications. Where less costly substitutions are permitted by the documents, it is almost certain they will be made. If there is a reasonable quantity of fixtures and light sources that must not be altered in any way, the designer must be prepared to defend them and to expedite their order and delivery, if necessary. In short, among the fifty or sixty lighting specifications in a project manual, it would be foolish to write more than a dozen "sole source" or proprietary specifications for a project that has a total of 500,000 square feet. This constraint becomes very harsh when applied to light sources because, for example, among the HID and low-voltage light sources, real equals cannot be found. A 175-watt warm deluxe white metal halide lamp bulb by General Electric does not give the same color and beam spread as the same lamp bulb by GTE Sylvania.

Time

The time span for the installation of a major project can create many problems. First, if there are several years between design and product delivery, new fixtures, light sources, and controls can prove unreliable for various reasons: their manufacturers can remove them from the market; their accessory components (like necessary ballasts) may not be available; their hardware may perform badly because quality control issues have not yet been identified by their manufacturers; and an inspector may not accept such items readily—or at all.

Second, the reasons for selecting certain fixtures or their locations may become blurred over time, both in the design office and on the construction site. This is yet another reason to keep a lighting design simple and self-apparent. A third problem is that the first and second difficulties mentioned here occur in all the other building trades as well and as accommodations are made, the original bid drawings become less and less representative of the actual work.

Ceilings

The construction details of a ceiling can greatly constrain a lighting design (Figure 3-2). The purpose of a ceiling is to define the upper limit of a space. A ceiling provides a thermal barrier, an acoustical barrier, and fireproofing, in addition to its potential as a location for light fixtures. It is essential that the designer know the type of ceiling to be used in a project and what functions its plenum (attic) performs. Proper locations for fixtures, the overall depth and appropriate flange for recessed fixtures, and the type of Underwriters Laboratory (UL) labeling all depend on proper identification of the ceiling system.

The location of lighting equipment is also compromised by other functions of plenum construction (Figure 3-3). For example, an air distribution device may be required by the mechanical engineer at the exact point on a ceiling that a fixture should occupy; or a plumbing pipe may be concealed in a plenum space just above a ceiling. Ascertaining the details of ceiling construction becomes even more important when sprinklers and accent lighting are specified (Figure 3-4). The correct fixture specification depends on the ceiling type. For instance, in a suspended ceiling, the runners of a 1-foot (30.48 cm) grid can be a severe problem if wallwashing fixtures are to be located 3 feet (91.44 cm) from the wall. One lighting fixture incorrectly specified because of inade-

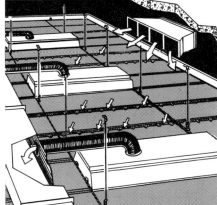

DUCTED SUPPLY/PLENUM EXHAUST

FIGURE 3-3: Typical Plenum Conditions
(a) To provide a less obstructed ceiling surface, designers may designate that the air supply and return registers be part of the lighting fixture. Fixtures which perform this function are known as "air handling." When they are required, a closer interface with the entire design team is vital. In such an instance, the needs of the mechanical engineer take precedence over the design needs.

PLENUM SUPPLY/DUCTED EXHAUST

(b) Selection of the fixtures depends upon whether the air movement should be accomplished through the fixture trim exclusively, or whether the air return should be handled through the lamp compartment and across the ballast housing. Air-handling fixtures are easier to use when the air movement does not pass through the lamp compartment. For maximum efficiency and increased light output, the fixture that passes the air through the lamp bulb compartment is best.

DUCTED SUPPLY/DUCTED EXHAUST

(c) If the plenum is used for air supply or return, the plenum and the structure must be fire-rated according to codes in most jurisdictions. These combination fixtures are particularly practical in spaces such as elevator lobbies, private offices, and hallways. Air-handling fixtures are available with incandescent, tungsten halogen, and HID sources, in addition to the fluorescent ones shown here. (Illustration by Reiko Hayashi.)

FIGURE 3-4: Ceilings as Design I
This hard-working Acoustone ceiling performs a myriad of functions. Sprinklers, air registers, and two kinds of lights are incorporated into the boldly textured pattern of overscale tiles. Less visibly, the tiles also control sound for conversational privacy and harmonize with room colors. (Photograph by USG Acoustical Products Company.)

FIGURE 3-5: Widgets and Gadgets of Suspended Ceiling Systems
Fixture manufacturers produce several different types of recessed fixtures for the marketplace. The three most common types are flanged trim, exposed grid trims, and regressed trim. Housings are formed with *flanged trim* to conceal raw, ugly cuts in the ceiling where the housing recesses into a wood or plaster ceiling. With *exposed grid* trims, housings are formed in a size and shape to drop into the metal suspension grid designated by one of the kinds of hangers: H-bar, T-bar, Z-bar, etcetera. When in place, the perfect match between fixture and grid conceals almost all metal parts of the fixture from occupants below. Housings for *regressed trim fixtures* are formed in the same manner as the exposed grid fixtures with the exception that the lowest plane of the fixture is higher than the ceiling plane. This is an excellent arrangement for fixtures that are too powerful or glaring, or for ceilings that are dark-colored. The regressed mounting component that makes it possible is inserted into the suspension grid before the fixture and then the fixture is mounted on top of it as if the component were a collar. (Illustration by Reiko Hayashi.)

EDGE DETAILS

TRIM EDGE

SQUARE EDGE
KERFED & BACKCUT

BEVEL EDGE
KERFED & BACKCUT

REVEAL EDGE

quate knowledge of a ceiling's construction can result in costly construction delays; delivery of fixtures that have a flange for an "H-bar" suspended ceiling instead of having the flange for a "T-bar" ceiling results in the entire quantity being returned to the factory for the welding of new flanges (Figure 3-5). Recent court cases have started to hold the designer liable for errors despite the fact that the designer may have no direct contract with the general contractor.

There is another way that ceiling type governs fixture type. Ceilings that are fire-rated impose additional restrictions on the lighting. The fixtures that are recessed into a fire-rated ceiling must be fire-rated themselves, or must be protected by employing fire-rated enclosures over the recessed fixtures. All fixtures that penetrate a fire-rated ceiling must be UL-labeled for recessed installation in such a ceiling.

Attached Ceilings. Ceiling systems are generally classified as *hung* or *attached* to the structure. The attached ceiling is the most simple; it can be made of lath and plaster, sheetrock, or wood. In some instances, the attached ceiling is exposed and the wooden tongue and groove boards are visible.

Exposed Beam Ceilings: In a residence, the most difficult ceiling the designer has to deal with is the exposed beam type. Its beams are structural members, and drilling, notching, or cutting them requires special care. The exposed beams support planking and a layer of sheathing. Before the final roofing is applied, insulation is placed on top. Regardless of the kind of roofing, once it is in place, any electrical circuits that have been built into it are costly to move. Lighting outlets have to be positioned before this final stage. A chandelier is frequently desired in these spaces, but its weight must be supported with adequate bracing placed on top of the sheathing, prior to the application of insulation.

Lath and Plaster, Sheetrock: These two are the most common forms of ceiling construction and they have two requirements in common. The first is that surface-mounted fixtures need UL-approved mechanical hangers to bear the fixtures' weight. The second is that because recessed fixtures' hangers are attached to a building's structure, they must have the fire-rating of the ceiling itself. Fire-ratings vary from one hour to three hours.

Acoustical Ceilings: The prevention of noise pollution has become a major concern in construction and design. Interior noise can be controlled through the use of acoustical

AIR SUPPLY DIFFUSERS

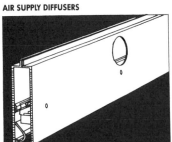

ELONGATED

CIRCULAR

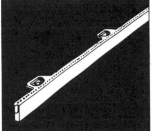

STRIP

FLAT SPLINE

WALL MOLDING

TEE SPLINE

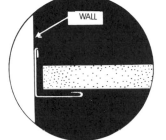

DOUBLE WED CROSS TEE

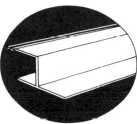

"Z" BAR

MAIN BEAM

FLAT STEEL SPLINE

ACCESS SPLINE

LAY-IN FIXTURES

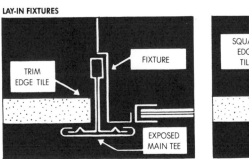

TRIM EDGE TILE

FIXTURE

EXPOSED MAIN TEE

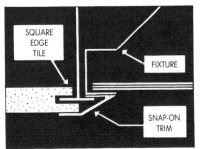

SQUARE EDGE TILE

FIXTURE

SNAP-ON TRIM

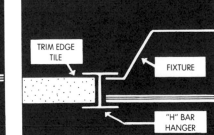

TRIM EDGE TILE

FIXTURE

"H" BAR HANGER

materials sprayed or applied to the ceiling. Penetration of this membrane by lighting fixtures will destroy its effectiveness. Acoustical shields also trap heat. For safety, fixtures must be UL-labeled for specific use with these ceilings because most fixtures generate heat that could be dangerous if confined by the acoustical membrane. The designer must also use precision in positioning recessed fixtures on acoustical ceilings; to reposition a fixture may require removing the sheetrock ceiling completely and then reconstructing and respraying it. Because acoustical material cracks when disturbed, track-mounted lighting is a good selection for such a ceiling.

Hung Ceilings. Hung ceilings are suspended from a building's structure to provide space for concealment of mechanical and electrical systems. Hung ceilings generally fall into two categories: nonfire-rated and fire-rated. The less regulated is nonfire-rated. But in regions where earthquakes or other trembler phenomena occur frequently, codes may require special hanger/clips which allow the fixture flexibility during such events. By comparison, fire-rated ceilings impose many restrictions on the de-

signer. For instance, fixtures that penetrate a fire-rated ceiling must be UL-labeled for the same hour-rating as the ceiling. In those instances where the designer uses a custom fixture, it is possible to have the fixture installation inspected and approved in the field by the Underwriters Laboratory. This practice is usually expensive and the arrangements must be made well in advance to avoid construction delays.

Suspended Grid Ceilings: The suspended grid ceiling is most often found in commercial buildings. The structure is first fireproofed; then the plenum is fitted with a fire-barrier ceiling with the cavity between ceiling and structure used for pipes, ducts, electrical wiring, communications wiring, and cables. The designer must know the locations of these to avoid interference with recessed lights.

Metal Ceilings: Metal ceilings are also more common in commercial structures (Figure 3-6). They are available in fire-rated and nonfire-rated types. Metal ceilings are generally lightly supported and if the designer plans to use heavy surfaces, pendants, or recess-mounted fixtures, additional support

from the building's structure might be needed. Ballasted or transformed fixtures having an "A" sound rating should be carefully selected; metallic ceilings will resonate the ballasts or transformers affixed to them, unless extreme care is taken in product selection and in cushioning installation.

Despite all the necessary precautions, ceiling systems can act as a centerpiece for the design of the interior. Standard moldings and fixtures can be assembled into surprisingly elegant constructions (Figure 3-7). Such a construction is often specified for a large space where people circulate continuously, e.g., ballrooms, stores, and transportation terminals.

CODE COMPLIANCE

Failure to comply with codes that protect consumer health and safety is one of the areas in which the law holds the licensed professional designer strictly liable. Ignorance of the law is not an acceptable defense. Contract clauses transferring the designer's responsibility to the contractor are seldom upheld by the courts.

To avoid these problems, the designer must comply with the codes that govern

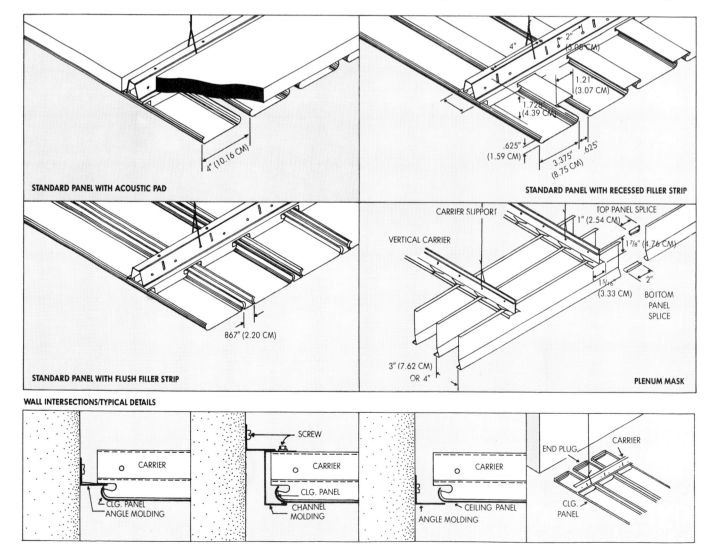

STANDARD PANEL WITH ACOUSTIC PAD

4" (10.16 CM)

STANDARD PANEL WITH RECESSED FILLER STRIP

STANDARD PANEL WITH FLUSH FILLER STRIP

867" (2.20 CM)

CARRIER SUPPORT

VERTICAL CARRIER

TOP PANEL SPLICE

1" (2.54 CM)

1 7/8" (4.76 CM)

2"

BOTTOM PANEL SPLICE

3" (7.62 CM) OR 4"

PLENUM MASK

WALL INTERSECTIONS/TYPICAL DETAILS

CARRIER

CLG. PANEL
ANGLE MOLDING

SCREW

CARRIER

CLG. PANEL

CHANNEL MOLDING

CARRIER

CEILING PANEL

ANGLE MOLDING

END PLUG

CARRIER

CLG. PANEL

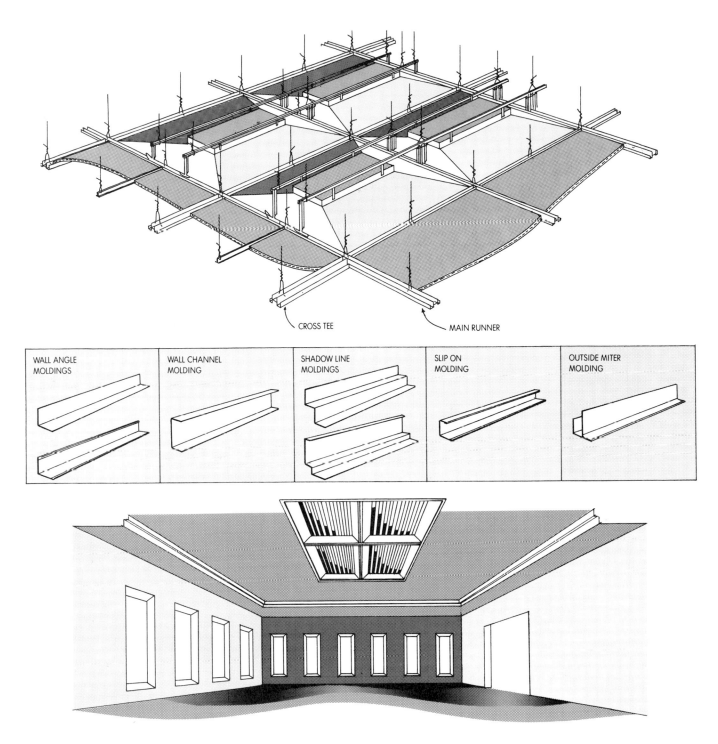

CROSS TEE   MAIN RUNNER

| WALL ANGLE MOLDINGS | WALL CHANNEL MOLDING | SHADOW LINE MOLDINGS | SLIP ON MOLDING | OUTSIDE MITER MOLDING |

FIGURE 3-6:   Metal Ceilings
(Left) As a design tool, these ceilings offer the designer an attractive alternative, but because of the extensive support system for the metal planks, the optimum point for fixture mounting may occur where a support channel is located. For this reason, the designer may find adjustable fixtures more adaptable in this situation. (Illustration by Reiko Hayashi.)

FIGURE 3-7:   Ceilings as Design II
(Above) The most familiar form of non-fire-rated ceilings are ones formed from T-bars. T-bar ceilings have metal runners of steel or aluminum which form a framework; fiber panels drop in the frame to close the ceiling cavity. The main Ts, or runners, carry the ceiling load. Building code often requires that the hung grid system have a support wire attached at each corner of the fixture to tie it to the grid and to the structure as well. (Illustration by Reiko Hayashi.)

his/her particular project. Although the current editions of the Uniform Building Code, Canadian Building Code, and National Electrical Code are always useful references, code requirements vary from community to community, depending on which edition of the National Standard was used as a model when the locality revised their ordinances. Many building codes often pertain to a single structure. Unfortunately, the dictates of one are not necessarily congruent with those of another. For instance, the State Hospital Code may require all hospital kitchen fixtures to be glass-covered, while the local electrical code requires easy bulb access for periodic inspections.

Obtaining Pertinent Code Data

It is important for the design team to know which codes will be applied to their project. To obtain the necessary information before the lighting design goes too far, many designers call the building inspection department in the locale where the project is to be constructed. Before calling, it is helpful to prepare a checklist of pertinent information about the project, so that the type of building can be correctly ascertained by the inspection department.

Some codes are more stringent than others; it depends on occupancy, usage, and size. The least restrictive codes are for single-family residences. High-rise, multifamily buildings are more thoroughly regulated. Office buildings, medical facilities, and retirement homes have even more stringent requirements to insure the health and safety of the occupants under emergency conditions. Places of public assembly such as theaters, churches, synagogues, and stores fall into yet another heavily regulated category (see Appendix B-2: Common Code Provisions and Appendix B-3: Special Code Conditions).

Once the designer has determined which regulatory bodies have jurisdiction and what their latest code is for a particular type of building, he/she can then investigate the possibility of getting the building inspection department to give advisory opinions on special lighting treatments. Often this preliminary interviewing will save many hours of redesign time—although advisory opinions are seldom rendered in writing. Only when the plans and specifications have been examined as a whole will a building inspection department approve them in writing. However, once they are approved, a more restrictive code which becomes operative at a later date does not affect the approved plans.

Basic Electrical Service

Although electrical wiring and circuitry must be designed by a consulting engineer, architect, or licensed general or electrical contractor, the designer should understand the distribution of electrical power so he/she can recommend practical switching patterns and lamping specifications for the lights.

Beginning at the property line, the local power company provides electrical service to a building's main panel. This equipment—called the *primary service*—may run underground or overhead. In most cases, the power company supplies, owns, and repairs all the electrical hardware up to and including the electrical meter. The main disconnect switch is at the meter. It feeds all the power distribution subpanels; in case of an emergency, its purpose is to provide a way to disconnect all electrical service to the building. Subpanels located throughout the structure are used to localize the control of electricity and to distribute the electrical circuits throughout the building. The meter base, disconnect switch, main panel, and all subpanels and distribution components (like switches and receptacles for plugs) are provided by the owner of the building. They are the *secondary service*.

Life Safety and Emergency Codes

All building codes include provisions for basic safety features. However, many multifamily residences, commercial offices, and public buildings will need to meet the more complex life safety codes. Most of these codes call for emergency lighting designed to lead occupants to safety—whether that consists of fire escapes, fire-rated stairwells, or exit doors.

The emergency lighting system for residential use usually contains three parts:

Emergency power supply, or battery

Transfer switch to reroute necessary fixtures from household electricity to battery-supplied electricity

Low-voltage light sources

When energized by the emergency battery, a low-voltage lamp bulb produces a penetrating beam of light to guide the way through dense smoke. These lamp bulbs generally sacrifice lamp life to achieve the required beam intensity. Therefore, emergency equipment lamps should be replaced after every use. For safety, emergency fixtures and illuminated exit signs should be checked on a regular schedule as recommended by the manufacturer or as sometimes required by OSHA (Occupational Safety and Health Administration) code. Whenever the designer has recommended emergency lighting, he/she should provide the client with a list of replacement bulbs needed for emergency lights.

Hotels. Life safety codes that govern hotels and other high-rise residential types of construction are among the most stringent. Designers should be fully conversant with the most recent recommendations of the American National Standards Institute and of the National Fire Protection Association codes for these facilities. Because one of the worst disasters in this type of building is nighttime fires, life support systems include emergency lighting in corridors, public areas, guest rooms, stairwells, fire escape columns, and other areas. Many codes will

---

CODE INFORMATION CHECKLIST
Note: Determination of the pertinent code depends upon identification of the project.

JURISDICTIONS	*Typical Inspecting Body*
☐ Project address	City building department
☐ Class	
(residential;	State licensing body;
health care;	county fire marshal
office; industrial;	
public assembly)	
☐ Occupancy	
(single; multiple)	City hotel/motel licensing body
☐ Use of the structure	
(presence of a cafeteria	County sanitation department
or other special use)	

HEALTH AND SAFETY ISSUES	*Typical Inspecting Body*
☐ Natural disasters	
(earthquake; flood; storm; etc.)	City building department
☐ Manmade disasters	County fire marshal
(fire/explosion/plague/pollution: air, water, noise, or light)	City air pollution control district
	County health department
☐ Special	
(disabled; sonic; energy; etc.)	State or city building department

SPECIAL INTERPRETATIONS

☐ New construction vs. remodel
(year of occupancy)

☐ Type of structural materials

☐ Number of stories

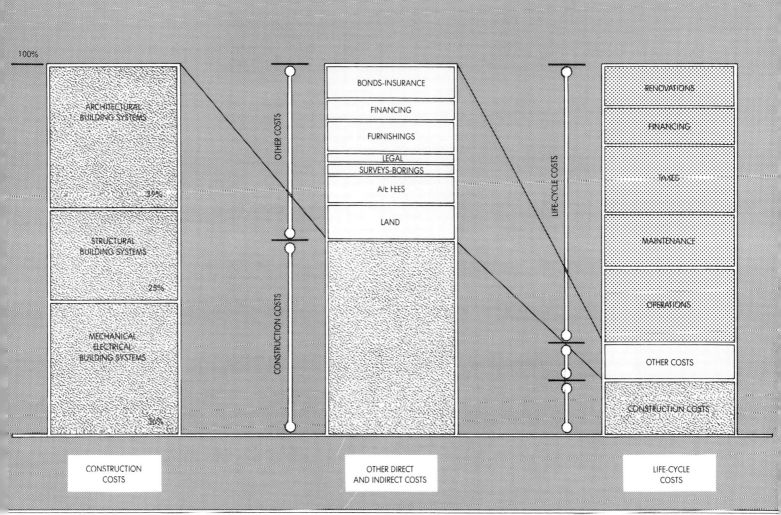

100%

ARCHITECTURAL BUILDING SYSTEMS	30%
STRUCTURAL BUILDING SYSTEMS	25%
MECHANICAL ELECTRICAL BUILDING SYSTEMS	30%

OTHER COSTS

CONSTRUCTION COSTS

BONDS-INSURANCE

FINANCING

FURNISHINGS

LEGAL

SURVEYS-BORINGS

A/E FEES

LAND

LIFE-CYCLE COSTS

| RENOVATIONS |
| FINANCING |
| TAXES |
| MAINTENANCE |
| OPERATIONS |
| OTHER COSTS |
| CONSTRUCTION COSTS |

CONSTRUCTION COSTS

OTHER DIRECT AND INDIRECT COSTS

LIFE-CYCLE COSTS

FIGURE 3-8: The Cost of a Building
Electrical costs vary between 5 dollars and 10 dollars per square foot; they are 10 percent to 15 percent of the total construction cost in a new building. Lighting makes up 11 percent of these electrical costs. But these figures will all vary according to the complexity of the project. (Illustration by Reiko Hayashi.)

require that these emergency light fixtures contain batteries with a push button and/or red indicator light on each unit for periodic inspections to determine whether the battery is fully functional.

Offices. The power source for the emergency lights is usually one of two kinds. The more elaborate of these involves standby motor generator sets and is found in hospitals, banks, and large corporate offices. The motor set is connected to a battery bank for immediate interim power until the more powerful standby generators reach the speed required to cause electricity to flow. The second, more common form of emergency lighting system for offices is one that uses remotely located self-contained battery packs and relay switches that turn the emergency lights on whenever power to the "e" (emergency electrical circuit) is disrupted. This e circuit is connected to an electrical panel reserved for emergency equipment. The quality of batteries used in the e circuit equipment varies widely, as does the quality of the automatic chargers. The designer should evaluate the differences carefully. Items to specifically check include:

Life of the battery

Length of time needed for the battery to fully recover once the system is operated

Degree of rotation of the light heads

Availability of replacement lamps and batteries

Projection distance of the light beam and its spread

BUDGET

One of the rewards of a successful lighting design occurs when an owner gets value received for the dollars spent on a given project. Therefore, the last, but most significant constraint on the lighting designer is cost, both in dollars spent and energy consumed. These have become synonymous since the cost of energy has become so expensive. The projected electrical bill is an important variable in the planning stages today (Figure 3-8). The budgeting of first costs is reworked several times during the design process.

First, an estimate is performed when the client program is completed by using the *current construction cost* multiplier times the projected square footage. Second, the schematic drawings are accompanied by a *probable cost projection* (PCP). Next, a revised probable projection cost is issued on the completion of the design drawings. Then at the conclusion of the working drawings and specifications, not before, bids are solicited. Additionally, specific *value engineering* studies may be conducted during construction.

For most professional designers, running over budget is a chronic problem. Because there are so many variables, the probable cost projection is difficult to predict. The most unpredictable variables are inflation, strikes, materials shortages, weather, cost of loans, and contractors' competing options to work on more lucrative local projects. Despite these difficulties, designers are compelled to explore conceptual design alternatives and system tradeoffs until cost targets can be realistically bracketed. When a design office goes considerably over budget, a project often must be redesigned to fall in budget, and this is done without additional design fees.

Computer Costing: Simple Projects

In a simple project like an office or showroom building, the lighting can be so straightforward that the layout of lighting fixtures can be instantly projected by computer. In return for the fixture order, many sales representatives are eager to perform this service for the design specifier at no cost. If the building is being built for speculation, first costs will be included in the computerized budget calculation, but owning and operating costs may not be.

Reducing Costs: Average Projects

The key factor in keeping the cost of a lighting system low is selection of a light source without expensive ancillary equipment like ballasts or special reflectors. A second factor is to select a simple fixture, like an adjustable track-mounted cylinder. The third factor involves easy acquisition and easy installation of a lighting system, because in general, the sooner a project can be completed, the more cost-effective it becomes.

Certain fixture lines pride themselves on being locally distributed and easily installed. As a group, these are called *contractor fixtures*. However, a design professional must be wary of the additional energy such inexpensive fixtures might consume, resulting in higher energy costs. For this reason, the cheap incandescent has been replaced on even the simplest projects by the more expensive, but far less energy consuming, fluorescent—often a 2-foot by 2-foot (61 cm × 61 cm) parabolic fixture that has U-shaped fluorescent tubes or an opal glass globe and uses the new compact "PL" fluorescent light source.

Life Cycle Costing: Complex Projects

Life cycle costing is an accounting method used to compare which of two lighting systems will give an owner better service for less money over time. It considers the total dollars spent on buying, installing, operating, and maintaining the system over its useful life. The results of life cycle costing is often expressed in *payback periods,* that is, the number of months before the more expensive system has offset its own cost.

In a more complex project like a hospital, several factors affect costs:

The smaller the building, the higher its unit cost

The more extreme the climate and site, the higher the cost

The greater the impact of the building on the public and users, the more costly the quality of materials and finishes

For complex projects, when the owner will continue as the building operator, the life cycle costing procedure is almost imperative (Table 3-1).

Because lighting is such a visible consumer of electricity, the lighting industry became one of the leaders in assembling the data used in life cycle cost analysis.

When energy costs escalated, it became apparent that lighting systems that are the least expensive to buy—ones that use incandescent light sources (see Chapter Four)—are often the most expensive to own because of the high energy consumption. On the other hand, for spaces with ceilings of 14 feet (4.3 m) or more, low-voltage incandescent and HID light sources (see Chapter Four) are thrifty in terms of life cycle costs. Their long life, energy efficiency, and precise (low-voltage) or abundant (HID) light output save enough money to offset the more expensive equipment and installation costs. But fluorescent light sources are the most cost effective for the wide range of lower ceilings in most cases.

Bidding

The formal bidding process and documents are described in Chapter Six, but the constraints that bidding places on lighting selections are summarized here. If a project is to be bid rather than negotiated, the winning contractor will have the upper hand; so it is best to keep the lighting design concept simple, bold, and foolproof. How is this accomplished?

First, fixtures and lamps equal to those specified should be available from more than one manufacturer and should be produced in a plant located in the same part of the country as the project. Additionally, fixtures with widely flanged fixture trims can be specified in the event that ceiling openings for recessed fixtures are less than perfectly round. To avoid confusion, symbols on the drawings should indicate which direction wallwashers and accent lights (see Chapter Five) should face. Also, a general note should direct installing electricians to mount wallwashers at distances shown from the wall; often walls are somewhat relocated in the construction process and the fixtures must follow.

There are several techniques by which certain fixture specifications can be preserved from the competitive and sometimes chaotic construction process. (These are discussed in Chapter Five, pp. 72-73.)

When the owner is not experienced, when potential bidders are not equally qualified, and when the drawings and specifications are not complete and accurate, it is better for an owner to negotiate a contract directly with a contractor. The advantages are that the contractor can assist in concluding the design; contingencies can be confronted and their cost estimated; and the contractor no longer has any reason to cut corners on the quality of the work or on products. On the other hand, the general contractor has no real incentive to keep costs down either. (Some owners offer to share a percentage of the savings over a stipulated sum if the contractor can create the savings.)

Value Engineering

Effective cost control is a creative process that integrates design decisions with cost decisions. It is attained only when the participants in the design and construction process commit themselves to a continual and profound respect for the owner's ability to pay and his/her right to receive full value. Even after construction has started, the owner may still be concerned about whether his/her money is being well spent. Large corporate clients often have a staff of value engineers who can isolate certain sections of the specifications for cost/benefit review.

This value engineering is based on the maxim that the greatest value to the owner is achieved when an *essential function* is obtained at minimum cost. An essential function includes user needs and community impact as well as other social values not envisioned in the specifications. Once levels of quality have been set for a particular function, design alternatives can be investigated to find the lowest costs commensurate with the defined objective. The net result is that an owner's value engineers distill elements of the architect's program and then rewrite the attendant specifications to show an owner how money can be saved. Often the new, rewritten specifications are entered as change orders (see Chapter Six) after the construction has begun.

Energy-Use Budgets

Many states now require the submission of a lighting energy-use document. Federal, provincial, and some state governments have resorted to calculating the energy impact of lighting in terms of installed watts-per-square-foot. The reason for this approach is simplicity of calculation. One

TABLE 3-1 COMPLETE LIFE CYCLE COST
A comparison of two proposed lighting systems for a drafting area.

OPERATING CONDITIONS	SYSTEM A (Original)	SYSTEM B (Projected)
Size of area	12,775 ft^2	12,775 ft^2
Lighting type	General fluorescent	Task fluorescent
Design footcandles	175-200 fc	135 fc
Footcandles at work plane (maintained)	135-150 fc	100-130 fc
Fixture position	North/South	East/West
Workstation position	East/West	East/West
Veiling reflections	High	Low
Number of fixtures	824	312
Lamp type	60W HO (high output)	35W
Number of lamps	824	624
Rated lamp life		
at 3 hrs/start	12,000 hrs	20,000 hrs
at 12 hrs/start	18,000 hrs	20,000 hrs
Lamp replacement rate	0.33 lamp/yr	0.22 lamp/yr
Cost per lamp	$1.64	$0.8637
Ballast type	Standard	High-efficiency
Number of ballasts	824	312
Ballast life	12-15 yrs	30-45 yrs
Ballast replacement rate	0.067 ballast/yr	0.027 ballast/yr
Ballast installation cost	$55/ballast	$40/ballast
Lens type	Plastic prismatic	Metal parabolic
Fixture cleaning/relamping cycle	0.67/yr	0.67/yr
Fixture cleaning/relamping labor cost	$1.30/fixture	$1.43/fixture
Watts/fixture	77W	75.3W
Total space load	63.448kW	23.494kW
Operating hours	3,640 hrs/yr	2,704 hrs/yr
Energy consumption	230,951 kWh/yr	63,528 kWh/yr
Energy rate (averaged to include demand)	$0.037/kWh	$0.037/kWh
Worker productivity rate	0.091 drawings/hr	0.098 drawings/hr

CAPITAL INVESTMENT		
Fixtures (312 at $70)		$ 21,840
Lamps (624 at $0.8637)		539
Ceiling tile (at $1.50/ft^2)		19,163
Other labor, equipment, and materials		19,700
Salvage value of existing fixtures (824 fixtures at $15/fixture)		($ 12,360)
TOTAL CAPITAL INVESTMENT		$ 48,882

OPERATING COSTS (ANNUAL)		
Energy cost	$ 8,545/yr	$ 2,351/yr
Replacement lamp cost	446/yr	119/yr
Fixture cleaning/relamping labor cost	718/yr	299/yr
Ballast replacement cost	3,036/yr	337/yr
TOTAL OPERATING COST	$12,745/yr	$ 3,106/yr

ANNUAL COST BENEFIT OF SYSTEM B		
Energy cost savings		$ 6,194/yr (72.5%)
Replacement lamp cost savings		327/yr (73.3%)
Fixture cleaning/relamping labor cost savings		419/yr (58.4%)
Ballast replacement cost savings		2,699/yr (88.9%)
Productivity benefit improvement		235,290/yr (7.5%)
Reduced error reduction benefit		Unknown
Sick leave reduction benefit		Unknown
Improved employee morale benefit		Unknown
TOTAL ANNUAL VALUE OF BENEFITS		$244,929

SUMMARY		
Simple payback		0.2 yrs (73 days)
Simple ROI		501%/yr

Source: National Lighting Bureau, *Getting the Most from Your Lighting Dollars,* 2nd ed. (Washington, D.C.: NLB,1983) 25.

merely totals up the power requirements for all fixtures and divides by the gross square footage of the building. A designer should know the regulations for energy conservation in the states where he/she works. Although they differ, most state energy-use codes are as uncomplicated as the watts-per-square-foot standard.

For example, California now requires a lighting energy-use budget prior to the issuance of a building permit (Title 24 of the state's building code). One method for compliance in a simple project is to include the fixture list on the plans (see Chapter Six). A new column is added to the list to show the energy use of the fixtures. In this column, energy used by all fixtures and lamp bulbs must be included, except for lighting used in emergency and life-safety support systems. The column must rate the lighting at the maximum wattage of a fixture at its UL listing—even if the designer elects to specify a dimmer or a lower wattage bulb for aesthetic reasons. If, for instance, a wallwashing fixture is UL-rated to house a 150-watt flood bulb and the designer specifies that the bulb be a 100-watt flood lamp, the energy use should be based on the 150-watt value. The intent of this interpretation is to circumvent intentional underlamping at the permit stage of construction and inspection, and then have the owner increase the lamp bulb wattage at the first relamping of the fixtures.

Some states allow a designer to use any alternative lighting strategy that uses no more energy than the energy allotment allowed by their legislation. However, any measurement of lighting efficiency must be projected in kilowatt hours; such a calculation must also include the energy used by lighting devices like dimmers.

LOOKING AHEAD
The most exciting, most innovative lighting design will be worthless if it does not consider and comply with the constraints reviewed in this chapter. Creativity alone will not create a successful lighting design; it must be coupled with a high regard for what is practical and economical. In the following chapter, an important practical consideration in any lighting plan, the selection of a light source, will be examined.

SELECTING A LIGHT SOURCE

Chapter Four

THERE ARE SEVERAL categories of light sources: daylight, combustion, incandescence, gaseous discharge, and chemicals. Daylighting has already been discussed in Chapter One; the combustion source, gaslight, has become obsolete; and chemical sources are presently too costly. That leaves the designer with two main sources of light: incandescent lamps and gaseous-discharge lamps (Figure 4-1).

INCANDESCENT AND GASEOUS-DISCHARGE LAMPS

These two categories of light sources are the most practical sources available to today's designer. The incandescent bulb produces light when its small wire filament is heated by electric current—a simple process. On the other hand, gaseous-discharge lamp bulbs have no filaments at all. They produce light when an electric current arcs between two electrodes within a tube to excite the gases trapped within that tube.

Because these two categories of light sources produce light in such different ways, the properties of the light they produce are also quite different. Specific light source alternatives can be compared by means of these properties in order to determine which one is best for a given space. These properties fall into five major categories: optical efficiency, electrical efficiency, lamp life/dimming, color rendering, and invisible properties. These are compared in Table 4-1.

OPTICAL CHARACTERISTICS

The optical characteristics of a light source determine its potential for widening and softening, or lengthening and tightening the lamp's beam spread. These characteristics enable the designer to control the light and thus insure that an installed lighting system will deliver the preconceived appearance to a given interior (Figure 4-2).

Shape and Distance of the Beam

The light source that is most suitable for the designed appearance of a space is the one that gets the best surface brightness from the lowest possible wattage. The designer pursuing a nonuniform lighting concept often needs optical precision from the light source. The longest distance, smallest beam, and most versatile beam shapes are delivered by incandescent, "point" sources like tungsten halogen slide projector lamps and low-voltage auto headlights.

On the one hand, uniform general lighting in a high-ceilinged space is handled more efficiently by high-pressure gaseous-discharge (HID) light sources. In wattages of 175 and higher, such sources produce powerful beams, broadly dispersed. On the other hand, low-pressure light sources like fluorescent tubes and low-pressure sodium bulbs work better in situations that require a great amount of general light in spaces where ceilings are less than 10 or 12 feet (3.1 m or 4.2 m) high. Their beams are almost visually shapeless due to their soft-edged spread.

Burning Position

The optical characteristics of a light source sometimes depend upon its position, horizontal or vertical. Before selecting a source and technique, the designer needs to consider burning position.

For instance, some techniques require fixtures to assume an angular position, or to be adjustable. For most incandescent lamp bulbs and fluorescent tubes, this presents no problem. But metal halide lamps are not suitable; they are sensitive with regard to their burning position. Some of these high-pressure bulbs burn only base-up; other models burn base-down to horizontal. When lamp bulbs are burned in positions other than ones for which they have been developed, color, output, and lamp life are affected as well as the shape of the beam. See Appendix A-2: Beam Spread Charts.

ELECTRICAL EFFICIENCY

The electrical efficiency of incandescent lamps versus gaseous-discharge lamps cannot be measured without understanding

TABLE 4-1   SUMMARY OF MAJOR PROPERTIES OF TODAY'S ELECTRIC LIGHT SOURCES

	INCANDESCENT			GASEOUS DISCHARGE				
	120 VOLTS		≤50 VOLTS	LOW PRESSURE		HIGH PRESSURE		
	TUNGSTEN FILAMENT	KRYPTON GAS	HALOGEN GAS*	MERCURY "FLUORESCENT"	SODIUM	MERCURY	SODIUM	METAL HALIDE
Optical Characteristics								
Size	Point		Small Point	Linear		Large Point		
Burning position	No limitations		Some limitations	No limitations	Some limitations	No limitations	No limitations	Many limitations
Appearance of beam	Hard (clear) Soft (frosted)	Soft	Hard	Soft	Soft	Hard	Soft	Hard
Electrical Efficiency								
Type of electrical load	Line voltage		Transformer	Ballasted				
Lumens/watts (source)	Low 9/29	Low 9/24	Low 27/29 · 20	High 49/100	Highest 140/200	Medium 50/55	High 100/140	High 70/100
Lumens/system watts	17	17	19 + (10% of elec) · 19	79 + (22%)	150 + (38%)	49 + (15%)	125 + (30%)	85 + (24%)
Costs: first	Lowest	Low	Medium	Medium	High	High	High	High
owning/operating	Highest	Medium	Low	Lowest	Lowest	Medium	Medium	Medium
Lamp Life/Dimming								
Average life (hours)	Short 750-2,000	Medium 2,500-8,000	Short 300-2,000	Long 20,000	Long 18,000	Long 24,000	Long 24,000	Long 16,000
Dimmability	Easy/Cheap		Not continuously/ expensive	Expensive	Not applicable	Expensive	Expensive	Expensive
Changes by end of life	Color warms/less light		No change	Less light	Same light/more electricity	Color cools	Color warms/more electricity	Color varies
Maintenance	Easy		Difficult	Less easy	Easy	Easy	Easy	Easy
Color Rendering	Good (warm)	Good	Excellent	Excellent; 200 + colors (some warm, some cool)	Limited (gold only)	Fair (some warm, most greenish)	Good (warm)	Good (cool)
Invisible Properties								
Infrared heat in the beam	Some bulbs	A few bulbs	Many bulbs	A few bulbs	Many bulbs	Some bulbs	Some bulbs	Some bulbs
Ultraviolet	None	None	Some bulbs	Some bulbs	None	Many bulbs	None	Many bulbs

*Incandescent sources burning on low-voltage current (≤ 50 volts) do not behave the same as those burning on common household current (120 volts).

Source: Developed by the authors from an idea by David Malman.

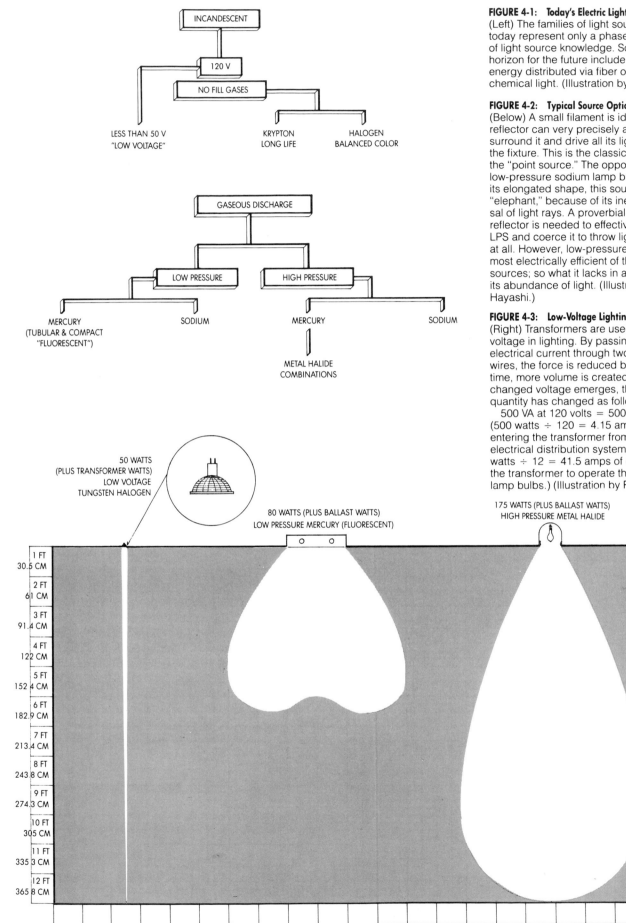

FIGURE 4-1: Today's Electric Light Sources
(Left) The families of light sources used today represent only a phase in the evolution of light source knowledge. Sources on the horizon for the future include stored solar energy distributed via fiber optic threads and chemical light. (Illustration by Reiko Hayashi.)

FIGURE 4-2: Typical Source Optics
(Below) A small filament is ideal because a reflector can very precisely and efficiently surround it and drive all its light rays out of the fixture. This is the classic performance of the "point source." The opposite is true of the low-pressure sodium lamp bulb (LPS). With its elongated shape, this source is an optical "elephant," because of its inefficient dispersal of light rays. A proverbial "bathtub" of a reflector is needed to effectively surround the LPS and coerce it to throw light any distance at all. However, low-pressure sodium is the most electrically efficient of the electric light sources; so what it lacks in agility, it gains in its abundance of light. (Illustration by Reiko Hayashi.)

FIGURE 4-3: Low-Voltage Lighting Systems
(Right) Transformers are used to change the voltage in lighting. By passing the building's electrical current through two sets of coiled wires, the force is reduced but at the same time, more volume is created. When the changed voltage emerges, the current quantity has changed as follows:
  500 VA at 120 volts = 500 VA at 12 volts (500 watts ÷ 120 = 4.15 amps of current entering the transformer from the building's electrical distribution system is equal to 500 watts ÷ 12 = 41.5 amps of current leaving the transformer to operate the low-voltage lamp bulbs.) (Illustration by Reiko Hayashi.)

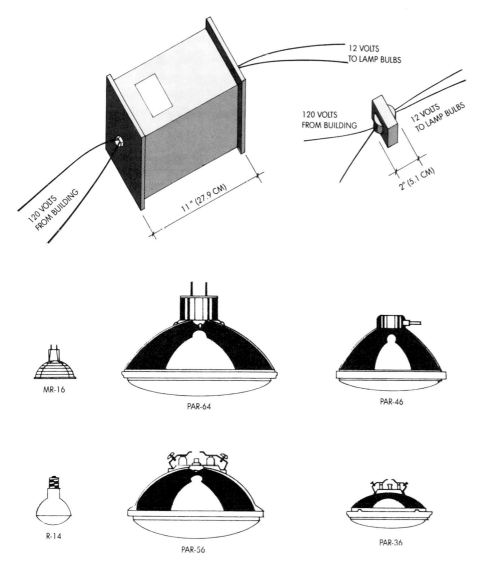

that discharge lamps must have ballasts. Therefore, in order to measure the amount of electricity they use, the current consumed by both the gaseous-discharge lamps and their ballasts must be calculated. For the low-voltage light sources, transformers perform a similar function (Figure 4-3).

Role of Ballasts

In an incandescent lamp, light is produced by heating a wire to temperatures high enough to make the wire glow. Useless and excessive heat results from the resistance of the wire to the free flow of electrical current. In an incandescent bulb this inefficient resistance is relatively fixed and eventually results in the destruction of the wire filament as the bulb "burns out."

On the other hand, in a gaseous-discharge lamp, the current arcs between two electrodes to excite gases. As the electrical current in the arc increases, the resistance decreases, which allows more current to pass. This process is too efficient. If the current were not limited by the ballast, it would destroy the lamp bulb (Figures 4-4 and 4-5).

Each type of gaseous-discharge lamp uses its own particular ballast (see Table 4-2). The designer will want a ballast that does the following:

1. Furnishes the correct electrical starting surge for the lamp

2. Provides the lamp with thermal fusing so it does not overheat (Class P)

3. Operates at high power factor to minimize energy (HPF)

4. Offers a long life

TABLE 4-2 BALLAST FUNCTIONS

BALLASTS	STARTER[1]	CLASS P[2]	HIGH POWER FACTOR[3]	LIFE[4]	HUM[5]	AUDIO INSULER[6]	SELF RADIO SUPPRESS[7]	SMALL/ LIGHT-WEIGHT[8]	DIMMABLE[9]	INSTANT RESTART[10]
FLUORESCENT										
DC transistor	No	Yes	Yes	Long	Quiet	Yes	Yes	Very small	Yes	Yes
Preheat	Yes	No	Yes	Short	Quiet	No	No	Standard	No	No
Instant Start (Slimline)	No	Some	Yes	Long	Slightly noisy	No	Yes	Standard	No	Yes
Rapid Start: Electronic	No	Yes	Yes	Inconsistent	Quiet	Yes	Yes	Small	Yes	Yes
Rapid Start: Core and Coil	No	Yes	Yes	Long	Quiet	Yes	Yes	Standard	Yes	Yes
High Output	No	Yes	Yes	Long	Slightly noisy	No	No	Standard	No	Yes
Very High Output	No	No	Yes	Long	Noisy	No	No	Standard	No	Yes
LOW-PRESSURE SODIUM	No	No	No	Medium	Noisy	No	No	Big/heavy	No	Yes
HIGH-PRESSURE MERCURY	No	No	No	Very long	Noisy	No	No	Big/heavy	Yes	No
Self Starting	No	Yes	No	Short	Noisy	No	No	Small	No	No
HIGH-PRESSURE SODIUM	Yes	Yes	Yes	Long	Some very noisy	No	Yes	Big/heavy	Some	Some
METAL HALIDE	Yes	Yes	Yes	Long	Some very noisy	No	Yes	Big/heavy	Some	No

Notes: (1) An auxiliary part to preheat the filaments prior to the electrical starting surge. (2) Internal fusing for the thermal protection of the ballast. (3) Timing that ensures that current and voltage are frequency "synchronized" to maximize the usefulness of the input watts. (4) Twelve to 15 years is normal; "high efficiency" and premium ballasts operate cooler and may burn 25 years. (5) Some hum is inevitable due to expansion of core and coil, but the sound rating should be "A," or at worst "B" for public spaces with hard surfaces. (6) The capability of the ballast to refuse passing audio signals. (7) All gaseous discharge lamp bulbs are possible sources of electromagnetic radiation at radio frequencies. The ballasts should suppress these noises. (8) Older ballast types are heavy. Newer ones are lighter and smaller but encased in old size cases, nonetheless. Electronic, solid state ballasts are both small and light. (9) Core and coil dimming ballasts can be substituted for certain standard ballasts. Both core and coil and electronic ballasts must be carefully matched to dimmers. (10) Cathodes may need either cooling or preheating before they will restrike an arc. This causes a significant delay.

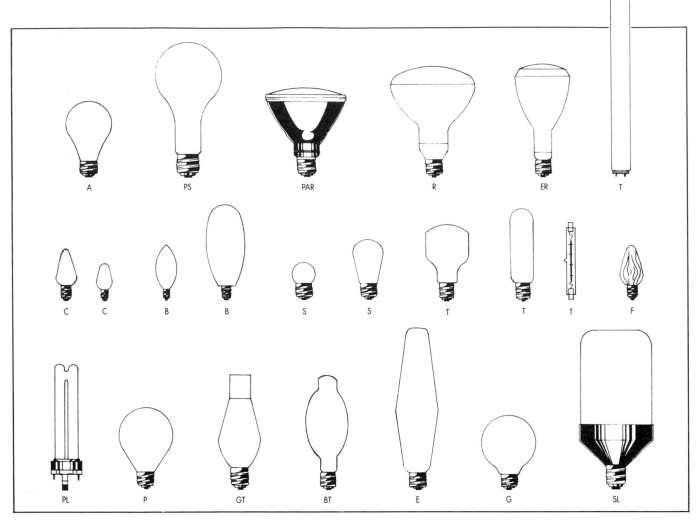

FIGURE 4-4:   Lamp Bulb Identification
Bulb manufacturers adhere to a standard lamp bulb identification system. The lamp wattage, bulb shape, and bulb diameter (in eighths of an inch) are listed in sequence and then followed by a slash (/). Other information about special features may follow the slash; this other information is usually explained in the footnotes as well, if it affects the companies' liability or warranty. This system is the one endorsed by the American National Standards Institute (ANSI). (Illustration by Reiko Hayashi.)

FIGURE 4-5:   Reading Catalogs of Large Lamp Bulbs
(Opposite page) Except for R, ER, and PAR lamps, most other shapes rely on the fixture reflector for the direction and thrust of the beam. If a lamp bulb is frosted, its beam characteristics will be diffuse and its throw distance will be shortened. If it is clear, its beam will project hard-edged shadows and patterns. (Illustration by Reiko Hayashi.)

5.   Generates very little noise of its own (A or B sound rating)

6.   Presents high impenetrability to passing audio frequencies

7.   Suppresses interference to nearby radios caused by its own gaseous-discharge lamps

8.   Be small and lightweight

9.   Can be dimmed

10.   Rapidly restart if the current is turned off and then back on.

Lumens-Per-Watt: One Measurement of Efficiency

One of the most important properties of any light source, due to the high cost of energy, is its efficiency in converting units of electricity into units of visible light. This can be determined by a measurement known as lumens per watt (l/w). For ballasted light sources this measurement really involves finding the lumens per "system watts."

Brightness as a Measurement of Efficiency

Another measurement of electrical efficiency is based on how much brightness a source delivers to key surfaces in a room. Smaller and more controllable "point" light sources give brighter surfaces with less light wasted. An example of recent developments in low-voltage, incandescent sources is the MR-16 and MR-11, low-voltage projector bulbs redesigned for precision architectural uses.

The Rewards of Electrical Efficiency

Lighting systems designed to use the lowest amount of energy have become popular because of the rise in the price of kilowatt-hours. Although standard voltage incandescent light may provide the most inexpensive lighting in terms of its initial costs, it is also the most energy inefficient of all the lighting systems. However, it is not equally true that the most energy-efficient light system—one using gaseous-discharge lamps—will cost more initially. For example, a project might need only a handful of sodium fixtures instead of a hundred incandescents, and would then cost less initially and be cheaper to maintain as well.

But the type of light source used is only one of two important factors that determine the relative costs of lighting systems. Strategy also plays a major role in determining costs. There are two such strategies: (1) the artistic one that uses the research of John Flynn to lower the number of fixtures and thereby reduce both initial and operating expenses; and (2) computerized life-cycle costing that compares savings in financed dollars against the same costs for an alternative system (see Chapter Three, p. 51). For comparisons to be valid, each lighting system must provide the same amount of light; a criterion that mitigates the comparison of strategy one to strategy two.

LAMP LIFE/DIMMING

The next major property by which light sources can be compared is their lamp-life and whether that life span can be increased by dimming. Lamp-life relates directly to operating costs of a lighting system. The cost of changing burnt-out bulbs can become significant if (1) labor is expensive; (2) a space is in use 24 hours a day and bulb changes are frequent; or (3) fixture mountings are almost inaccessible. Under such conditions, long-life, gaseous-discharge lamps are the most cost-effective and group replacement of all bulbs in a system, dead or not, is the most economical solution.

But short of replacing incandescents with gaseous-discharge lamps, the life span of incandescents can be increased by dimming. For instance, an incandescent lamp bulb, rated by its manufacturer to burn for 800 hours, may actually burn more than 10,000 hours if it is dimmed and burned continuously. This equation can be used to predict the approximate increase in incandescent lamp-life by dimming:

LAMP LIFE	LUMEN OUTPUT	LAMP COLOR
$\dfrac{\text{life}}{\text{LIFE}} = \left(\dfrac{\text{VOLTS}}{\text{volts}}\right)^d$	$\dfrac{\text{lumens}}{\text{LUMENS}} = \left(\dfrac{\text{volts}}{\text{VOLTS}}\right)^k$	$\dfrac{\text{color}\cdot}{\text{COLOR}\cdot} = \left(\dfrac{\text{volts}}{\text{VOLTS}}\right)^m$

Notes: (1) Capital letters represent rated values from manufacturers' catalogs. (2) d = 13; k = 3.4; and m = 0.42.

Source: John E. Kaufman, ed., *IES Handbook Reference Volume 1981* (New York: Illuminating Engineering Society, 1981) 8-9.

Dimming Benefits

Reducing current and, therefore, wattage is certainly one of the benefits of dimming a light source. But its most important benefit is the flexibility it gives to both designer and client. When a designer is not sure what level of intensity the light should have in a given space, he/she will often specify more than enough light. For a high-budget project, the experienced designer will specify both dimmers and toggle switches, but locate the dimmers inconspicuously. When the project is completed, the designer will use the inconspicuous dimmers to create the best light effect. Thereafter, each time the client enters the space, he/she will only need to flip one of the regular toggle switches to get the planned effect.

There are many situations in which the client will need the flexibility offered by dimming. For example, a client who uses the same conference room for audio visual presentations and board meetings will need light sources that will dim.

Dimming Problems

There are several reasons to hesitate before rushing to use dimming controls:

They can be expensive

Their electronic parts can be unreliable

They are incompatible with some ballasts or transformers

Their use is limited by the inherent characteristics of some light sources

Regarding the latter, only certain wattages of metal halide and sodium bulbs can be dimmed. Even then, dimming cannot proceed below a minimum level because the electric arc that produces light in such bulbs cannot be maintained below that level. The easiest HID lamp to dim is mercury, but the dimming module and its control add wattage losses to the system; also, most mercury-dimming components are noisy.

Dimmers for fluorescent bulbs have been in the marketplace for over 20 years. Special ballasts and sockets used to be required for these bulbs, but are no longer necessary. However, such bulbs cannot be dimmed all the way off because the electrodes of the lamps must be kept heated. If

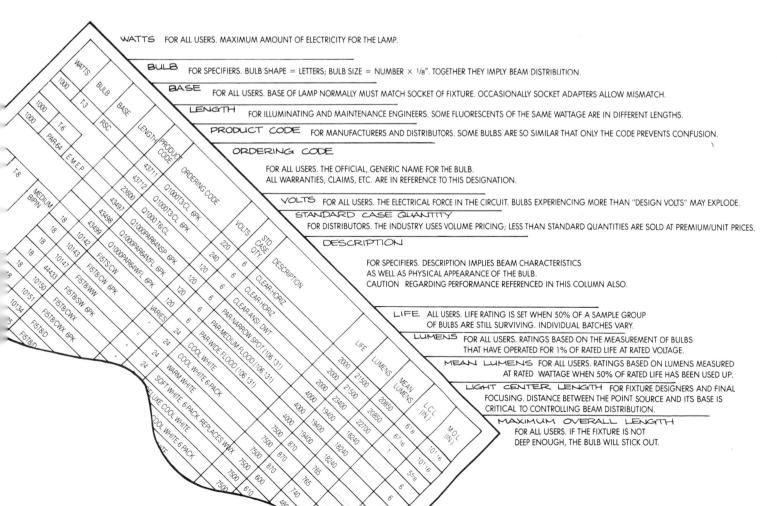

the lamps are dimmed too low, the light will flicker and spiral within the tube. This shortens lamp life. To dim equally, all the lamps on the same dimmer should be new simultaneously and of the same length and manufacturer.

Incandescent bulbs are the easiest to dim, but even these have problems. Special dimmers must be used for low-voltage light sources and the double-ended tungsten halogen sources will often lose their ionization cycle, curl up, and fall out of their fixtures if they are subjected to dimming that is too low or too prolonged.

Selecting Dimmer Controls
The practical way to control the light source, that is, to dim it, is by controlling the electrical input. Such controls operate by one of two methods: (1) the amplitude of the electrical current can be compressed; or (2) the current can be interrupted rhythmically. Figure 4-6 illustrates these methods.

There are several different types of dimmers, each with advantages and disadvantages: the simple resistance dimmer, the autovariac (a complex form of resistance dimmer), and solid state dimmers.

The resistance dimmer is electrically reliable and cheap. On the other hand, it heats up, wastes energy, and must be carefully matched to its loading to dim evenly. It is also large and heavy.

The autovariac does not require careful loading; it dims large or small loads equally well, does not heat or waste energy, and is very reliable. However, it is expensive, heavy, large, and must have its brushes cleaned occasionally.

Solid state dimmers are small, cheap, readily available, energy efficient, unaffected by loading below their capacity, and need no cleaning. The solid states' disadvantages include their fragility, that is, their components "fry" with very little provocation. This malfunction often creates electri-

cal hazards in connected circuitry. They also create noise in other parts of the circuit. Filaments on the circuit may start to "sing" in protest to the jarring of endless on/off electrical pulses or radio frequency interference may be picked up on nearby stereo or television equipment as static. One way to diminish both these difficulties is to buy "specification grade" electronic dimmers from the electrical wholesaler rather than the "consumer grade" sold at hardware stores (Figure 4-7).

Alternatives to Dimming
When selecting electronically controlled dimmers and other devices, it is best to keep them simple. Multilevel fluorescent ballasts are available that offer two or three light intensity levels. Easy user control can be achieved by using one wall switch for each intensity level.

Ultrasonic and Infrared Personnel Detectors. These devices have intensity settings and delayed off functions that can turn lights on when workers walk in and off when they leave. Time clocks and photocells are reliable indoors and out. Photocells, in particular, are simple, seasonally self-adjusting, require no electric power and minimum maintenance—although they do need washing once a year or so.

Low-Voltage Switching. This is not to be confused with low-voltage incandescent lighting, but it is equally useful. It provides a way to inexpensively control one load from many locations. In many code jurisdictions, wiring for low-voltage switching is permitted to run without benefit of conduit.

Time Switch. This device has recently become more available and less expensive. It must be operated manually to turn the lights on, but it will turn them off by itself in 30 minutes. New state energy codes often require one switch per space or more. The time switch is often a good selection for

spaces that are used infrequently such as bathrooms or stock rooms.

COLOR RENDERING
This is the fourth physical property by which light sources can be compared. There are three aspects to the colors of light:

1. The color appearance of the light source itself

2. The light interreflected throughout the interior at large

3. The color rendering capacity of the light source on specific objects

Temperature Kelvin measures the first aspect, the color appearance, and implies the third aspect, warm or cool color rendering. Although such a measurement is sometimes convenient, it is somewhat inaccurate for all light sources except incandescent. The second general shift in the color of light affects color contrasts in a real environment. It is a phenomenon caused as much by the color of the walls, ceiling, and floor acting as color filters as by the spectrum of the lamp bulbs themselves.

Color-Rendering Capacity
To an interior designer, the specific color of the interior surfaces is always critical. Palette selection is one of the designer's proprietary skills, so the specific color-rendering characteristics of a light source are very important; they can alter or enhance that color palette. The light source and the finish colors of an interior are mutually dependent on one another to create each of the several million discernible colors.

Color measurements used by the lighting industry—like temperature Kelvin and the color rendition index—are often meaningless because the degree of color-shift between the laboratory's color-rendering standard and that of the lamp-at-hand provides no indication as to whether either one

FIGURE 4-6: Dimming the Sine Wave
Compressing the amplitude of the sine wave can be done with either a resistance dimmer or a variable (autovariac) transformer. The resistance dimmer is connected in series with the lamp. The voltage that the lamp "sees" is equal to the supply voltage minus the voltage dropped across the dimmer. The resistance dimmer, then, is using the energy not passed along to the lamp and it is heating up accordingly. The autovariac does not use up the energy it saves.

The typical electronic dimmer consists of a pair of solid state thyristors connected so that each one conducts electricity for only one half of the alternating cycles of the current. Their on/off timing is activated by a tiny DC signal pulsing a silicon-controlled rectifier (SCR). The rhythm of this on/off signal to the thyristors needs to be balanced because a light imbalance may cause connected ballasts or transformers to self-destruct. (Illustration by Reiko Hayashi.)

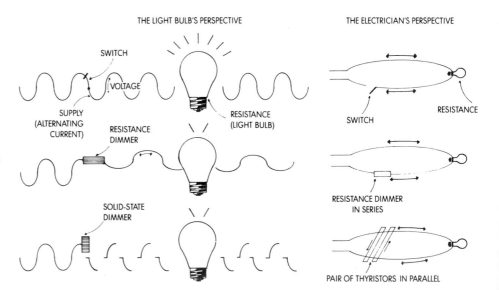

THE LIGHT BULB'S PERSPECTIVE

SWITCH

VOLTAGE

SUPPLY (ALTERNATING CURRENT)

RESISTANCE DIMMER

RESISTANCE (LIGHT BULB)

SOLID-STATE DIMMER

THE ELECTRICIAN'S PERSPECTIVE

SWITCH

RESISTANCE

RESISTANCE DIMMER IN SERIES

PAIR OF THYRISTORS IN PARALLEL

TABLE 4-3   COLOR APPEARANCE OF THE LIGHT SOURCE

LIGHT SOURCE	COLOR TEMPERATURE (Kelvin°)
Candles	1900° ±
Fluorescent lamps	2600°-7500° (Apparent K°)*
Tungsten filament lamps	2700°-2900°
Film and projection lamps ("quartz")	2850° ± -3200°
Moonlight	4100° (Apparent K°)*
Daylight (sun and clear noon sky)	5800°-6500°
Clear blue sky	10,000°-26,000° (Apparent K°)*

*Color temperature is a term used to describe the color appearance of a light source by comparing it with the color of a black body radiator as it is heated from a cold black to a white-hot state. Only if a light source is a thermal radiator, e.g., an incandescent lamp, does its color temperature give information on its spectral energy distribution. When the temperature Kelvin (K°) is applied to a gaseous discharge source, e.g., a fluorescent lamp, it is only as a guide to its apparent warm color or cool color habits. (The temperature Kelvin of any group of lamp bulbs emerging from the assembly line may vary as much as 500K° from published data.)

Source: J. B. deBoer and D. Fischer, *Interior Lighting,* revised 2nd ed. (Antwerp: Philips Technical Library, 1981) 96.

will flatter a particular finish in the palette (Table 4-3). To obtain direct information on the expected color appearance of individual objects to be lighted by a particular light source, the designer must turn to the spectral distribution chart for that light source.

Spectral Distribution Chart

At present this is the most useful standard. It is a graphic depiction of the specific wavelengths, or colors of light, emitted by a particular light source, as well as the relative strength of each color. These charts are produced by the manufacturers of lamp bulbs and are available for a specific lamp upon request. If the lamp wattage is listed, these charts can be quite detailed and accurate. (See Color Plates 2 and 3.)

Working Samples

The best way for the designer to anticipate how colors will look under a specific light source is to obtain a working sample of the light at the wattage under consideration from its manufacturer. The selection of which working sample to obtain can be made by first evaluating the information found on the spectral distribution charts. Then, the designer can mount the sample and finalize his/her palette under the actual light source.

Matching Spectral Distribution to the Palette

This point is the key to designing the lighting of a space to suit its occupants, and cannot be overemphasized. A good match maximizes visual impact and minimizes energy usage. A bad match causes color distortions (Color Plate 4).

Energy is saved when almost all the light from the light source is efficiently converted to reflected brightness in the space. By closely matching palette colors to a light source's colors, very little electricity is wasted because the lamp generates only colors of light that will be reflected, and few that will be absorbed and disappear into a room's surfaces.

Brightness on surfaces and objects creates maximum visual impact. And that impact can be exaggerated by using finish colors in a combination that establishes powerful contrasts between objects and background. But the light source must support both of the contrasting colors and not gray or distort them.

INVISIBLE LIGHT

To a degree, everything and everyone is affected by light energy. Light has wavelengths that are seen as either colors or brightness. But there are ultraviolet and infrared wavelengths of light that can only be seen by observing their effects. The bleaching or peeling of house paint is such an effect caused by ultraviolet light.

These invisible wavelengths of light and their effects provide the fifth and final physical property of light to consider when selecting a light source. These effects of invisible light fall into two categories: (1) *photodegradation,* the destructive effects of visible and invisible light on things; and (2) *photobiology,* the sometimes beneficial, sometimes harmful, effect on people.

Photodegradation

The deteriorating effects of light take place at varying rates. These rates vary according to the color, texture, and chemistry of the material upon which the light falls, according to the intensity and duration of that light. (See Table 1-2 in Chapter One for the effects of daylight in fading fabrics.)

Light damage can be assessed in two ways: (1) the fading and bleaching caused by all of the shortwave light frequencies, but especially ultraviolet light (Color Plate 5), and (2) the peeling and other dehydrating effects caused by longwave light frequencies, especially infrared light. This latter form of invisible light is typical of combustion light sources and those at high pressure; whereas ultraviolet light is produced as a necessary side effect of vaporized gases, like mercury, used in gaseous-discharge lamps. Table 4-1 charts the likelihood of ultraviolet and infrared output from each light source.

Controlling Photodegradation. Since both fading and heat damage occur from visible as well as invisible light, they cannot be entirely prevented except by storing particularly valuable artifacts in lightless, ventilated, and humidity-controlled vaults. This is seldom feasible, so methods which slow down photodegradation, rather than eliminate it, must be found. These can include: (1) controlling the amount of time that light is allowed to strike an object; (2) controlling the spectral output of the light source; and (3) controlling the amount of light absorbed by the object.

To combat fading, for instance, the designer could do the following:

Use a light source with little or no ultraviolet, such as incandescent or Ultralume fluorescent bulbs.

Provide the fixtures with glass or acrylic lenses that retard transmission of ultraviolet light.

House artifacts in custom cases of UF-3 acrylic. This special material is from the Rohm and Haas Company.[1]

Use personnel sensors that control display spotlights so that they only turn on when visitors are present.

Protect the artifact with blackout cloth that can be lifted by visitors for viewing and then replaced.

To combat the effects of infrared heat, the designer may want to do the following:

Select lamp bulbs with dichroic reflectors that reflect as much as 60 percent of the heat from the rear of the fixture.

Consult with a conservator about raising local humidity to absorb a portion of the heat.

Darken the interior generally or switch lights off until visitors enter. Use personnel-detecting switches to turn lights on as people enter.

Be sure that articles are restored periodically by professionals using proper emollients.

Protecting objects from light damage while displaying them to the best advantage is really a very special problem for the designer. See Case Study Seven on display lighting for the techniques that can be used to solve this problem.

Photobiology

The invisible light that most affects humans is in the ultraviolet or near ultraviolet range. These are the erythemal and sub-erythemal wavelengths commonly known for their ability to burn and tan the skin.

Beneficial Effects. This range of light is known to have beneficial effects on infant jaundice, rickets, and the calcium-absorbing capacity of older people. Some of these

FIGURE 4-7: Switches and Dimmers

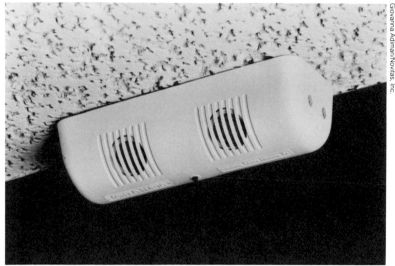

Giovanna Adimari/Novitas, Inc.

Uniquely angled transducers allow the Light-O-Matic ultrasonic motion sensor to turn lights on and off in many different room configurations. Where lighting is controlled by dimmers, the device will dim and brighten lights automatically.

Home Control System includes a wall-mounted programmable controller for total home or area control; a wall-mounted manual controller for area control; and a wall switch module and wall receptacle module (receivers). System installation uses existing AC wiring.

Leviton Manufacturing Co. © 1982

The Enertron light switch automatically turns off the lights after a preselected time period. If the 5-, 15-, or 30-minute time intervals are not suitable, other models offer 1, 1½, or 2 hours, or 2, 3, or 4 hours. The switch is appropriately named "Time Out."

Tork Time Controls

The portable, plug-in time switch is original from Tork controls. The timer plugs directly into a wall socket and the lamp cord is plugged into the outlet on the face of the unit. Features include a seven-day programmable control and an override that delivers manual operation to the user without affecting the week's schedule.

Enertron

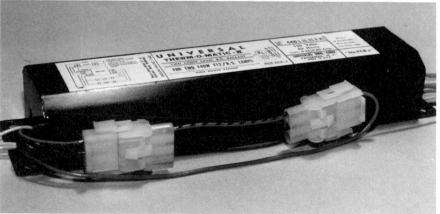

R. C. Powell

This Universal fluorescent ballast operates two 4-foot (121.9 cm) tubes. When the grouping of workstations changes, it can be rewired to deliver a high or low light level as needed.

Infracon® turns office lighting on and off, according to room occupancy, by detecting and responding to changes in radiated heat caused by the presence and movement of human bodies. The bezel of the passive infrared sensor measures 2.6 inches (6.6 cm) in diameter.

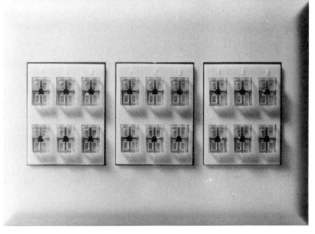

For years, low-voltage switching by means of magnetic relays has been the most convenient and energy-efficient way to switch many lights from one location or one light from many locations. These energy-saving control systems by Touchplate automatically turn out selected lighting at preselected times, but late workers need only reach for a nearby switch to override the master system and turn on the lights that they may need.

Lutron's hand-held controller operates on infrared frequencies to send instructions to a wall receiver. Each channel of the receiver can be programmed to turn on a different combination of lights at full output or at preselected dimming levels.

effects are thought to be hormone related. This supposition is based on a theory that a photoreceptor located in the depths of the eye, but unrelated to vision, cues the pituitary and pineal glands which, in turn, regulate glandular activity, hormonal balance, and body chemistry.[2]

It has been alleged by John Ott, a banker, author, photographer, and public speaker, that invisible light also benefits the sight, strength, mood, and mental alertness of many individuals.[3] Studies at Cornell University found that college students exposed regularly to fluorescent tubes emitting ultraviolet light increased in visual acuity and decreased in fatigue as compared to students in classrooms with standard cool white fluorescent tubes.[4]

Adverse Effects. Controversy here revolves around how much near ultraviolet light is good—that is, how intense a dose of ultraviolet is needed and for how many hours? Excessive irradiation causes skin allergies and skin cancers. In fact, the American Cancer Society finds that the very same frequencies thought to stimulate cortical activity (mental alertness and responses) are those causing the most common human cancer, melanoma. Moreover, some people require very little exposure to these wavelengths to contract this cancer. Although fluorescent, high-pressure mercury, and metal halide light sources are energy conserving, they would not be good choices for the office or home of people whose families are known to have had skin cancers.

LOOKING AHEAD
All these physical properties of a light source are important: photobiology and photodegradation, electrical efficiency, optical efficiency, lamp life, and color rendering. Each must be considered in order to select the proper source for a given project. Once these priorities have been assessed, it is relatively simple to select the proper bulbs from lamp catalogs. The next consideration, the selection of lighting fixtures that convey the chosen light source, will be explored in the following chapter.

CHAPTER NOTES
[1]Rohm and Haas Company, *Plexiglas in Museums and Galleries* (Bristol: Rohm and Haas, 1979).

[2]Faber Birren, *Light, Color and Environment* (New York: Van Nostrand Reinhold, 1969) 41.

[3]John Ott, *Health and Light: The Effects of Natural and Artificial Light on Man and Other Living Things* (Greenwich: Bevin Publishing, 1973).

[4]J. B. Maas, J. K. Jayson, D. A. Kleiber, "The Effect of Spectral Distributions in Illumination on Fatigue," *Journal of Applied Psychology*, October 1974: 76-87.

Chapter Five

SELECTING FIXTURES

THE LIGHTING FIXTURE houses the lamp bulb and shapes its beam of light. The fixture includes all the necessary parts for adjusting and protecting the bulb and for connecting it to the electrical supply (Figure 5-1). From the thousands of fixtures available, how can the designer choose the right ones for a given project? First, it is helpful to know that any fixture can be considered on the basis of five criteria:

Direction of its light beam

Type of mounting

Initial and maintenance costs

Appearance (or disappearance)

Electrical safety

BEAM SHAPES

The Illuminating Engineering Society of North America (IESNA) uses six categories to describe the direction of a fixture's beam of light. These classifications are illustrated in Figure 5-2. Also, we have added a few more categories by dividing the "direct" category into narrow, medium (asymetric), and wide beam spreads. These new divisions distinguish accent lights from wallwashers and/or downlights. To perform the lighting techniques described in Chapter Two's section on lighting composition, this distinction between the width and orientation of the direct beams is critical. Today's emphasis on producing the designed appearance of interiors by delivering brightness to specific surfaces and objects requires this more precise information.

To determine what type of beam spread is produced by an unfamiliar fixture, the designer can obtain its photometric profile (*candlepower distribution curve*) from the manufacturer (Figure 5-3). Knowing the candlepower distribution not only helps to select the fixture for a particular lighting technique, it also helps to identify which fixture will deliver poor task lighting. For instance, indirect glare occurs when overhead fixtures emit light in the zero degree zone (refer back to Figure 1-16). And direct glare can be anticipated from fixtures with candlepower emitted in zones above 45 degrees (Figure 5-4).

Candlepower distribution curves can also predict good task lighting. In the 1970s, lighting research revealed that particular angles of light emphasize task contrasts. For example, when the angle of the light helps to emphasize the print on a page, reading becomes easier. One particularly beneficial angle is described by some as "27 degrees from vertical to the task." Some fixtures and lenses—those with "batwing" candlepower profiles—are designed to deliver as much light as possible in the "good reading zone" and as little as possible in the zones that create glare (Figure 5-5).

MOUNTINGS

There are seven common types of mountings by which fixtures may be attached to a building: recessed, surface-mounted, wall-bracketed, suspended, track-mounted, portable, and structural. They all have advantages and disadvantages (Figure 5-6).

FIGURE 5-1: Lighting Fixtures: Past and Present
There are three considerations involved
when specifying lighting fixtures. First,
materials and construction must be suitable
to the microclimate of the space; for example, UL "wet location" labeled fixtures would
be needed for a sauna. Second, mounting
locations should accommodate each of the
dimensions of a fixture. If a ceiling is 7 feet, 6
inches high, suspension of an indirect fixture
that is mounted on an 18-inch stem will
radically alter traffic patterns in that space.
Third, the right accoutrements for installation
must be available; for example, if a project
has a shed ceiling, is the fixture selected
available with sloped ceiling adapters?
(Illustration by Reiko Hayashi; modeled after
"Lighting Fixtures Then and Now," by Daniel
Blitzer, Lightolier; a presentation to Designers Lighting Forum, Saturday Seminars
Program, San Francisco, 1980.)

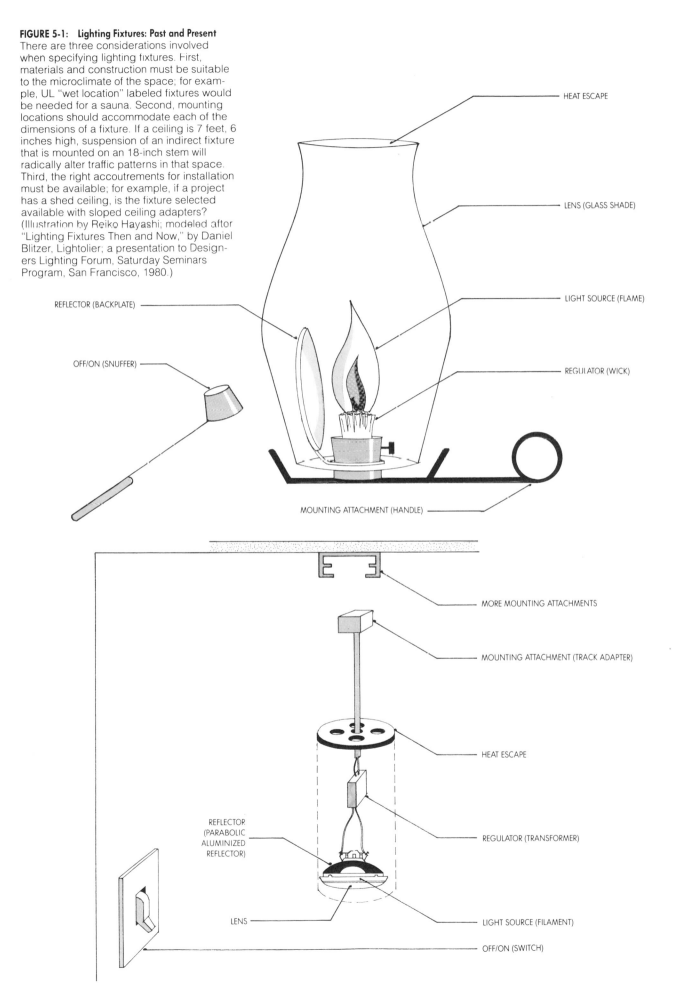

FIGURE 5-2: Common Fixture Types (continued)

	FIXTURE TYPE	BEST USES	WORST USES

Semi-Direct:

Although some light is directed upward, it is less than 40 percent. If the designer thinks of downward light as task lighting, then it seems that the upward light serves as ambient lighting. It softens shadows and maintains the brightness contrasts in the room at comfortable levels for work or play.

The semi-direct fixture is the most practical for task lighting levels and for uniform lighting levels because it delivers most of its light down to the task while a smaller percentage goes up to alleviate glare.

Although it is hard to find a space for which the semi-direct fixture is ill-suited, it is not used in spaces where design is important unless a board room, dining room, or executive office needs light both as the focal point of the space and for tasks.

Direct (wide):

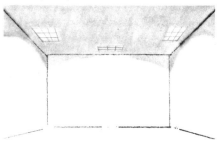

Fixtures directing more than 90 percent of their light downward fall into this category. Although fixture energy efficiency is generally in inverse proportion to the degree to which the light is directional, the direct fixture tends to be one of the most energy conserving because of the width of its beam.

Some architects use direct fixtures with a wide beam spread in a grid pattern to uniformly light a space because the fixtures can be recessed out of sight. An obvious choice for both task and nontask space when interest is only on horizontal surfaces like desks or tables.

The architect's strategy can produce an uninhabitable space wherein the glare becomes intolerable due to (1) dark ceiling colors; (2) cheap fluorescent lenses or louvers; or (3) room geometry that puts the entire ceiling plane within view of most occupants. Well-shielded direct lighting can cause the ceiling height to be less apparent just as indirect light causes it to become more apparent.

Direct (medium asymmetrical):

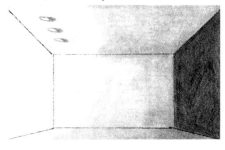

For the designer, the wallwashing technique and its derivatives are powerful tools; they depend upon throwing the light to one side. The Flynn research indicates that vertical brightness in the line of sight affects behavior most. Asymmetrical beam distribution produces such brightness the most efficiently and effectively because it does not brighten the whole space; only the intended surface.

The wallwasher fixture is the workhorse of the interior designer or architect. It draws attention to one side of a space and causes occupants to arrange themselves around it or move toward it. The wallwashing technique is often used to distract the eye away from a narrow hallway by lighting only one long wall.

Never use wallwashing in a space where the actual ceiling height is too low. Never use wallwashing to augment a textured wall or wall finish; the broadside angle of light flattens texture by denying its shadow formations.

Direct (narrow):

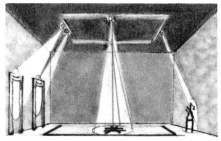

The ability to achieve a narrow beam spread depends upon several devices: the reflector, a lens, and/or the position of the lamp in the fixture. The incandescent light source is an electrical energy extravagance but readily amenable to optical manipulations. For various reasons, however, the same narrow beam cannot be developed from other light sources. Incandescent light bulbs are used largely for accent or focal lighting. Only the incandescent can deliver the "pencil beam."

The best use of the narrow beam is the fashionable low-voltage lighting in homes, museums, restaurants, and upscale stores. Slender beams pick out a balanced pattern of objects and backgrounds from the blackness. Only significant features of the design are lighted so that no light is wasted. Both the technique and the equipment conserve energy.

Such spaces are not safe for those whose footing is insecure or who are sensitive to glare. Designers should combine low-voltage incandescent lighting with other techniques in public spaces or for spaces used by people over 50 years old.

LEGEND: MOUNTINGS: S/W/P (ETC.)

R = RECESSED   W = WALL BRACKET   TYPICAL ENERGY UTILIZATION:
C = CEILING SURFACE   T = TRACK   A = 70–100 LUMENS/WATT
S = SUSPENDED   P = PORTABLE   B = 50–80 LUMENS/WATT
                       N.A. = NOT APPLICABLE C = 30–60 LUMENS/WATT
                                              D = LESS THAN 30 LUMENS/WATT

TYPICAL INCANDESCENT HOUSING	TYPICAL FLUORESCENT HOUSING	TYPICAL HID HOUSING	CANDLEPOWER DISTRIBUTION

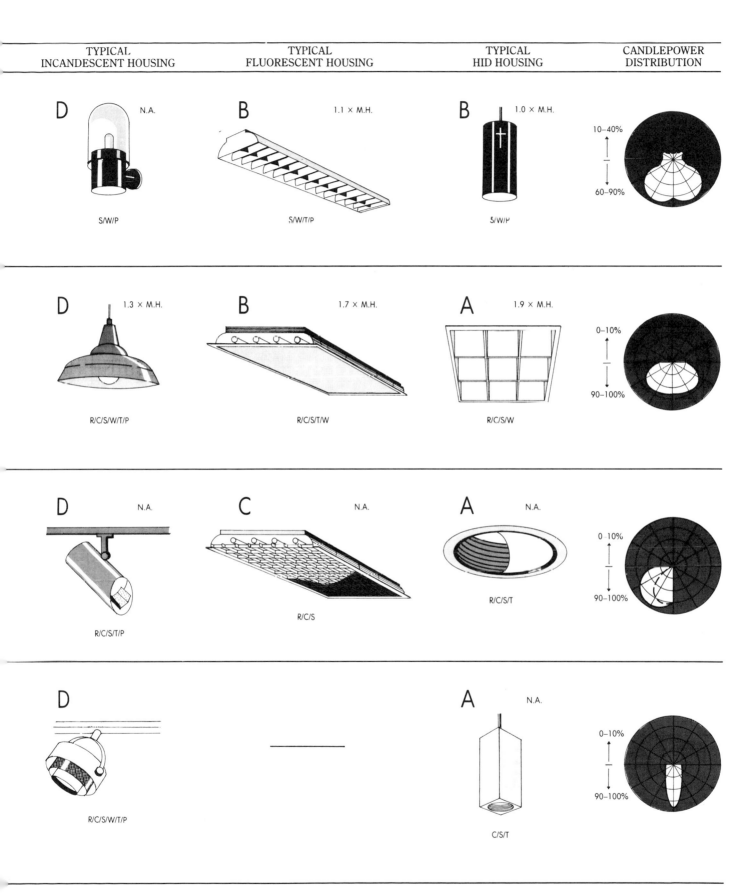

D   N.A.

S/W/P

B   1.1 × M.H.

S/W/T/P

B   1.0 × M.H.

S/W/P

10–40%
60–90%

D   1.3 × M.H.

R/C/S/W/T/P

B   1.7 × M.H.

R/C/S/T/W

A   1.9 × M.H.

R/C/S/W

0–10%
90–100%

D   N.A.

R/C/S/T/P

C   N.A.

R/C/S

A   N.A.

R/C/S/T

0–10%
90–100%

D

R/C/S/W/T/P

A   N.A.

C/S/T

0–10%
90–100%

SPACING CRITERION: 1.0 × M.H. (ETC.)
MULTIPLIER TO DETERMINE THE "ON CENTER" DISTANCE BETWEEN
FIXTURE UNITS WHEN UNIFORM LIGHT DISTRIBUTION IS NECESSARY.

M.H. = "MOUNTING HEIGHT" OR DISTANCE FROM THE
FIXTURE TO THE DESK TOP OR OTHER TARGET.

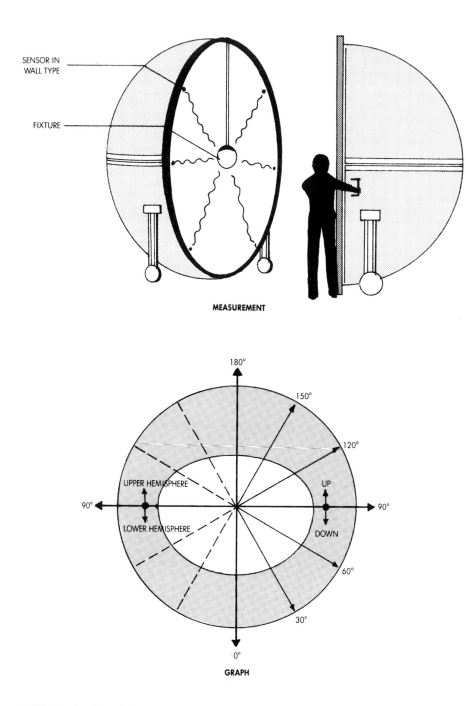

FIGURE 5-3: Graphing of Photometric Data
The "candlepower distribution curve," a graphic representation of the shape and direction of the light coming from a fixture, can be used to estimate the light from that fixture that will arrive at a distant location. The fixture is placed at the center of a photometric testing sphere. Sensors around the edges of the sphere divide its central cavity into zones. The quantity of light received into each zone is recorded. A designer familiar with the recorded candlepower distribution curves can tell at a glance how the light will behave when the fixture is installed. (Illustration by Reiko Hayashi.)

Recessed

The most seductive advantage of a recessed fixture is its appearance, or more precisely its disappearance from the field of view. In fact, recessed fixtures that have a shiny black phenolic interior not only prevent glare but are almost invisible on a dark colored ceiling.

Because recessed fixtures are relatively inaccessible, they have several disadvantages. These include increased installation, operating, and relamping costs. The aggravated entrapment of both heat and light within the fixture wastes electricity. Lamp bulb and ballast life may be shortened slightly. In using certain recessed fixtures, there is also some loss of flexibility. The recessed accent light, in particular, can only tilt up to about 40 degrees. Therefore, it usually cannot illuminate objects high on the wall except by very exact placement of the fixture in the ceiling quite close to its target. In some complex construction projects, it is exactly this kind of placement precision that is likely to be lost.

Surface-Mounted

The surface-mounted fixture may be the most popular, and there are several reasons for this. First, the surface-mounted fixture lights a space very efficiently. Neither light nor heat is impeded. Also, its ceiling-hugging location can allow it to be quite bright, much brighter than a fixture mounted lower, which would fall into the line of sight and cause discomfort. Its light beam can be directed in a wide pattern. Finally, installation and relamping usually are easy and relatively inexpensive. As for disadvantages, such surface-mounted fixtures lower the effective height of a ceiling. Most light sources are available in fixtures that offer a surface-mounted option.

Wall-Bracketed

One common use for this type of mounting is to bring sidelight to a "target"; for example, lighting the faces of visitors outside the door of a residence or at the mirror in an entryway. Wall bracket fixtures are also selected for spaces with exceptionally high or low ceilings. If a ceiling is too high, the recessed or surface-mounted fixtures might be hard to maintain and relamp. If a ceiling is very low, the clearance for passersby may be impeded even if there are fixtures extending down a short distance.

However, the reasoning in both cases is spurious. With a very high ceiling, a suspended fixture is often a better solution. And with a very low ceiling, recessed downlights with black phenolic interiors would provide light without brightness on the ceiling or obstacles to passersby.

Wall-bracketed fixtures have some disadvantages. First, only light sources and fixture lenses of low brightness should be used because the mounting location is directly in the line of sight. (But when low

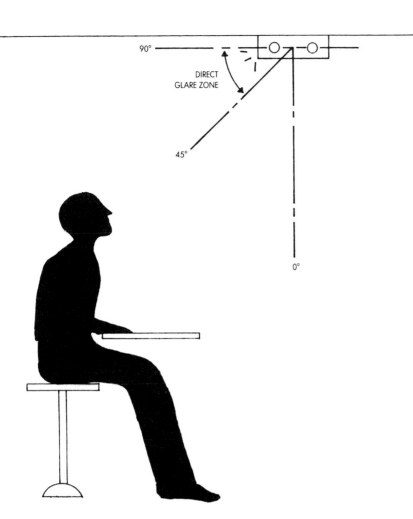

FIGURE 5-4: Direct Glare
(Left) This results when the geometry of the room is combined with an individual's line of sight. For instance, a high ceiling will increase the number of fixtures that enter the field of view. But the fixtures are less likely to be seen—unless an individual has reason to look up. Visual Comfort Probability (VCP) is the measurement currently accepted as the standard for evaluating the potential for glare in a room. A VCP value of 70 indicates that 70 percent of the people in the space would not complain of glare, even if they were seated in the most vulnerable location; 70 VCP or higher is considered adequate for most lighting installations unless the occupants are older persons. (Illustration by Reiko Hayashi.)

FIGURE 5-5: Batwing Distributions of Light
(Below) A cross section through the shorter width of this fluorescent fixture illustrates the batwing shape of light for which the fixture was designed. The lens of the fixture blocks the downward light beam and splits it into right and left beams that strike the tasks below at a desirable 27-degree angle. *(a) Linear batwing distributions* produce a nominal batwing shape only in a cross section through the width of the fluorescent fixture. *(b) Radial batwing distribution* shows the batwing beam configuration in a cross section through the length of the fixture as well. (Illustration by Reiko Hayashi.)

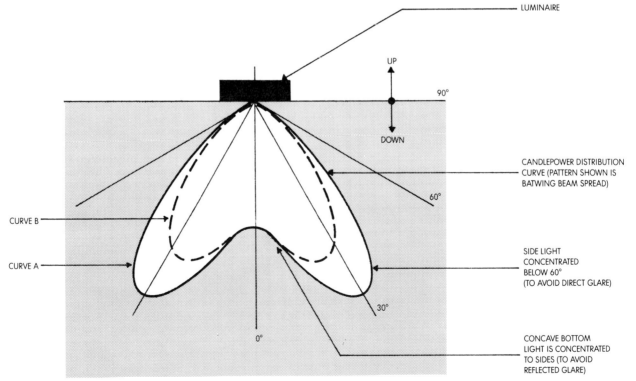

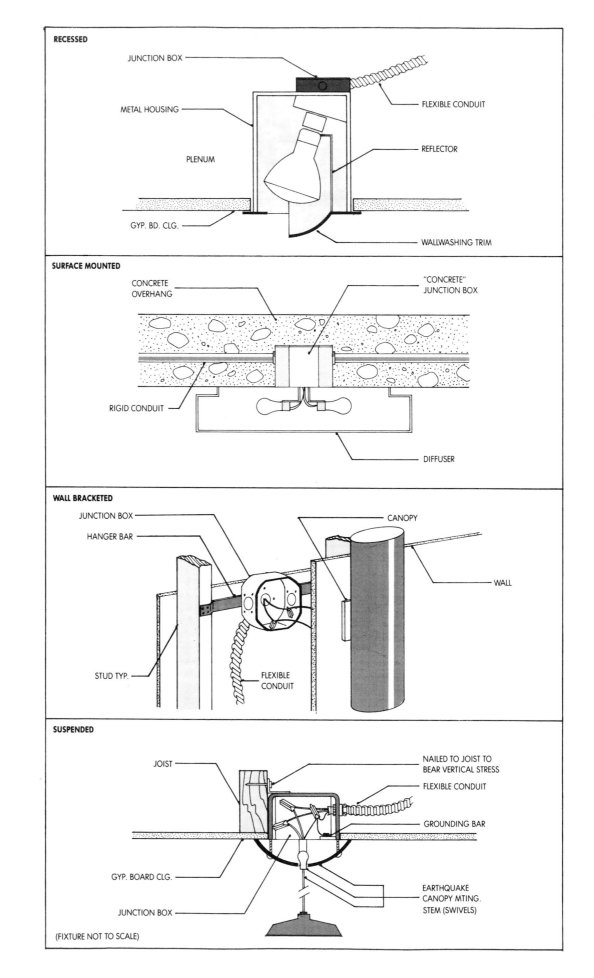

RECESSED

JUNCTION BOX

METAL HOUSING

PLENUM

GYP. BD. CLG.

FLEXIBLE CONDUIT

REFLECTOR

WALLWASHING TRIM

SURFACE MOUNTED

CONCRETE OVERHANG

"CONCRETE" JUNCTION BOX

RIGID CONDUIT

DIFFUSER

WALL BRACKETED

JUNCTION BOX

HANGER BAR

CANOPY

WALL

STUD TYP.

FLEXIBLE CONDUIT

SUSPENDED

JOIST

NAILED TO JOIST TO BEAR VERTICAL STRESS

FLEXIBLE CONDUIT

GROUNDING BAR

GYP. BOARD CLG.

JUNCTION BOX

EARTHQUAKE CANOPY MTING. STEM (SWIVELS)

(FIXTURE NOT TO SCALE)

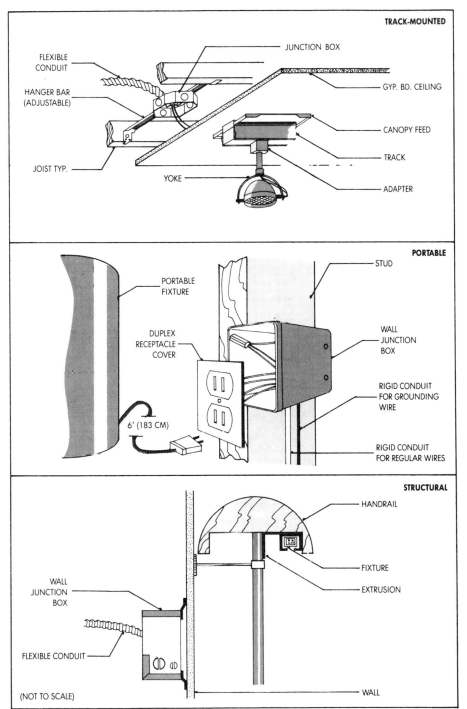

FIGURE 5-6: Electrical Mountings
The location of most fixtures must be determined in advance. Next to each fixture location is a 4-inch by 4-inch by 2-inch junction box which contains the wires to be spliced to that fixture. These junction boxes are usually nailed into place when the ceiling and/or walls are open and the space unfinished. If these boxes have to be moved later, the expense and mess produced when a finished ceiling or wall is carved up to permit the pulling of new wires around and through studs and joists can be disastrous. This immobility is shared by most types of mountings except track and portable. (Illustration by Reiko Hayashi.)

brightness light sources are used, additional room lighting will be required.)

Another disadvantage is the wasted light absorbed into the wall and the accompanying flare of pointless brightness that occurs on the wall just above them. The most recently designed fixtures incorporate a decorative reflector plate against the wall to reflect the extra light and to create a focal point for the flare of brightness.

Suspended
One major advantage of fixtures with suspended mountings is their appearance. Many such fixtures can be considered "lighted ornaments." Wherever lighting fixtures act as thematic accessories in an interior, such as a restaurant or church, it is always the suspended, or "pendant," fixture that is dramatically dropped into full view. Although there are thousands of gorgeous ones to choose from, only lately have manufacturers begun to design a lighted ornament that also provides good task or architectural light.

The disadvantages of fixtures with such mountings are obvious. Being in full view, such a fixture easily becomes glaring if its brightness is not controlled. But there is a paradox here: although the suspended fixture is in the midspace of the room, it seldom is close enough to any room surface to make it bright. For example, in a dining room such a fixture must often be turned up to illuminate the food, but when that illumination is achieved, the fixture is then much too bright. Two solutions are possible; select a pendant fixture with good lateral shielding or use separate functional lighting.

Separate functional lighting is a particularly attractive complement to the decorative fixture suspended in a stairwell. Such a fixture creates a potential glare problem to those above, below, and alongside it. Therefore, it can seldom be as bright as necessary to effectively light the stairs. Separate lighting can create the additional brightness that's needed.

Another disadvantage of the suspended fixture can be the greater cost of its installation. Often the fixture must be leveled. Some codes require suspended fixtures to have "earthquake" hangers; these special stems allow the fixtures to sway but not break loose in the event of a disaster.

Track-Mounted
Track is often the answer to a mounting quandary; it is an electrified wireway. Lighting fixtures mounted on track are code approved for many uses and places, and have three important advantages: versatility, economy, and flexibility.

In terms of versatility, the track can be recessed, surface mounted, stem supported, or attached to a wall. It can even be purchased with a cord and plug as a portable fixture. There are tracks so small that they are used under shelves, and others so big that they can conceal air ducts. The track itself comes straight or curved and in more than a dozen finishes.

Its economy is multiple: it is easy and cheap to install, which accounts for its great popularity, and it is also inexpensive to buy and maintain. Existing wiring often does not need to be altered because the track houses the electrical circuit—or even two, three, or four circuits—with dimming. Its flexibility rests on the many and varied fixtures that can be installed by attaching them to the track. These include fluorescent, incandescent, tungsten halogen, low voltage, and decorative fixtures. Even illuminated signs, shelves, and stereo speakers can be attached to the track. Almost every lighting technique described in Chapter Two can be accomplished with track lighting.

Now the disappointments. There is a bare "nuts and bolts" appearance to track lighting that is acceptable in a high-tech design scheme but less so in a more traditional one. Second, successful track lighting depends on the know-how of its user. Too often, track-mounted lighting results in a miniature landing field of garish spotlights, harsh shadows, and direct glare. When objects are each spotlighted to exactly the same brightness, they do not establish any visual priorities or direction for a lighting design. It is important to remember that the purpose of a lighting design is to compose the visual field into a unified and logical scene.

Another problem with track-mounted lighting is that it is easy for the person who cleans these fixtures to refocus them accidentally. Finally, track lighting requires the correct selection of a myriad of small parts. One way to deal with this problem is to carefully identify and call out each piece in the original specifications; another way is to specify generally. For example: "Contractor to inspect site, verify field dimensions, and furnish material to mount two lengths of 8-foot (2.5 m) track: Halo #1256-P; five wallwashers: Halo #1722-P; and two low-voltage accent lights: Halo #1728-P." The second system is actually more workable because field dimensions often change during construction.

Portable
Portable lighting fixtures are sold primarily at the consumer level and reflect current fashion trends more than other types of fixtures. Portable fixtures can have an almost infinite variety of different looks. For example, an HID uplight in a 6-foot-tall (183 cm) cylinder can be covered with fabric. A wall sconce can be faux marble, faux malachite, or faux common rock. There are even luminous benches, tables, and boulders. The cost of portables is just as variable as their appearance. Competition among manufacturers promotes minimum pricing, because most portables that sell successfully when introduced are soon copied and sold at lower prices. Maintenance costs for

portables are nominal and installation costs are nonexistent.

The strategy of using the portable fixtures to provide working light close to the task and ambient light to soften room contrasts originated in the home. Task lighting was provided by a table lamp next to the reading chair while ambient light flowed from the opal glass fixture overhead. In the 1970s, this concept was modified and popularized for office lighting when lighting designer Sylvan Shemitz introduced lighted office furniture—portable work stations that incorporated task lighting and indirect ambient lighting in one desk unit.

As it became apparent that the 4-foot (123 cm) fluorescent tubes built into the furniture caused reflections on the task and had a limited beam spread, designers added the jointed task light to their workspaces. Recently, miniature but powerful fluorescent and incandescent lamp bulbs have produced another generation of more stylish fixtures. Today, such fixtures in postmodern shapes and colors are seen throughout offices across the country.

Some office settings are better for built-in task-ambient lighting than others. In an influential technical paper by Noel Florence, the results of tests made on five kinds of task ambient lighting systems were given.[1] Combinations of direct task lighting with furniture-mounted indirect ambient lighting used the most watts-per-square-foot. On the other hand, for a dense layout of work stations (60 square feet [18.3 m] for each) the combination of one F40 fluorescent in the workstation for task lighting with one ceiling-mounted F40 fluorescent tube for ambient lighting was best (1.48 watts-per-square-foot), if the ceiling fixture had a parabolic batwing louver. For a more generous layout of work stations (180 square feet [55.0 m] for each), the economy of the previous system was the same as that of a system that offered two (two-lamp) overhead parabolic fixtures to each workstation. Each system required less than one watt-per-square-foot.

Although a furniture-integrated lighting system such as Shemitz's workstation is not always the most energy efficient, it has been successful for many reasons:

Easy maintenance

Can be moved

Localized switching saves hours of use

Qualifies for investment tax credits

Structural
Structural lighting includes not only the soffits, coves, and valances illustrated in Appendix A-1: Structural Lighting Charts, but also handrails, lighted coffers, lighted niches, and other places where the lighting is integral to the construction. Like recessed lighting, the chief advantage of structurally mounted lighting is its appear-

ance. Being built in, it is relatively unseen. The light can be controlled to enhance the brightness balances of the room without creating glare in the field of view.

However, there are several disadvantages to structural lighting. Although it can be dimmed, it is otherwise inflexible. Also, its initial costs are high. These include higher design fees, in addition to the carpentry, painting, and wiring costs. Finally, there is the concern that structural lighting will use too much energy because even when lighting cavities are painted matte white, the flow of light from them is not efficient.

FIXTURE COSTS
Like all quality products, fixtures that have the best craftsmanship and materials are usually more expensive. Nonetheless, comparing fixtures of equal cost is easy if the designer remembers that (1) the light source is encased inside a metal can, but (2) the beam of light is needed in the space—not in that can. Either the features of fixtures force the light beam into the room or the lamp bulb itself projects the light beam out. This latter type is the least expensive. Such fixtures depend on the reflector of the bulb or tube to jettison the light into the space. Their disadvantages include the necessity for costly, timely, and exact duplication of the lamp bulb when it burns out.

More expensive fixtures use reflectors and lenses to project the light from the can, but these reflectors and lenses must be cleaned periodically, therefore, higher initial costs are augmented by recurring maintenance costs. The most expensive fixtures are those that require ballasts and transformers. This extra electrical management increases their initial cost but lowers their owning and operating costs in a direct ratio to the increased life of the light source and the decreased use of electricity. (See the section on life cycle costing in Chapter Three.)

Substitutions for Specified Fixtures
A designer's professional performance can be measured in three ways: the beauty of a designed space, how well that space functions, and how much the completed project costs. To perform well in any of these areas, the designer must control his/her project from its concept to its completion. Exercising such control over the lighting system is difficult because of the contractors' practice of substituting fixtures for those specified by the designer. And such substitutions are hard to prove because most designers cannot identify the fixtures after installation. On major projects, the effort to do so is seldom attempted, unless a lighting designer is involved, because the risk of holding up the construction schedule is too costly.

But why do contractors make such substitutions? The answer lies in an understanding of the lighting industry which consists of two very different markets. It is the existence of these two markets that creates the practice of making substitutions.

The first market is the specifier market; it's a more profitable one for manufacturers, although they tend to be smaller than commercial/industrial manufacturers. Here fixtures are produced to order, and such orders must be placed eight weeks in advance. Custom fixtures are also in this market and most new kinds of fixtures are introduced here. These fixtures are shown and sold (1) in design showrooms by agents of the manufacturer, or (2) in specifiers' offices by commissioned territorial representatives. To obtain these fixtures for construction, they also must be ordered in advance.

The other market is the commercial/industrial one. Although there is less profit here, manufacturers tend to be large. They make their money by selling volume quantities of their product, which is very efficiently manufactured, to distributors at a small profit per unit. In turn, the distributor sells from stock to the electrical contractor when construction is in progress. To protect the economies of scale offered only by large production runs, the manufacturer of commercial/industrial fixtures insures his/her market by requiring customers (the distributors) to inventory sizable quantities of his/her product line at all times.

Many small to midsize distributors can only afford about a dozen such lines. So these distributors take advantage of the urgency of a contractor's construction schedule; they "package" a project by substituting the lines they carry on their shelves for those named in the specifications. Together the distributor and the contractor may approach an owner, architect, or general contractor to offer a lower cost and a "credit" on the lighting if the owner will accept the cheaper substitutions. If the owner does not accept, the project will be delayed, since the specified products require eight weeks from order to delivery. Sometimes the cheaper fixtures are suitable alternatives; usually they are not because their distribution of light differs, although they may be similar in appearance to the specified fixtures. Usually the owner does not receive the full savings in his credit, either, because of the legitimate costs of the contractor's and distributor's time in making up the package.

Controlling Costs and Rescuing Specifications
The notion of weighing initial costs against owning and operating costs is academic unless the specifier can hold his/her specifications. In real life, both initial costs and operating costs depend upon installation of the specified product. Professional lighting consultants have developed a few tactics that reduce "substitutions" and packaging.

The first one involves creation of a partnership with the field representative of specification grade fixtures.

If the designer determines that the fixtures from one or two of these manufacturers are crucial to his/her project, the designer can then interest the representatives in the project and write up the remainder of the specifications to include "equals" for the less important fixtures around the lines carried by those representatives. When the field representatives are familiar with a project and know they have a large commission riding on it, they will hound the project's contractor to write the fixture orders soon enough to accommodate the necessary 8-week delivery schedule.

Another tactic protects the crucial fixtures only. Using this tactic, the designer writes exclusive and proprietary specifications for less than a dozen fixture types; the rest of the fixtures are written with generous, low-priced equals—three or four equals for each fixture type. When the bidding process begins, the "Instructions to Bidders" includes a form that lets every bidder know that all proposed substitutions and credits are to be listed on the form and returned with the bid package. "No other substitutions will be approved." Later, before the "certificate of substantial completion" is signed, the designer can have fixture substitutions not accepted on the substitution form pulled out of the project and replaced with the specified item at the contractor's cost.

A third tactic for rescuing specifications saves a key fixture type or two by having the owner buy and furnish them to the job after "substantial completion" of construction. This is a traditional and frequently used tactic when any of three sets of circumstances exist: (1) in projects having a large quantity of customized, but identical, decorative fixtures; (2) in projects where expensive dimming controls can upgrade the use of cheaper fixtures; and (3) in projects that have complicated systems of "tinker toy" parts that must be assembled on the site. In the last instance, the owner may not only buy the small parts, but he/she often hires an electrical contractor to install them. The manufacturer can recommend nearby installers or can send his/her own installer to the project.

APPEARANCE
When selecting fixtures on the basis of appearance, the designer might want to review some assumptions about the space to be illuminated:

1. Will the interior design be enhanced by making the lighting system visible? If not, structural lighting and recessed lighting will conceal the fixtures.

2. If the fixtures should be seen, should they make a statement in the space? A

major statement can be made by fixtures suspended into the line of sight. A minor statement might be one in which wall bracket fixtures flank a mirror.

In these examples, it is important to remember that when fixtures are lighted, their appearance and decorative contribution to a space are controlled by the pale or dark color of the background against which they are seen. If the contrast of lighted fixtures to a dark background is too extreme, the visual detail will be lost in glare. On the other hand, if the contrast between lighted fixtures and their pale background is too bland, the fixtures may blend in and be visually lost (Figure 5-7).

The appearance of the fixtures unlighted must also be considered. The molding that rims the cavity of a structural fixture; the silver, black, or gold reflectors or louvers in the aperture of a recessed fixture; or the materials and finishes of the surface-mounted or suspended fixture—these are the decorative "skin" on a lighting system. Just as it is foolish to select a lighting system purely on the basis of these decorative attributes, it is also foolish to ignore them.

SAFETY
Another important factor to consider when selecting fixtures is their safety. Fixtures not only shelter the lamp bulb from weather and other hazards, but also protect curious children, wooden joists, and other sensitive and flammable materials from the heat of the lamp or ballast. So, to ensure the public's safety, fixtures and their installation are inspected. Underwriters Laboratories in the United States and the Canadian Standards Association in Canada perform tests on fixtures to certify them as safe for a particular use; for example, use for "wet locations" would apply to those fixtures certified for shower stalls. Once a fixture is certified, its manufacturer is permitted to affix a blue "UL" label to all fixtures of that type (in Canada, it is the green "CSA approved" label). Most new and remodeled commercial projects require the use of fixtures bearing these labels.

If fixtures are altered in any way, this safety certification may become void. The liability for the fixtures' safety then falls upon those who participated in the change. Often an interior designer becomes unknowingly entangled in litigation, because products liability is much stricter than professional liability. One way to re-ensure public safety and avoid such liability is to submit a sample of altered fixtures to a local electrical testing laboratory for certification. Another way is to draw the attention of the building department's field inspector to the eccentric installation and request that he/she certify the fixtures "as installed." With this latter tactic, the designer must be prepared to correct fixtures or their mount-

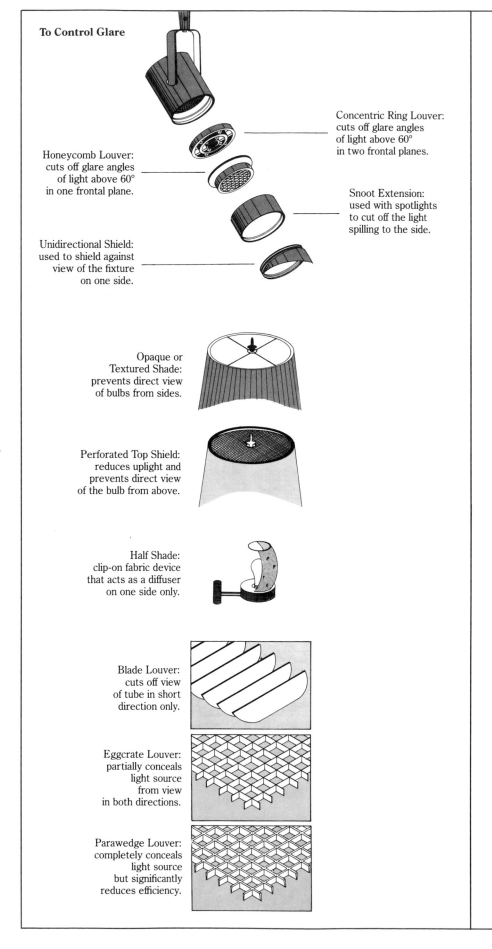

To Control Glare

Honeycomb Louver:
cuts off glare angles
of light above 60°
in one frontal plane.

Concentric Ring Louver:
cuts off glare angles
of light above 60°
in two frontal planes.

Snoot Extension:
used with spotlights
to cut off the light
spilling to the side.

Unidirectional Shield:
used to shield against
view of the fixture
on one side.

Opaque or
Textured Shade:
prevents direct view
of bulbs from sides.

Perforated Top Shield:
reduces uplight and
prevents direct view
of the bulb from above.

Half Shade:
clip-on fabric device
that acts as a diffuser
on one side only.

Blade Louver:
cuts off view
of tube in short
direction only.

Eggcrate Louver:
partially conceals
light source
from view
in both directions.

Parawedge Louver:
completely conceals
light source
but significantly
reduces efficiency.

FIGURE 5-7:   Accessories
Fixture accessories always add flexibility;
often accessories are required to properly
light a project. These include many devices
that were originally created to direct glare
away from an individual's line of sight. Soon,
such accessories were joined by others that
originated in the theater to change the effect
of the light beam. There is also a third group
of accessories that are just ornamental. One
way or another, most of these accessories
can be attached to fixtures, but the designer
should test their visual results before specifying them, because such results differ from
one fixture to another. (Illustration by Reiko
Hayashi.)

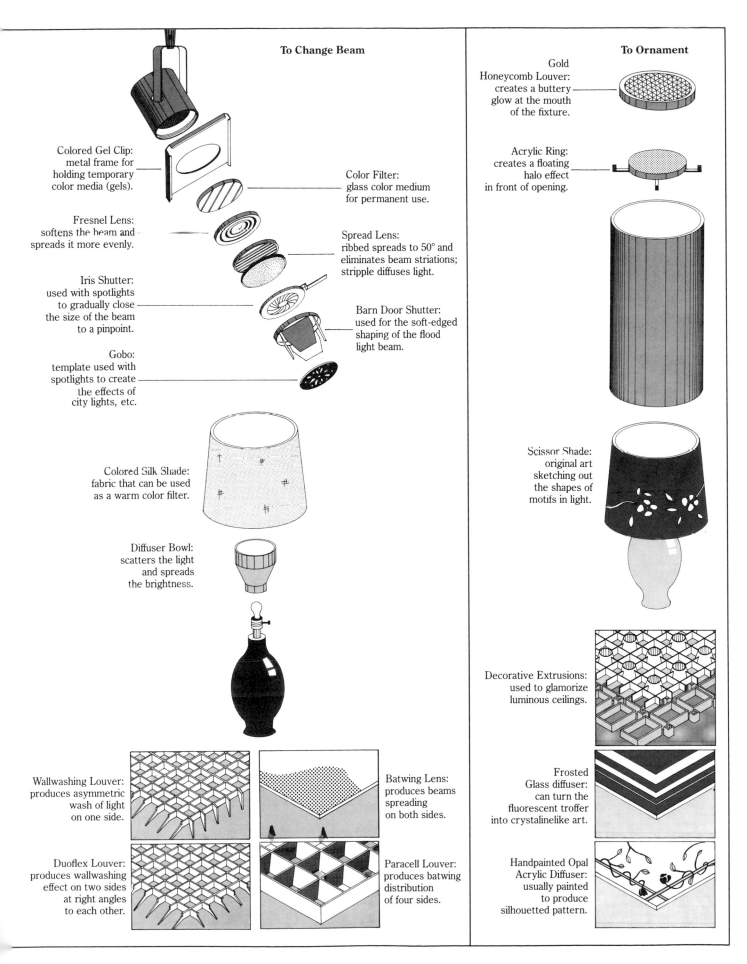

To Change Beam

Colored Gel Clip:
metal frame for
holding temporary
color media (gels).

Fresnel Lens:
softens the beam and
spreads it more evenly.

Iris Shutter:
used with spotlights
to gradually close
the size of the beam
to a pinpoint.

Gobo:
template used with
spotlights to create
the effects of
city lights, etc.

Color Filter:
glass color medium
for permanent use.

Spread Lens:
ribbed spreads to 50° and
eliminates beam striations;
stripple diffuses light.

Barn Door Shutter:
used for the soft-edged
shaping of the flood
light beam.

Colored Silk Shade:
fabric that can be used
as a warm color filter.

Diffuser Bowl:
scatters the light
and spreads
the brightness.

Wallwashing Louver:
produces asymmetric
wash of light
on one side.

Duoflex Louver:
produces wallwashing
effect on two sides
at right angles
to each other.

Batwing Lens:
produces beams
spreading
on both sides.

Paracell Louver:
produces batwing
distribution
of four sides.

To Ornament

Gold
Honeycomb Louver:
creates a buttery
glow at the mouth
of the fixture.

Acrylic Ring:
creates a floating
halo effect
in front of opening.

Scissor Shade:
original art
sketching out
the shapes of
motifs in light.

Decorative Extrusions:
used to glamorize
luminous ceilings.

Frosted
Glass diffuser:
can turn the
fluorescent troffer
into crystalinelike art.

Handpainted Opal
Acrylic Diffuser:
usually painted
to produce
silhouetted pattern.

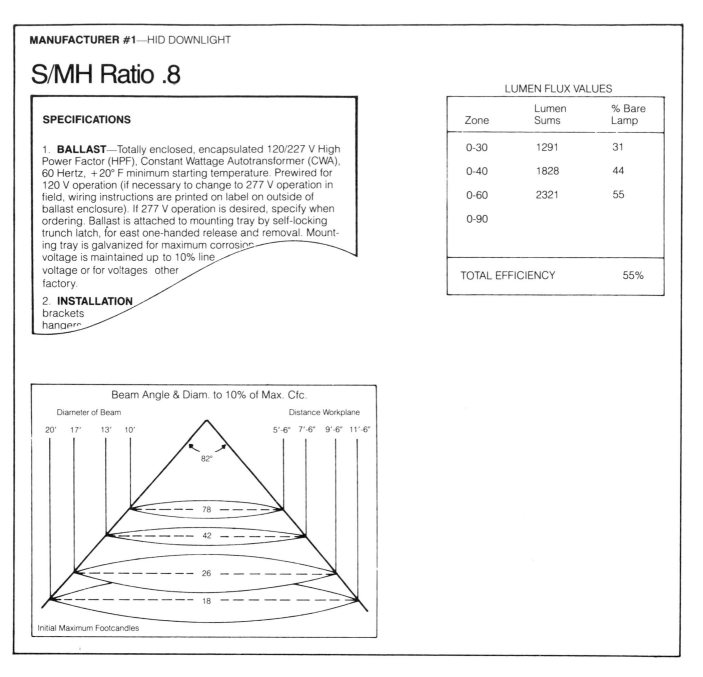

MANUFACTURER #1—HID DOWNLIGHT

S/MH Ratio .8

SPECIFICATIONS

1. **BALLAST**—Totally enclosed, encapsulated 120/227 V High Power Factor (HPF), Constant Wattage Autotransformer (CWA), 60 Hertz, +20° F minimum starting temperature. Prewired for 120 V operation (if necessary to change to 277 V operation in field, wiring instructions are printed on label on outside of ballast enclosure). If 277 V operation is desired, specify when ordering. Ballast is attached to mounting tray by self-locking trunch latch, for east one-handed release and removal. Mounting tray is galvanized for maximum corrosion voltage is maintained up to 10% line voltage or for voltages other factory.

2. **INSTALLATION**
brackets
hangers

LUMEN FLUX VALUES

Zone	Lumen Sums	% Bare Lamp
0-30	1291	31
0-40	1828	44
0-60	2321	55
0-90		
TOTAL EFFICIENCY		55%

Beam Angle & Diam. to 10% of Max. Cfc.

Diameter of Beam   Distance Workplane

20'   17'   13'   10'   5'-6" 7'-6" 9'-6" 11'-6"

82°

78

42

26

18

Initial Maximum Footcandles

FIGURE 5-8: Catalog Aids
Note: The catalog aid used most by the designer is the map showing the footcandles wallwashing a vertical surface. On a one-foot grid, if the footcandles vary more than 33 percent, look for a smoother distribution of light from another manufacturer's wallwasher. (Illustration by Reiko Hayashi.)

ings as directed by the field inspector. Failure to comply can result in the installation's failure to pass inspection, which can cause the "Certificate of Public Occupancy" to be withheld.

READING FIXTURE CATALOGS
The interior designer's increasing responsibility for lighting decisions has led to an increase in the number of demonstration showrooms run by electrical distributors and manufacturers. However, most designers still select fixtures through fixture catalogs. Such catalogs must deliver enough information so that the designer can make confident selections. Important information any catalog should provide about fixtures includes:

1. UL or CSA labels for a given type of location

2. IBEW (International Brotherhood of Electrical Workers) labels, which unionized cities require

3. Acrylic lenses; "styrene" lenses are not permitted in some code jurisdictions

4. Recessed height (for recessed fixtures); for thermal safety, fixtures must have an inch or more of clearance in the plenum above the ceiling

5. Fixture flange; it must be appropriate for a project's type of ceilings

6. Top access; installation of such fixtures will require crawl space above the ceiling

7. Length and width; some fixtures may not fit between the ceiling joists

8. Plaster frame; this must be available

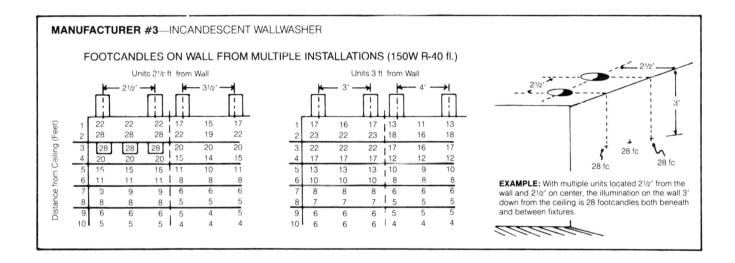

MANUFACTURER #2—HID DOWNLIGHT

Initial Footcandles

100WE-23½

Area Per Fixture in Square Feet

RAPID ESTIMATE ILLUMINATION CHART

Use for quickly approximating the number and spacing of units for any desired level of illumination. Computed for D room index with 50% ceiling, 30% walls, and 10% floor reflection factors.

MANUFACTURER #3—INCANDESCENT WALLWASHER

FOOTCANDLES ON WALL FROM MULTIPLE INSTALLATIONS (150W R-40 fl.)

Units 2½ ft from Wall

Distance from Ceiling (Feet)	2½′			3½′		
1	22	22	22	17	15	17
2	28	28	28	22	19	22
3	28	28	28	20	20	20
4	20	20	20	15	14	15
5	15	15	15	11	10	11
6	11	11	11	8	8	8
7	9	9	9	6	6	6
8	8	8	8	5	5	5
9	6	6	6	5	4	5
10	5	5	5	4	4	4

Units 3 ft from Wall

	3′			4′		
1	17	16	17	13	11	13
2	23	22	23	18	16	18
3	22	22	22	17	16	17
4	17	17	17	12	12	12
5	13	13	13	10	9	10
6	10	10	10	8	8	8
7	8	8	8	6	6	6
8	7	7	7	5	5	5
9	6	6	6	5	5	5
10	6	6	6	4	4	4

EXAMPLE: With multiple units located 2½′ from the wall and 2½′ on center, the illumination on the wall 3′ down from the ceiling is 28 footcandles both beneath and between fixtures.

from the manufacturer when the project has new plaster ceilings

9. Wide trim ring; if a fixture must be cut into an existing ceiling of old plaster, this will disguise the uneven hole

Fixture catalogs also include cutaway photographs of the installed fixtures to show how they look and how they are mechanically seated into a particular type of ceiling. A fully dimensioned cross section illustrates internal structure, alternate positions in different ceiling types, and the optical train or physical flow of light. A plan view is also included for each fixture, which allows the designer to see whether recessed fixtures will fit between the 16-inch space between ceiling joists, or if the joists will have to be "boxed."

A candlepower distribution curve is also found in most catalogs to show the relative shape of a fixture's beam of light. And finally, a variety of estimating aids are given to help the designer determine how many fixtures will be needed, eliminating the need for the designer's own calculations. Often model specifications are offered which, if copied exactly and enforced stringently, will prevent competitors' products from receiving approval as equals. These estimating aids are shown in Figure 5-8.

LOOKING AHEAD
Selecting fixtures is not hard. The nature of the project predetermines their selection. For instance, a lighting system for a newspaper office with a 20-foot ceiling, VDT tasks located everywhere, and an owner who hates maintenance, will have to use HID light sources in low glare recessed

fixtures. Why? Because mercury light sources are the only ones that can economically deliver the blanket of low-level ambient light. Maintenance is eased by their 24,000-hour life, and recessed mountings keep them out of sight. To increase such a lighting system's flexibility, inexpensive, individual task lights can be added to aid in reading copy or performing other non-VDT tasks.

This imaginary project, like most real ones, almost selected its own fixtures. Once you understand the problem presented in lighting a given space, the answers to it become obvious.

CHAPTER NOTE
[1]Noel Florence, "The Energy Effectiveness of Task-Oriented Office Lighting Systems," *Lighting Design and Application*, January 1979: 28-36.

COMMUNICATING YOUR DESIGN

Chapter Six

DRAWING NAME	# OF DRAWING
REFLECTED CEILING PLAN Most common for large commercial work and for other complex ceiling systems	Numbered as an "A" sheet Follows last floor plan
LIGHTING PLAN Residential and commercial projects	Numbered as an "E" sheet Precedes plans for power distribution
ELECTRICAL PLAN Also known as power and signal Residential and commercial jobs	Numbered as an "E" sheet Follows last lighting plan
LIGHTING DETAIL Used in both residential and commercial projects whenever the design criteria creates the need for precise information	Numbered as an "E" sheet Follows the final electrical plan
APPROVAL DRAWINGS Also known as shop drawings	Not in bid package

Note: ANSI: American National Standards Institute

A DESIGNER'S OBJECTIVE is to produce the highest quality work in the shortest time span. Simple lighting statements and lighting drawings lead not only to better communication between designers and the construction trades, but also to a more consistent profit for the designer.

Traditionally, there are two vehicles by which the designer communicates with the installers: the project drawings and the project manual. Each plays a precise role.

The project drawings show the location of the lighting and its relationship to the site, the structure, and to other systems of building components. To work well as visual communication, they must be uncluttered. Therefore, some conventions and rules must apply; information is given only once and is shown in the most logical place. Only generic materials references, like "track lighting" or "acoustic tile," appear on the drawings.

The specifications in the project manual, on the other hand, clearly identify the type and quality of each of the lighting products, its technical description, qualifying criteria, and any other information on product performance and installation methods that would lead to proper and complete cost evaluation and installation. Together with the other legal documents in the manual, the specifications identify who will do what, how and when they will do it, and how much they will be paid.[1]

DRAWINGS

There are five types of lighting drawings:

    Reflected ceiling plan

    Lighting plan

    Electrical plan

    Detail sheet

    Approval drawings (see Table 6-1)

The two for which interior designers and lighting consultants are most frequently re-

	* Design phases:	4. Documentation
	1. Programming	5. Bidding
	2. Schematic	6. Construction
	3. Development	7. Postconstruction

TABLE 6-1 THE FIVE LIGHTING PROJECT DRAWINGS

RESPONSIBLE DESIGNER REQUIRED STAMP	PREPARED BY	DESIGN PHASE* (when)	PURPOSE	SHOWS	PREFERRED SCALE	ACCOMPANYING SPECIFICATIONS METHOD
Registered architect	Architectural drafter	Rough drawing/ Phase 2 or 3 Final drawing/ Phase 4	For designers and consultants to check coordination of building systems in complex ceilings. The centering dimensions shown here control all spatial relationships affecting the ceiling systems.	Changes in ceiling elevations and materials . . . walls, partitions, and soffits that intersect with the ceiling . . . lights, sprinklers or HVAC registers that attach to or penetrate the ceiling. (Switches and other control devices may also be shown.)	1/8″ = 1′-0″ 1/4″ = 1′-0″ for residences and remodels. (May be reduced scale where uncomplicated.)	Specific method varies with project and trades However, integrated ceiling systems often found in Division 13/ Special Construction.
Registered architect Electrical consultant (residential or commercial) Installing contractor (small residential) Electrical consultant (large commercial)	Registered architect Interior designer Space planner Lighting consultant or supplier Electrical contractor (estimator)	Phase 2, 3 or 4 Phase 4, 5, or 6	For designers, consultants, and installers to illustrate the lighting concept and its components. Usually an advisory document; information often transferred to electrical drawings.	Lighting fixtures . . . Lighting controls and fixtures assigned to each control. (May show special features needed for correct lighting placement.)	1/8″ = 1′-0″ 1/4′ = 1′-0″ for residences and remodels.	Proprietary (one brand only) Reference standard (ANSI or ASTM or reference manufacturer & model) Performance
Same as above	Registered architect Electrical consultant Electrical contractor (estimator)	Phase 3 Phases 4, 5, and 6	For electrical bids and permits and to provide a basis for pricing and to guide electrical construction.	The electrical service, single line diagram, main switchboard, and materials, distribution and motor control switchboards, panelboards, electrical outlets, conduit and wire. All power going to all electrical equipment. Telephone service and distribution outlets, conduits, communications, security systems, fire alarms, transformers, and stand-by generators.	1/4″ = 1′-0″	Residential: Proprietary (high budget) descriptive cash allowance Small commercial: proprietary descriptive reference brand or equals Large commercial: performance (high budget) reference brand(s) and equals descriptive (low budget) Publically funded: three approved manufacturers
Registered architect or Electrical consultant	Registered architect Interior designer Space planner Lighting consultant	Phase 3, 4, or 6	For electrical wiremen performing the installation.	Enlargements of lighting fixture or its mounting or installation method.	1 1/2″ or 3″ = 1′-0″ or at smallest scale that will be easy to draw and easy to read without wasting sheet space or crowding sheet appearance.	Proprietary Reference brand(s) and equals
None	Lighting manufacturer	Phase 5 or 6	Submitted to the specifier by the manufacturer and/or contractor to indicate whether the proposed product meets the intent of the design.	Mechanical diagram and complete data on a fixture to show its construction or required shop procedures for special finishes and materials.	Varies (see Figure 6-12) Custom fixture submit: 1 1/2″ or 3″ = 1′-0″ or full scale.	Performance Reference standards Reference brand(s) and equals Descriptive

ASTM: American Society of Testing Materials

sponsible are the lighting plan and the detail drawings. The technical knowledge and visual skills required to produce these should be within the interior designer's area of competency.

Creating the other three kinds of lighting drawings—reflected ceiling plan, electrical plan, and approvals drawings—involves legal relationships and skills for which many interior designers have not been trained or licensed. But designers should be able to read such drawings, even though they may not be able to assume sole responsibility for having created them.

Reflected Ceiling Plan
A mirrored floor would show viewers the

reflection of the ceiling above: this view is the *reflected ceiling plan* (Figures 6-1 and 6-2). It is used to check on the ceiling appearance and the coordination of ceiling-mounted building systems. Although the entire ceiling is seldom seen at one time, some architectural designers consider the shape of the ceiling plane and the pattern of its fixtures, sprinklers, and registers to be a significant part of the environmental experience. Specific fixture placement is determined by (1) the client's need and (2) the appearance of the space at eye level. Minor adjustments to these fixture locations can create (3) a ceiling plane that is logically patterned as well (Figures 6-3 through 6-5).

FIGURE 6-1: Reflected Ceiling Plan/Commercial
It was hard for subcontractors from different trades to maintain the installation tolerances necessary to create the visual and functional relationships indicated on this reflected ceiling plan. Here, the task is compounded further by the folded configuration of the ceiling (see Figure 6-11 also). (Illustration by Reiko Hayashi.)

LEGEND:
FLUORESCENT FIXTURE	
RECESSED INCANDESCENT	
JUNCTION BOX	
SPRINKLER	
SINGLE POLE SWITCH	

CHECKLIST OF DRAWINGS CONVENTIONS

IDENTIFICATION
1. Underlined titles are preceded by a boxed **bold** letter to allow reference to them to be concise.

2. Titles should not be so bold as to compete with the drawing; lettering should be simple and readable.

3. Titles of details should be specific and should include the room number.

4. Titles should indicate how the drawing is oriented, that is, "vertical section" or "plan section."

5. Any enlarged drawing is a detail; use of the word "detail" in a title seems redundant.

6. On the detail sheet, one drawings specialist divides the sheet into a 16-part standard grid with titles and alphabet sequenced from left to right and from upper to lower.

7. Because reproductions enlarge or reduce sheet size, graphic scales that also enlarge or reduce are preferred.

8. Drawings are scaled only for general reference; dimensions necessary for estimating or for construction are always stated.

9. Dimensions for the spacing of fixtures are given as "on center" to the fixture opening. Three types of on-center dimensions are common:
   from center of fixture "A" to center of fixture "B"
   from center of fixture "A" to centerline of the room
   from center of fixture "A" to the finished face of a vertical surface

10. Placement of fixtures within the grid of a suspended ceiling is usually read as the relationship of the fixture to the ceiling tile unless otherwise indicated. (The designer should remember that the ceiling installer prefers to cut the partial tiles at the wall in order to adjust for irregularities in wall alignment.)

READABILITY
1. Lines showing fixture groups assigned to the same control switch are to be curved.

2. Line weights can be used to lend clarity:
   heavy lines show fixtures
   light lines show furniture and backgrounds
   heaviest outlines describe the perimeter of the materials in a detail.

CAUTIONS
1. When consultants work during the design phase they are disadvantaged in having to begin before the architectural changes are complete. Specifications benefit from a clause requiring the contractor to scale only the architectural plans to locate fixtures and controls. Alternatively, designers may require the contractor to verify all dimensions in the field and report any discrepancies from the drawings.

2. Because designers offer ideas, rights in the designs are often protected by a clause on the drawings such as "designs submitted by design office for this project shall be and remain the property of the Designer, together with any and all drawings, models, specifications, and samples furnished by the Designer. These copyrights are subject to the exclusive rights of Client as contained in the Designer/Client Agreement dated _____ ." (Designers should see their own attorney for similar language.)

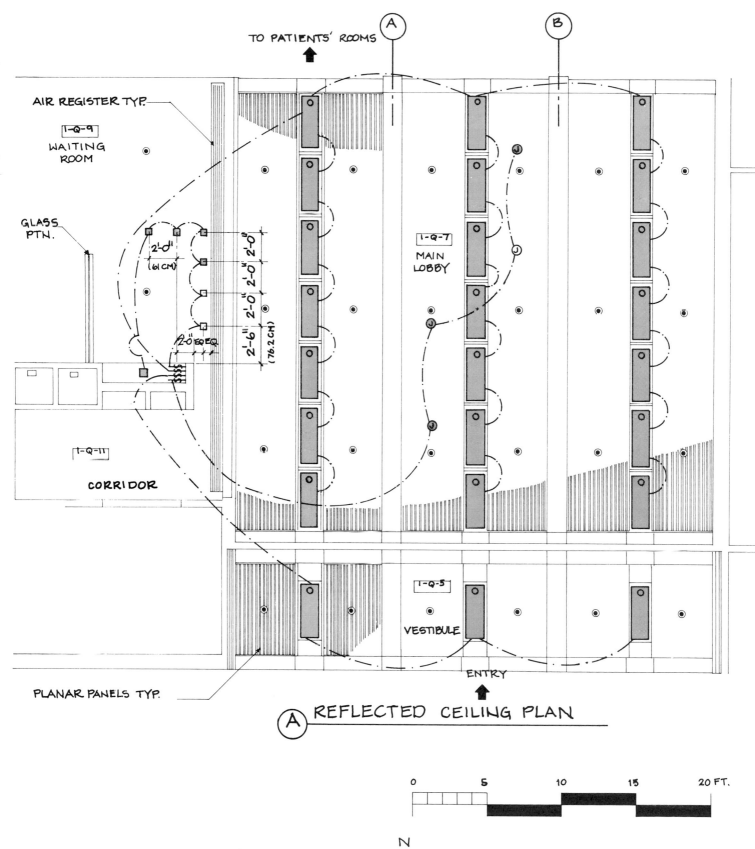

TO PATIENTS' ROOMS

(A) (B)

AIR REGISTER TYP.

1-Q-9
WAITING
ROOM

GLASS
PTN.

2'-0"
(61 CM)

2'-6"
(76.2 CM)

2'-0" EQ EQ

1-Q-7
MAIN
LOBBY

1-Q-11

CORRIDOR

1-Q-5

VESTIBULE

PLANAR PANELS TYP.

ENTRY

(A) REFLECTED CEILING PLAN

0   5   10   15   20 FT.

N

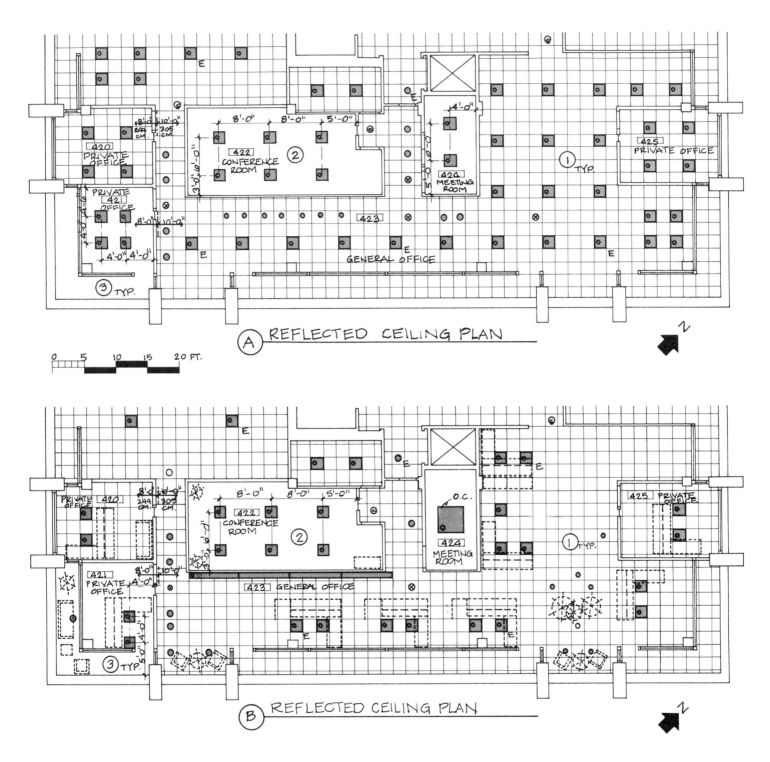

Ⓐ REFLECTED CEILING PLAN

0 5 10 15 20 FT.

Ⓑ REFLECTED CEILING PLAN

FIGURE 6-2: Reflected Ceiling Plan/Landscape Office
Often, the fire sprinkler heads are not indicated on the designer's drawings because the spacing, locations, and connecting pipes are so rigidly controlled by the fire codes that the designer finds it too confusing. Then, during construction, a licensed sprinkler subcontractor will design the sprinkler system to meet code using a minimum number of heads. He/she submits the layout to the governing fire authorities and to the design office for approval.

Invariably, the design office adds heads in an attempt to get the sprinklers to fall geometrically into the ceiling pattern. Because all of this occurs after the contracts are signed, the additional heads are charged to the owner.

The solution is for the reflected ceiling plan to indicate "typical acceptable locations." Although the sprinkler subcontractor will need to increase his/her bid to accommodate the heads needed for the acceptable pattern, the bid will not be as high as the extra costs for change orders. (Commentary courtesy of Jo Drummond, CCS/CSI; Illustration by Reiko Hayashi.)

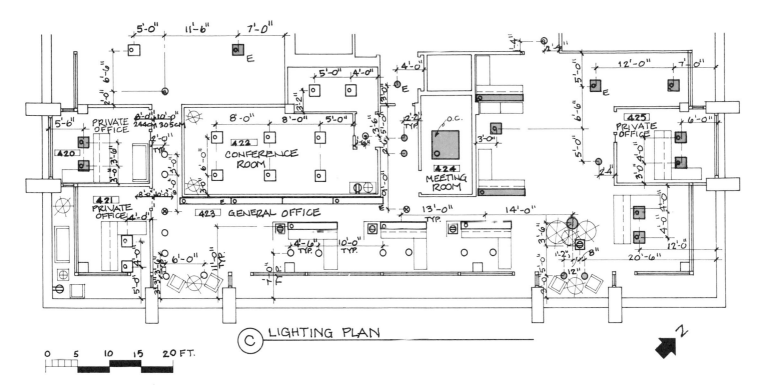

LIGHTING PLAN

0 5 10 15 20 FT.

LEGEND:

2X2 RECESSED FLUORESCENT (61 CM. X 61 CM.)	
1X4 RECESSED FLUORESCENT (30.5 CM. X 122 CM.)	
RECESSED INCANDESCENT	
EXIT LIGHT	
SMOKE DETECTOR/ ALARM	
2X2 RECESSED FLUOR. ON NIGHT CIRCUIT & EMER. POWER	
1X4 RECESSED FLUOR. ON NIGHT CIRCUIT & EMER. POWER	
RECESSED INCAN. ON NIGHT CIRCUIT & EMER. POWER	
① ACOUSTICAL TILE 2'X2' (61 CM. X 61 CM.)	
② SHEET ROCK 5/8" (15.8 MM)	
③ AIR BAR	
--- DENOTES FURNITURE FOR DWGS. A & B	
WALL MOUNTED DUPLEX RECPT. OUTLET	
FLOOR MOUNTED DUPLEX RECPT. OUTLET	
___ DENOTES FURNITURE FOR DWG. C	

FIGURE 6-3: Lighting Plan/Same Landscape Office
Alternative lighting layouts (Figures 6-2, 6-3, and 6-4) for the same offices offer several obvious cost differences as well as some that are not obvious For example, Plans B and C require that fixtures and desks be relocated together when employee groupings change. (Comparison courtesy of Jan Lennox Moyer ASID/IIES.) (Illustration by Reiko Hayashi.)

Plan A: General Ambient Lighting
3 watts/square foot: fixture cost = $1.58/square foot

Plan B: Specific Task Lighting
2.13 watts/square foot: fixture cost = $2.56/square foot

Plan C: Furniture-Integrated Lighting
3.3 watts/square foot. fixture cost = $3.53/square foot.

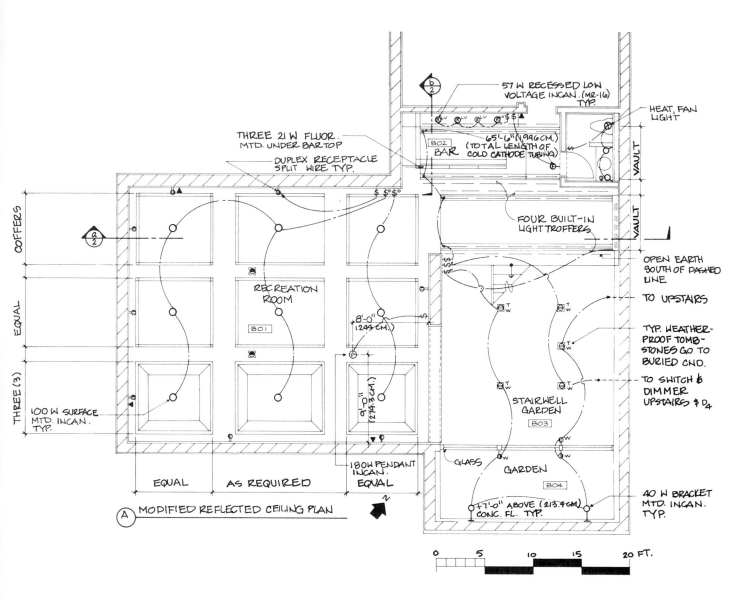

THREE 21 W FLUOR.
MTD. UNDER BAR TOP

57 W RECESSED LOW
VOLTAGE INCAN. (MR-16)
TYP.

HEAT, FAN
LIGHT

DUPLEX RECEPTACLE
SPLIT WIRE TYP.

65'-6"(1,996 CM.)
(TOTAL LENGTH OF
COLD CATHODE TUBING)

BAR
B02

VAULT

COFFERS

FOUR BUILT-IN
LIGHT TROFFERS

VAULT

a
2

RECREATION
ROOM

B01

OPEN EARTH
SOUTH OF DASHED
LINE

TO UPSTAIRS

EQUAL

8'-0"
(244 CM.)

TYP. WEATHER-
PROOF TOMB-
STONES GO TO
BURIED CND.

TO SWITCH &
DIMMER
UPSTAIRS & D₄

THREE (3)

100 W SURFACE
MTD. INCAN.
TYP.

9'-0"
(274.3 CM.)

STAIRWELL
GARDEN
B03

EQUAL   AS REQUIRED   EQUAL

180 W PENDANT
INCAN.

GLASS   GARDEN
B04

40 W BRACKET
MTD. INCAN.
TYP.

A MODIFIED REFLECTED CEILING PLAN

+7'-0" ABOVE (213.4 CM)
CONC. FL. TYP.

N

0   5   10   15   20 FT.

LEGEND			
▢	SURFACE FLUORESCENT	┤S	SINGE POLE SWITCH
○	SURFACE INCANDESCENT	┤S³	THREE-WAY SWITCH
⊗LV	RECESSED INCAN.-LOW VOLTAGE	┤S⁴	FOUR-WAY SWITCH
℗	PENDANT INCANDESCENT	┤S⁰ᵗ	FOUR-WAY DIMMER SWITCH
⊗	HEAT, FAN LIGHT	┤⊖	DUPLEX RECPT. OUTLET
┤○	WALL BRACKET INCAN.	┤⊖	DUPLEX RECPT.-SPLIT WIRED
┤⊘	WALL MTD. FAN	┤⊖ᵂ	DUPLEX RECPT.-SPLIT WIRED*
═══	COLD CATHODE	⊡ᵂ	WEATHERPROOF TOMBSTONE OUTLET
◄	TELEPHONE OUTLET	⊡	FL. MTD. DUPLEX RECPT.-SPLIT WIRE

*WEATHERPROOF

FIGURE 6-4: Modified Reflected Ceiling Plan/Residential New Construction
In residential projects, it is particularly hard for the designer to restrict the lighting system to only those fixtures that can be mounted to the ceiling. (1) In the multistory Stairwell Garden seen here, weatherproof electrical receptacles normally used outdoors will provide electricity to the lights staked into the garden soil which illuminate the 25-foot trees through which the staircase ascends. (2) On the other hand, the adjacent recreation room features a traditionally coffered ceiling, so lighting locations in this space must be dimensioned to the coffers. (3) In the meantime, the barrel vaults with their built-in lighting require not only plan views but also section and detail views. (Illustration by Reiko Hayashi.)

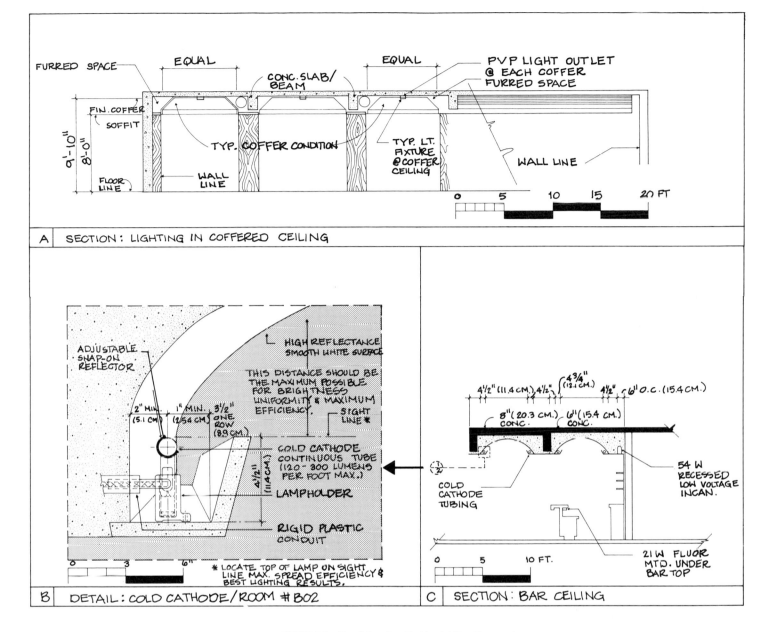

FIGURE 6-5: Detail Drawings/Residential New Construction
Because this story is below grade, bidding electrical subcontractors are hesitant about using their standard price guidebooks unless they can assess to what extent concerns like conceal-ment for the conduit and dimensions for the coves have been addressed. Therefore, the information from sections (a) and (c) will tend to standardize prices, but the precision of the cold cathode lighting dimensions shown on (b) the detail drawing will increase prices. (Illustration by Reiko Hayashi.)

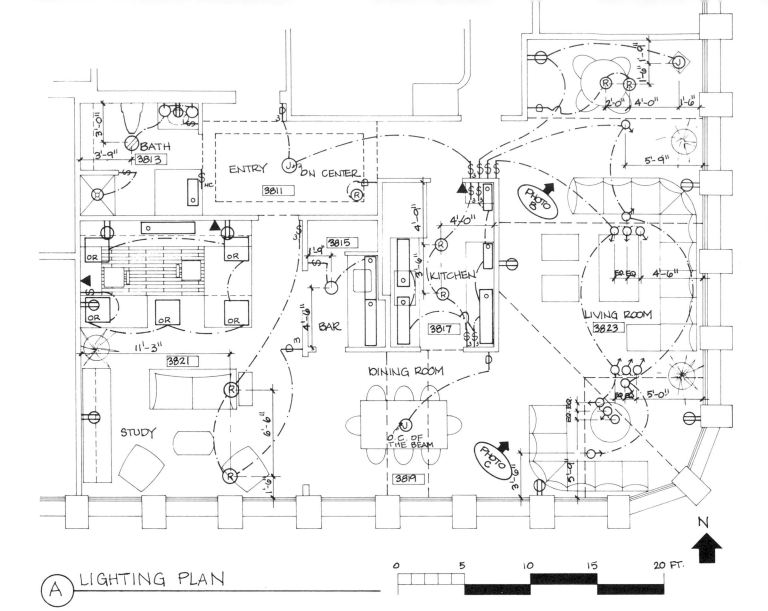

A LIGHTING PLAN

0   5   10   15   20 FT.

N

FIGURE 6-6: Lighting Plan/Residential Remodel
In contemporary residences that have
ceilings nine feet high or less, the visual
relationship of the lighting to the furnishings
is profound. For this reason, the installer
should know not only the dimensions by
which to locate fixtures on the ceiling, but
also how the fixtures relate to the furniture
pieces by having them indicated on the
drawings. When the furniture is not indicated, the wiring installer has to use his/her
own judgment to "correct" fixture locations.
(Illustration by Reiko Hayashi.)

LEGEND:

SYMBOL	DESCRIPTION
▢	RECESSED FLUORSCENT
OR	SURFACE FLUORSCENT
○	SURFACE INCAN.
Ⓡ	RECESSED INCAN.
Ⓙ	JUNCTION BOX
⊘	HEAT, FAN LIGHT
⚲	LOW VOLTAGE INCAN. SPOT
⊫◯	DUPLEX RECEPTACLE
◀	TELEPHONE OUTLET
⊢S	SINGLE POLE SWITCH
⊢S³	TWO-WAY SWITCH
⊢D	DIMMER
⊢D³	TWO-WAY DIMMER
⊢S MC	MOMENTARY CONTACT SWITCH

b

c

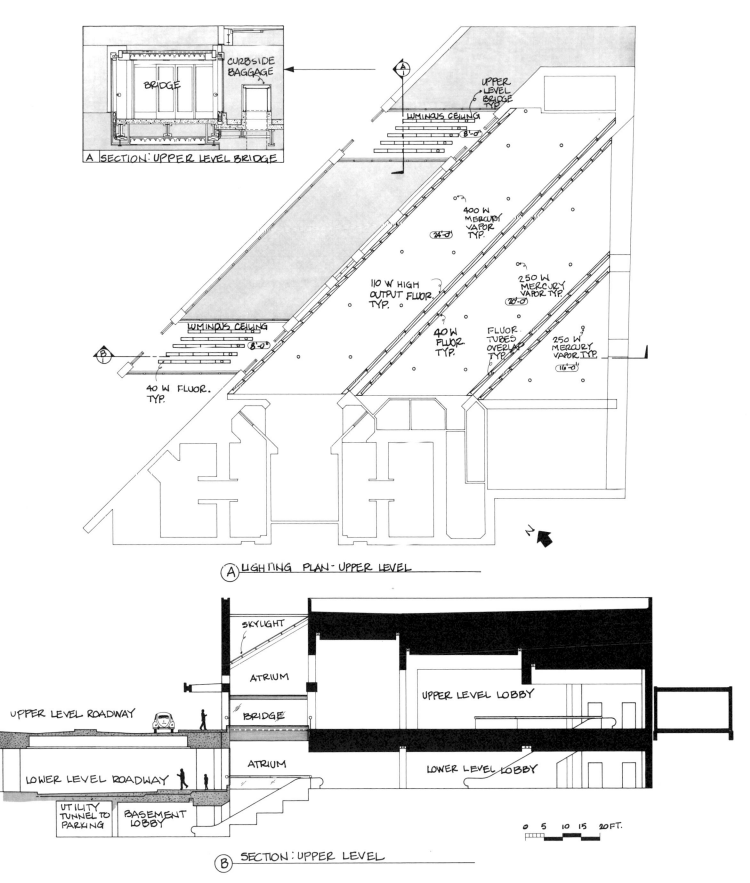

A | SECTION: UPPER LEVEL BRIDGE

BRIDGE
CURBSIDE BAGGAGE

UPPER LEVEL BRIDGE TYP.

LUMINOUS CEILING
8'-0"

400 W MERCURY VAPOR TYP.
24'-0"

110 W HIGH OUTPUT FLUOR. TYP.

250 W MERCURY VAPOR TYP.
20'-0"

LUMINOUS CEILING
8'-0"

40 W FLUOR. TYP.

FLUOR. TUBES OVERLAP TYP.

250 W MERCURY VAPOR TYP.
16'-0"

40 W FLUOR. TYP.

A | LIGHTING PLAN - UPPER LEVEL

SKYLIGHT

ATRIUM

UPPER LEVEL LOBBY

UPPER LEVEL ROADWAY

BRIDGE

ATRIUM

LOWER LEVEL LOBBY

LOWER LEVEL ROADWAY

UTILITY TUNNEL TO PARKING

BASEMENT LOBBY

0 5 10 15 20 FT.

B | SECTION: UPPER LEVEL

FIGURE 6-7: Lighting Plan Plus Sections/Multistory Commercial
Because the ceiling here is at several different heights above grade, the full set of drawings includes three plan views: upper, lower, and basement, but only the basement plan shows a single contiguous ceiling plane. For reasons such as this, some drawings are called lighting plans rather than reflected ceiling plans. (Illustration by Reiko Hayashi.)

TABLE 6-2   SELECTED SYMBOLS THAT APPEAR ON LIGHTING DRAWINGS

LIGHTING OUTLETS

CEILING WALL

○	○	SURFACE INCANDESCENT
♂	♂	ACCENT LIGHT
◑		WALL WASHER
Ⓡ	Ⓡ	RECESSED INCANDESCENT
○LV	○LV	LOW-VOLTAGE INCANDESCENT
○E	○E	INCANDESCENT ON EMERGENCY POWER
Ⓙ	Ⓙ	JUNCTION BOX
○L PS	○L PS	LAMP HOLDER WITH PULL SWITCH
Ⓥ	Ⓥ	OUTLET FOR HIGH-INTENSITY DISCHARGE
Ⓧ	Ⓧ	EXIT LIGHT OUTLET

TRACK LIGHT WITH LIVE END

SURFACE OR PENDANT INDIVIDUAL FLUOR. FIXTURE

RECESSED INDIVIDUAL FLUOR. FIXTURE (EMERGENCY POWER)

SURFACE OR PENDANT CONTINUOUS ROW FLUOR. FIXTURE.

RECESSED CONTINUOUS ROW FLUOR. FIXTURE

FLUORESCENT CEILING

PANELBOARDS

FLUSH MOUNTED PANELBOARD & CABINET

SURFACE MOUNTED PANELBOARD & CABINET

RECEPTACLE OUTLETS

- SINGLE RECEPTACLE OUTLET
- DUPLEX RECEPTACLE OUTLET (+12" AFF)
- DUPLEX RECEPTACLE TOMBSTONE OUTLET
- QUADRUPLEX RECEPTACLE OUTLET
- DUPLEX RECEPTACLE OUTLET - SPLIT WIRED
- SINGLE SPECIAL PURPOSE RECEPTACLE OUTLET
- RANGE OUTLET
- CLOCK OUTLET [SPECIFY VOLTAGE] (+90" AFF)
- FLOOR SPECIAL PURPOSE OUTLET
- FLOOR TELEPHONE OUTLET- PUBLIC
- FLOOR TELEPHONE OUTLET- PRIVATE
- FLOOR SINGLE RECEPTACLE OUTLET
- FLOOR DUPLEX RECEPTACLE OUTLET

SWITCH OUTLETS

- S SINGLE POLE SWITCH (+48" AFF)
- S₃ THREE-WAY SWITCH
- S₄ FOUR-WAY SWITCH
- S_LV LOW-VOLTAGE SWITCH (SOLDER CONTACTS)
- S_DIM DIMMER SWITCH (+48" AFF)
- S_D AUTOMATIC DOOR SWITCH
- S_MC MOMENTARY CONTACT SWITCH
- S_RC REMOTE-CONTROL SWITCH
- S_WP WEATHERPROOF SWITCH
- S_F FUSED SWITCH
- S_T TIME SWITCH
- S_K KEY-OPERATED SWITCH
- S SWITCH & SINGLE RECEPTACLE

SIGNALING SYSTEM OUTLETS RESIDENTIAL OCCUPANCIES

- PUSH BUTTON
- BUZZER
- BELL
- OUTSIDE TELEPHONE
- INTERCONNECTING TELEPHONE
- TELEPHONE SWITCHBOARD
- ELECTRIC DOOR OPENER
- Ⓢ SMOKE DETECTOR/ ALARM
- TV TELEVISION OUTLET
- Ⓜ MICROPHONE OUTLET
- Ⓣ THERMOSTAT (+46" AFF)

PANEL CIRCUITS

- LIGHTING PANEL
- POWER PANEL
- Ⓜ MOTOR
- T TRANSFORMER (OR DRAW TO SCALE)
- F FIRE-ALARM BELL
- F FIRE-ALARM STATION
- A₅ AUTOMATIC FIRE-ALARM/SMOKE DETECTOR
- CITY FIRE-ALARM STATION
- FS AUTOMATIC FIRE-ALARM DEVICE
- UNDERGROUND DUCT LINE
- HFL HEATER FAN LIGHT

INSTITUTIONAL COMMERCIAL & INDUSTRIAL OCCUPANCIES

- PAGING SYSTEM DEVICES (ANY TYPE)
- FIRE ALARM SYSTEM DEVICES (ANY TYPE)
- ELECTRICAL CLOCK SYSTEM DEVICES (ANY TYPE)
- PUBLIC TELEPHONE SYSTEM DEVICES
- PRIVATE TELEPHONE SYSTEM DEVICES
- SOUND SYSTEM

GEOMETRIC SYMBOLS

- ∠ ANGLE
- ℄ CENTERLINE
- ⊥ PERPENDICULAR
- ∅ ROUND, DIAMETER
- ⊘ SQUARE

MISCELLANEOUS

- #XXXX ROOM NUMBER B-BELOW GRADE 100+ STREET LEVEL OR LOWEST MAIN FLOOR 200+ SECOND FL.
- FIXTURE TYPE QUANTITY OF THIS TYPE IN THIS SPACE (OR WATTAGE CONSUMED BY A SINGLE UNIT- LARGE COMMERCIAL PROJECT)
- SUPPLY AIR HVAC
- RETURN AIR HVAC
- ROOF PITCH
- REMOVE TREE (8" [20.3 CM.] DIAMETER)
- TREE TO REMAIN
- CHANGE IN CEILING LEVEL

Lighting Plan

The lighting plan recommends equipment and equipment locations that fulfill the needs of the client's program. In many states, it may not be used legally for electrical construction unless it has been stamped by a licensed architect or engineer—or unless the installing contractor has assumed liability under his license. To prevent misuse, in some design offices it is customary for those executing lighting plans to use *curved lines* to indicate which fixtures are to be controlled by which switch. The curved lines help to distinguish between this advisory document and the formal electrical plan which uses *straight lines* to designate circuits and wiring (Figures 6-6 and 6-7).

Types. In both lighting plans and electrical plans, each kind of fixture is identified with a capital letter of the alphabet. This letter is known as the fixture's "type" (Table 6-2); on the symbols' list a hexagon or circle can be used to show the fixture type. Whenever any party to the construction discusses a fixture, they refer to it by its alphabet letter. If one fixture is identical to another—that is, from the same manufacturer but differing in length or color—then the designer designates the same type on the drawing but adds a number. This facilitates counting and ordering the fixtures (Table 6-3).

The Electrical Plan

The purpose of the electrical plan is to illustrate the proper distribution of electricity to meet the building's needs. In most jurisdictions, the number, size, and location of the wires are all regulated by codes. The electrical plan becomes a document for construction only when stamped by a professional whose competency has been examined by the state or province where the building is being constructed.

In residential or small commercial projects, an unlicensed designer may have drawn the electrical layout and given it to a contractor to estimate the costs of installation, but it is the contractor's license that allows him/her to assume responsibility for the safety of the installation of the electrical system. If the contractor is not licensed and the designer has hired him/her, it is the designer who may be found liable for electrical faults—even after several years have passed.

In a midsize commercial project, or a remodeling project, the electrical plan may be done by the architect and interior designer together, but it is the architect's stamp that indicates that he/she has assumed responsibility for fire safety, electrical safety, seismic safety, and the operation of the building under emergency conditions.

In a large commercial project, the interior designer is often invited, during the design development phase, to recommend lighting strategies and the equipment with which to execute them. But it is the consulting engineer's office that will stamp the working electrical plans and assume responsibility (Figures 6-8, 6-9, 6-10).

Detail Sheets

Usually the intent of the lighting detail is to illustrate a mounting location for lighting that is to be built-in or otherwise artfully concealed. Designing lighting details is not difficult if the designer has a respectful understanding of physics. There are three areas of concern:

1. Can the heat radiated by the light source and its ballast (if any) escape upward? In close surroundings, a 4-inch whisper fan on the same off/on switch as the lights often can help the heat to escape.

2. Is heat conducted to any adjacent materials that have low kindling temperatures?

TABLE 6-3 DESIGNATING A FIXTURE BY TYPE

TYPE	RIGHT	WRONG
Lightolier L-31-P (4'-0" track)	K-1	
Lightolier L-21-P (2'-0" track)	K-2	
Lightolier L-J-P (joiner piece)	L	K-3
Lightolier L-356-P (cylinder light)	M	K-4
Lightolier L-716-P (optical projector)	N	K-5

Note: Certain alphabet letters are not used to designate fixtures or controls:
E/e which is reserved for emergency circuits
I/i is often confused for the number 1
O/o is often confused for the number 0
X/x is reserved for emergency lights and circuits

DRAWING A LIGHTING PLAN: A CHECKLIST OF STEPS

COMPOSING THE LIGHTING SHEET
Select the sheet size
Lightly enclose areas for:
    plan view
    symbols legend
    general notes
    title block and border
    detail drawings
Draft vertical planes that intersect with the ceiling onto the plan view

DOING THE PRELIMINARY LAYOUT (tissue overlay)
On the reverse side of the tissue (right reading) draw the obstacles:
    indicate joists above the ceiling to ensure clearance of recessed fixtures
    show suspended ceiling grid to be sure fixtures are clear of the runners
    illustrate skylights, rafters, trusses, and changes of ceiling plane
        to show possible attachment locations for fixtures
        to prevent unintended scallops of light

On the front side of the tissue draw the lighting system:
    arrange and rearrange the fixtures to get the best combination of
        lighting for safety needs
        lighting for task needs
        lighting that reinforces the design strategy
        lighting that creates a logical pattern of fixtures on the ceiling
    draw the final arrangement of fixtures to scale

DRAFTING THE FINAL SHEET
Trace the final grid pattern and skylights (etcetera) on the reverse side of the lighting sheet
Trace the final fixture pattern on the front side of the lighting sheet
Show the switching/dimming recommendations with curved lines or lowercase letters
Hand letter the "type" designations for each kind of fixture near a typical fixture unit
    (Also list the type on a rough copy of the fixture list; alternate between lighting sheet
        and fixture list, confer with catalogs to decide on manufacturers and equals.)
Print symbols legend and general notes
Ink title block and border

Check plan: insert margin notes only where the intent of the drawing is unclear.

[Drawings and specifications are legal documents and since some of the methods suggested herein may not be traditional, each reader/user must decide on the appropriate employment of these methods. Neither the author nor the publisher hereby assumes any legal obligation or liability for the use of any methods, suggestions, or data in this book.]

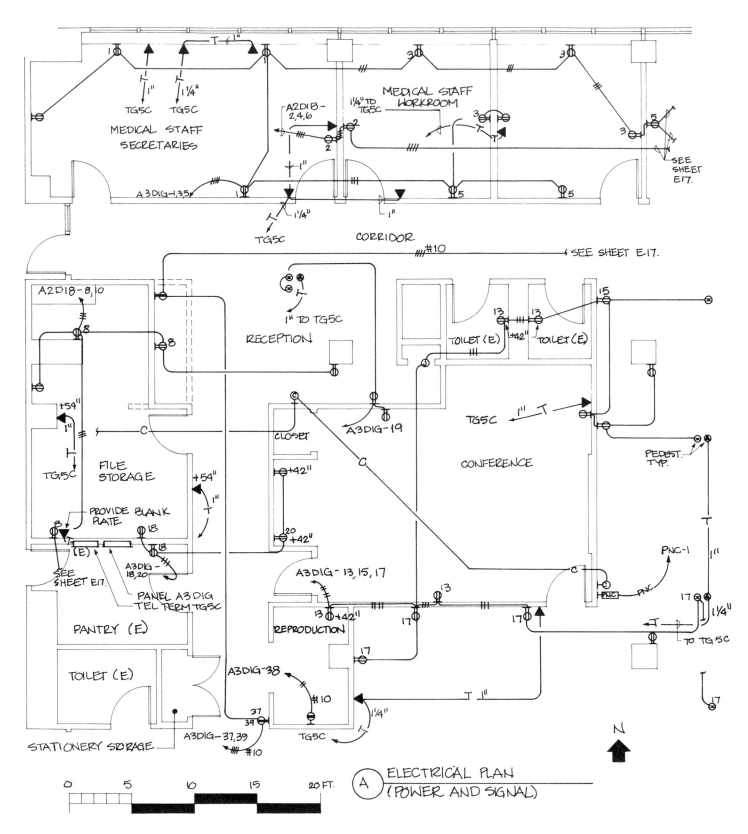

ELECTRICAL PLAN
(POWER AND SIGNAL)

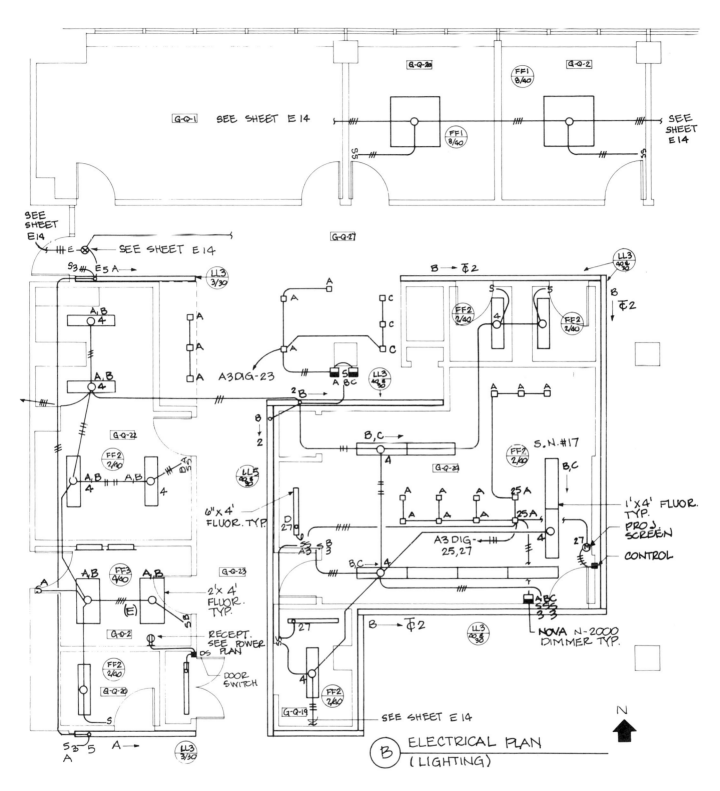

**FIGURE 6-8: Electrical Plan (Power and Signal)/
Commercial Remodel**
The office tasks performed here require not
only electrical receptacles for typewriters but
also the typical network of communications
wiring for telephones and computer mo-
dems. The break up of AT&T has resulted in
the need for designers to provide even more
communications-related design services
than in the past. (Illustration by Reiko
Hayashi.)

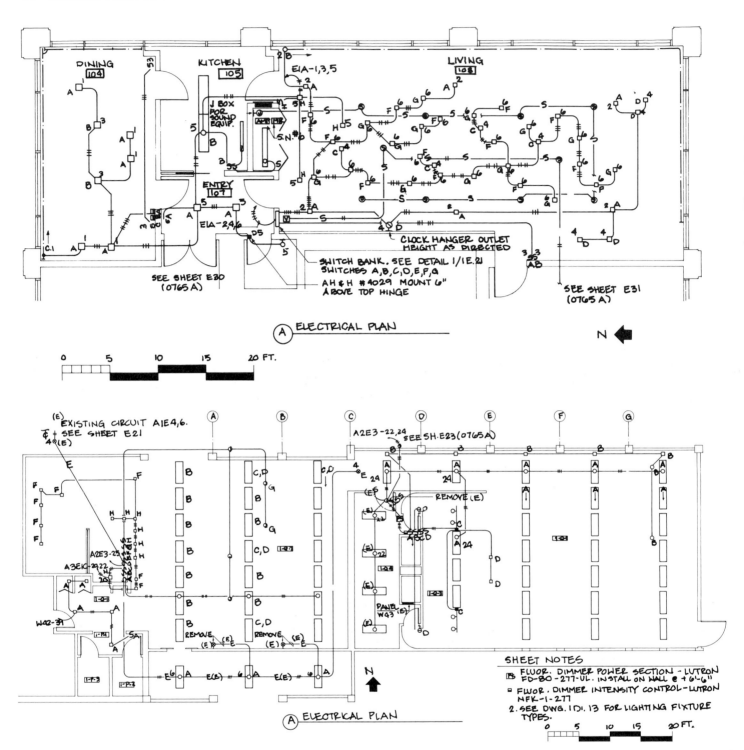

FIGURE 6-9: Electrical Plan/Residential
(Top) In residential kitchens, the codes often require that lighting and appliance circuits be separate. One of the advantages of this is that the lights do not dim when the refrigeration unit starts to cool the refrigerator/freezer. (Illustration by Reiko Hayashi.)

FIGURE 6-10: Electrical Plan/Commercial
(Above) Although the lighting plan and electrical plan seem similar in many ways, they convey different information. The electrical plan shows how the lighting system is to be wired; the lighting plan shows why the lighting system is designed in that way. (Illustration by Reiko Hayashi.)

FIGURE 6-11: Detail Drawings and Elevation/Commercial
(Right) Although the architectural appearance of the north elevation is continuous, the left three modules are incorporated into a glass and granite lobby with living trees, while the right three modules are a part of the chapel with its red suede wall fabric and upholstery and blond oak seating. Because these interior treatments are so different from one another, the lighting treatment at the north wall changes accordingly, despite the burden of mounting two different fixture types to the concrete folded plate ceiling. (Illustration by Reiko Hayashi.)

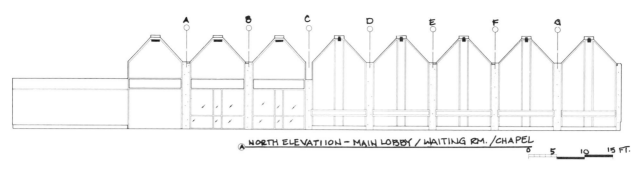

Ⓐ NORTH ELEVATION - MAIN LOBBY / WAITING RM. / CHAPEL

0   5   10   15 FT.

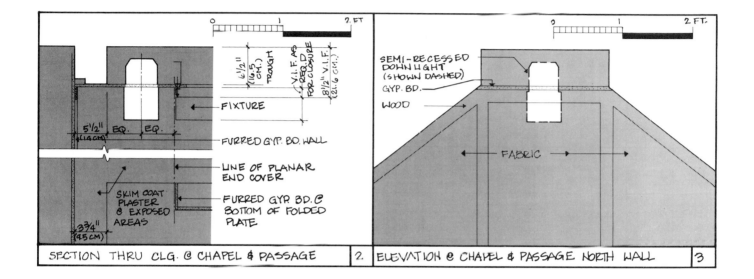

SECTION THRU CLG. @ CHAPEL & PASSAGE   2.   ELEVATION @ CHAPEL & PASSAGE NORTH WALL   3

Section thru clg labels:
- TROUGH
- 6½" (16.5 CM.)
- V.I.F. AS REQ.D FOR CLOSURE
- 8½" (21.6 CM.)
- FIXTURE
- 5½" (14 CM)
- EQ. EQ.
- FURRED GYP. BD. WALL
- LINE OF PLANAR END COVER
- SKIM COAT PLASTER @ EXPOSED AREAS
- FURRED GYP. BD. @ BOTTOM OF FOLDED PLATE
- 3¾" (45 CM)

Elevation labels:
- SEMI-RECESSED DOWN LIGHT (SHOWN DASHED)
- GYP. BD.
- WOOD
- FABRIC

0   1   2 FT.

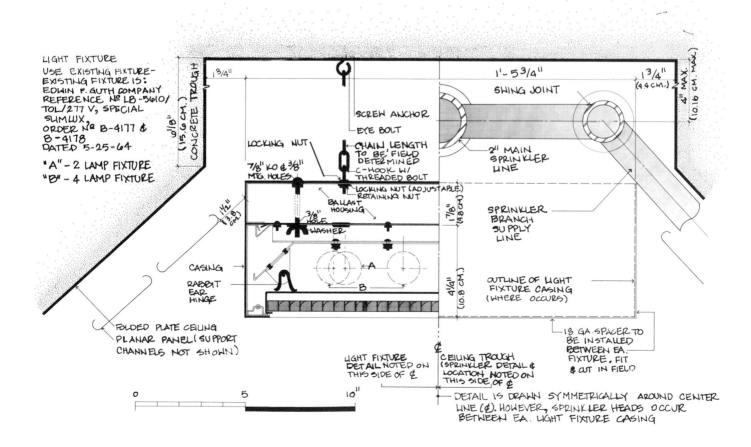

LIGHT FIXTURE
USE EXISTING FIXTURE-
EXISTING FIXTURE IS:
EDWIN F. GUTH COMPANY
REFERENCE № LB-5610/
TOL/277 V, SPECIAL
SLIMLUX,
ORDER № B-4177 &
B-4178
DATED 5-25-64

"A" - 2 LAMP FIXTURE
"B" - 4 LAMP FIXTURE

- CONCRETE TROUGH
- 1¾"
- 9⅛" (15.6 CM.)
- 1'-5¾"
- SWING JOINT
- 1¾" (4.4 CM.)
- 4" MAX. (10.16 CM. MAX.)
- SCREW ANCHOR
- EYE BOLT
- CHAIN LENGTH TO BE FIELD DETERMINED
- C-HOOK W/ THREADED BOLT
- LOCKING NUT (ADJUSTABLE) RETAINING NUT
- 2" MAIN SPRINKLER LINE
- LOCKING NUT
- 7/8" KO & 3/8" MTG. HOLES
- BALLAST HOUSING
- 3/8" HOLE
- WASHER
- 1½" (3.8 CM.)
- 7/8" (4.8 CM)
- SPRINKLER BRANCH SUPPLY LINE
- CASING
- RABBIT EAR HINGE
- A
- B
- 4¼" (10.8 CM.)
- OUTLINE OF LIGHT FIXTURE CASING (WHERE OCCURS)
- FOLDED PLATE CEILING PLANAR PANEL (SUPPORT CHANNELS NOT SHOWN)
- LIGHT FIXTURE DETAIL NOTED ON THIS SIDE OF ℄
- ℄
- CEILING TROUGH (SPRINKLER DETAIL & LOCATION NOTED ON THIS SIDE OF ℄
- 18 GA. SPACER TO BE INSTALLED BETWEEN EA. FIXTURE, FIT & CUT IN FIELD
- DETAIL IS DRAWN SYMMETRICALLY AROUND CENTER LINE (℄). HOWEVER, SPRINKLER HEADS OCCUR BETWEEN EA. LIGHT FIXTURE CASING

0   5   10"

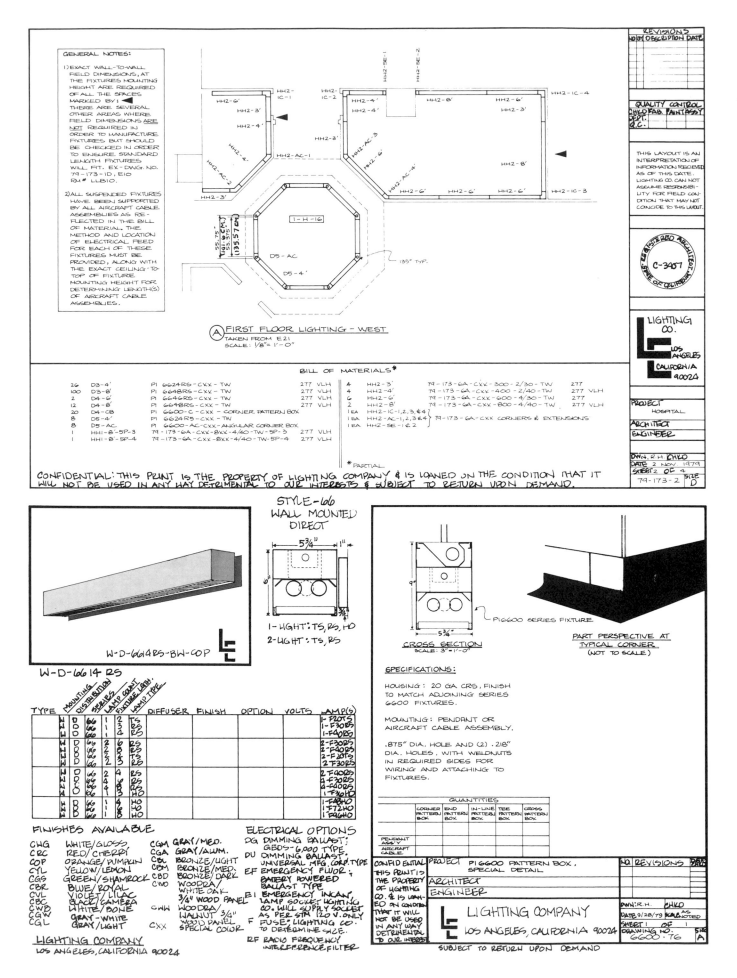

Inserting pads of inert material between the source of the heat and any combustible material is useful here.

3. Can the lamp bulb or tube be easily replaced? Try to visualize or sketch the angles of insertion (Figure 6-11; also refer back to Figures 6-5 and 6-6).

Approval Drawings
Most design drawings transmit information from the designer to those who will build the project. The approval process reverses this flow of information (Figure 6-12). For the designer's approval, the manufacturer, the field representative, or the contractor submit technical information on particular fixtures because they want to be sure that the fixture is acceptable before the order is placed with the distributor. Either of two criteria should be met before approval is given by the designer: (1) the submitted fixture is the physical reality of the fixture type specified many months ago during the design development phase; or (2) the submitted fixture is "equal to" the one named in the specification of the type. (See Appendix B-4: Specific Language Regarding Substituted Items.)

The rules governing the submission of approval items are found in the project manual under "General Conditions of the Contract for Construction" published by the American Institute of Architects (AIA) as Document A201 (1976) in Supplementary Conditions and in "Division One/General Requirements" of the Specifications. Together they establish requirements for submittals: the required number of approval drawings, whether reproducible sepias are preferred by the design office, etc. Additional specific requests for fixture and lamp bulb information may be included in Division Sixteen/Electrical Specifications. Often a list of all electrical items for which approval submissions are required will be included in

this section. If the designer expects the submission of preprinted fixture catalog sheets, he/she usually will ask for "product data"; if he/she wants original drawings for the fabrication of a custom fixture, the approval list will refer to "shop drawings." Last, physical fixtures are called "samples." They should be able to be lighted and should be submitted with the lamp bulb that is recommended by their manufacturer.

In a design office, according to specialists in construction specifications, the submission of approval drawings is one of the most frequently mishandled activities. The underlying problem is that by the time the drawings are submitted, the designers are working on their next project. No one has time to refresh themselves on the previous project and comment properly on such drawings (Figure 6-13).

PROJECT MANUAL DOCUMENTS
As technology has advanced, the number of choices and decisions a designer must make has multiplied enormously; choices involving finishes and materials, installation strategies, and competing codes have made lighting and interior design a more complex process. Channeling this avalanche of information has become the most pressing problem in design today. One solution for handling it is the creation of better working procedures—procedures that everyone involved in the design and construction process can follow. To this end, the project manual has become a vehicle for organizing information and directing the installation of a project. The project manual contains nine documents necessary to complete a project successfully:

1. Invitation to Tender (bid)
2. Instructions to Bidders
3. Tender or Bid Forms
4. Bond Forms

5. Forms of Agreement (copyright: AIA)
6. General Conditions of the Contract for construction (architecture, AIA) for furniture, furnishings, and equipment (AIA, ASID)
7. Supplementary Conditions of the Contract for construction (architecture, AIA) for furniture, furnishings, and equipment (AIA, ASID)
8. Specifications
9. Addenda

When the drawings are almost done, the design office that will be responsible to the owner for construction contract administration prepares to issue the project manual. It goes out with the drawings to those contractors who will be tendering bids. Not all of the documents in the project manual are defined as "contract documents"; only the Agreements, the General and Supplementary Conditions, the Specifications, the Addenda, and Change Orders become contractual.

The drawings and these contractual documents in the project manual are complementary. Although the standard forms of the Conditions, copyrighted by the AIA and the ASID, do not state which governs in case of conflict, legal precedent often says that the specifications supersede the drawings. Nonetheless, conflicts are perilous and costly. In order to reduce conflict, brevity, consistency, and lack of redundancy are sought in all of the project documents, especially in the specifications.

Invitation to Tender
This document is also known as the advertisement for bids, request for proposals, and invitation to bid. It is designed to attract qualified bidders and to help them in deciding whether or not to tender an offer of

Date	Type	Manufacturer	Designer	Due	Approved/Disapproved	Date	Notify (Mfg./G.C./Rep)*
6/19	L	CAPRI	JOE	6/26	MANUFACTURING TOLERANCE 3/32" WARRANTY 2YRS.	6/23	LTG. TECHNOLOGIES 328 N. FIRST, S.F. 90023

Notes: (1) All submittals are received by the office manager and dated, logged, and distributed to the person responsible for the lighting system with a time limit for his/her response. (2) When the time limit is reached, the manager reminds the reviewer and permits a short extension if necessary. (3) When the approval or disapproval is given, those fixtures in the disapproval column of the log are referred by the manager to the project captain. (4) The project captain notifies the submitter of the need for revision and resubmission, and the process begins again.

*For this system to work well, the approval stamp used by the design office should require only a minimum number of carefully selected entries to be made by the reviewer.

FIGURE 6-12: Approvals Submittal/Commercial
(Left) In this manufacturer's approvals package, the design office will check the dimensions on document A stringently. The difficulty of properly joining suspended fixtures is particularly difficult if the gauge of the metal is too thin or the dimensions and angles of the components are not exact. (Illustration by Reiko Hayashi.)

FIGURE 6-13: Approvals Log
(Above) These formal procedures assist the designer to perform his/her postdesign responsibilities for product approvals. (Illustration by Reiko Hayashi.)

labor and materials for the project. The invitation performs three functions:

It briefly describes the project

It states where the project documents can be secured and the amount of the drawings deposit

It discusses the bidding procedure

Instructions to Bidders

This second document contains "the requirements with which the bidder must comply" in tendering his/her offer. It also describes "conditions affecting the award of the contract." Whenever a designer requests bids from installers, some instructions to bidders are given. In the smallest projects, informal verbal advice may let the bidders know how to apportion their prices, when and where bids are due, and that other bidders are in receipt of the same instructions. In larger projects, or in publicly funded projects, written instructions will delineate bid formats, procedures, and cautions.

The lighting design may be affected by several portions of the Instructions to Bidders. These are the following:

The tour of the site

The procedures by which "queries" are to be made

The basis upon which alternates or substitutions will be accepted

First, wisdom dictates that the person who designed the lighting should participate in any group tour of the site by bidders. When the electrical estimator or installer understands the lighting design concept and the expectations of the designer, a more accurate bid results.

Second, queries from bidders about the intent of the lighting documents are often referred to the designer, regardless of the fact that the lighting may have appeared formally on electrical drawings prepared by the engineer. The designer is the one who can most clearly respond because he/she originated the lighting strategy. Usually the queries are requests for the clarification of ambiguities or notification of errors. No matter how informally the inquiry has been submitted, the individual who is responsible for the lighting should respond in writing. The written response is sent to the administrating designer. In fairness to the bidders, the administrative designer copies all responses to all bidders in the form of an addendum. Addenda must be issued by the design office that issued the original contract documents, so that it becomes clear that the addendum is an addition or correction to the agreement.

Third, the lighting design is affected by the procedure which allows the owner to accept alternates and substitutions. With regard to substitutions, one experienced specifier provides a form, along with the Instructions to Bidders, on which all substitutions for designated fixtures and controls must be listed by the bidder. Substitutions not listed on the form when it is returned with the bid package will not be approved for the project (refer back to Appendix B-4.) This allows the substitutions to be reviewed by the owner and specifier before the contract is awarded. As for alternates, an alternate fixture type or installation method allows the owner and designer to reshape the bid by accepting a less expensive alternate in one place in order to have a more expensive alternate elsewhere.

However, when alternatives to the lighting types are permitted, the lighting designer should assume that the lower cost alternate will be accepted by most owners. So, the designer should be sure that the cheaper alternate works well with the other fixtures in the lighting design.

Bid Forms

The usual bid form is a letter addressed to the owner from the contractor. This pre-printed form furnished by the design office contains blanks for project identification and acknowledges that the bidder (1) has the bid document, (2) has the addenda, and (3) has examined them, and the site. Additional blanks provide spaces to list the bid life, proposed contract amount, signatures, and a list of attachments. One attachment that affects the lighting design is the name and qualifications of the electrical contractor on the attached listing of subcontractors. Another is the proposed schedule for submittal of product data, shop drawings, and samples (Appendix B-6: Submittals).

The Agreement

The signing parties agree to five items:

1. Identification of the parties to the Agreement

2. Description of the work to be performed

3. Description of considerations

4. Statement of time allowed for performance

5. Signatures of the agreeing parties

There are several preprinted agreement forms copyrighted by the AIA and some jointly by the AIA and ASID. The preprinted blank spaces should be filled in by the design office, except for the name of the contractor who is to win the work, the date of completion, and the price. There are several types of agreements: (1) work done for a stipulated sum; (2) work done for cost plus a percentage for overhead and profit; and (3) work done for a percentage of the installed cost of the project.

Text continues on page 113

COLOR PLATE 1: Seven Color Contrasts
The Bauhaus colorist, Johannes Itten, isolated seven basic color contrasts which are illustrated here:

(a) Contrast of Hue: When the three primary colors are used adjacent to one another, they deliver the strongest and most vigorous effects. A background of shadow will cause them to appear paler and brighter.

(b) Light/Dark Contrast: Dark or unlighted surfaces and colors appear to recede because their low reflectancy returns less light to the eye, just as distant surfaces would do. Conversely, pale and bright surfaces seem closer, because more reflected light reaches the eye. In dark environments, if only one wall is pale, that wall not only expands and advances, it may even seem to generate light by itself, that is, become a "secondary" light source.

(c) Cold/Warm Contrast: Warm colors next to cool ones exaggerate each other. For example, when a warm-colored object is seen against a cool-colored background, the object seems warmer. To light these adjacent warm/cool surfaces, the designer should select a light source that reinforces both sides of the spectrum.

(d) Complementary Contrast: Complementary colors are those that are diametrically opposed to each other on the color wheel. When they are placed side by side, they excite each other to maximum vividness. A complementary contrast is always a warm/cool contrast and should be lit as above.

(e) Simultaneous Contrast: A pure chromatic color tends to push a neighboring color—or an adjacent shadow—toward its opposite, or complementary color. This phenomenon is important because in any lighting plan, the gray areas of shadow reinforce the drama of an adjacent color that is lit.

(f) Contrast of Saturation: When an intense or pure color is placed adjacent to the same color but in a diluted version, the viewer experiences a contrast between dull and vivid. As saturation increases, color value shifts as well. To create impact, the designer should be sure to establish at least four steps of value difference between colors used for a target object and those used as backgrounds. This ensures that one color will be dark while the other is pale. One will absorb light while the other reflects it. For impact, concentrate the light on the reflective color.

(g) Contrast of Extension: Certain colors have more power or impact on the eye. Two colors should be combined in proportions that bring their brilliance or impact into balance by a corresponding variation in the extent of surface covered by each color. (Illustration by Reiko Hayashi.)

	VISUAL IMPRESSION	AN EXTREME EXAMPLE	MUNSELL NOTATION
a	Cheerful	Red Yellow Blue	5R5/6 5Y5/6 5B5/6
b	Dramatic	Purple Yellow	5PB1/6 5Y9/14
c	Stimulating	Blue Orange	5B5/6 5YR5/6
d	Sophisticated	Red Green	5R5/6 5G5/6
e	Bold	Gray Yellow	5N5/ 5Y5/6
f	Harmonious	Gray Blue	5N5/ 5B5/6
g	Varies with Proportions	Red Dots Field of Green	5R5/6 5G5/6

COLOR PLATE 2: Spectrum Profiles I: The Colors of Electric Light

There are more than 200 different fluorescent color spectra available in North America. Designers often combine two or more to produce the best color reinforcement for their finish colors. By mixing tubes, almost any color effect can be duplicated—even that of an incandescent.

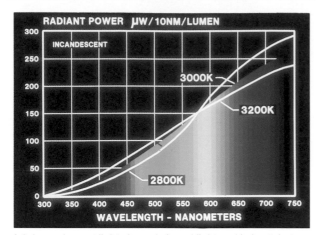

(a) Incandescent light abounds in red light and in heat, but shows little reinforcement for blue hues. (Courtesy of General Electric Company.)

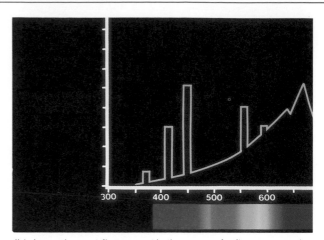

(b) Incandescent-fluorescent is the name of a fluorescent tube that renders finish colors much as if they were lighted with incandescent bulbs. Like other warm phosphored fluorescents, efficiency in lumens per watt has been sacrificed (49 lumens/watt). (Courtesy of G.T.E. Lighting Products.)

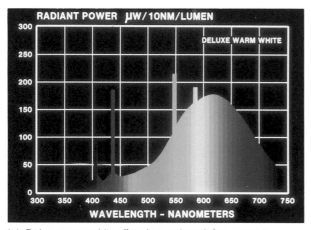

(c) Deluxe warm white offers less color reinforcement to objects in the deepest reds and blue-greens. It is often used where people or woods need to look attractive. (Courtesy of General Electric Company.)

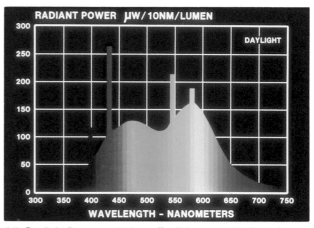

(d) Daylight fluorescent tubes offer little support to the colors with red in them, but it is one of the best reinforcements for blue colors. (Courtesy of General Electric Company.)

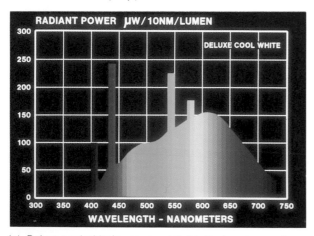

(e) Deluxe cool white is very special. It is the lone low-cost fluorescent that can render both warm and cool colored finishes well. For this reason, it is preferred for cost conscious but color critical interiors like hospital examination rooms. (Courtesy of General Electric Company.)

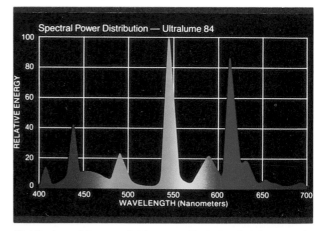

(f) Ultralume 84, a new light source, illustrates that the opposition of adjacent colors to one another is the key to color vitality. Although the tubes are expensive and should be replaced every few years to maintain color quality, the discontinuous spectrum and "Tristimulous" phosphors cause both warm and cool "colored" surfaces to become vibrant. (Illustration reproduced with the permission of North American Philips Lighting Corporation, copyright owner.)

HID light sources are infamous for unpredictable variations in color from lamp to lamp and over the life of an individual lamp. Many of these variations, however, will cancel each other in the color rendering of a sizable space. To control color quality, the designer can specify an installation of lamps from a common assembly run and can insist that all bulbs are to be changed at one time.

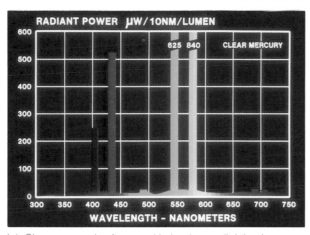

(a) Clear mercury is often used in landscape lighting because of its affinity for greens. (Courtesy of G.T.E. Lighting Products.)

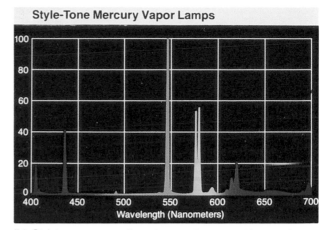

(b) Styletone mercury offers strong color support for certain warm colors, but care must be used in selecting just those colors. (Illustration reproduced with the permission of North American Philips Lighting Corporation, copyright owner.)

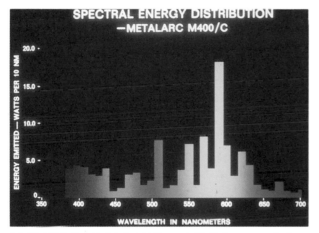

(c) Metalarc C was the first of the metal halide sources that was well balanced for both warm and cool colors. (Courtesy of G.T.E. Lighting Products.)

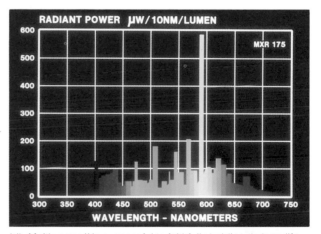

(d) Multi-vapor II is successful in faithfully holding its long life, rendering warm colors and minimizing the lamp to lamp variations that are notorious in the metal halide group. (Courtesy of General Electric Company.)

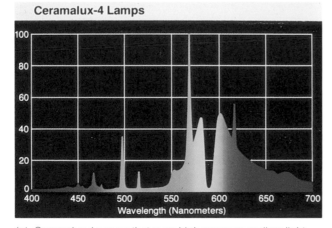

(e) Ceramalux 4 proves that even high pressure sodium light sources can deliver a warm/cool color scheme if the designer utilizes a robin's egg blue in the palette. (Illustration reproduced with the permission of North American Philips Lighting Corporation, copyright owner.)

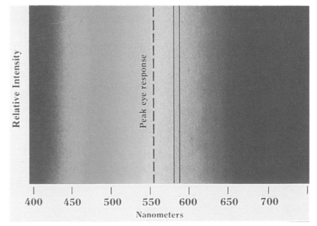

(f) Low pressure sodium is used successfully indoors in only a few high fashion interiors. Rochester Institute of Technology uses it as a wallwashing source in the main lobby. Normally, the narrowness of its yellow color band is just too limiting for even the most exotic palette of colors. (Illustration reproduced with the permission of North American Philips Lighting Corporation, copyright owner.)

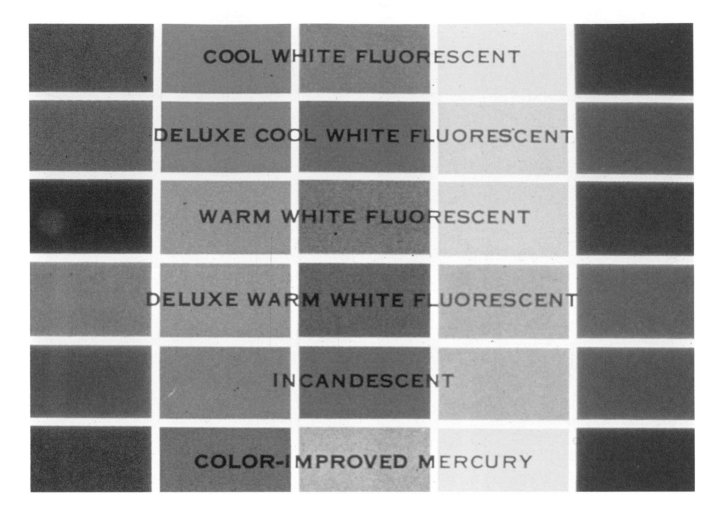

COOL WHITE FLUORESCENT

DELUXE COOL WHITE FLUORESCENT

WARM WHITE FLUORESCENT

DELUXE WARM WHITE FLUORESCENT

INCANDESCENT

COLOR-IMPROVED MERCURY

COLOR PLATE 4:   Color Shifting: Five Colors Under Six Light Sources
(Above) There are only five colors here: grape, bristol blue, avocado, lemon yellow, and cherry red. They appear as 30 different colors because of the color shifts caused by each of the six different light sources with which they are lighted. This shifting of color appearance makes the matching of interior colors risky unless the color matches are selected and installed under the same kind and wattage of light source. A particular concern here is the phenomenon of "metamerism." Two colors can appear to match under one light source, but refuse to match when both are lighted under another light source. Both colors will have shifted, but not in the same direction. (Illustration by Reiko Hayashi.)

COLOR PLATE 5:   Fading and Fugitive Colors
(Below) In order to maximize energy efficiency and color vibrancy, the designer should select a light source that provides the same colors of light as the colored finishes he/she intends to use in the interior. However, when the finishes contain blue and the light sources put out ultraviolet light, fading is likely to occur unless the blue dyestuff is unusually well bonded by its host. Blue and colors incorporating blues are fugitive: they are inclined to fade under daylight and certain electric lights. (Illustration by Reiko Hayashi.)

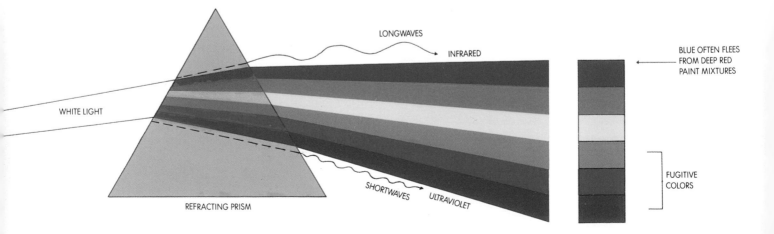

LONGWAVES

INFRARED

WHITE LIGHT

REFRACTING PRISM

SHORTWAVES   ULTRAVIOLET

BLUE OFTEN FLEES FROM DEEP RED PAINT MIXTURES

FUGITIVE COLORS

COLOR PLATE 6: La Entrada, South View
In a small space, every element of the interior designer's composition has to contribute to the desired effect. Here the warmth of the oak chest and tile floor are exaggerated by their contrast with the blue lighting. (Photograph by Mary E. Nichols.)

COLOR PLATE 7: Creating Light with Color
(Above) Light colors and shiny surfaces are not very porous; they offer high brightness and reflectance, while porous textures and dark colors are nonreflective. The latter will sponge up light and decrease brightness and reflecting light. However, when an object is light colored and shiny and its background is dark and porous, brightness contrast is maximized and the object has the visual impact that it would have had if it were individually spotlighted. (Photographs by Mary E. Nichols.)

COLOR PLATE 8: The Color of Daylight
(Right) These two photos show summer and winter sunlight. In North America, summer sunlight is normally indirect and reflects into a building from outdoor surfaces. In the winter, the sunlight is a warmer color and penetrates directly and deeply into spaces with south-facing windows.

COLOR PLATE 9: *Luminous Tapestry,*
by Joan Hathaway
(Above) These luminous panels that separate the living room from the all-glass entry serve several purposes. From the street side, the blue 13-foot (396.2 cm) acrylic panels function as one part of a show-stopping facade. From the living-room side, the panels establish the unique scale and exotic mood of the room. (Photograph by Dan Forer.)

COLOR PLATE 10: *Drive-In,* **by Lili Lakich**
(Left) This 18-foot by 10-foot (548.6 cm × 304.8 cm) neon sculpture combines neon with brass, cooper, honeycomb aluminum and the fender of a 1957 Chevy. It illustrates that neon is a medium unique in its forcefulness. Because Lakich often explores the color and reflective qualities of metals, her neon pieces are as interesting in the daytime as at night. (Photograph by Lili Lakich.)

COLOR PLATE 11: *Illusions in Color,* by Dan Flavin
One place to experience a real interaction with color has been the Hausermann Furniture Showroom in the Pacific Design Center in Los Angeles. This company generously provided showroom space for a maze of corridors illustrating imaginary color effects. (Photograph by Toshi Yoshimi.)

COLOR PLATE 12: Enhancing Merchandise
(Above) The combination of energy conserving metal halide with low voltage MR-16 incandescents produces the reinforcement for a broad but cool range of fashion colors. Aptly this store is called ICE (see Case Study Six). (Store design by Philip Schwartz.)

COLOR PLATE 13: The Work of Motoko Ishii
(Right) Motoko Ishii, IALD, is much admired among her professional lighting colleagues for the easy grace and style of her lighting designs. For her 1981 commission for the Northwestern National Life Insurance Company Building in Minneapolis, Minnesota, Ishii devised one of the large and sparkling creations similar to those of the Osaka World's Fair which first brought her international recognition. (See Chapter Nine for a discussion of Ishii's later work with laser lighting.) (Photograph provided by Motoko Ishii International.)

COLOR PLATE 14:   Highlighting an Entry
(Above) This space functions not only as an entrance, but also as
the anteroom for an ancient chapel. The sculpture *Portrait of a
Condemned Soul*, by Harriet Moore, dominates one view, while the
bas-relief panels seen here echo the fires of damnation. Almost
hidden in the negative space lies the sign of the cross (see Case
Study One). (Photograph by Mary E. Nichols.)

COLOR PLATE 15:   *Private Laserium*, by Tully Weiss
(Right) Laser performance holds the essence of both theater and
art. Some of the 24 preset dimming effects spin sheets of light into
the air that seem to restructure the residence with their colored
beams. (Photograph by Doug Tomlinson.)

a

COLOR PLATE 16: *AMBA,* **by James Turell**
The excitement associated with Turell's work is due both to its experimental and experiential nature. On entering the gallery, the viewer who is new to Turell's work may "see" *(a)* three pastel canvases in mitered frames while those who are familiar with Turell's work and that of other California School artists will know instantly that whatever they are seeing is not what it appears to be. A real understanding of whatever they are seeing *(b)* will come to them only if they wait for their eyes to get used to the light levels in the space. (Photograph by Nance Calderwood.)

b

112

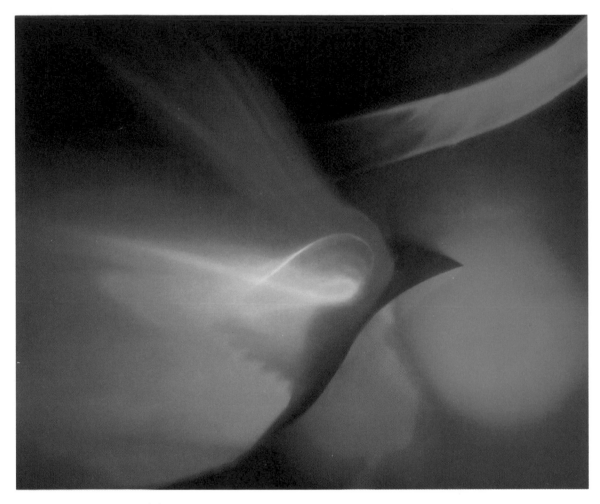

COLOR PLATE 17: *Lumia: A Study from "The Firebirds",* **by Thomas Wilfred**
"A great visual music can be composed and played," declared Wilfred. Indeed, his swirling figures sweep over and through the viewer's senses in rhythm with music. (Photograph by permission from T. D. Jones, *The Art of Light and Color* (New York: Van Nostrand Reinhold, 1972).

The General Conditions

The Agreement is based only on these five points, so the role of the General Conditions that follow in the project manual is to amplify those points. Therefore, the General Conditions consist of almost twenty closely packed pages of very small print. Usually these discussions of administrative matters are based on AIA Document A 201 (1976). There are several advantages for standardizing them this way:

They can be preprinted.

The majority of construction problems are identical, and therefore can be economically addressed as a group.

Legal precedents are known so that legal costs are saved if litigation arises.

In lighting specifications, there should be no statements that duplicate these General Conditions. For instance, some consultants devise paragraphs of general conditions-for-lighting that often create ambiguities and are in conflict with the AIA's General Conditions of the Contract. If the intent of the electrical or lighting consultant in adding such paragraphs is to include contract conditions that will apply to the entire project, those conditions should be forwarded to the design office that will be issuing the project manual.

Supplementary Conditions

Other requirements specific to the project will go into Supplementary Conditions—such as the format for shop drawings. Supplementary conditions contain three kinds of information:

Deletions from the General Conditions

Modifications of the General Conditions

Additions to the General Conditions

In contrast to the preprinted General Conditions, the supplementary conditions are always newly prepared for each project. Most of those tendering offers on big projects are familiar with the preprinted General Conditions form, but they must read the specifics of the Supplementary Conditions to discover how the specifier has changed the preprinted form. Matters like wage rates, participation in the contract by minority subcontractors, and other Equal Opportunity regulations are found in the Supplementary Conditions. These Supplementary Conditions should always be reviewed by the client's legal counsel.

Specifications

Within the project manual, it is the specifications that qualify the products and guide the installation procedures. In recent years, the writing of specifications has become consistent through the efforts of the Construction Specifications Institute (CSI). The establishment of a uniform practice for all construction specifications enables better communication between designers and

other parts of the industry. Also, it helps define legal precedents regarding the "following of accepted professional practice," and improves the quality of bidding.

Within the 16 standard divisions of the CSI Masterformat, specifications can be written broadly or narrowly; actually, most final sets of working specifications are mixtures of broad and narrow scope categories, but each specification is written around the lowest common denominator in general use in construction. For instance, within the Electrical Division, lighting specifications (Section 16500) can be divided into other sections as diverse as: 16535 Emergency Lighting; 16545 Pool Lighting; and 16580 Theatrical Lighting, in addition to the more basic sections, like 16501 Lamp Bulbs; 16502 Ballasts; and 16510 Lighting Fixtures. If the sections are "narrow," or very specific and appropriately sequenced, they may even become useful as subcontracts. To assist in this process, each section is further divided into three parts: General, Products, and Execution. Each part has its own subsections. The structure of the CSI Masterformat, from division through subsection, provides a framework that can accommodate a great deal of information (Appendix B-7: Sample Lighting Specifications).

Division One. Four places in the project manual discuss administration issues that relate to lighting:

1. The preprinted General Conditions

2. The modifications found in Supplemental Conditions

3. The first part of Division Sixteen/Electrical, usually entitled General

4. Division One of the Specifications, called "General Requirements"

Division One is a compendium of the rules governing the construction of the project (refer back to Appendix B-6). As consultants are hired, rough drafts of Division One are sent to them for their reference because it deals with the three issues that are chronically troublesome: equals, substitutions, and nonavailability.

Equals are a recurring dilemma in North American construction. In the U.S., recent decisions of the Supreme Court have been helpful in solving some of these problems. The justices have held that a proprietary specification (one brand only) is not a violation of anti-trust law. They comment that technically few brands of specified items are exactly alike. If the specifier decides to limit his/her specifications to one source, he/she has the responsibility to do so and to enforce it. The court ruled that other suppliers can qualify "or equal" only when the specifier chooses to waive his/her specifications. It has been clearly stated that the contractor can not decide that another supplier is "equal to" the brand specified—only

the specifier is charged with this judgement and responsibility.[2]

Nonetheless, there are three occasions when the phrase ". . . or approved equal" might still appear:

When the project is publicly funded

When the project is urgently rushed

When the specifier welcomes help

The lighting specifier is always interested in a better job for the same money or an equal job for less money. The technique of welcoming equals without succumbing to unwanted substitutions can be reinforced by including a no-nonsense section on Submittals and Substitutions in the Specifications under Division One.

Although more than 90 percent of today's lighting documents are written as proprietary specifications or as reference standards (or as a combination of the two), there are actually five different ways that lighting specifications can be written:

1. Proprietary. A method in which only one fixture and lamp bulb is designated by manufacturer and model number (Figure 6-14).

2. Reference standard. A method by which either (a) one or two manufacturers' products are listed by model or trade name; or (b) any product or material is accepted which will meet the requirements for technical specifications as determined by the American Society for Testing and Materials (ASTM) or the American National Standards Institute (ANSI).

3. Cash allowances. A method by which bidders are asked to include a fixed sum for the purchase, delivery, or installation of a product to be selected by the owner or designer later. (Often used for the dining area chandelier in tract homes.)

4. Performance standard. A method by which the attributes, purposes, and other qualifications of a product or material are described, but bidders are left free to find their own items to comply with these specifications. (This shifts a share of the professional liability for selection to the bidder.)

5. Descriptive. A method that attempts to describe the features of a selected material without naming the manufacturer and/or model, but actually limits acceptable products to the one described. (This method is the manufacturer's favorite because it allows him/her to suggest a description to the specifier that includes features that are exclusive to his product. When the feature is not relevant to the needs of the project, its inclusion sometimes limits competition unfairly.)

Changes

Once the project manual is completed, a change can occur in any of three ways: addendum, change order number one, or other change orders.

PROJECT:

SHEET   OF

DATE:

ROOM NO.	TYPE	QTY	VOLTS	WATTS	LAMP	FIXTURE	MOUNTING	SWITCHING	REMARKS
B-10	A	4	120	250	Q250T3 BY MFG.	RED DOT	PORTABLE ON	4-WAY SWITCH	ACCENT LIGHT FOR MULTISTORY HANGING ON
						MLV250-GS	GROUND STAKE	W/DIMMER AT	NORTH WALL. TO BE APPROVED FOR WET
						WITH LAMP		FIRST FLOOR	LOCATIONS. TO BE PROVIDED WITH VISOR
									SHIELDING BY MFG.
B-11	B	1	120	40	40A19	THOMAS IND.	RECESSED 6⅞"	WITH LIGHTS @	2.5 SONES SOUND RATED. SUBSTITUTE ONLY
						T342 FAN LITE		DOOR	APPROVED ON 2.5 SONES OR LESS/50 CFM
B-12	C	3	120	21	ONE F8T5	ALKCO #138-RSW-	SURFACE UNDER	SEE REMARKS	GANG THREE UNITS TO SINGLE MANUAL
					ONE F13T5	CO-W	BAR TOP		SWITCH ON NORTH UNIT
103	D	1	120	100	A19	HALO H7-416	RECESSED 11½"	TOGGLE WITH	WEATHERPROOF
								TYPE E	
104	E	1	120	276	F40/WW	PRUDENTIAL	RECESSED 11⅝"	AS ABOVE	OVERLIGHTED AREA FOR SECURITY
				INCL.		#P-2946-X-2C			FORCE AT NIGHT
				BALLAST					

FIGURE 6-14: Fixture List
When the fixture list appears as a chart or schedule, it often facilitates the contractors'
bidding and ordering. *Note:* Remarks column should include only items that cannot be
identified by (1) information on fixture list; (2) notes on drawing; or (3) details. (Adapted from
Luminae by Reiko Hayashi.)

Addendum. This is a change that occurs in response to a bidder's inquiry or, if it is substantial enough, affects the bid. An addendum is issued by the design office responsible for the project manual. It can be issued only prior to the signing of the contract. In fact, because it benefits the owner to have addenda bid upon equally by all bidders, many design offices allow as much as a week between the last addendum and the bid opening in order to give each contractor enough time to discuss the change with his/her suppliers and subcontractors. Although addenda may be issued on colored paper for clarity and attention, they become a legal part of the contract documents.

Often an addendum is accompanied by a change in the drawings. A "cloud" is drawn around the change and a delta revision number is assigned to the cloud to help distinguish it from later revisions.

Change Order Number One. This is a minor modification that results from a bidder's inquiry but is unlikely to affect pricing. It can be negotiated with the successful bidder as soon as possible after the awarding of the contract, before orders for materials or furnishings have been placed.

Other Change Orders. These are changes required after the construction or installation process is underway. These are numbered in sequence but become much more complex and costly as the construction proceeds. In the lighting industry, even the friendliest electrical distributor is going to charge his/her customer a 20 percent to 80 percent cancelation or restocking charge. In fact, the total cost of a change order can be more than ten times the amount of the product or material involved. Most of the additional sums are legitimate handling costs, bookkeeping costs, and penalties of various kinds. Collectively, such charges make the contractor appear—however unfairly—that he/she is pocketing money without any commensurate benefit to the owner.

The Best Project Manual

Project manuals can be conveniently divided into three kinds: (1) The loosely constructed, rapidly written, descriptively specified manual that harbors hundreds of potential substitutions and change orders; (2) the exactingly detailed, proprietarily specified manual with heavily annotated drawings that require "Work" only the gods could build; and (3) the documents package that calls for detailed craftsmanship clearly but infrequently, that welcomes "equals" for as many fixture types as is reasonable, and that contains specifications that have been formulated with regard to the owner's financial situation.[3] Like the porridge of the three bears, the first type of project manual is too troublesome for any but the most unscrupulous contractor; the second is too impractical for any but the most lavish budget. Only the last is just right—and it is the result of at least 20 years' experience.

LOOKING AHEAD

Drawings and documents are the formal parts of the contractual agreement. No matter how carefully or professionally they are prepared, errors, omissions, misunderstandings, and historical accidents will cause disruptions in the installation process. When these occur, the reason, integrity, and willingness of each party to see that the others get a square deal will go a long way toward the successful completion of the project. Ultimately, a process as complex as lighting design and electrical construction depends on both good documents and good will.

CHAPTER NOTES

[1]"Bidding Requirements (MP-1-2)," *Construction Specifications Institute Manual of Practice* (Alexandria: Specifications Institute, 1980) 1-21.

[2]Whitton Corporation v. Paddock Pools (Massachusetts, U.S. District Ct., 1983, decision upheld by U.S. Supreme Ct., 1983).

[3]Hans W. Meier, *Construction Specifications Handbook*, 2nd ed. (Englewood Cliffs: Prentice, 1981) 31.

LIGHTING SPECIFIC INTERIORS

Part Two

Once the designer has carefully analyzed a given project and worked out compositional techniques, selected light sources and fixtures, and communicated his/her lighting plan to the various trades through documents and drawings, then the actual work of implementing that lighting plan can begin.

The nine case studies in this section present a wide spectrum of actual lighting designs that have been devised for a variety of different lighting situations—from the entry of a private residence to the lobby of a major hotel, from the dining room of a San Francisco town house to that of a busy restaurant. The designers represented by these case studies also present a varied cross section of professional styles and working methods.

A standard format has been devised for presenting these case studies. Each one contains (1) data and physical specifications; (2) an analysis of the design program; (3) the specific composition/lighting strategy; (4) the constraints under which the project was undertaken; and finally (5) lighting tactics such as light sources, fixtures, beam angles, beam shapes, mountings, costs, etcetera.

Lighting design is an applied art. While a knowledge of lighting theory and an analysis of a given project are essential for any designer, it is the practical application of this knowledge that determines a designer's success. These case studies offer the opportunity to see how designers work and think, to witness the application of theory, and to discover how these ideas and theories materialize in private and public environments.

Store design by Philip Schwartz

HIGHLIGHTING AN ENTRY

LA ENTRADA

INTERIOR DESIGN: Reiko Hayashi and Fran Kellogg Smith, ASID/CSI

LIGHTING DESIGN: Reiko Hayashi

A well-designed entry impresses visitors, makes them feel comfortable, and encourages them to return. To accomplish this, the lighting must (1) create that important first impression; (2) provide cues on how to use the space; and (3) provide light for tasks.

The entry in this case study was transformed into a unique space by opposing red and blue colors of light and by lighting two of the focal centers from below. Additional refinements include the use of added resistance on the electrical circuit to extend lamp life and warm lamp color.

DATA/PHYSICAL SPECIFICATIONS

This entry is found in an old adobe house that was built in the late eighteenth century by Franciscan priests from Spain who came to win converts to Christianity. Although the adobe has been continuously occupied and remodeled for more than two hundred years, this "entrada," or entry, is thought to be one of the original rooms (Figure C1-1). The adobe is listed in the National Registry of Historic Places.

The entrada's ability to produce a memorable first impression is disproportionate to its size: 8 feet by 20 feet by 10½ feet (2.4 × 6.09 × 3.20 m) high. Its tile flooring, overscale baseboard, and matte white walls are historically accurate, but the plaster ceiling is not.

ANALYSIS/PROGRAM

Client Image. The owner wants this entry to evoke the hush of an art museum without losing touch with the adobe's history. Because this space is not only an entrance, but also an anteroom for the chapel, art and antiques are used to establish a religious ambiance. The sculpture *Portrait of a Condemned Soul* by Harriet Moore sets forth the theme, while the bas-relief panels reinforce it with their allusions to the fires of damnation. The sign of the Cross is found in the negative space of the panels (see Color Plate 6).

Client Vision. Typical guests are the owners' adult children and their friends. Older persons with impaired vision are not anticipated.

Daylighting. The entry's only outside opening, a door, admits practically no daylight to this room due to its northern orientation. Such an exposure, coupled with a wide overhang outside, prevents the heat of the Southern California sun from being troublesome. At night, double hung, heavily carved shutters are closed to prevent heat loss.

Color. Because the walls and flooring are authentic, but the ceiling is not, the focus is away from the ceiling; the eye is instead drawn toward the hand-thrown tile flooring. Unfortunately, the floor's color is both dark and subtle; it does not visibly stand forth. So, the warm, burnished red of this tile is enlarged with the warm gleam of an old Spanish dowry chest. While the dark finish of the 12-inch baseboard is also not authentic, it too is used to extend the size and visual importance of this tile floor.

Activities. *Tasks:* Two tasks commonly performed in residential foyers are (1) checking one's appearance in the mirror, and (2) identifying callers before admitting them. The first task requires light at the mirror. The second one needs light that allows the householder to identify callers when answering the door.

Traffic: This entrance is a major passage for the house. The double opening in the east wall leads to the visitors' usual destination, the living room. Because the opening to this room is large, the light level in the entry must be high enough so that the relatively brighter adjoining room does not magnetize the visitors and compel them to speed through the entry without savouring it (see Figure C1-2).

Mood. The entry's mood should be hushed, reverent, and unique.

FIGURE C1-1:   South View
Here, the sculpture, *Portrait of a Condemned Soul* by Harriet Moore, sets forth the entry's ecclesiastical theme, reflecting the heritage of the adobe house in which it is located. (Photograph by Mary E. Nichols.)

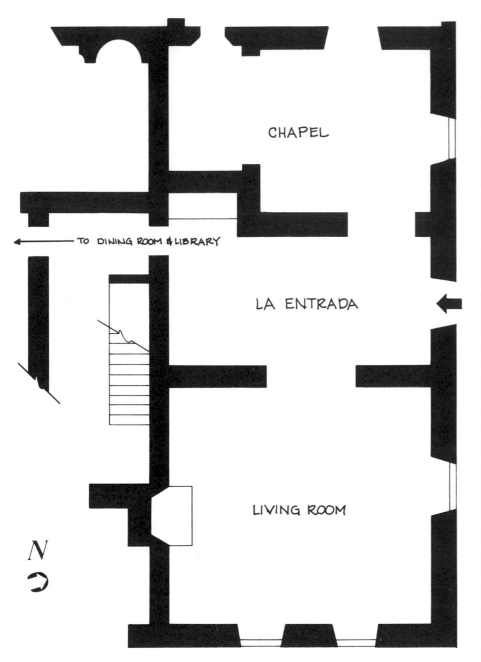

CHAPEL

← TO DINING ROOM & LIBRARY

LA ENTRADA

LIVING ROOM

N

FIGURE C1-2: Plan View
Seen in this plan view of the interior, La Entrada has four directions of transit and three major points of view. The primary view is from the front door toward the south wall (see Color Plate 6). (Illustration by Reiko Hayashi.)

COMPOSITION/STRATEGY
The most common lighting strategy for entryways is to create a single bold lighting effect that combines the creation of directional cues with the necessary task lighting.

Of the four doors that open into the entrada, three of them offer good views of the room. The view of the south wall from the north door is primary in creating that important first impression. The second most important view is the one seen from the living room toward the west wall. The least important view is of the north wall which is seen by those coming from the depths of the house. Both the brightness level and the uniqueness of the lighting effects should follow the same sequence of importance—from brightest and least unique to least bright and most unique (south wall, west wall, north wall).

White light with blue highlights has been

selected because the blue will contrast strongly with the reddish warmth of the tile flooring and help to establish the visual importance of the tiles. Luminous pedestals not only present the thematic Moore sculpture in museum-like fashion, but also provide the needed light for viewing oneself in the mirror.

CONSTRAINTS
Code. There are few code liabilities on this project because (1) code variances are normally given for historic buildings, if the work is not patently unsafe; and (2) although the historic building is opened to the public from time to time, the structure is still "private" according to the codes.

Life Safety. Many structures built before electrical conduit was commonly used have old-fashioned knob and tube wiring . . . and mice. Such a combination leads to electrical hazards because the mice munch at the insulation—leaving exposed copper wiring. To avoid fires, circuits should be checked in their entirety when new electrical work is done, and replaced when necessary.

Energy. In some states, energy-efficient light sources of at least 24 lumens-per-watt must be used in lighting new and remodeled residential kitchens, baths, and laundries. Although none of those areas is involved here, no homeowner wants to pay for more energy than is necessary. In addition to economic concerns about energy, an older structure, such as this 1776 adobe, presents a special case for energy conservation. It has an outdated allotment of electrical service from the utility: an allotment that did not anticipate the electrical burdens of forced air or a toaster-oven, much less a hand-held 1,200-watt hair dryer. The net effect is that there is seldom enough power in such a house, so energy-conserving light sources are usually necessary to avoid fire hazards that might result from overloading the circuits.

Budget. Although this is the home of a private designer rather than a showplace for demonstrating innovative designs, expense is still a concern. A budget of 1000 dollars was established.

Schedule. Four weeks was allotted for the completion of this entryway.

Feasibility. Two problems often make the relighting of older structures economically impractical. The first is the need to bring additional electricity into the main electrical panel. The other is the discovery of safety hazards in the electrical wiring. Since neither of these occurred here it was no problem to complete this project on schedule and near budget.

TACTICS

Light Sources
For this entry, incandescent light sources have been chosen because a grazing tech-

nique is used on its south wall to draw the visitor's eye to it. Such a technique requires the beam control that only an incandescent's small filament provides. Without color filters, incandescent light sources are also naturally abundant in red, which helps to bring out the color of the floor tiles.

Beam Angles. In order to draw the eye to it, the beam angles for the south wall will be made the brightest. Wallwashing and grazing are the most powerful lighting techniques for achieving a sheet of vertical brightness. Of the two, grazing is the more unusual. Two 50-watt low-voltage MR-16 lamps provide the needed incandescent light at a grazing angle from below.

Certain pieces of sculpture, such as the

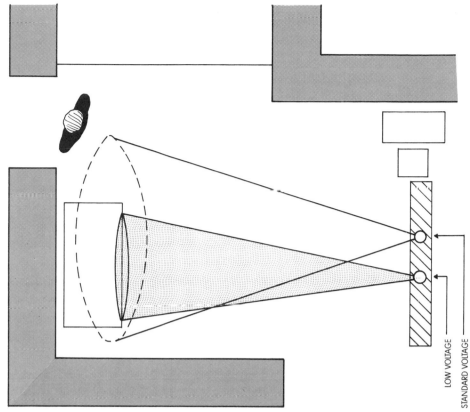

Moore sculpture displayed against the west wall, respond very well to intense lighting from one direction and diffuse lighting from the other. The intense highlighting (1) reveals the piece's finest features; (2) sculpts its three-dimensional curves in shadow; and (3) creates brightness that attracts the eye. Because this sculpture is so porous, however, these highlights from overhead can be caused only by a very intense source like a low-voltage incandescent. Diffuse lighting from the pedestals below softens the shadows, preventing them from masking portions of the piece. A standard voltage (120v) 50-watt R20 incandescent lamp bulb produces the glints of color diffused through the frosted and stippled glass tops of the pedestals.

Incandescent track lights of normal voltage might be used to emphasize the frontal aspect of the antique chest on the floor, but people coming from the south door will look directly into the glare. Luckily, the very narrow beams of low-voltage incandescent lamps will help here. At least the glare angle will be more narrow and controlled (Figure C1-3).

Lamp Life. The normal short lamp life of many of these low-voltage PAR lamps is a definite drawback. Such lamps often are dimmed to extend their life. To do so, the addition of 42 watts of resistance to the conductors between the transformer and the lamp bulbs is a permanent, inexpensive, and tamperproof way to dim them. This reduces the 12 volts of electrical force from the transformer to 10 volts at the lamp bulb

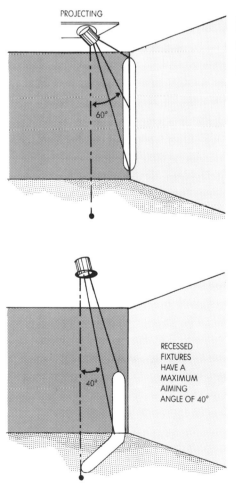

FIGURE C1-3: Aiming Angle Studies
The very narrow beam of a low-voltage lamp frequently can be used to limit the number of glare angles that might otherwise distract passersby. (Illustration by Reiko Hayashi.)

FIGURE C1-4: North View
The dark finish of the 12-inch (30.5 cm) baseboard is not authentic to the adobe's heritage, but is used to extend the size and visual importance of the tile floor which is also dark. (Photograph by Mary E. Nichols.)

and extends bulb life from 300 hours to 3850 hours.

Lamp Color. Incandescent light sources are naturally abundant in red. When they are dimmed, the reduced voltage will redden not only the color of the light, but also the color of the floor tiles it falls upon. Other light sources in the room are boosted with blue filters to create the blue light effects which provide a unique contrast to the red floor tiles (Figure C1-4).

Invisible Effects. The Moore sculpture is only minimally sensitive to fading. On the other hand, the heat of infrared wavelengths from the MR-16 lamp bulbs will dehydrate the antique dowry chest. So, the back of the chest is protected by an application of aluminum foil "armor." The stream of light projected onto the wall of the northeast corner produces no damage because the wall's white paint reflects the light away.

Fixtures

Luminous pedestals and low-voltage highlighting are lighting techniques usually associated with museums. However, these techniques can work equally well in residences.

Beam Shape. The overhead PAR lamps control their own beam shapes. The beams from the pedestal-enclosed R20 incandescents have been selected not for shape, but

for the red and blue jewel-like color of their light; so the insides of the pedestals have been covered with an application of crinkled silver foil to increase the reflectance of these cavities, and thereby increase the glints of color.

Mounting. The particular low-voltage "special effect" lamp chosen for the northeast corner requires that the fixture be surface mounted in order to aim the beam at a high enough angle. Therefore, all the low voltage lampholders are surface mounted as a group rather than locating one prominent little fixture in the ceiling by itself (Figure C1-5).

Costs. *Equipment:* This typical low-voltage pan fixture replaces an incandescent fixture that had been using standard voltage at the same location. The wholesale cost of this low-voltage fixture was 400 dollars while the two furniture pedestals were 350 dollars each.

Installation: Because the wattage of the pan fixture, with its low-voltage PAR lamps, is considerably less than that of the decorative lantern it replaces, the electrical contractor needs only to find a remote location for the transformer and add the resistance to the circuit to replace an existing dimmer. This involves about half a day's work for the electrician. The existing dimmer is unusable anyway because it is not UL-rated for low-voltage equipment.

Owning/Operating: For 300 watts burning for 3,850 hours, the operating costs are

less than those of owning the previous 360 watts, which needed random lamp bulb changes at an average of every 800 hours. The fixtures, including the pedestals, function best if they are cleaned once a year. Although the lamp bulbs do not need replacement, dirt should be removed. Dirt alone can destroy as much as 80 percent of the brightness of a lamp bulb.

Appearance. The fixtures and ceiling are intended to be unseen, so the surface mounted low-voltage unit is painted to match the ceiling's color. Portable fixtures are concealed behind the dowry chest and the R-20 bulbs are enclosed inside the luminous pedestals.

CONCLUDING THOUGHTS

There are several reasons the lighting design for this entry is so successful. First, the designer was able to satisfy the client's desires. Second, she did so in a way that was not only beautiful but also economical in terms of installation and maintenance costs. Energy consumption was also reduced to ease the electrical loading in an old structure.

FIGURE C1-5: Lighting Plan
Low-voltage lighting was used because a precise light beam was needed for the Moore sculpture, only a controlled beam could resolve the glare problem at the south doorway, and an additional low-voltage, special effect lamp could be used to create a simple, inexpensive treatment for the northeast corner. (Illustration by Reiko Hayashi.)

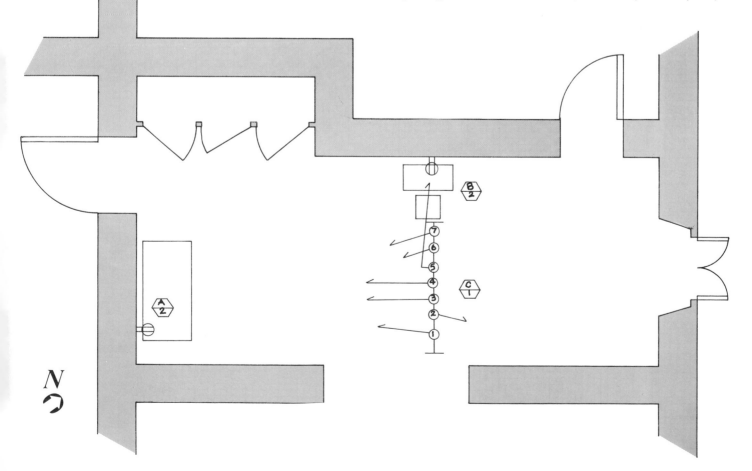

Case Study Two

INTERACTING IN PUBLIC

MARRIOTT HOTEL LOBBY

ARCHITECTURE: Rayburn, Hatch, Portman, McWhorter, Hatch & Raugh, Inc.

INTERIOR DESIGN: Trisha Wilson & Associates, Inc.
Jim Looney, AIA and Connie Jackson, ASID

LIGHTING DESIGN: C. M. Kling & Associates, Inc.
Candace M. Kling, MIES/ASID-IF/IALD

The lighting for a hotel lobby's very public space must fulfill the same three functions as lighting for a private residential entry: (1) create a first impression; (2) welcome guests while cuing their use of the space; and (3) provide light for tasks. In addition to these functions, lighting in a lobby must facilitate interaction among the guests, and between the guests and hotel staff.

It is very difficult to create an elegant but practical space on a moderate working budget, but by using highly reflectant colors for equally reflectant hard surfaces, this interior designer has created a very gracious and practical space. The use of lighting controls is a major part of this lighting plan and a significant part of the budget.

DATA/PHYSICAL SPECIFICATIONS

This 10-story, 300,000 square foot hotel contains 504 guest rooms on a choice site not far from the Orlando Convention Center, the Orlando Airport, and Disneyworld. The lobby of this hotel is 4,000 square feet; three quarters of this volume is open to a 25-foot ceiling. Two types of architectural features interrupt the line of sight: a line of seven columns and a pedestrian bridge crossing the space at its second story. This bridge/mezzanine offers guests a walkway and a series of conversation areas on round, cantilevered balconies. On the west and east walls, plate glass rises the full width and height of the space. This project has won awards both for architecture and interior design.

ANALYSIS/PROGRAM

Client Image. The owners of this project, Marriott Hotels and Johnson Properties, visualized a very "Florida" experience for their guests. The hotel projects a bright, airy, and cheerful ambiance that is open to the Florida sunshine and flowers. Their target guest is the conventioneer who attends conference activities while his/her family enjoys Disneyworld. Because of the family appeal, the interior cannot be so fragile or overly sophisticated that the guests will feel uncomfortable.

Client Vision. The patrons of this hotel are generally middle class and college educated. Most are traveling with their young families and are under 50. Vision limitations of such patrons are minimal and not paramount to the success of a lighting design. In fact, acoustical problems are more likely to occur. Hard building surfaces often amplify sound but are necessary to resist the wear and tear of children.

Daylighting. Florida evokes an image of sunlight for most people, so it is important for the hotel to be flooded with light. An abundance of daylight enters from two full-height glass walls in the Lee Vista lobby. Even on overcast days, photocells will raise the levels of electric lights up to full strength to dispel gloom (Figure C2-1).

Color. To achieve the desired airy Florida ambiance, colors used on surfaces are highly reflectant to enable daylight to penetrate deeply into the space and reflect freely. Building materials include light colored woods with painted surfaces of white and cream. A rainbow of vivid colors are used for decorative accents and in gardens filled with tropical plants and blooming annuals.

Activities. *Tasks:* Task lighting is needed at many locations within the lobby (Figure C2-2). The staff at the registration desk has a variety of writing, typing, and filing jobs to be performed rapidly. The bell captain and concierge must be able to read very small print at night and during the day. Guests will also need to read maps, tickets, or itinerary schedules in the lobby. In the daytime these tasks are all assisted by daylight, but at night they must be specifically aided by the lighting designer.

Traffic: The lobby is a hub for traffic; the pedestrian flow across it is constant. Since

FIGURE C2-1: Daylighted Entry
The vaulted volumes of this entry and the high cost of electricity are both good reasons to select HID light sources or daylighting. Nevertheless, the owners feared added heat loads and the unfamiliar colors of light that such HID sources create, so the more familiar incandescent light sources were chosen instead. (Photograph by Rion Rizzo.)

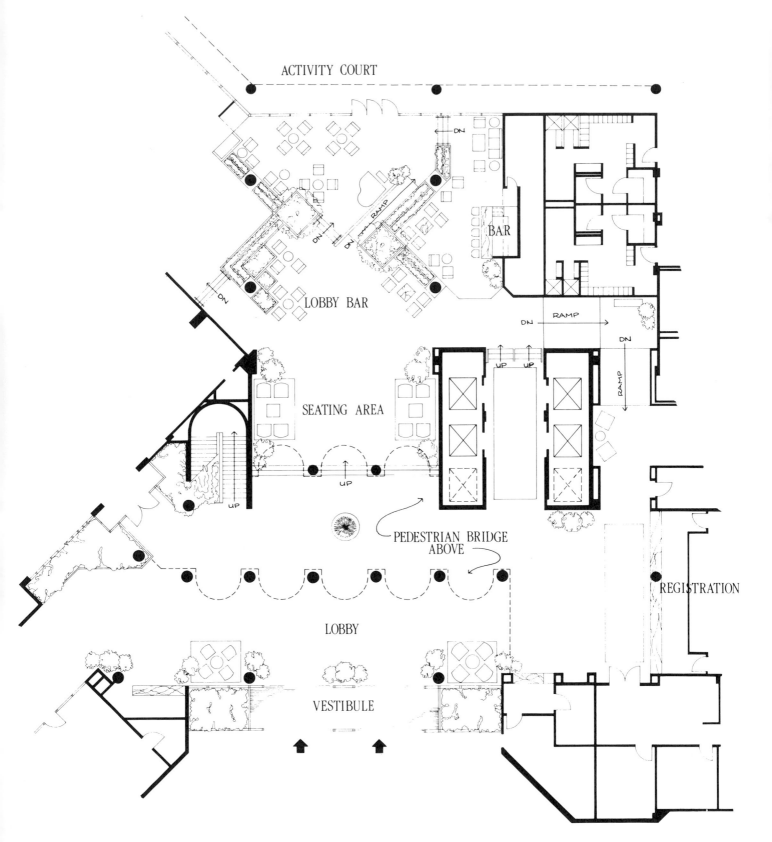

ACTIVITY COURT

BAR

LOBBY BAR

SEATING AREA

PEDESTRIAN BRIDGE
ABOVE

REGISTRATION

LOBBY

VESTIBULE

FIGURE C2-2: Plan View
(Above) When an entry's focal point is
hidden, as shown in this plan view, the
designer must boldly create that important
first impression without it. (Illustration by
Reiko Hayashi.)

FIGURE C2-3: Nightlighted Entry
(Right) At night, incandescent lighting draws
attention to the colorful banners floating
overhead. Their lighthearted vitality compen-
sates for the loss of the Florida sunlight.
(Photograph by Rion Rizzo.)

a guest may cross the lobby four to six times each day, the lobby's appearance should change significantly as the day passes to add variety.

Mood. In the lobby, the designer's principle goal is to deliver an immediate and unmistakeable welcome to the arriving guest. This first visual impression must be one of a cheerful, airy, and colorful space settled naturally and comfortably into the warm Florida landscape. On the other hand, the lighting of the nighttime lobby must be a definitive contrast; it could be segmented into areas of intimate activity.

COMPOSITION/STRATEGY

Because the Florida image is intended to pervade the guests' every daytime experience, their eyes must be continually directed to the higher brightnesses of the plantings and the gardens seen through the glass walls. To achieve this, the interior lighting needs to be a blended and uniform level of brightness that does not stop the eye with highlights or shadows. Uniform lighting will also assist the multitude of seeing tasks in the lobby.

However, the overhead mezzanine cre-ates an obstacle to the lighting designer's accomplishment of this uniform light level. The upper side of the bridge can catch the light that comes from the ceiling and become too bright, while the space beneath remains dark.

At night, the lighting must change to create pools of brightness which break up the spatial volume of the lobby. The warmer color of incandescent light may help to establish a contrast between the daylighted lobby and the nightlighted one (Figure C2-3).

CONSTRAINTS

Schedule. This project has been designed and built in 15 months. Such fast-track schedules telescope the (1) architectural design services and (2) the construction process into a single schedule of quasi-coordinated phases. To start and finish a project as soon as possible, the construction is begun before the design is finished. Thus, the shell defines the shape of interior spaces, rather than the reverse.

Construction. Although this building is not a skyscraper, a lack of construction precision can be anticipated because of the schedule.

Fast-track construction often has the same limits on design niceties as high-rise construction. That is, oversights or errors in the architectural documents or in the workmanship of the construction crew snowball into situations that can only be resolved by gross adjustments to the building—for example, by moving a wall a few feet from the location specified on the blueprints. Often, the quality of the lighting is sacrificed because good lighting requires that the walls, floors, and ceilings be built where indicated on the blueprints. (The location of lights versus surfaces is critical for success.)

Code. Hotels are facilities to which both the guest and the general public are invited, causing them to be rife with code requirements. Florida legislation requires local codes to be at least as stringent as ASHRAE 90-75—an advisory document prepared by the American Society of Heating, Refrigerating, and Air Conditioning Engineers in 1975; the section of this document that concerns lighting was authored by the IES and promotes lighting performance standards that maximize energy efficiency. HUD (U.S. Department of Housing and Urban Development) Minimum Prop-

erty Standards and Appendix J of the Florida Standard Building Code are also in effect in Orlando.

Life Safety. In a hotel, exceptional efforts are made to properly light staircases, ramps, and all other exits to be used in a crisis situation, such as a fire. Fixtures along these egress routes are usually circuited to an emergency generator or to batteries that automatically provide power in the eventuality of a power outage (Figure C2-4).

Energy. In order to reduce energy consumption, the lighting designer for this project went beyond a simple lighting layout and specification and studied the control capacity of the entire lighting system. She was aware of the fact that the energy consumption in any building is determined by its use. "Lights must be turned off or down to save energy."

Budget. Among the lighting designers who specialize in hotels, the Kling office is particularly admired for their ability to manipulate tight budgets, such as the one for this hotel. In this case, the designer balanced the expense of dimmer controls against the savings that dimming would permit in inexpensive incandescent fixtures, their low maintenance, and their reduced energy consumption. The use of such incandescent fixtures would have been impossible without such dimming controls.

Feasibility. Clearly the lighting design for such a fast-track project must be simple, fail-safe, and economical as well as energy-efficient (Figure C2-5). Basing the lighting strategy on the dimming system limits the possibilities for errors.

TACTICS

Light Sources
One alternative to incandescent light might have been HID light. In spite of their obvious cost savings, energy savings, and applicability to high ceiling spaces, there is a lingering reluctance to use HID sources in important public rooms. This reluctance is apparent within the hospitality industry.

Beam Angles. For ceilings of 25 feet, the ability of high-intensity discharge light sources to deliver light to distant spaces below is unrivaled—except by certain incandescent sources.

Lamp Life/Controls. HID sources require infrequent replacements, but the same can be true of incandescent sources—if they are controlled by dimmers.

Lamp Color. However, in a hotel lobby where guests spend a lot of time, the color limitations of HID sources can be disastrous. Hotel owners don't want to take risks with the unfamiliar color and shadow patterns these light sources can create. Because

FIGURE C2-4: Egress Lighting
In a crisis like a hurricane or fire, lights on stairs and along exit routes are the only ones that operate. Their paths of light lead the guests, who are unfamiliar with the surroundings, to the exits and safety. (Photograph by Rion Rizzo.)

their colors and beam characteristics are familiar and residential, incandescent sources are still the most commonly used for a "home away from home" effect. As a consequence, reductions in costs and energy consumption are often required elsewhere to offset the higher operating costs and energy requirements of the incandescent fixtures.

Invisible Effects. Incandescent light sources generate less light and more heat per watt than HID sources, but they contribute very little ultraviolet to the space.

Fixtures
Hotel entry lighting traditionally uses decorative pendant fixtures to hold these incandescent light sources. Often the appearance of the fixture is used as a major thematic accessory to the entry's first impression function. However, such fixtures need frequent cleaning and relamping, but are relatively inaccessible. Another problem with decorative pendant fixtures is their high cost.

In this hotel lobby, however, another way was found to create the same decorative effect. Banners that could be illuminated beautifully were more convenient and cost effective.

Beam Shape. Powerful, narrow, incandescent downlights will throw needed illumination 25 feet (7.60 m) without wasting light where it has no purpose. In this project, incandescent downlights brighten the lower lobby without flooding the intimate circular

seating areas on the mezzanine and pedestrian bridge above. (HID beams would have been much more difficult to control.)

Mounting. Adequate depth for recessing fixtures is available throughout the main ceiling except in the lowered portion over the pedestrian bridge, which is filled with mechanical ductwork. Under the bridge, the designer had to use very shallow fixtures to continue the pattern of recessed downlights. Sometimes the lighting designer will overlay the reflected ceiling plan with the mechanical drawings to ensure that the plenum depth is clear in those locations where fixtures are to be recessed. But in fast-track construction, the ductwork frequently shows up in unplanned locations.

Costs. *Equipment:* The initial cost of the recessed incandescent fixtures offers a great savings. Normally this savings is canceled out by electrical inefficiency and by the cost of frequent lamp bulb replacement, but in some cases, like this hotel lobby, such frequent replacement can be minimized. Here the designer, Kling, specified greater wattages than what was needed for appropriate lighting. In this way, the incandescent lamp bulbs could always be kept dimmed, which greatly lengthened their lifespan, thus reducing replacement costs.

Installation: Incandescent fixtures are among the least expensive to install. Having no ballasts, they are much less complicated to wire than HID fixtures. Among the mounting options, recessed mountings on accessible suspended ceilings are not unusually labor intensive.

Owning/Operating: The key to this lighting system is its dimming controls. Although expensive, their cost is easily justified by (1) the longer life they add to incandescent lamp bulbs; (2) the reduced maintenance, and (3) the increased flexibility of light levels that they provide to the building's operator. The maintenance schedule for these incandescent sources, when they are dimmed to 50 percent of normal voltage, should be only a little more costly than that of the alternative HID light sources.

Appearance. Because the fixtures are recessed, they are not intended to be seen, which enhances the clean ceiling and airy impression of the space.

CONCLUDING THOUGHTS
This designer's use of dimming controls allows the lighting system to enliven the space with day-versus-night and sunny-versus-overcast variations, while at the same time realizing savings on operations, energy consumption, and prolonged bulb life. This strategy is typical of lighting designers who have theatrical backgrounds, but it is also appropriate and workable here, in the lobby of the Lee Vista Hotel.

FIGURE C2-5: Reflected Ceiling Plan
This plan for the lobby shows how the lighting designer balanced the expense of the needed dimmer controls against the savings in (1) inexpensive incandescent fixtures; (2) low maintenance costs; and (3) reduced energy consumption. (Illustration by Reiko Hayashi.)

Case Study Three

CREATING A MOOD

WILLSON DINING ROOM

INTERIOR DESIGN: David Winfield Willson, IALD

LIGHTING DESIGN: David Winfield Willson, IALD

Three men can be credited with opening the way for low-voltage lighting in architectural uses. The first was Marvin Gelman, president of Lighting Services, Inc., a New York manufacturer of miniature theatrical fixtures that use low-voltage lamp bulbs. The second was LeMar Terry, IALD. He was the first person to turn out the floodlights in display windows, museums, and stores to dramatize objects with the slender beams of low-voltage lights. The third was David Winfield Willson, IALD, who quickly realized the impact low-voltage lighting would have in energy-conscious architecture. His lighting design for the dining room of his San Francisco town house used only 49 watts and became a lighting landmark of the 1970s. Soon restaurants, hotels, and many other types of spaces were dramatically illuminated with the focal lighting techniques made possible by low voltage.

DATA/PHYSICAL SPECIFICATIONS

David Winfield Willson frequently entertains small groups of friends at dinner in this intimate dining room which is also used to showcase lighting systems for prospective clients (Figure C3-1).

The dining room measures approximately 12 by 15 feet (3.66 × 4.57 m) and is 8½ feet (2.60 m) high. Exterior landscape lighting would have been helpful to visually enlarge the perceived size of the space, but only if it could be done without allowing the viewer to see the quickly rising slope outside too accurately.

ANALYSIS/PROGRAM

Client Image. On a first visit to this room, guests immediately recognize the urbanity and talent of their host. The controlled presentation of the oriental porcelains and colorful centerpiece announce his superb taste.

Client Vision. Typical guests are between 35 and 60 years of age. Vision problems are probable among people of that age range, but their tasks and traffic patterns are quite apparent and predictable in this uncomplicated space.

Daylighting. The bay window faces west. While the soft, diffuse sunset glow is pleasant, it presents no heat or glare concerns, because the steep, ivy-covered hillside cuts out all direct light.

Color. Here the use of color is unsurpassed. A rich, warm, matte red encourages the ambient light to bury itself in the walls; by contrast, the cool gloss of white porcelain reflects its smooth luster. This combination of an absorptive surface behind a reflective one creates the visual impression that the vases are thrusting forward.

Activities. *Tasks:* When dining, the guests' interest becomes the food and the people. Not only should lighting make both appear interesting, it must also provide enough illumination for diners to cut and eat their food.

Traffic: A room of this size is not a thoroughfare. The passage space needed to claim one's chair is sufficient. The only hazard is created by the porcelains; they will need to be lighted to ensure their safety.

Mood. The mood should be relaxed and intimate. The Flynn research on light and psychology concludes that such spaces are created with dimmed downlight and bright end walls.[1] Here Willson's landmark space confirms Flynn's feeling that appropriate lighting angles and intensities deliver predictable impressions and behavior.

COMPOSITION/STRATEGY

Willson created the lighting plan for his dining room around two viewing locations. The first is a scene viewed from the doorway: a collection of handsome porcelains

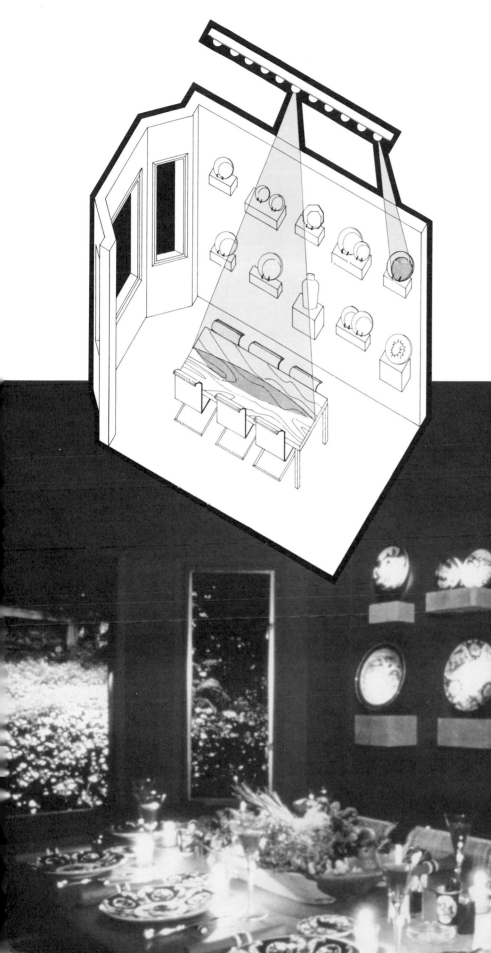

FIGURE C3-1:   Low-Voltage Lighting
(Below) This intimate dining room in a San Francisco town house was designed by David Winfield Willson who also designed its lighting. (Interior Design/Lighting Design by David Winfield Willson.)

FIGURE C3-2:   Strategy
(Left) Two scenes are developed here. The first is a still life viewed from the doorway. The second scene is the one viewed by the seated guest as he/she enjoys both the dinner and the dinner companions. (Illustration by Reiko Hayashi.)

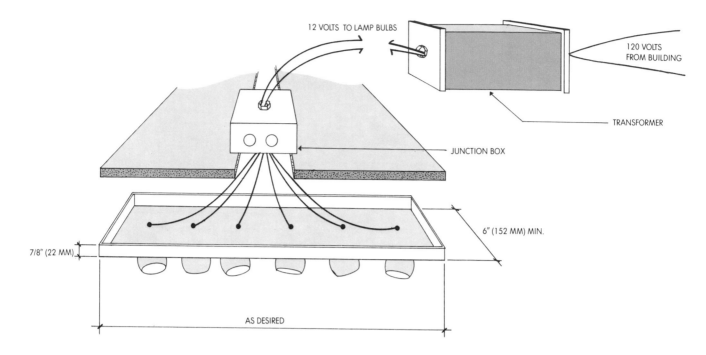

FIGURE C3-3: The Pan Fixture
(Above) Track is a decorative wireway, but so are these custom-built pans. As long as the pan projects at least 7/8 of an inch from the ceiling, it can act as a channel for the management of wires running from the junction box to each lamp head. (Illustration by Reiko Hayashi.)

FIGURE C3-4: The Traditional Look in Low-Voltage Lighting
(Below) More costly mountings include recessed 2-foot by 4-foot prefabricated panels containing multiples of as many as six recessed low-voltage accent lights attached to one transformer. These can be recessed into suspended ceilings or built into the ceiling plane with architectural detailing. (Illustration by Reiko Hayashi.)

dominates, while the dining table provides interest in the foreground (Figure C3-2). The landscape outdoors contributes an illusion of distance. Once they are seated, the guests concentrate on a second scene: the food and their dinner companions. The setting is so relaxed the guests may sit at the table for hours.

The color of the light source is warm enough to flatter skin tones, but not so warm as to distort the cool accent colors that vitalize the centerpiece. Indirect lighting found in many restaurant dining rooms (see Case Study Nine) is not advisable because a white tablecloth would enlarge the table and cause it to visually press against the dark walls. Instead, the table is left bare and votive candles light faces directly from below.

Exceedingly flat exterior lighting, spread evenly across the ivy covered hillside, washes out three dimensional shadows and makes the distance between the house and the hill appear larger than it really is. Lacking both shadowing and horizon line, perspective is hard to establish.

CONSTRAINTS

Code. The lighting done by designers in their own homes is often innovative. Many code restrictions do not apply to work done by the householder, unless some part of the building is used commercially. So, the designer tends to use his/her own home as a laboratory. Here he/she can work out details or imaginative concepts and still minimize liabilities.

Life Safety. This is one of the code areas that does not apply to a private residence, unless the residence is owned by others, for example, a hotel or a condominium.

Energy. Energy codes do not apply here, but even so, lighting that conserves electrical resources is both professional and desirable.

Budget. By keeping the cost of lighting low, the designer was able to demonstrate his skill in delivering an elegant and expensive look for less money than his peers.

Schedule. Since a designer sells his/her time, valuable time taken from clients to design his/her own home needs to reward him/her with marketing potential as well as personal satisfaction. Completion of a project like this should be as rapid as possible.

Feasibility. This project was not easy to build. Because many extraordinary but unorthodox lighting effects must be seen to be

discussed, much less sold, a designer's private home is often the only feasible proving ground. This home put residential low voltage before the design world.

TACTICS

In the 1970s when Willson first created the lighting for his dining room, his use of contrasting brightnesses was highly innovative. He achieved these brightnesses by selecting focal points, and illuminating them with low-voltage incandescents in an otherwise darkened interior.

Light Sources

Beam Angles. Only low-voltage incandescent sources can deliver the 10-inch (25.40 cm) spot of light needed for the porcelains. Willson elected to use 12-volt PAR-36 auto headlights (#4405). These bulbs have small stubby filaments that respond precisely to reflector control. This type of focal lighting has become so popular lately that many new bulbs are manufactured for this type of use. Today's competitors might include the 6 volt PAR-46 display spot, the 5.5 volt PAR-36 display spot, the 12 volt PAR-36 narrow spot, and the Halostar series of lamp bulbs introduced by Osram from Europe.

Lamp Life. In the 1970s, however, only the #4405 lamp made possible the controlled use of light that has won so much recognition. To lengthen the lamp's relatively short life more than a hundredfold, Willson used a transformer to provide an input current of 5 volts instead of the design voltage of 12 volts. The remote transformer supplying the 5 volts is located in a nearby kitchen cabinet. Its absence from the dining room ensures noiseless operation as well as reduces the physical size of the fixture on the dining room ceiling.

Lamp Color. One of the by-products of reducing the voltage to the lamp bulb is that the color of the light becomes ruddier, warming the red walls, the wood of the table, and the skin tones of guests. Best of all, it causes the color of the electric lights to match the color of the candlelight at each place setting.

Invisible Effects. Having only incandescent light and candles might cause a designer to review the heat removal capacity for the space. However, the transformation of the 12-volt system to 5 volts reduces the electrical wattage of the lamp bulbs to an awesome low of 49 watts (167 BTUs).

Fixtures

Beam Shape. The shapes of the beams are actually determined by the PAR lamps. Like all PAR lamps, the #4405 is a complete and enclosed optical system.

Mounting. One of the nicest features of surface-mounted low-voltage systems is that they can replace the ceiling fixture at the center of the room. These custom-built pans are actually decorative wireways (Figure C3-3).

Costs. *Equipment:* Fixtures come in several price ranges. A system can be as simple as the painted one here that blends into the ceiling plane, or for a higher price, it can be as eye catching as those finished in brass and copper.

Installation: Because the wattage of the new system is invariably less than that of the previous dining room fixtures, rewiring costs are low. In fact, the installation cost of these systems is sometimes no more expensive than the cost of changing fixtures.

Owning/Operating: When these systems are dimmed on special low-voltage dimmers, the life of the lamp bulbs is extensively lengthened, keeping electric bills and maintenance costs low.

Appearance. Because most of these systems are surface-mounted, appearance is an important issue. There are four choices:

1. To minimize the size and distraction of the hardware by painting it to match its surroundings

2. To project a fashion image by using costly finishes

3. To present the hardware in a traditional setting by building panels bearing low voltage fixturing into the ceiling plane with architectural detailing (Figure C3-4.)

4. To use track for a lean, inexpensive high-tech look

CONCLUDING THOUGHTS

The creative use of precise focal lighting techniques enabled this designer to create a dramatic effect without sacrificing budget. The energy savings he achieved through use of low-voltage incandescent sources made his lighting design innovative, functional, trend-setting, and beautiful.

CHAPTER NOTES
[1]John E. Flynn, "A Study of Subjective Responses to Low Energy and Nonuniform Lighting Systems," *Lighting Design and Application* 7, No. 2 (1977): 6-15.

Case Study Four

MULTIPLYING PRODUCTIVITY

CALIFORNIA FIRST BANK

ARCHITECTURE: Skidmore, Owings and Merrill, San Francisco
Charles Basset, FAIA, partner in charge

INTERIOR DESIGN: Skidmore, Owings and Merrill, San Francisco
Murray Charles Pfister, ASID
Andrew Belschner, project manager

LIGHTING DESIGN: Horton Lees Lighting Design, Inc.
Jules Horton, IALD, lighting designer
Shaper Lighting Products
Hans Shaper, custom fixtures

A custom lighting fixture such as the one seen in Figure C4-1 may look simple in its completed form, but it represents the consideration and resolution of a myriad of details. By selecting such a fixture, not only does the designer determine the light in the space, but the fixture itself becomes a dominant element of the interior design. As with most design projects, the concept is only the initial step; careful collaboration is needed at every step to ensure success. This collaboration usually involves the architect or interior designer, the lighting designer and/or electrical engineer, and a manufacturer.[1]

During the design development phase, more than one manufacturer may be involved, but once the fixture's design is established, a single manufacturer should be selected to actually fabricate the fixture type. At this point, many details still need to be worked out by the manufacturer, some of which may affect the building's structure, its power supply, and circuiting requirements (Figure C4-2). The time and knowledge the manufacturer provides in working out these details will become part of the fixture cost, and it is unethical for the designer to ask more than one manufacturer to perform services from this point forward.[2]

DATA/PHYSICAL SPECIFICATIONS

The head office of the California First Bank is located along San Francisco's prestigious "bankers' row," California Street. This twenty-one-story building is the hub of a financial network that includes 133 branch offices in California, and assets in excess of five billion dollars. The main banking hall is

almost 100-feet (30.48 m) square and 40 feet (12.19 m) high.

"The circle within a square" characterizes the Skidmore, Owings and Merrill approach to this space. The enormous hall has been softened and warmed with a concentration of curves that start with the radial tellers' bank, 38 feet in diameter, and continue to the radius ends on the cabinet files. At the axis, guarded by the ring of tellers, rises a polished steel tower. Its 14-foot height allows an elevator to noiselessly glide up from the cash vaults below (Figure C4-3).

ANALYSIS/PROGRAM

Client Image. The California First Bank is Japanese-owned and operated. Its parent company, The Bank of Tokyo, Ltd., wanted to establish a contrast to their traditional and conservative California Street neighbors by creating a contemporary and comfortable building. Although the bank was designed to seem airy and friendly, management also wanted the facility to project a sense of efficiency.

Client Vision. Young, urban professionals working in the financial district are more likely to bank here than senior citizens. However, Jules Horton, president of Horton/Lees, believes that designing for the anticipated users of a space will lead to lighting that doesn't accommodate change. He designs for the broadest range of possible uses and users.

Daylighting. A space such as this, with south and west glass walls, must be lighted to balance the apparent brightness outside with affective brightness deep inside the

FIGURE C4-1:   The Tellers' Line
The most spectacular of the concentric circles that unify this massive banking hall is the polished steel ring that houses the tellers' lighting fixtures. The alignment of its 18 sections must be flawless because any errors in fit will be seen in the altered reflections of its polished finish. (Photograph by Jaime Ardilles-Arce.)

FIGURE C4-2: The Fixture Ring

(a) Section: Because the ring is suspended on slender reflective rods, it fills the hall with an almost weightless presence. Locating the lights so closely above the tellers' deal plates, cash drawers, and other task surfaces is an extra benefit. Also, its continuous housing allows these task lights to be mounted at precisely the right angle to the task.

(b) Details: One of the most interesting and critical details is the ring's indetectable swivels that will permit it to sway without breaking loose in the event of an earthquake. (Illustration by Reiko Hayashi.)

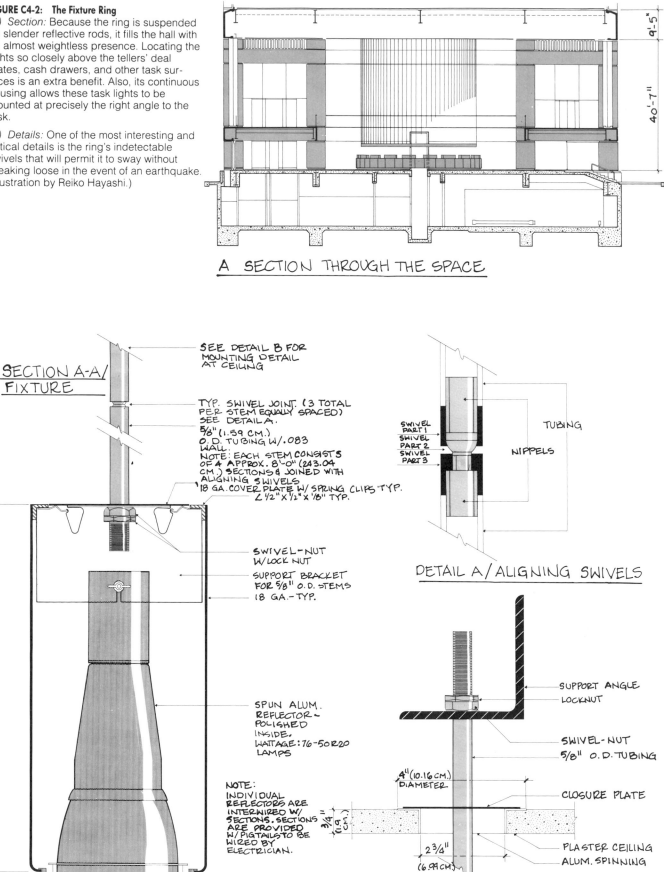

A SECTION THROUGH THE SPACE

SECTION A-A/ FIXTURE

SEE DETAIL B FOR MOUNTING DETAIL AT CEILING

TYP. SWIVEL JOINT. (3 TOTAL PER STEM EQUALLY SPACED) SEE DETAIL A.
5/8" (1.59 CM.) O.D. TUBING W/.083 WALL.
NOTE: EACH STEM CONSISTS OF 4 APPROX. 8'-0" (243.04 CM.) SECTIONS & JOINED WITH ALIGNING SWIVELS
18 GA. COVER PLATE W/ SPRING CLIPS TYP.
∠ 1/2" X 1/2" X 1/8" TYP.

SWIVEL-NUT W/LOCK NUT

SUPPORT BRACKET FOR 5/8" O.D. STEMS 18 GA.-TYP.

SPUN ALUM. REFLECTOR - POLISHED INSIDE. WATTAGE: 76-50 R20 LAMPS

NOTE: INDIVIDUAL REFLECTORS ARE INTERWIRED W/ SECTIONS. SECTIONS ARE PROVIDED W/ PIGTAILS TO BE WIRED BY ELECTRICIAN.

12" (30.48 CM.)

5 3/4" (14.6 CM.)

18 GA. COVER

DETAIL A/ ALIGNING SWIVELS

SWIVEL PART 1
SWIVEL PART 2
SWIVEL PART 3
TUBING
NIPPELS

DETAIL B/ MOUNTING @ CEILING

SUPPORT ANGLE
LOCKNUT
SWIVEL-NUT
5/8" O.D. TUBING
CLOSURE PLATE
PLASTER CEILING
ALUM. SPINNING

4" (10.16 CM.) DIAMETER
3/4" (1.9 CM.)
2 3/4" (6.99 CM.)

interior. This has been accomplished brilliantly by using HID uplights (Figure C4-4).

Colors. In addition to the tellers' Carrara marble counter, the polished steel elevator tower, and the other fine building materials typical of Skidmore, Owings and Merrill's work, a palette of clear, primarily warm colors emphasizes the bank's cordial and contemporary image. Rose, pink, carnelian, and a deep vivid blue are used here, but the vibrant Venetian red in the conference rooms and the carpeting dominates.

Activities. *Tasks:* The task lighting for tellers is very demanding. Sharp vision is required daily to identify forgeries and counterfeit bills, to tally dispensed and deposited cash. Good lighting is also needed at the checkwriting stands, at the officers' desks, and in the conference rooms.

Traffic: Most people will have no hesitation in orientating themselves, deciding on a direction of movement, or relating to the scale of the space. The unique configuration of the tellers' counter is seen by the patrons immediately upon entering the building.

LIGHTING CONCEPT/STRATEGY

For task lighting, the designers agreed on a large ring to suspend downlights over the tellers' counter. The officers on the platform benefit from recessed downlights that supplement the daylight from the west. To balance the brightness outside, and to provide ambient lighting to the space, powerful HID uplights reflect light from the ceiling into the midspace (Figure C4-5).

CONSTRAINTS

Schedule. Approximately two years elapsed between the commission of the lighting design and the completion of construction. This schedule was sufficient for both design and construction. Jules Horton comments that real professionals like the architects at Skidmore, Owings and Merrill do not delay decisions. Because of this prompt and attentive interaction between the two design organizations, the project stayed on its relatively tight schedule.

Construction. The size of this space, and the size of the project as a whole, make a large custom fixture an appropriate selection. The fixture helps to fill the space and bring it to a more human scale. But, because the custom fixture will be constructed off the job site by its manufacturer, the lengthy construction schedule will endanger only the exactness of the ceiling slots for the recessed downlights. If the specification is modified to allow for adjustable accent lights, then the lights can be manually focused to counteract any misunderstanding in the location of the light slots.

Code. In San Francisco, the building code has very explicit provisions on the proper support of fixtures during earthquakes.

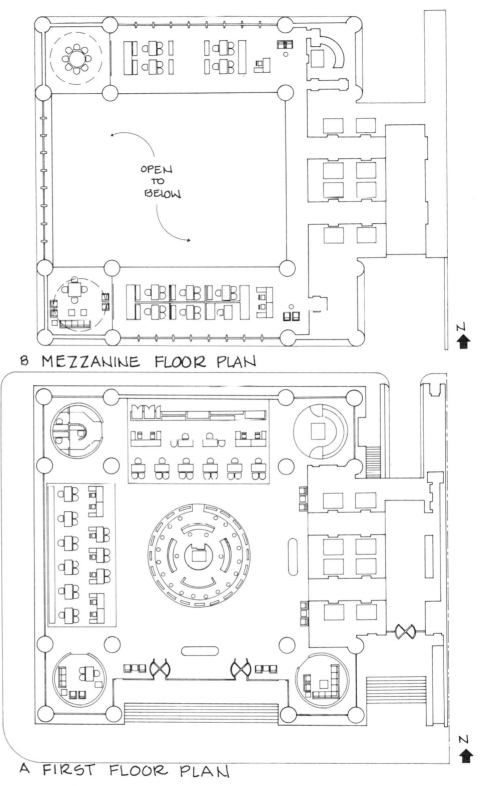

B MEZZANINE FLOOR PLAN

A FIRST FLOOR PLAN

FIGURE C4-3: Plan Views

(a) First Floor Plan View: Even if the curious eye did not move from left to right and top to bottom, the daylight at the west windows would still attract the eye to the cluster of desks where bank officers are readily available to the customer.

(b) Mezzanine Plan View: The great round drums over the conference rooms visually dominate the upper space seen in this plan view. They are lined in seven shades of Venetian red silk and enclosed with clear glass panels to create spaces with acoustical privacy but visual impact. (Illustration by Reiko Hayashi.)

The custom fixture may need to be inspected as many as three times:

1. As a design drawing that needs advisory approval

2. As a prototype fixture segment at the factory

3. Upon assembly at the site

Because San Francisco is a unionized city, IBEW labels on the custom fixture as well as UL labels are also necessary. In regard to energy codes, designer Horton states that the design documents were approved for permits before Title 24, California's energy code, became effective.

Budget. This client, like many financial institutions, was seeking a space that was substantial but not opulent. Similarly, Horton has again proven himself proficient at specifying fixtures whose performance is essential to the project, but which are not extravagantly priced.

Energy. The designers used HID, energy-conserving light sources where they could. Otherwise, because of the volume of the space, filling it with light necessitated a large budget for electrical operating costs.

Feasibility. Skidmore, Owings and Merrill and Horton/Lees Lighting Design have worked together on several monumental projects; their mutual respect and reliance contributes not only to the feasibility of any project they undertake together, but also to its probability of success.

TACTICS

Light Sources

Beam Angles. Because the lighting strategy revolves around using a suspended ring to bring task lighting close to the task surface, beam shape and distance are not important. In fact, if the 4-foot, 8-inch (17 m) distance from suspended fixture to task can be guaranteed, a 50-watt R-30 incandescent flood will be ample. At the other extreme, the distance from the recessed light slots to the officers' desks at the west wall is more than 38 feet (12 m). Only incandescent and HID light sources can travel such a distance and deliver a precise beam (Figures C4-4 and C4-6).

Control/Lamp Life. Because the recessed light sources are delivering their maximum candlepower as task lights, it is unlikely that dimmers would be beneficial. In the ring and beneath the mezzanine, however, the 50R30 downlights are close to their targets; so a specification that calls for these light sources to be the type that are designed for 130 volts will insure permanent dimming life. When they receive the normal current, only 110-120 volts, both this dimming and a significant extension of bulb life is the result. San Francisco's fog burns away by midmorning, so the lighting system also has

FIGURE C4-4: The Glasswalls
Although San Francisco's fog and the nearby buildings moderate the natural light, solar glass was augmented with a sunscreen. Once in place, this screen is hardly visible, and yet it cuts overhead glare for those seated next to the glass. (Photograph by Jaime Ardilles-Arce.)

FIGURE C4-5: Customer Service Desks
The warm white deluxe mercury uplights mounted into the top of the elevator tower are invisible to banking customers, yet they contribute immeasurably to the lighting of the space. Their light bridges the gap between the color of daylight and that of the incandescent light sources; they add ambient light to the space which softens the shadows and balances the task lighting. By drawing the visitor's eye to the ceiling, these uplights engender an appreciation of the volume of this enormous space. (Photograph by Jaime Ardilles-Arce.)

typical *daylighting circuits* that shut off the recessed fixtures at the west and south wall slots when the needed level of light has been supplied by nature. Because of the giant proportions of the banking hall, switching of many lighting circuits is accomplished with low-voltage relay switches for economy (see p. 58, Chapter Four).

Colors. The color of San Francisco's daylight is crystalline and cold because of the year-round moisture in the air, but the palette of the interior colors is warm. What to do? Designer Horton varied his selection of light sources. Where the light strikes the ceiling above, he has chosen a warm deluxe white mercury, the HID source with the longest life. This source acts as a color mediator between the warmth of the incandescent sources and the cool but sometimes bright daylight outside.

Invisible Light. Infrared radiation, or heat, is generally welcome in San Francisco, so light sources emitting infrared frequencies are helpful. Ultraviolet radiation would be a problem if it struck employees at high intensities continuously or faded fabrics. However, both the red conference room canopies and the tellers' areas are lighted with incandescent light sources that have no ultraviolet radiation. In fact, the only sources of ultraviolet light are the natural daylight and the mercury uplights. Moreover, the mercury beams strike a white painted ceiling where titanium dioxide in the paint reduces the ultraviolet frequencies before shedding the light to the people below.

Fixtures

Beam Shapes. *Glare:* Because of the high ceiling, direct glare is unlikely since the ceiling is not in the normal line of sight. The fixtures in the ring suspended 7 feet, 4 inches (223.50 cm) from the floor and those recessed in the 8-foot high ceilings under the mezzanine are not located at angles where their brightness would cause difficulties in vision either.

Task Angles: On the other hand, the fixtures suspended in the steel ring are perfectly placed to cast the highest quality of cross lighting to the tellers' tasks. In most cases, two fixtures flank each opening in the tellers' counter.

Mounting. Three mountings are unusual in this project: the uplights in the elevator tower, the light slots in the ceiling, and the suspended ring (Figure C4-7).

Costs. The Edison Price fixtures that have been specified for the light slots are costly but necessary. Few manufacturers command the optical knowledge or manufacturing precision to deliver an accent light that will focus at 38 feet. The Horton office stresses, however, that other fixtures on this project offer off-the-shelf availability and standard pricing—except for the custom ring.

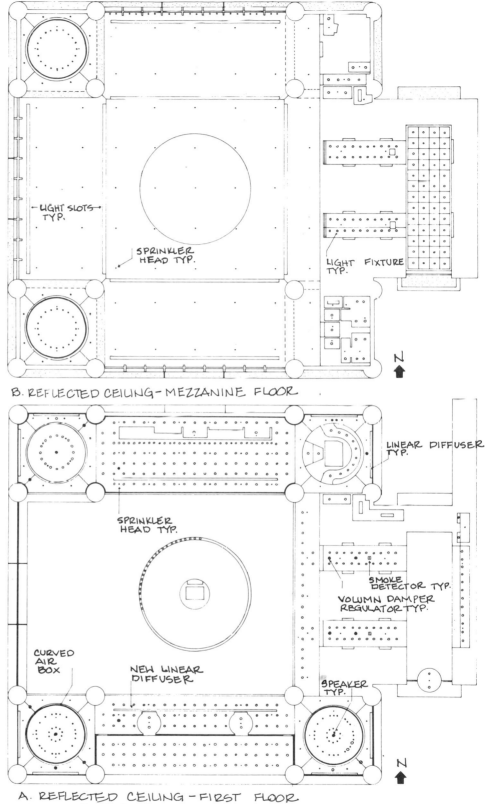

FIGURE C4-6: Reflected Ceiling Plans

(a) First Floor: Each downlight in the first floor ceiling houses only a 50-watt bulb.

(b) Mezzanine: The ability to have clean purposeful light slots at the points at which each slender fixture support rod soars through the air with no visible attachments was a very simple detail of special concern to the designers at Skidmore, Owings and Merrill. (Illustration by Reiko Hayashi.)

Appearance. The polished steel ring is as critical to the designed appearance of this space as the light it casts. Both architects and lighting designer speak of the cooperation that led to this key concept. The fixture fills the spatial volume, reinforces the "circle in the square" theme, echoes the polished finish of the elevator tower, and still manages to cross light the tasks.

Maintenance. This outstanding fixture is also easy to maintain because it is practically within reach from the floor. Is it as easy to change the bulbs of the adjustable accent lights 38 feet away? It is. Theatrical catwalks in the plenum area above the ceiling make these fixtures easily accessible too (Figure C4-7a).

Safety. One of the greatest challenges in the design and manufacture of a suspended fixture of this size and weight is earthquake safety. Where subways or earthquakes rock the streets, special fixture hangers are required that will allow suspended fixtures to roll with the movement, but not shift or jounce hard enough to disconnect themselves or swing out of control. Devising the special hangers for this custom fixture required ingenuity and perseverance. But still more talent was required to convince the inspector that the stresses had been properly calculated for an object of this weight and span.

CONCLUDING THOUGHTS

The lighting of the California First Bank is thoughtful, thorough, and professional. But the originality of the design is due to the circular counter, the elevator tower, and the polished steel fixture ring. This last element is a perfect illustration of the best kind of cooperation among the architect, engineer, lighting designer, and fixture manufacturer. Although the use of large scale custom fixtures requires extra time and care, they lend a special distinction to an interior, as this case study demonstrates so well.

CHAPTER NOTES

[1]Randolph Borden, personal telephone interview, July 1985.

[2]Randolph Borden, same interview.

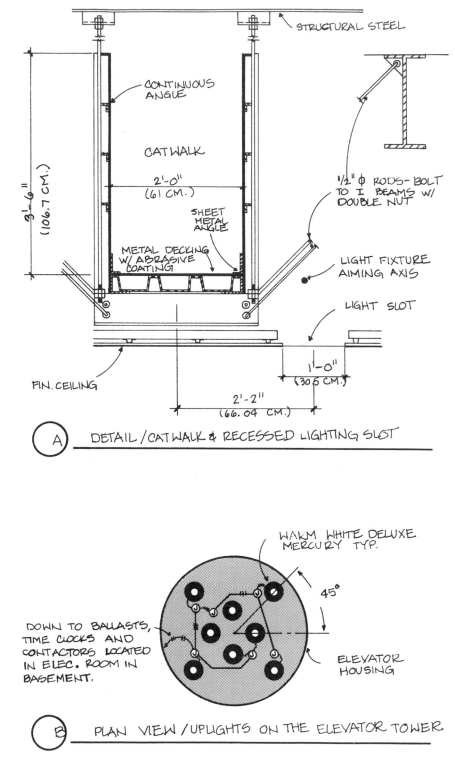

A DETAIL/CATWALK & RECESSED LIGHTING SLOT

B PLAN VIEW/UPLIGHTS ON THE ELEVATOR TOWER

FIGURE C4-7: Unusual Fixture Mountings
(a) Recessed Lighting Slots: Although catwalks are seldom used, they must securely hold a person's weight without damaging the ceiling below.

(b) Uplights on the Elevator Tower: Because of patterns of electrical interference that are compounded by the presence of the elevator machinery below, the ballasts' clock control and low-voltage switching contactors are all located some distance away from the mercury uplight fixtures they govern.

(c) Custom Fixture Ring/Plan View: This segment of the fixture ring has removable covers to provide access when necessary. (Illustration by Reiko Hayashi.)

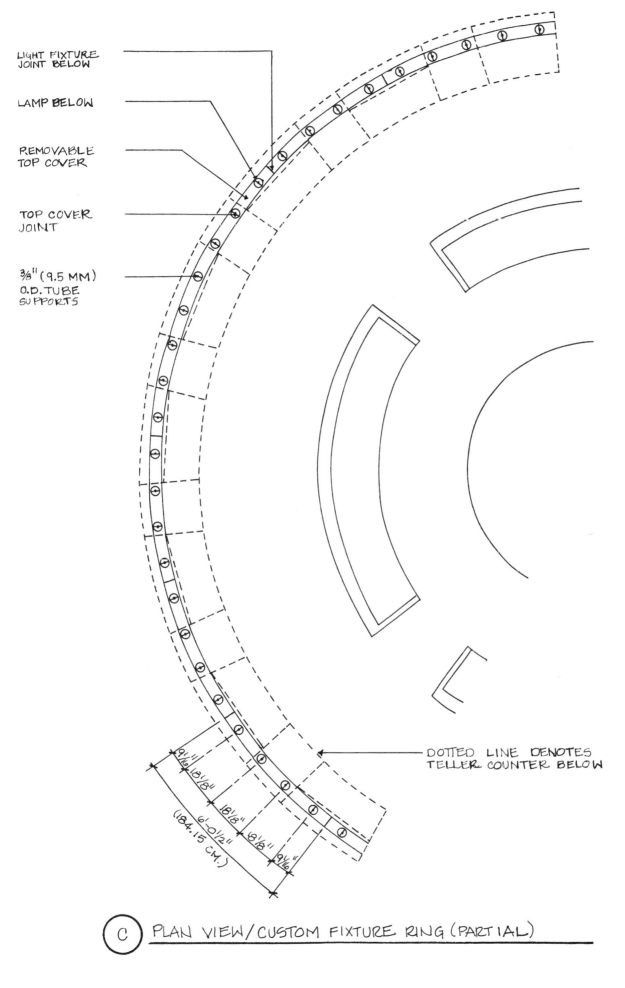

LIGHT FIXTURE
JOINT BELOW

LAMP BELOW

REMOVABLE
TOP COVER

TOP COVER
JOINT

3/8" (9.5 MM)
O.D. TUBE
SUPPORTS

DOTTED LINE DENOTES
TELLER COUNTER BELOW

9/16"

18 1/8"

18 1/8"

9 1/2"

9 1/4"

6'-0 1/2"
(184.15 CM.)

9/16"

C   PLAN VIEW/CUSTOM FIXTURE RING (PARTIAL)

Case Study Five

DAYLIGHTING AN OPEN OFFICE

LOCKHEED MISSILES AND SPACE COMPANY

ARCHITECTURE: Leo A. Daly Planning/Architecture/Engineering

Lee S. Windheim, AIA

Robert J. Riegel, AIA

Kyle V. Davy, AIA

INTERIOR DESIGN: Lockheed project design team

LIGHTING DESIGN: Leo A. Daly Architecture

Michael D. Shanus, MIES

This office building is a monument to creative lighting design. Deep, penetrating daylighting is encouraged by the design of the building which incorporates skylights, interior and exterior light shelves, and two atria. Coupled with a judicial use of fluorescents for task lighting and to even out light levels, the lighting design for this building attests to the energy savings that can be realized with daylighting.

DATA/PHYSICAL SPECIFICATIONS

Building 157 at Lockheed Missiles and Space Company in Sunnyvale, California supports the activities of 3,000 engineers and technicians.

ANALYSIS/PROGRAM

Client Image. This space-age employer competes with the other high-technology corporations in Silicon Valley for the best engineers and technicians. As a result, this building's state-of-the-art working environment and its creature comforts must work to attract prospective employees (Figure C5-1).

Client Vision. Lockheed employees are both young and old and their vision requirements vary.

Daylighting. Steven Selkowitz, Ph.D., states, "The use of deep daylighting techniques can dramatically reduce electrical energy use in large office buildings. Successful daylighting design, however, requires faithful commitment and a firm understanding of climate, site, orientation, building configuration, and an overriding concern for the human activity taking place within the building envelope."[1] (Figure C5-2).

Sunnyvale has mild temperatures typical of California's Bay Area so heat gains and losses are not severe. The building's location also enables its designers to benefit from the most advanced daylighting research, funded by the Pacific Gas and Electric Company and the Lawrence Berkeley Laboratories of the University of California. "Without their interest and guidance, the project wouldn't have been possible," says the Daly office.[2] (Figure C5-3).

Color. Against the endless expanses of matte white so typical of daylighted spaces, cool greens are a vibrant contrast. Workstations in a practical almond color and light oak finish look well juxtaposed to the live plantings of ficus benjamina and cascading ivy.

Activities. Since Silicon Valley is the native habitat of the American computer, it is not surprising that every workstation could house a terminal. Although the VDT user at Lockheed is often young, glare, visual accommodation, and veiling reflections are problems that can impede productivity and damage health. The user is involved with as many as five visual tasks. He/she may need to see: the monitor, the keyboard, hardcopy source materials, hardcopy output, and additional reference sources. Severe eyestrain often results from visually switching between the high visual contrasts of these tasks—especially if they are improperly positioned and/or poorly illuminated (Figure C5-4).

Mood. The mood is understated but very sharp and upbeat.

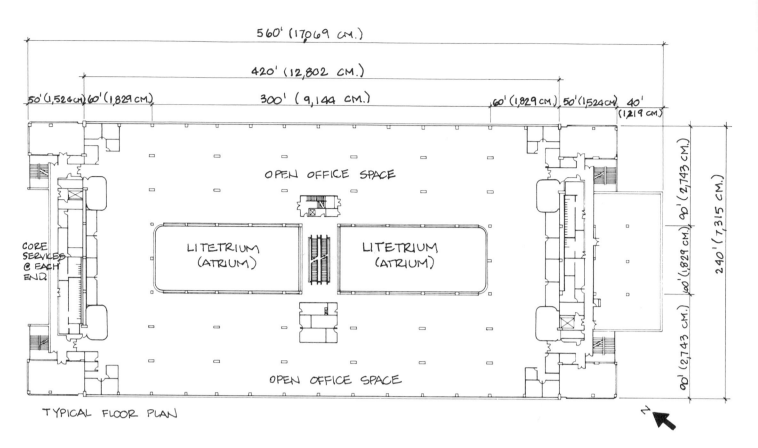

TYPICAL FLOOR PLAN

FIGURE C5-2: Typical Floor Plan
(Above) To permit bilateral daylighting of the open office plan, glass walls face north and south. Heat gains and direct sun penetration are minimized by blocking east and west exposures with banks of service facilities. (Illustration by Reiko Hayashi.)

FIGURE C5-3: Cross Section/Lockheed Building 157
(Below) The building's configuration is shown in this cross section. The atrium parallels the windows to admit daylight while sloped ceilings help to integrate their footcandles gradually into the mid-space. The skylights' sloped glass panels face south to diffuse direct sunlight while vertical panels of clear glass face north to admit a consistently high quality of skylight. (Illustration by Reiko Hayashi.)

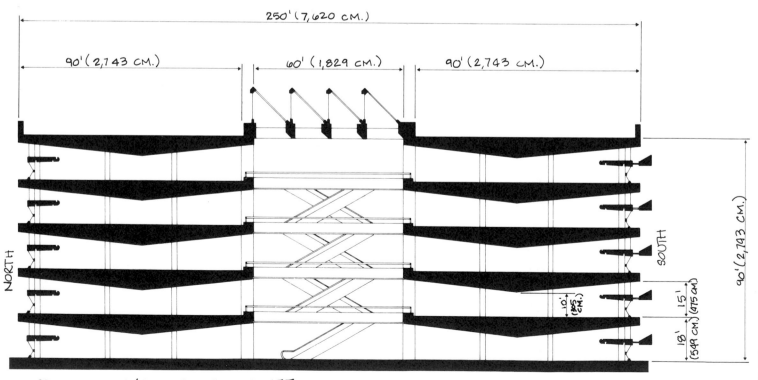

CROSS SECTION / LOCKHEED BUILDING 157

COMPOSITION/STRATEGY

The goal of the design concept was to optimize the energy efficiency of the building and improve the effectiveness of the work environment. The substitution of daylighting for electrical lighting was the primary strategy for accomplishing these ends. But daylighting is like fire, says Shanus, "it is extremely beneficial when used correctly; but uncontrolled, it can be disastrous."[3] Inevitably, daylight is accompanied by heat and glare.

Glare. The three-pronged attack on glare used here attempts to achieve a uniform distribution of 30 to 35 footcandles throughout the space: adjustable window coverings, exterior shading devices, and tinted glazing reduce perimeter light levels at the windows. Meanwhile, rows of fluorescent fixtures controlled by photocells do the fine tuning to even out the midspace light levels (Figure C5-5). Task lights within the workstations boost light levels for particular tasks when needed.

Heat. The designers anticipated the increase in solar heat, and included such heat removal features as exhaust vents at the top of the skylight to create a modified chimney effect in the atrium, return air vents on the high side of the sloped ceiling and above the light shelves, and "solar cool" glass below the light shelves (Figure C5-6).

CONSTRAINTS

Code. Due to the expanses of glass and lack of roof and wall insulation, Lockheed Building 157 did not conform to California's pre-

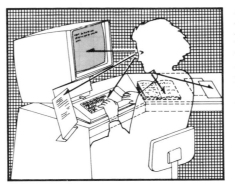

FIGURE C5-4: Five Specific VDT Seeing Tasks
(Above) Several objects in adjacent locations require the intermittent concentration of the VDT operator. Because each of the objects has a different brightness, a different shininess, and is at a slightly different distance from the operator, eyestrain can be acute. In fact, it can be so acute that some ergonomic studies (National Institute for Occupational Safety and Health, *Working with Video Display Terminals: A Preliminary Health Risk Evaluation*, Cincinnati, 1980) recommend mandatory rest periods for VDT operators of 15 minutes in each two-hour work period. (Illustration by Reiko Hayashi.)

FIGURE C5-5: Lighting Strategy Cross Section
(Below) This cross section shows how a continual light level of 30 footcandles on the desks' surfaces is produced by photocells. They face downward to read the level of light available on the desk tops and they dim the fluorescents, so these fluorescents only supplement the daylighting. Only by keeping electric lighting turned down or off is energy saved. (Illustration by Reiko Hayashi.)

scriptive energy code, Title 24. However, the state offers an alternative approach known as the *energy budget*. This permits energy saved in one area to be expended in another as long as the budget allowance is not exceeded overall. California enforces their energy code by refusing building permits at the local level until energy calculations are approved. This "energy budget" was the option used by the Lockheed building team.

Life Safety. Because the 600,000 square-foot (5573 sq.m) building has 5 stories, life safety issues are a paramount concern. These were effectively addressed by the application of full fire sprinkling, and the use of exterior staircases.

Energy. Even in mild climates, over 50 percent of the total energy consumed by an office building may be used by the lighting. This estimate does not include the quantity of additional energy needed to remove the heat created by the lighting system. Preliminary forecasts—both graphic (Figure C5-7) and computerized (DOE 2.1a)—promised a potential savings of 70 percent of the electricity normally needed for ambient lighting if daylighting were used. Title 24 allows 2 watts-per-square-foot (2W/929.00 sq.cm); computer projections promised .92 watts-per-square-foot (approximately .01W/sq.cm)—less than half the allowance.

Budget. Using the DOE 2.1a software, the building's annual energy savings were estimated at 21,000 BTU per-square-foot. (This savings was later verified by monitor-

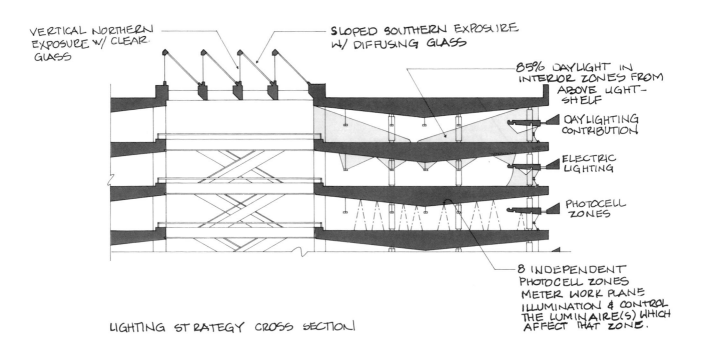

VERTICAL NORTHERN EXPOSURE W/ CLEAR GLASS

SLOPED SOUTHERN EXPOSURE W/ DIFFUSING GLASS

85% DAYLIGHT IN INTERIOR ZONES FROM ABOVE LIGHT-SHELF

DAYLIGHTING CONTRIBUTION

ELECTRIC LIGHTING

PHOTOCELL ZONES

8 INDEPENDENT PHOTOCELL ZONES METER WORK PLANE ILLUMINATION & CONTROL THE LUMINAIRE(S) WHICH AFFECT THAT ZONE.

LIGHTING STRATEGY CROSS SECTION

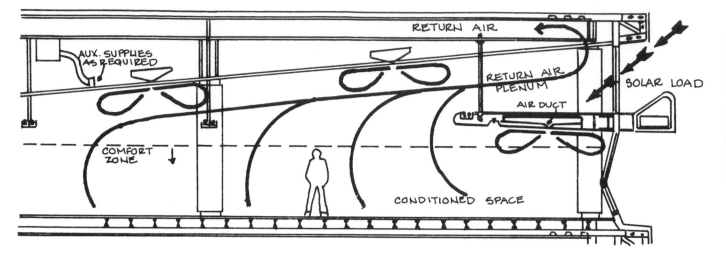

FIGURE C5-6:   HVAC Cross Section
A large portion of the solar heat gain dissipating above the light shelves is shown here. The designers' approach, therefore, was to treat these spaces as a part of the pathway for air return. By allowing these locations to heat to as much as 95 degrees F (35 degrees C), a 20-percent savings in the volume of supply air was achieved as compared to the volume that would have been required to maintian these overshelf areas at the temperature of the occupied zone. (Illustration by Reiko Hayashi.)

FIGURE C5-7:   Daylight Prediction Graph
A sequence of graphic aides, such as this one, were used to project the daylight available inside Building 157 The curves represented all seasons of the year as well as all weather conditions. After the control schemes are developed, sensor zones are determined and the energy savings are predicted. Energy savings result from the integration of daylighting with fluorescent lighting to provide 30-35 footcandles of ambient illumination. (Illustration by Reiko Hayashi.)

SUPPLEMENTAL LIGHTING CONTROL

DIMMING

STAGED

ON/OFF

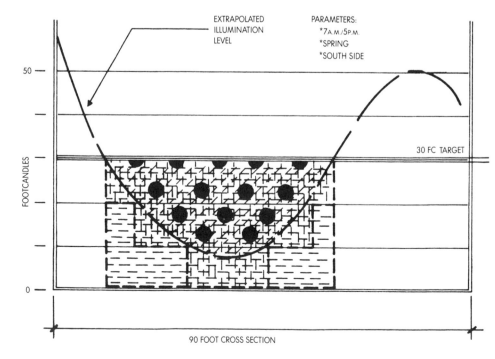

ing the completed building.) Using this input, the payback period on the additional cost of light shelves, sloped ceilings, and interactive fluorescent dimming was calculated at eight years. It is hoped that another 5 to 15 percent savings will accrue through the increased productivity of the building's high-tech employees.

Schedule. Although the facility is not for speculation or for commercial lease, the schedule for design and construction is as stringent as any. This tends to be the case even when corporations build facilities for their own occupancy.

Feasibility. Although first costs of lighting this building are high, Lockheed knows that a state-of-the-art structure projects a winning image. This quality work space helps to attract and keep quality employees.

TACTICS

Light Sources

Beam Angles. *Daylight:* The optical train of the daylighting is made up of the top surface of the light shelf with its reflective matte white finish and the matte white sloped ceilings. Together they act as one enormous fixture to deliver daylight to the midspace.

Electric Light: Fluorescent tubes are used in a direct/indirect fixture overhead as well as for task light at the workstations.

Lamp Life. Daylight is forever; fluorescents last for 20,000 hours. Because the fluorescent lights supplement lighting requirements only (1) when daylighting is insufficient and (2) when the space is occupied, they should last many years. This is an excellent illustration of the use of controls to save energy and extend lamp life.

Color. The color of daylight in the bay area is on the cool side because of the constant moisture in the atmosphere. To blend with the daylight, cool white fluorescent tubes were selected for the building's ambient lighting. The cool colors in the designers' palette are more vibrant because of the coolness of these light sources. To add additional warmth and sparkle in the workstations, warm white fluorescent tubes are used in the task lighting fixtures.

Invisible Effects. The heat load calculation includes the infrared heat anticipated from the fluorescent tubes and fluorescent ballasts as well as that from electronic equipment used in the space. In open offices, the increased productivity of smart electronics is equal to great increases in wires and cables and their accompanying heat.

The invisible ultraviolet wavelengths of daylight are sufficiently filtered and absorbed so that little fading damage could occur: indirect daylight admitted by the clear glass above the light shelves is reflected several times from matte white finishes containing titanium dioxide which absorbs the ultraviolet; direct daylight admitted below the light shelf is filtered by tinted solar glazing.

Fixtures

Beam Shape. The distribution of light from fluorescent tubes can be radically and efficiently altered. In the suspended system here, the uplight tubes can benefit from low-brightness spread-lenses that disperse the light more widely across the ceiling. In both the suspended system and the system of fluorescent task fixtures, batwing refracting lenses distribute light at the best angles for achieving visual contrasts. In both instances, horizontal angles of light dispersion are avoided because VDT screens will reflect them as glare.

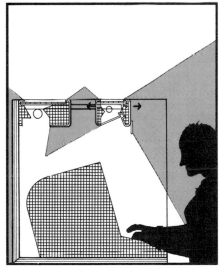

FIGURE C5-8: Lighting the VDT Station
The front fixture, mounted on drawer glides, is fitted with an adjustable baffle to cut off light that would otherwise reflect from the operator's clothes onto the screen. The permanently affixed rear fixture brightens the workstation's background behind the screen so that the brightness contrast is no higher than 3:1 from white VDT screen to light-colored background panel. (Illustration by Reiko Hayashi, inspired by the thoughts of Sylvan R. Shemitz, patent pending by Sylvan R. Shemitz, West Haven, Connecticut.)

Mounting. Because the daylighting concept uses the sloped ceiling as a reflector, it is logical that fluorescent uplights be mounted on stem suspension in order to continue the inboard penetration of indirect lighting. At Lockheed the mounting location of undercabinet fluorescent task lights is not unusual. For more problematic spaces were VDT locations are fixed one designer suggests a system of dual fluorescents (Figure C5-8).

Costs. *Equipment:* The entire building could be considered an expensive daylight fixture. The suspended fluorescents are carefully lensed, and therefore are also somewhat expensive. The workstations have built-in task lights, also carefully lensed but their costs are not extraordinary. The lighting controls are expensive, and in some cases, experimental, but Lockheed's experience with this system has proven that they are effective.

Installation: None of the equipment is unusually difficult or expensive to install. Installing suspended fixtures can be difficult because they must be leveled; but the workstations are portable and are easily plugged in. Wire management is handled within the furniture.

Owning/Operating: The entire lighting system, and in fact the entire building, has been analyzed for a payback period of eight years. Although Lockheed Building 157 is a technological landmark, it is also an aggressive investment characteristic of the leadership of Lockheed.

Appearance. The building looks like the efficient no-nonsense think tank that it is. The adage, "form follows function," could not be more evident than it is in this paragon of daylighting technology.

CONCLUDING THOUGHTS

By effectively controlling the undesirable by-products of daylighting—heat and glare—the designers created a system that was dramatic and cost-effective. The intelligent use of fluorescent fixtures to light tasks and even out light levels also proved to be economical.

CHAPTER NOTES

[1]Pilar Viladas, "Through a Glass Brightly," *Progressive Architecture* 11 (1981): 138.

[2]Michael D. Shanus *et al.,* "Going Beyond the Perimeter with Daylight," *Lighting Design and Application* March 1984: 40.

[3]Shanus *et al.* 40.

Case Study Six

ENHANCING MERCHANDISE

THE BOUTIQUE ICE

INTERIOR ARCHITECTURE: L.A. Design
Phillip Schwartz, IBD, designer

LIGHTING DESIGN: Luminae Lighting Consultants
Richard Harms, designer

The primary function of any retail space is to sell merchandise. Current research has shown that more than 80 percent of all retail sales are made on impulse; so the designer should provide an ambient light level that allows line-of-sight visibility of merchandise throughout. At the same time, the ambient light should not be so intense that it washes out the brightness accents on special merchandise displays.

DATA/PHYSICAL SPECIFICATIONS
ICE is a boutique that specializes in Italian fashions for women and is located within the Beverly Center; an upscale shopping mall, in Beverly Hills, California.

ICE is located on the top floor, and its ceilings rise to 13 feet. Store frontage measures 30 feet with one 2-foot column interrupting its continuity (Figure C6-1). On the 3,000-square-foot (259 sq. m) sales floor, a variety of merchandise is displayed on free-standing racks in the midspace and on waterfall racks attached to soffited walls. There are dressing rooms in the center section of the space and seating in the rear.

ANALYSIS/PROGRAM
Client Image. The experienced owners of this boutique feel that it should project a very avant-garde image—one that is racier and younger than their other two properties in the same shopping complex.

Client Vision. This store sells the latest fashions, so its typical customer is between fifteen and forty years of age. Therefore, the designers can presume that such young customers will have good eyesight.

Daylighting. The top floor of the mall is skylighted. Although no sunlight penetrates to the interior of the store, seasonally, at very specific times of day, the sunlight brightens the walls of the malls' skywells to glare levels. This could be a potential problem if such glare can be seen from within the store. However, a cross-section sketch of sun angles and reflections seen from

within the store reassures the designers that such glare will not be a problem and, therefore, tinted glass will not be needed to control it (Figure C6-2).

Color. In retail situations, walls, ceiling, and floor finishes are simply backgrounds, or foils, for the merchandise, so the palette is kept neutral. An interesting and lustrous pattern of blue-gray tile with a contrasting white grout directs visual attention downward and guides the eye into the interior depths (see Color Plate 12).

Activities. *Tasks:* The primary task for this space is to sell merchandise. Lighting must attract customers and display the merchandise to its best advantage.

Traffic: In retail stores, the normal traffic objective is to draw customers as deeply into the space as possible. This pattern of movement maximizes their opportunity to purchase.

Mood. Clearly, the mood for this boutique should be upbeat and nontraditional. Hints of postmodern entablature set this tone.

COMPOSITION/STRATEGY
For most retail spaces, a lighting strategy should establish the highest and most interesting brightnesses in their depths. In this way, passing customers are drawn into such spaces by appealing to their subconscious curiosity. On the conscious level, customers see bursts of *highlighting* throughout the space created by accent lights which are focused on featured merchandise (Figure C6-3).

Comfortable but controlled *downlighting* in the midspace does the following:

Enables the floor-standing displays to be moved anywhere

Ensures impulse purchase opportunities because all merchandise is visible

Blends the accent brightnesses into a unified visual whole

FIGURE C6-1:   ICE
This boutique, specializing in Italian fashions for women, is located in the Beverly Center, a shopping mall in Beverly Hills, California. (Store Design by Philip Schwartz.)

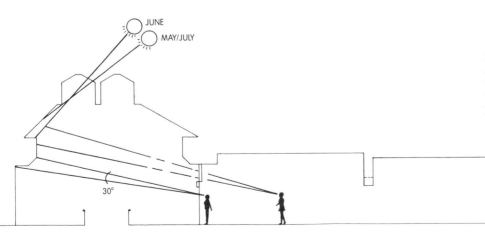

FIGURE C6-2:   Sight Line Sketch
A check of the glare angles shows that tinted glass will not be needed. Because of the opaque fascia, even unusually high visual angles will not bring the bright sidewalls of the skywell into view. (Illustration by Reiko Hayashi.)

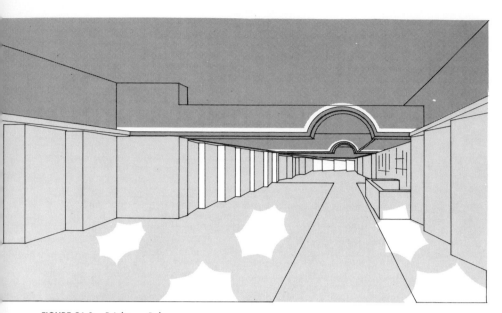

FIGURE C6-3: Brightness Balances
A parade of brightnesses is intended to lead the eye into the depths of the boutique. At the same time, an overall level of general illumination is interspersed by bursts of brightness on the merchandise, so that impulse buying can flourish. (Illustration by Reiko Hayashi.)

All the lighting for ICE must be in a cool vein, but the coolness must not overpower the colors of the neutral backgrounds or the merchandise.

Blue neon tubing is used to emphasize the three-dimensional sculpting of this post-modern interior and to enlarge the space. The Flynn research suggests that downlighting plus diffuse overhead lighting and peripheral wall lighting result in visual impressions of spaciousness.

CONSTRAINTS

Code. Designs for a commercial space, such as this, on the top floor of a seven-story shopping complex, should meet building and safety codes in a straightforward and un-complicated manner. Unusual lighting tactics and fixtures without UL labels will be questioned since such conspicuous and potentially hazardous facilities are always inspected thoroughly.

Life Safety. In California, both lighted exit signs and lights that will illuminate at least two pathways to safety are required by

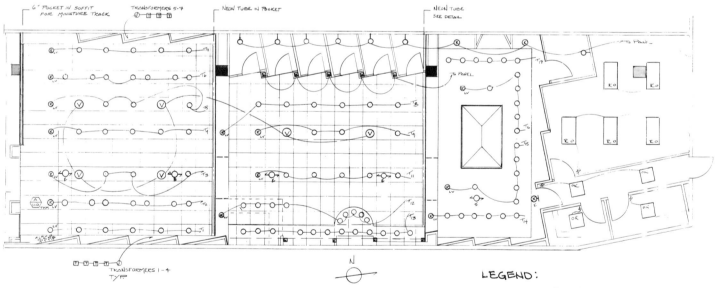

FIGURE C6-4: The Lighting Plan
The fixtures are strategically placed to create brightness on the merchandise. For this reason, the MR-16 accent fixtures are patterned throughout the space. The metal halide downlights are widely spaced because the ambient light is not to overpower the accentuated displays. Special fluorescents are mounted vertically at the mirrored fitting room doors; they have been selected in cool white deluxe to blend with the cool ambience of the space without sacrificing too greatly the warmth of skin tones. A row of adjustable MR-16 accent lights augments the illumination cast by the artificial skylight, producing the brightness needed to attract customers into the depths of the store. Window displays at the front of the store are lighted from the pocket-encased track. Neon tubing over the arches adds a note of architectural reinforcement and upbeat fun. (Illustration by Richard Harms.)

LEGEND:

- RECESSED INCANDESCENT
- RECESSED METAL HALIDE VAPOR
- WALL-BRACKETED INCANDESCENT
- WALL-BRACKETED EMERGENCY EXIT
- SURFACE-MOUNTED EMERGENCY EGRESS LIGHT
- MINIATURE TRACK
- NEON TUBING
- VERTICALLY MOUNTED FLUORESCENT
- RECESSED FLUORESCENT
- RECESSED LOW VOLTAGE
- TRANSFORMER
- JUNCTION BOX
- WALL SWITCH

code. Because customers are on the top floor of an unfamiliar building, this type of safe egress routing can save lives in a fire or earthquake.

Energy. Title 24 limits the wattage that may be committed to lighting a space in California. A retail space, however, may exceed the usual allotment of two watts-per-square-foot because added wattage is allowed for merchandise displays. The California Energy Commission recognizes the commercial need for additional brightness.

Budget. Fashion retailers are averse to high initial lighting costs. Procedures like life-cycle costing, which spread and justify costs over time, are wasted on these clients because their financial success is measured in periods of one year—or even one season—not in ten-year payback periods.

Schedule. This particular project is governed by an opening date only ninety days in advance of the working drawings. While not impossible, no foreseeable delays can be accommodated.

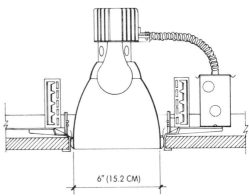

FIGURE C6-5: Fixture Angles
The angle at which the light beam strikes the merchandise is critical. An open A lamp downlight in the soffit directly overhead provides a soft edged, wide distribution of light and very high electrical efficiency. This beam spread will flatter certain kinds of vertically displayed merchandise by emphasizing its texture. Kurt Versen and Indy manufacture a wide range of square downlights that look well in such soffits, but for a California store with a tight schedule, the round Lightolier fixture, shown here, is more quickly available. However, a wider angle would be preferable for merchandise projecting from the wall on waterfall hangers. MR-16 fixtures are located here so as to broadcast a more intense, hard edged beam diagonally across the waterfall displays. Such an angle and beam emphasize colors and lend sparkle and luster to fabrics. (Store Design by Philip Schwartz; Illustration by Reiko Hayashi.)

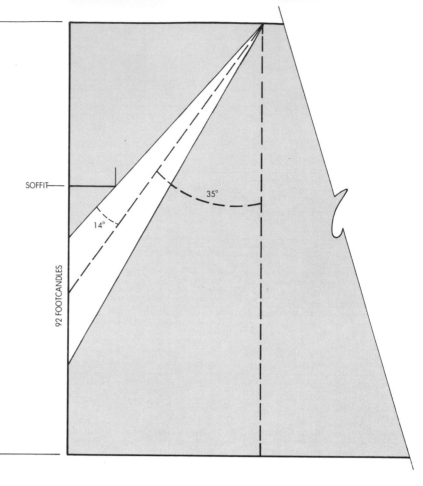

Feasibility. The schedule and budget limitations are severe, but not prohibitive (Figure C6-4).

TACTICS

Light Sources

Beam Angles. Because the ceiling's height is 13 feet, high-intensity discharge (HID) light sources offer a natural choice to provide uniform ambient light. Highlighting is provided by low-voltage lamps with their narrow, well defined beams.

Fluorescents are a better choice for the seating area in the rear, however, because they won't cast harsh, unattractive shadows over the customers seated there. For the same reason, fluorescent tubes are preferred for the mirrored fitting rooms.

Lamp Life. The client here is opposed to the high maintenance costs for replacing bulbs, so lamps with a long life like HID and fluorescents are the best choices. The low-voltage lamp bulbs will need some technical adjustment to extend their life.

Lamp Colors. In order to enhance the slightly cool look of the interior of ICE, lamps with a slightly cool color rendering are the most suitable. Metal halide lamps are the coolest

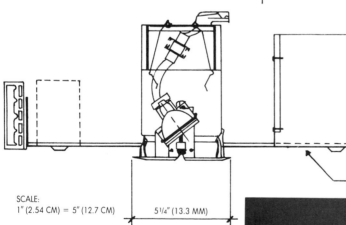

LAMP:
MR-16 (EXT)
50 WATTS
BEAM SPREAD: 14°
(2'-4" at 10'-0" [71.1 CM at 304.8 CM] THROW DISTANCE)

TRANSFORMER

SCALE:
1" (2.54 CM) = 5" (12.7 CM)   5¼" (13.3 MM)

FIGURE C6-6: Fixture Selections
These miniature round fixtures, using energy-conserving, high-intensity, low-voltage MR-16 bulbs, provide a controlled beam of exceptional brilliance. They adjust to 40 degrees off vertical with a 358 degree rotation and all adjustments may be made with a common Phillips screwdriver from below. The Capri unit was chosen because still further economies can be gained by linking several fixtures to a single transformer; Capri's outboard location for its transformers makes fixture ganging easy. (Store Design by Philip Schwartz; Illustration by Reiko Hayashi.)

of the three available HID sources. In incandescents, krypton and MR-16 lamp bulbs have a slightly cool cast as well. Among the fluorescents, there are many cool bulbs to choose from.

Invisible Effects. Fading problems are unlikely in this very fashionable shopping complex, because in order to pay the high rentals, shops such as ICE have to move merchandise very quickly, allowing little time for fading. Therefore, light sources that have a moderate amount of ultraviolet output, and therefore the potential for fading, can still be considered.

Fixtures

Beam Shape. To create the downlighting in the midspace, a fixture that has a broad beam distribution will be the most energy- and cost-effective. Fixtures such as open, silver cone downlights are the logical choices. The silver of the cones' reflectors keeps the color of the light cool. For the narrow beams to project highlights, adjustable low voltage fixtures such as those originated by the Capri Company can be used (Figure C6-5).

Mounting. Although the fixtures will need to be recessed in order to preserve the clean, modern expression of the interior design, glare will not be a problem because large expanses of the ceiling plane need not fall within the line of sight. This, however, would not be true without the division of the ceiling into thirds by the use of stylized fascia.

Costs. *Equipment:* Because of the small number of fixtures needed, HID downlights cost the least initially and also have the lowest operating costs. However, the fluorescents are less powerful and more diffuse, so quite a few fixtures are needed. The low-voltage accent lights have been grouped to common transformers to reduce first costs, but are still the most expensive fixture in this project (Figure C6-6).

Owning/Operating: The electrical cost is controlled by the limitations of watts-per-square-foot imposed by California's energy code. Maintenance costs should be low because the low-voltage accent bulbs are dimmed and the other light sources are naturally long-lived. The low-voltage lights should not be used as night lights, however, no matter how appealing the merchandise looks. Too many burnouts will occur.

Appearance. For this project, most fixtures are either recessed or structurally built in. Even the blue neon tubing is somewhat hidden away (Figure C6-7).

CONCLUDING THOUGHTS
As obvious as this lighting strategy seems, it is still experimental. As the metal halide light source's color spectrum improves, the combination of metal halide HIDs with dichroic low-voltage MR-16s will become more common.

FIGURE C6-7: Designing to Sell
In Beverly Hills, the firm of L. A. Design unveils its newest look with the boutique, ICE—a cool setting for hot fashions. (Store Design by Philip Schwartz.)

DISPLAYING FOR POSTERITY

Case Study Seven

THE VATICAN PAVILION OF THE LOUISIANA WORLD EXPOSITION

ARCHITECTURE: Ronald B. Blitch, AIA

CURATOR: Most Reverend Val A. McInnes, O.P. PH.D.

DIRECTOR OF EXHIBIT DESIGN: Stuart Silver Associates
Clifford LaFontaine, designer

LIGHTING DESIGN: Terry/Chassman Associates
LeMar Terry, designer

Museum artifacts are not the only objects that can be damaged by light (Color Plate 5). Common household items like textiles, leather, feathers, paintings (especially watercolors) are all susceptible. On the other hand, jewelry, metals, and minerals as well as substances like ceramics, enamels, glass, and stone are practically impervious to light.

Whenever light touches an object, some damage occurs—from visible and invisible light. To minimize this *photodegradation* (the damage from light), the designer needs to know the fundamental factors that cause it. These include:

1. The intensity of the light

2. The duration of the exposure

3. The spectral or color characteristics of the light

4. The absorptive, or porous, characteristics of the affected material

Also, three environmental influences can speed the photochemical damage caused by light: high humidity, high temperature, and active atmospheric gases like oxygen and ozone. In a general way, the response of the designer should always be to minimize the effect of these factors on his/her clients' valued objects.[1] Some of the preventive lighting techniques employed by the museum designer and conservator can also be utilized in residential spaces.

DATA/PHYSICAL SPECIFICATIONS

This 15,000 square foot exhibit was housed in the Vatican Pavilion at the Louisiana World Exposition and contained almost 200 sacred artifacts imported from the collections of the Roman See. The pavilion was designed and constructed as a temporary home expressly for the exhibit.

The galleries in the Vatican Pavilion vary in size and in ceiling height. There are also a number of room configurations—from round to trapezoidal—to capture the interest of the visitor. Gallery One even forms a cross in plan view. Another gallery, decorated with freestanding divider/planters, opens along its length to an outdoor atrium enclosing a sculpture and fountain. Still another mimics the catacombs of ancient Rome (Figure C7-1).

ANALYSIS/PROGRAM

Client Image. A few years ago, *La Pietà* by Michelangelo was exhibited in another setting outside the Vatican—one that the press criticized as being tasteless and contrived. Because of this, the Roman Catholic Church was anxious to convey an atmosphere of conservative dignity and artistic purity for this next exhibit.

Client Vision. Representatives of the Most Reverend Phillip M. Hannon, Archbishop of New Orleans and president of the New Orleans Vatican Pavilion, informed the designers that many of those visiting the exhibition would be older and perhaps infirm. Certainly during the previews, visiting groups showed that this was indeed the case. The designers therefore planned wide aisles to accommodate wheelchairs and the walking companions for the infirm and a light level that would never leave visitors in complete darkness.

Daylighting. Levels of daylight affect the exhibit at three locations (Figure C7-2). First, at the entrance where gallery visitors are coming from bright daylight, a vestibule of midlevel lighting helps them adjust to the low levels of lighting that they will encounter in the inner galleries. These low light levels protect the delicate nature of the textiles displayed in Gallery One. Because adapting to changes of light level is slow among the elderly, the vestibule reduces the light level gradually in two stages. Sec-

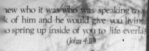

FIGURE C7-1: Christ and the Woman of Samaria
By positioning this famous sculpture by Ivan Mestrovic in the atrium, daylight was permitted to enter Gallery Two. As in other galleries where daylighting occurred, both the amount of light and the spectral content were carefully controlled, not only to reduce glare and preserve the lighting design, but also to conserve the artifacts against damage. (Photograph by Frank Methe, *Clarion Herald*.)

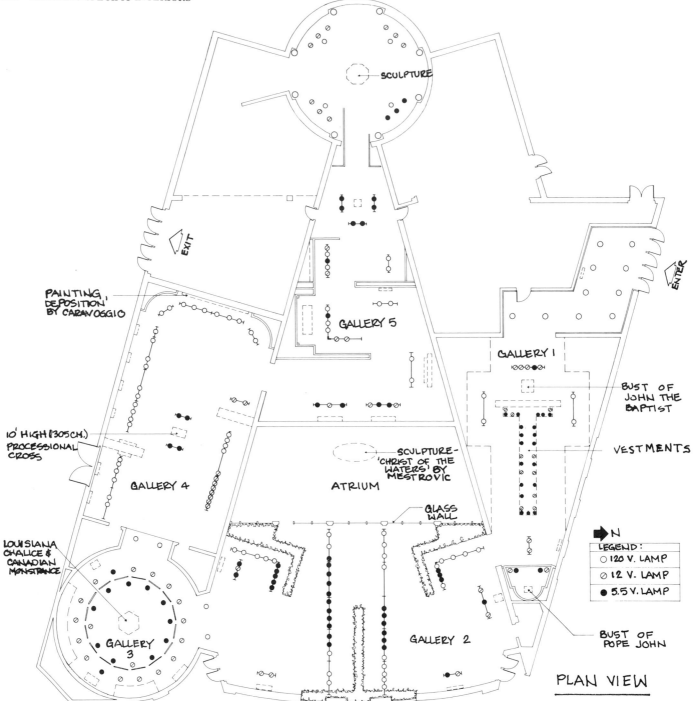

SCULPTURE

EXIT

PAINTING,
DEPOSITION
BY CARAVOGGIO

GALLERY 5

10' HIGH (305 CM.)
PROCESSIONAL
CROSS

SCULPTURE-
'CHRIST OF THE
WATERS' BY
MESTROVIC

ATRIUM

GALLERY 4

GLASS
WALL

ENTER

GALLERY 1

BUST OF
JOHN THE
BAPTIST

VESTMENTS

LOUISIANA
CHALICE &
CANADIAN
MONSTRANCE

N

LEGEND:
○ 120 V. LAMP
⊘ 12 V. LAMP
● 5.5 V. LAMP

GALLERY
3

GALLERY 2

BUST OF
POPE JOHN

PLAN VIEW

FIGURE C7-2: Plan View
The architect had hoped to open two windows across the gallery from the atrium to balance Gallery Two with bilateral daylight, but the lighting designer felt that one long side having daylight would be difficult enough to control, and he also suggested that the exterior of the glass wall be coated with reflective tinting to further control the daylight. It is only this reflective coating that keeps the lighting design from being obliterated by washes of daylight. (Illustration by Reiko Hayashi.)

ond, in Gallery Two, a long wall of glass allows visitors to view the complex sculpture of *Christ and the Woman of Samaria* from several angles and distances. The piece is exhibited in a reflecting pool outside in the atrium. Finally, in the last gallery, clerestory windows encircle the domed ceiling and allow light to enter from overhead. The designer was not unhappy with this lighting effect, but the admittance of daylight raised questions about the preservation of the artifacts.

Color. For this particular exhibition, there were very few brightly colored finishes. Walls were muted to gray, cool white, or

neutral beige, so as not to compete with the artifacts. One exception occurred in Gallery Five where a more dense profusion of smaller artifacts called forth the only vivid color contrasts in the exhibit. Within the display cases, dark blue and dark green velvets were used behind gold artifacts while a deep gray velvet appeared behind silver ones. In one instance, where the artifacts themselves were brightly colored, Director Silver chose to create a background from a neutral-colored linen fabric.

Activities. *Tasks:* The major assignment of the lighting designer here was to light the sacred artifacts so that they could be clearly seen, but in such a way as to allow visitors to relate to the artifacts appropriately.

Traffic: Additionally, the lighting plan was required to invisibly move the visitors along the viewing route promptly. The total amount of time spent within the exhibit space (or *dwell time*) by the average visitor to enjoy the collection was 45 minutes to an hour. Terry varied his light levels with this in mind; like an oasis, each relatively bright focal center is just a visible distance from the previous one.

Mood. The lighting must evoke different moods as determined by the artifacts themselves. For example, the splendor and pageantry of the ceremonial vestments produces awe for some, exhilaration for others. Certainly the mood evoked by *The Deposition* by Caravaggio is contemplative or sad. Through thoughtful placement of the artifacts in relation to the gallery space and to each other, the exhibit designer establishes a sequence of emotional experiences. The lighting designer must reinforce these emotions through selection of appropriate light sources and use of compositional lighting techniques.

CONCEPT/STRATEGY

LeMar Terry is sometimes referred to as the "prince of darkness"; his usual style is to blacken a gallery and light only the artifacts. Because of the elderly viewers at this exhibition, he augmented the low-voltage track lighting for the Vatican artifacts with incandescent downlights for selected architectural features. Together, the two kinds of accent lighting created a modest ambient light level. Where daylight was admitted, both the amount and the spectral content of the light was carefully controlled.

CONSTRAINTS

Construction. There are many advantages to a short-life, single purpose structure such as this one, but some advantages can have negative effects also. For instance, track lighting was anticipated from the outset, so there was very little plenum available to receive the penetrations required by recessed fixtures. Where there was plenum space, it was reserved for HVAC ducting. Because the original design concepts were so clear, there was little flexibility in the design to accommodate later changes.

Code. Temporary buildings are excluded from many provisions of the Unified Building Code, but in the case of this exhibition structure, designed to receive thousands of guests daily, the inspection department re-included some of the provisions normally excluded to ensure that the structure could be safely used for this purpose.

Life Safety. Despite the temporary life of the structure, requirements for lighted exits, for lighted emergency evacuation routes, and for the lighting of other path-finding features necessary to guide unfamiliar gallery visitors to safety were high on the inspector's checklist. At the Vatican Pavilion, the electrical engineer and architect decided to put the lighting designer's recessed fixtures onto emergency power circuiting to meet some of these needs.

Energy. A unique aspect of museum exhibits is that energy codes have practically no effect on them. Long before the watts-per-square-foot energy limitations could be reached, the limitations on allowable light levels curtail wattage consumption. The curator of such an exhibit is protecting his/her artifacts for posterity by limiting light levels, but the husbandry also assists the lighting designer in saving energy.

The low-voltage incandescent light sources chosen by the designer produce 29 lumens-per-watt; the quartz light sources produce 12 to 18 lumens-per-watt and the 65-watt flood lights give off 9 lumens-per-watt. None of these sources are electrically-efficient; all are optically efficient, but so little light is allowed on the artifacts that energy consumption is not a prime concern.

Budget. First costs have the greatest impact in a temporary exhibit such as this. Although the fixtures will later be reused to

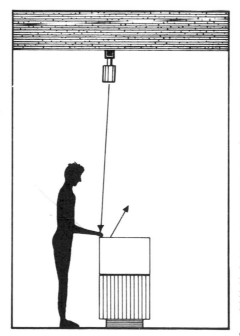

FIGURE C7-3: Glass Display Cases
In the lighting of glass display cases or vitrines, the strategy is one of avoidance. First, the light should not come from too far in front of the display objects or the glass will reflect the beam into the viewer's eyes. Instead of precious objects, the viewer will see the bright image of the overhead fixtures in the glass. Second, the light should not brighten the frontal aspect of the viewer or else his/her own bright image will be mirrored in the glass. Finally, the light should not come from behind the viewer or else his/her shadow will cover the display. (Illustration by Reiko Hayashi.)

light a parish schoolroom, the Church money was donated expressly for the Pavilion. After the initial costs for the schematic design were estimated, the participating designers were asked to make cuts in the cost of the project wherever they could. Terry was able to make a valuable contribution by (1) reducing the quantity of fixtures slightly, and (2) by asking a small fixture manufacturer to handle this order on a special basis. By changing manufacturers, the fixtures were acquired without sacrificing either focusing features, like adjustability or the ability to fit special beam modifying accessories onto the fixtures, and without sacrificing quality.

Schedule. The urgency of the construction schedule often increases the construction costs of the project at the last minute. This can be prevented if the lighting designer remains communicative and responsive in spite of his/her distance from the project. When the general contractor wanted to rush the ordering of 19,000 dollars in fixture changes, the lighting designer managed to correct a few erroneous figures, reorganize the fixture quantities, and reduce the cost to less than 3,000 dollars—all within several days (see Appendix B-8: Sample Additional Work Clause).

Feasibility. With an adequate budget, an appropriate (although demanding) schedule, and a building dedicated only to the exhibition, the lighting challenges were centered on aesthetics and the conservation of the artifacts (Figure C7-3). Because no unusual problems were anticipated, the lighting designer was able to estimate his time closely (Appendix B-9: Sample Worksheet for Projecting Designers' Hours).

TACTICS

Light Sources

Beam Angles. The style of Terry's work presumes the tight clean beam of low-voltage lighting. At 5.5 volts, a 4-degree stream of light from a "bullet beam" PAR lamp can deliver an intensity of 50,000 candlepower to the gemstones of a papal ring. Other artifacts, such as antique vestments, require both a wider beam and lower footcandles.

The designer's use of spread lenses evened out the field of light across the width of the low-voltage beam. But still, the resulting footcandles were far too high for the faint quotations on the walls of Gallery One; for these, Terry selected 65-watt PAR flood lamps that have 60-degree beam spreads.

Lamp Life. Although the designer's specifications included both standard and low voltages of quartz light sources as well as incandescent light sources, none of these bulbs are known for their long life, which is typically about two thousand hours, so maintenance may be frequent. Dimmers

FIGURE C7-4: The Mitre
In Gallery One the textiles received no more than 5 footcandles of light. Although they received and reflected so little light, they seemed quite bright in the darkened gallery. This particular illusion is one that has long been associated with the designer, LeMar Terry. It makes use of the greater sensitivity of the viewer's eye to brightness when the eye is dark-adapted by the light level in the dim gallery. (Photograph by Frank Methe, *Clarion Herald*.)

choosing electric dimming, which reddens the light. Instead, the designer used fly screen held over the face of the fixtures by accessory clips to mechanically reduce the amount of light. (Copper screening warms the light slightly, silver screening cools it, but black fly screen merely reduces the quantity of light without greatly affecting its color.)

Invisible Effects. The invisible ultraviolet and infrared light waves are a nightmare to the curator, because they destroy the artifacts that these professionals are committed to preserve. Because photons of radiant energy at the shorter blue and ultraviolet wavelengths contain more energy than those of the longer red and infrared wavelengths, ultraviolet light causes fading and other similar losses of chemical bonding. Daylight has the most ultraviolet light per lumen.

To filter out ultraviolet light in Gallery One, Terry has used a stepped acrylic ceiling of DP-30 acrylic for the vitrines that house the fragile mitres, liturgical vestments, and other fabric objects. In Gallery Two, he has suggested solar glazing, as discussed previously, and has also used UF-3, an ultraviolet filtering acrylic available both in clear sheet and powder form (made by Rohm and Haas). In Gallery Six, the glass bricks of the clerestories have been frosted to filter ultraviolet light by applying a pliant gel sheeting, made by the Rosco Company, inside the glass.

The most fragile artifacts in this exhibit were the textiles. Under the rules governing the Louisiana World Exposition, the hours that an exhibit was open could not be curtailed, so the length of time that these delicate objects were exposed to light could not be shortened to reduce the effects of photodegradation. Instead, the designer limited the intensity of the light (Figure C7-4). Sometimes a second objective in lighting textiles is to ensure that the light is evenly distributed across the fabric because uneven stresses would cause it to tear in its more weakened places.

Fixtures

Beam Shape. Because the low-voltage beams used in the exhibit are so narrow, there are few angles in the room from which viewers can be blinded by the direct glare that comes from looking directly into them. On the other hand, the 65-watt flood lights with their broad beam angle need to be carefully located and focused to keep viewers from being momentarily blinded when looking upward. Usually louvers on the fixtures are necessary to shield viewers from an uncomfortable visual experience. In many exhibits, another kind of glare, indirect glare, can be a problem when light ricochets from the top of glass display cases. Again careful location and focusing can solve the problem and prevent veiling reflections (Figure C7-5).

often prove too flexible as well as too costly. Although they would extend lamp life, they also make it possible for gallery attendants to turn the lights too high.

Lamp Color. Quartz light sources are used because of their excellent color. The ability to reinforce both warm colors and cool ones is an important qualification of lighting in exhibit design. Often a warm-colored object will be displayed against a cool-colored background to emphasize its visual impact. In these instances, the light source needs to reinforce both the warmth of the object and the coolness of the backdrop in order to enrich the contrast between them. Preserving and reinforcing the natural color of the artifacts is another reason for not

Mounting. Track mounting is flexible, versatile, and economical. It is easier to use track to achieve precise aiming angles and they can be easily reinstalled and reused when the exhibit comes down.

Costs. *Initial:* Because track-mounted fixtures are so common, they were respecified for this project at a lower cost, merely by changing manufacturers. However, each low-voltage track fixture needs its own integral transformer and that is expensive. Although affixing several fixtures to a single, large transformer is sometimes a savings, designer Terry frequently mixes 5.5-volt fixtures on the same track as 12-volt fixtures. Such a mix complicates the installation of shared transformers unless the tracks have more than one circuit, which also raises their cost.

Installation: To limit installation costs, track mounting was recommended throughout. In a few galleries, track could not be used. For instance, at the entrance, recessed fixtures were specified where the ceiling was both low and conspicuous due to a lack of powerful visual distractions in the same space.

Owning/Operating: The major items were the cost of electricity, which was limited by the allowable light levels, and the cost of changing bulbs.

Appearance. One of the benefits of a darkened gallery is that the fixtures are seldom noticed unless they are incorrectly placed. Incorrect placement includes any location that causes the visitor to walk directly toward the beam of light. Even in a gallery where the fixtures are visibly mounted, the height of the ceiling often keeps them from falling into full view of the normal (30 degrees) lines of sight. In other galleries, the designer took precautions to conceal fixture placement entirely (Figure C7-6).

CONCLUDING THOUGHTS

Having lighted most of the famous collections touring North America over the last decade, LeMar Terry's approach is experienced and astute as well as distinctive. He blends his artistry with an understanding of the damaging chemical effects caused by light striking fragile museum artifacts. The hallmark of his mastery is that the visitor notices none of the painstaking focusing, filtering, and budgeting; the visitor sees only beautiful objects, beautifully displayed.

CHAPTER NOTES

[1] Robert L. Feller, "Control of Deteriorating Effects of Light upon Museum Objects," *Museum* 17, No. 2 (1964): 71-98.

[2] Laurence S. Harrison, "An Investigation of the Damage of the Hazard in Spectral Energy," *Illuminating Engineering* 48 (1954): 253; and W. B. DeLaney and A. Makulec, "A Review of Fading Effects on Museum Fabrics," *Illuminating Engineering* November 1963: 676-684.

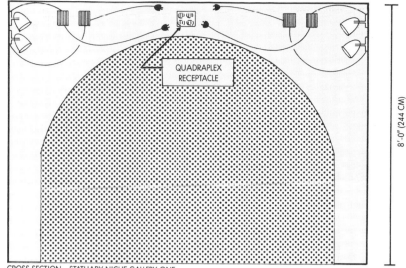

CROSS SECTION   STATUARY NICHE GALLERY ONE

8'-0" (244 CM)

QUADRAPLEX RECEPTACLE

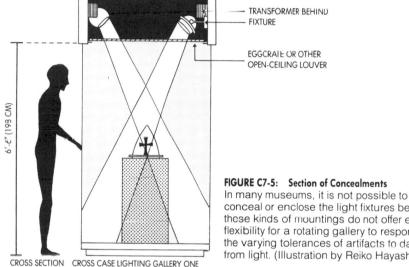

CROSS SECTION   CROSS CASE LIGHTING GALLERY ONE

6'-4" (193 CM)

TRANSFORMER BEHIND
FIXTURE

EGGCRATE OR OTHER
OPEN-CEILING LOUVER

FIGURE C7-5: Section of Concealments
In many museums, it is not possible to conceal or enclose the light fixtures because these kinds of mountings do not offer enough flexibility for a rotating gallery to respond to the varying tolerances of artifacts to damage from light. (Illustration by Reiko Hayashi.)

FIGURE C7-6: Gallery Five
Precise lighting enhances the "Treasures of the Vatican" in each of the six galleries in the pavilion. These are truly "beautiful objects, beautifully displayed." (Photograph by Frank Methe, *Clarion Herald*.)

LIGHTING WITH CARE

Case Study Eight

THE CHARTER HOUSE RETIREMENT CENTER

ARCHITECTURE AND PLANNING: Design Through Research, Inc.
Jack L. Bowersox, president
Dale Treimain, vice president and project architect

INTERIOR DESIGN: Design Through Research, Inc.
Dale Treimain, project design coordinator
Pat Hoaglund, ASID

Lighting design for the elderly must take into account not just their physical disabilities or visual limitations, but also their emotional and psychological well being. The designers of the Charter House Retirement Center in Rochester, Minnesota carefully incorporated these needs into their lighting plan which is based on delivering task lighting while consistently avoiding glare. Many of the Charter House residents are part of the medical community associated with the Mayo Clinic; they seek new interests in their retirement and pay rigorous attention to health care.

DATA/PHYSICAL SPECIFICATIONS

The residents of this model complex of congregate living must be 62 years of age or older. The Center includes not only 300 apartment units but also a 48-bed facility that offers both skilled and intermediate care (Figure C8-1).

This 2-story nursing facility is attached to a 22-story apartment tower. Four dining rooms are located on the tower's top floor and a party room and lounge adjoin them. Meal service is also provided in the third floor private dining room or in the assisted living facility located on the third and fourth floors. Tray service meals can be brought to any of the 18 residential floors of the apartment tower. In addition to a library, lounge, and exercise spa, there is also a darkroom, woodworking shop, textile workshop, and ceramics studio. Year-round gardening is made possible by an indoor greenhouse (Figure C8-2).

ANALYSIS/PROGRAM

Client Image. Realizing that the aging process is both individual and gradual, the Council on Aging of the client's parent corporation, Rochester Methodist Hospital Health Services, Inc., felt that community housing for the elderly should offer the fullest range of adaptive responses to the changing emotional and physical needs of the residents. Because the residents have their health and psycho-social needs provided while living in their own apartments, most can delay or avoid being cared for in the skilled care unit altogether. "The costs to the system and to the resident are greatly reduced by this approach."[1]

Client Vision. The residents of the center have special visual needs:

They are glare sensitive

They require light levels three times higher than normal

They require correct beam angles to perform visual tasks

They will perceive blues and blue-greens as muted or even brown

Additionally, moving from one room to another, the residents' ability to adapt to rooms of a significantly higher or lower light level is slow, raising the possibility of accidents, especially falls.

Daylighting. Because of the residents' visual limitations, direct beam sunlight could cause many glaring effects, so daylighting is handled with great care. Exterior overhangs are supplemented by flexible window coverings similar to pull-down shades. In the south-facing dining room, tinted glass and a double layering of sheer glass curtains baffle and filter the penetration of sunlight. On one floor, glass clerestories on the inboard side of a daylighted corridor allow the interior room to "borrow" daylight—but the borrowed light is indirect (Figure C8-3).

Color. "Bright colors may be clearly read as contrasts on neutral backgrounds," says Jack L. Bowersox. Here, warm colors like

FIGURE C8-1:   The Charter House Retirement Center
Because the aging process affects each individual in a different and unpredictable way, independent living, assisted living, and a skilled nursing facility are all available at this retirement center. (Photograph Courtesy of the Charter House.)

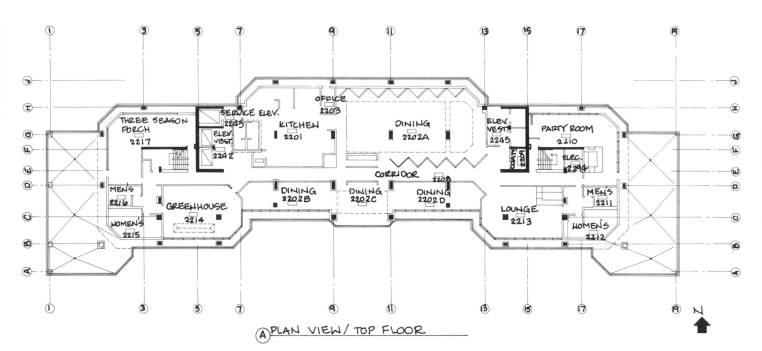

A PLAN VIEW / TOP FLOOR

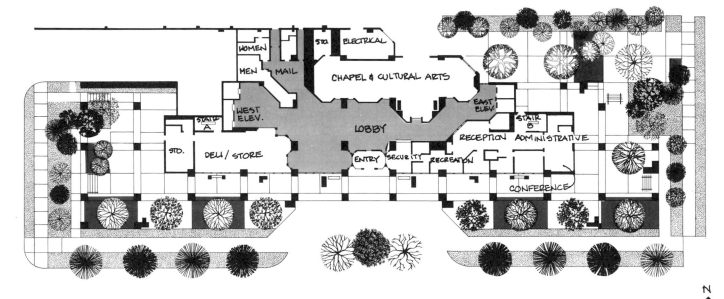

C PLAN VIEW / FIRST FLOOR & PLAZA

FIGURE C8-2: Plan Views/Representative Floors
The aging process is slowed down in elderly people who engage in daily activities and recreation. The Charter House seems more like a multifaceted country club or resort because it emphasizes a wide range of living options and recreation. (Illustration by Reiko Hayashi.)

crimson, coral, and pumpkin on cream convey a typically residential rather than institutional atmosphere. Value contrasts are low, however, and all finishes are matte to restrict reflected glare.

Activities. Because there are so many activities in a facility like the Charter House, only a few representative ones are treated here.

Tasks: Among the tasks associated with *independent living,* those connected with the bathroom mirror are particularly important for the elderly, for example, applying makeup and shaving. Each morning the resident recaptures his/her self image in the mirror. Because the aging process reduces skills, agility, sight, and memory, finding a positive self image in that mirror becomes increasingly difficult but increasingly important. The architects have used incandescent lighting to give the resident a healthy warm image in the mirror.

Among the tasks associated with *assisted living,* those at the bedside become all important. Bowersox makes the point that the bedside stand should contain an assistance call button and a bedside light. Because these conveniences are attached to furniture rather than to the wall, there is greater flexibility in adjusting and relocating them (Figure C8-4).

Among the tasks associated with socialization among small groups of two to four people, conversation ranks high (Figure C8-5). For socialization among large groups, assemblies for worship or cultural enrichment are common. Both activities will occur in the Cultural Arts Center (Figure C8-6).

Traffic: Two groups populate the corridors: those who are familiar with the building and those who are not. Since the latter receive explicit directions from the security person at the entry, they only need directional signs to prompt them. It is the residents themselves who are more inclined to lose their way. For them, low mounted signs 48 inches (101.6 cm) above the carpet have letters in bas-relief or in recessed carving; such three dimensionality can be reinforced with light and shadow, but as vision fails with increasing age, the tactile senses become more reliable. Bowersox suggests that as short- and long-term memory losses begin to occur, orientation to time and place becomes more important to the resident psychologically. Hallways become neighborhoods and can best be identified by environmental clues such as by gripping a handrail that has an unusual cross section or texture.

Pathways: Ramp lighting was not considered for the Charter House. "Ramps should be avoided because chairbound older persons do not have the upper body strength or proficiency to use them. This is only one of the standards for handicapped accessibility that has been developed to meet the

FIGURE C8-3: The Hallway
The principles of borrowed daylight are illustrated here. By means of a skylighted ceiling, daylight is admitted to this matte white corridor. The white surfaces in the corridor encourage beam daylight to reflect and reflect again. In so doing, the quality of the light becomes diffuse and shadowfree. Only then is the light allowed to enter the examination rooms on the inner radius of the circular corridor. Note that the clerestory windows to the examination rooms have an overhang to prevent direct sunlight from entering and creating unwelcome shadows. (Photograph by Paul S. Bednarski)

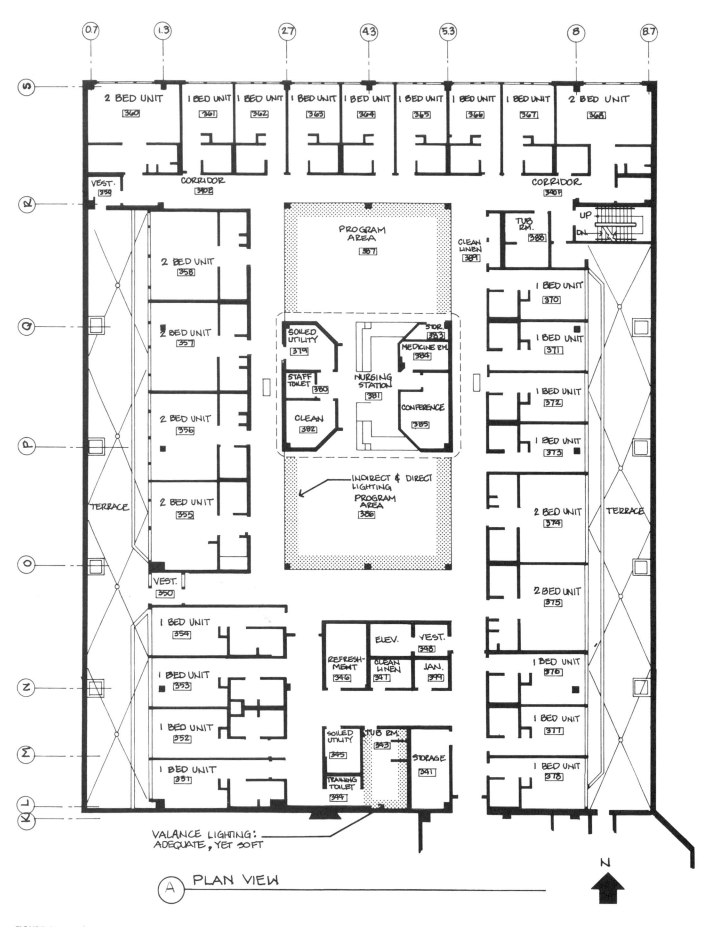

0.7 1.3 2.7 4.3 5.3 8 8.7

S

2 BED UNIT 360   I BED UNIT 361   I BED UNIT 362   I BED UNIT 363   I BED UNIT 364   I BED UNIT 365   I BED UNIT 366   I BED UNIT 367   2 BED UNIT 368

VEST. 359

CORRIDOR 340B   CORRIDOR 340F

R

PROGRAM AREA 387

TUB RM. 388

UP

DN

CLEAN LINEN 389

2 BED UNIT 358

I BED UNIT 370

Q

2 BED UNIT 357

SOILED UTILITY 379

STOR. 383

MEDICINE RM. 384

I BED UNIT 371

STAFF TOILET 380

NURSING STATION 381

P

2 BED UNIT 356

CLEAN 382

CONFERENCE 385

I BED UNIT 372

I BED UNIT 373

TERRACE

2 BED UNIT 355

INDIRECT & DIRECT LIGHTING PROGRAM AREA 386

2 BED UNIT 374

TERRACE

O

VEST. 350

2 BED UNIT 375

I BED UNIT 354

ELEV.   VEST. 398

N

I BED UNIT 353

REFRESH- MENT 346

CLEAN LINEN 347

JAN. 399

I BED UNIT 376

I BED UNIT 352

I BED UNIT 377

M

SOILED UTILITY 345

TUB RM. 343

STORAGE 341

I BED UNIT 351

TRAINING TOILET 344

I BED UNIT 378

K L

K

VALANCE LIGHTING: ADEQUATE, YET SOFT

N

A PLAN VIEW

FIGURE C8-4: Plan View/Assisted Living
Although the residents of the Charter House receive many individual kinds of assistance from
one another and from the staff, two special floors have been planned for residents whose
need for help many be higher than that of the others. (Illustration by Reiko Hayashi.)

needs of younger, stronger, and healthier handicapped persons," declares the project architect, Bowersox.[2]

Mood. The parent corporation felt a conservative, sophisticated mood would help to convey confidence in the resident, so that the self-assured individual wouldn't ask for help before he/she actually needed it.

COMPOSITION/STRATEGY

Avoiding glare is the first priority of the lighting strategy and delivering task light where needed is the second. Ambient light is reflected from walls and ceilings to fill the rooms with indirect light from invisible sources. Where additional light is needed for conversation, reading, or other activities, specific task lighting from plug-in fixtures provides convenient, efficient, and adjustable illumination.

CONSTRAINTS

Schedule. For this project, the schedule for design was long, but the schedule for construction was short. More than a year was spent on preprogramming. Another year was spent in schematics, and still another in design development. But when financing was suddenly completed, the schedule switched to fast-track.

FIGURE C8-5: Recommended Conversation Relationships
Conversation grouping must allow encounters to be face to face; it is often painful for older persons to turn their heads and shoulders to the side. (Illustration by Reiko Hayashi.)

FIGURE C8-6: The Cultural Arts Center
Although some residents would rather observe than actively participate, the potential for glare in the many viewing angles is apparent. Such a condition makes this space very difficult to light properly. Track-mounted lighting fixtures offer the greatest range of adaptability because they can be hand focused and changed when needed. (Photograph courtesy of the Charter House.)

Construction. Along with the architect's administration of the contract, there was a separate owner/contractor value engineering program related to the negotiated agreement on a guaranteed maximum price. Although the architect maintained effective control over the expense of the project by means of the certificates for payment, the value engineering program raised issues that led to budget cuts.

Code. No special building codes were applied to this project.

Life Safety. The strictest possible interpretations of the existing life safety codes were enforced by the office of the fire marshal for this project. The combination of a high-rise building and an elderly occupancy required that all precautions be taken.

Energy Code. As in many states whose codes are based on ASHRAE 90-75, energy budgeting is the practice in Minnesota. Within the building envelope, the architect and engineers can calculate average energy consumption by borrowing wattage from one area or building system to be spent in another.[3]

Budget. Since the not-for-profit project was financed through bond sales, the cash flow was sporadic. Over the fast-track part of

the design and construction process there were several major cuts in the budget. Ultimately, however, first costs of construction were less than 50 dollars per-square-foot, which is very economical.

Feasibility. The Charter House is the kind of sophisticated retirement project that presumes the presence of an appreciative market. Such facilities are likely to be found in urban communities with a large, health-conscious upper middle class population.

TACTICS

Light Sources

Beam Angles. The architect's lighting strategy avoided glare by using lighting effects that were blended and soft. Therefore, the hard edges of precisely controlled beams were inappropriate.

Lamp Life/Controls. By choosing built-in fluorescents for ambient lighting, the architect was able to make use of their long 20,000-hour lamp life. Where lights were visible to the residents, the shorter lived incandescent was preferred. Dimming controls were used where needed.

Lamp Color. How people appear to themselves and to one another was of the utmost importance. The warmth and modeling given to the face and complexion by incandescent light sources was the decisive factor in their selection. Correspondingly, all fluorescents were warm white. Warm tones were also chosen for major room finishes.

Invisible Effects. No attention was given to the issue of whether ultraviolet radiation is beneficial in forestalling the effects of aging on bone chemistry.[4]

Maintenance. The burden of consistently servicing incandescent fixtures was discussed in the design development phase.

Because no other light source could deliver the same warm color and familiar shadowing, lamp changes were accepted as a necessity.

Fixtures

Beam Shapes. For this project the beam delivered by the fixture needs to be variable or adaptable for several reasons: (1) the function of a particular room may change as its occupants become older and (2) the vision capabilities of the residents will also change. In some instances the architects have chosen fixtures that easily adapt to reflect the beam in a new direction, for example, wallwashers that can become downlights by revolving the reflector.

Mounting. A third reason for choosing adjustable fixtures is seen in the Cultural Arts Center where the blended wash of indirect light intended to fill the room requires the overlapping of beams. In other spaces, indirect light is provided by structurally mounted fluorescents built into soffits, walls, valances, and coves (Figure C8-7).

All over the Charter House, portable incandescent fixtures are not only movable, swing-arm adjustable, of three-way variable intensity, and low glare, they are also reminiscent of the residents' previous homes. The one great frustration of the architects was that so few manufacturers offered switches that were easily operated by the less dexterous fingers of the elderly.

Costs. Although the original lighting strategy was already very economical, during the fast-track portion of the design and construction three substantial budget cuts affected the lighting.

Installation: Recessed fluorescent lighting in perimeter light slots was deleted because of its excessive installation costs.

Equipment: Although no other significant

fixture types were cut from the project, the deletion of a textured wallcovering from the apartment corridors presented an unexpected lighting problem. Without that wallcovering, light from the fluorescent valances overhead struck the wall at a grazing angle and highlighted every tape joint. Whereas the textured grasscloth wallcovering would have been enhanced by the grazing angle, the naked wall was not. (See Chapter Two, Grazing Light.)

Owning/Operating: The maintenance and electrical cost of operating incandescent light sources was accepted by the owners. However, the inconvenience and expense of these incandescents was reduced as much as possible by generating greater quantities of ambient light from long-life, low-energy fluorescents.

Appearance. The appearance of the retirement facility is clublike. Table lamps, floor lamps, and chandeliers are effective as decorative accessories as well as lighting. The visible use of incandescents is combined with the invisible use of fluorescents.

CONCLUDING THOUGHTS

The strongest feature of this lighting system is the viability of the strategy. The architectural office feels that the emotional well-being of the residents is paramount to their physical well-being. Therefore, lighting is very residential in its quality—just like in a country club or resort.

CHAPTER NOTES

[1]Jack Bowersox, address, "High Technology and Its Benefits for an Aging Population," a hearing before the select committee on aging, U.S. House of Representatives, Ninety-Eighth Congress, May 22, 1984: 98-459.

[2]Bowersox, 98-459.

[3]Minnesota Energy Agency, 740 American Center Bldg., 160 East Kellogg Blvd., St. Paul, MN.

[4]John Ott, *Health and Light: The Effects of Natural and Artificial Light on Man and Other Living Things* (Greenwich: Bevin, 1973).

FIGURE C8-7: *The Staircase*
For the aged, it is easier to see steps when their treads are lighted and their risers are shadowed as shown here; this is also true for outdoor stairs in natural light. Some of the artistic lighting treatments for stairs—such as putting neon beneath each stair lip—is very confusing to older eyes and should be avoided. (Photograph by Jack L. Bowersox.)

DINING IN STYLE

ANTHONY'S RESTAURANT

INTERIOR ARCHITECTURE: Hellmuth, Obata & Kassabaum
Guy Obata, principal in charge design
Michael L. Willis, project interior designer

LIGHTING DESIGN: Hellmuth, Obata & Kassabaum
Eugene Fleming, IALD, lighting designer

Restauranteurs have become more intrigued with lighting design since the cost of energy has risen. The objective, of course, is to reduce expenses. This case study demonstrates how energy-efficient and economical lighting can also be beautiful—and make both food and diners beautiful as well (Figure C9-1).

The success of a restaurant depends upon its suitability to the marketplace. But lighting can do the following:

Make the food appear more tantalizing

Enhance the interior designer's efforts

Broaden a restaurant's appeal to prospective customers by providing enough light for diners of more than middle age

However, to achieve these objectives, the lighting system should still be cost-effective, flexible, and easily maintained.

DATA/PHYSICAL SPECIFICATIONS

Anthony's is a small restaurant on the street level of the 20-story Equitable Life Insurance Company in St. Louis. Anthony's offers seating for 126 patrons within its 1,500 square feet. Although Anthony's is not large, transparent panels divide its interior into sections to create the illusion of a bigger space (Figure C9-2). Ceilings are 10 feet high; plate glass windows face into the building's skylighted atrium. Its French a-la-carte menu with flaming specialties attracts gourmet diners of medium to upper income. Anthony's has won awards for its cuisine and its design.

ANALYSIS/PROGRAM

Client Image. Anthony's is a second property for its owners, the Bommarito brothers. Drawing on their experience with their first restaurant, they knew that a simple, but warm, contemporary design would place the focus on the food. The architect Obata agreed. A restaurant of such simplic-

ity would seem as modern as the mirrored silver office tower it occupies.

Client Vision. This restaurant's patrons are well established and often more than middle-aged. The vision problems of such patrons need to be considered since such patrons will be sensitive to glare.

Daylighting. The restaurant's west-facing windows are on the east side of the building's atrium known as the Garden Court, and consequently are sheltered from direct daylight penetration. Only at luncheon in late spring and early summer are daylight levels significant.

Color. The clients here have specified warm hues, but the lightness or darkness of those hues can be used to direct light to the people and the food. The textures of a dark acoustical ceiling and a dark absorbent carpet on both floors and walls will absorb much light and ensure that the only brightnesses will be created by light bouncing off the white tabletops.

Activities. *Tasks:* If there is enough light on the tables, reading the menu and cutting food should be easy, even for older people. Because the tables must sometimes be moved, lights must be equipped to move with them.

Traffic: Returning to a table in an unfamiliar and darkened interior can prove difficult, especially for older people. On the other hand, there are no stairs, ramps, or other hazards present here for which specific lighting would be required to ensure safety.

Mood. "Warm" and yet "clean and modern" seem to be conflicting moods but HOK has created a design so abstract that the two blend. Added elements of intimacy and serenity are also felt in the hush facilitated by the absorbent surfaces of the ceiling, floor, and walls.

FIGURE C9-1: Design Philosophy
(Above) "The design philosophy is really a simple one," declares Guy Obata of HOK, "the interest is in the food and the people." By focusing brightness on the table, the food is featured and the uplight reflected from a light-colored tablecloth erases lines and wrinkles from diners' faces. (Project Design by Hellmuth, Obata & Kassabaum, Inc.; Photograph by William E. Mathis.)

FIGURE C9-2: Preserving the Nighttime View
(Below) When all interior lighting is discretely confined to one carefully shielded fixture per table—such as a pendant fixture dropped deeply over the table, a hooded portable one, or louvered low-voltage accent lights aimed away from the panels or from equally treacherous glass windows—then such illusions are preserved. (Illustration by Reiko Hayashi.)

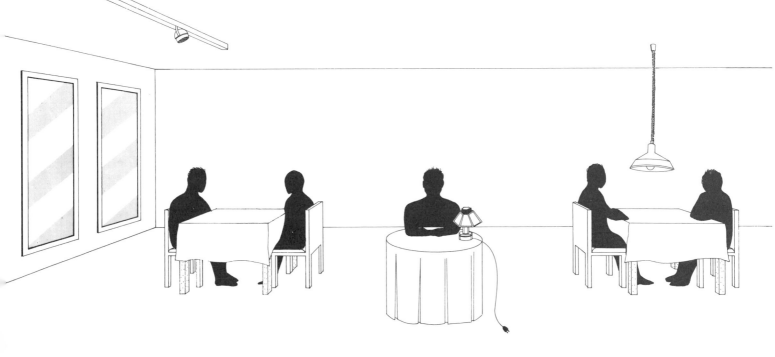

FIGURE C9-3: **Preserving Lighting Illusions**
It is very difficult to separate the proper lighting for this restaurant from its colors and textures; they are so masterfully coordinated. Ambient light would also destroy the illusion of a larger space created by the bronze transparent panels, so light-absorbing carpet and dark colors are used on floor and walls so as to make any generalized brightness impossible. (Photograph by William E. Mathis.)

COMPOSITION/STRATEGY

Using color to coordinate the lighting design involves the use of dark finishes on room surfaces—whose colored pigments and textures absorb the light—and light table-cloths—whose pigments reflect the light—to create the brightness contrasts that draw attention to the tabletops.

Therefore, lighting design at Anthony's need only follow the superb color and texture cues of its interior. By pumping enough light onto the only reflective finish—the white tablecloths—the designer can highlight the food with direct light and still bounce indirect light onto the seated diners. A few brighter objects are needed to develop a sense of the space (refer back to Figure C9-1 and see Figure C9-3).

CONSTRAINTS

Construction. In constructing a high-rise building like the Equitable Building, precise dimensioning is often lost because of the complexity of the project. The use of suspended ceiling and track mounting allows electrical power for the lighting to be allocated and distributed, but the location of each fixture can be determined later, during the interiors installation when information on fixture and furniture location is more complete.

Codes. In spaces like these a number of codes can apply simultaneously. Health, occupational, and life safety ordinances must be satisfied in addition to the normal electrical codes regulating new commercial construction.

Life Safety. The emergency exit route is easy at Anthony's because it has no steps and is on the street level. Two exits and exit routes are normally required by most safety codes, and usually they must be marked with illuminated "exit" signs. Although these signs are ugly, the code dictates that they be visible to all diners (Figure C9-4).

Energy. The technique used at Anthony's requires only one light source for each table. On that basis, each table could use as much as 60 watts and still leave enough wattage to illuminate serving stations, plants, or art objects.

Budget. Budget is the biggest constraint on restaurant lighting. Due to the spectre of so many over designed, but bankrupt restaurants, an owner's main concern is keeping initial costs down. Typically, lighting constitutes 11 percent of the total electrical expense, out of the 25 percent allocated for HVAC and electrical expense. Restaurateurs prefer to spend more for the kitchen or foodstuffs.

Savings. A restaurant owner can save 15 to 40 percent on electrical bills by planning

FIGURE C9-4:   The Problematic "Exit" Sign
Exit signs in brass, chrome, and clear acrylic
are attractive in a high general lighting level
like that found in a coffee shop, but almost
no illuminated exit sign is attractive in a
darkened space. In one historic negotiation
between a lighting designer and the city
inspector, it was agreed that the code called
for an exit sign of a certain brightness, but
did not put limits on how the requisite
brightness was to be achieved. They agreed
on low-voltage spotlights that automatically
turn on painted exit signs whenever the
emergency electrical system is activated.
The benefit is that neither the exit signs nor
the spotlights are lighted unless there is an
emergency. (Illustration by Reiko Hayashi.)

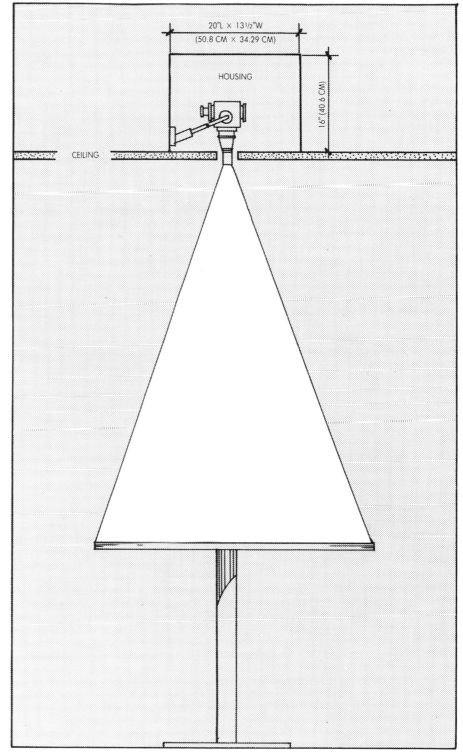

lighting carefully. Because restaurants are
high-energy users, designs using (1) low-
energy lighting, (2) passive solar techniques like daylighting, and (3) proper insulation between kitchen and dining room can
accrue big savings.

Anthony's has employed the lighting
technique that saves the most energy—that
of highlighting only the tables by using low-
wattage fixtures. White table linens provide
the catalysts that enable low-wattage fixtures to be effective: at night they become
tabletop reflectors.

Schedule. Because HOK was asked to design the new restaurant early in the planning stages, the design schedule proved to
be of no concern.

Feasibility. With a generous completion
schedule, an appropriate budget, and a
strong design concept, the only nagging
problem is the almost totally black traffic
areas. If the actual lighting specifications
can conserve enough wattage, there should
be enough left for downlights to assist patrons returning to their tables.

TACTICS

Light Sources
There are three considerations when selecting the best lighting source for dining:

1. The ability to control the light source's
beam

2. The color rendering capability of the
light source

3. Its amenability to electrical control

The last consideration is the most important; different dining times and patrons of
differing ages require different lighting levels. Diners reading the *Wall Street Journal*
at breakfast will require more light than
young lovers sharing an intimate late sup-
per. A versatile lighting plan should involve
dimmers, multiple switching, or supple-

FIGURE C9-5:   The Optical Projector
Even if the exact table locations had been
known, it would have been unlikely that
recessed fixtures could have been cut into a
plaster or sheet-rock ceiling so that they
were centered over each table. The lights
would also have been unable to move when
tables were shifted. (Illustration by Reiko
Hayashi.)

FIGURE C9-6: "Special" Fixtures
Energy limitations for this kind of project are often 2 watts-per-square-foot. When new legislation of 1½ watts-per-square-foot takes effect, it may be mandatory to use custom fixtures, or specials, in order to move the light source as close as possible to its target. In restaurants, recessed track allows the fixtures to be relocated whenever tables are rearranged. Note, however, that the transparent bronze partitions prevent those movements from becoming too extreme in this particular floor plan. (Illustration by Reiko Hayashi.)

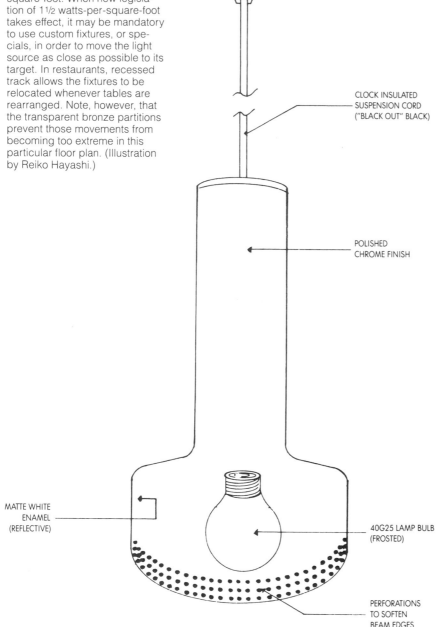

TRACK COUPLER

CLOCK INSULATED
SUSPENSION CORD
("BLACK OUT" BLACK)

POLISHED
CHROME FINISH

MATTE WHITE
ENAMEL
(REFLECTIVE)

40G25 LAMP BULB
(FROSTED)

PERFORATIONS
TO SOFTEN
BEAM EDGES

mentary lighting systems to adapt the space for these different lighting needs.

Beam Angles. Dimming is important in this restaurant because less light is required for dinner than for luncheon. For dimming ease, reliability, and economy, incandescent lamp bulbs are best. But which incandescent light source?

Because the light should spread broadly over the white tablecloths in order to catch the individual place settings in its beam, the best choice is either one recessed optical projector per table that uses tungsten halogen lamp bulbs (Figure C9-5) or a pendant fixture that uses a frosted nonglare bulb. The optics of the tungsten halogen alternative depends on manually adjusted shutters

inside the fixture; they will need to be readjusted as the metal "fatigues." The pendant fixture derives the spread of its beam by virtue of the distance from the table to the bulb. This distance has to be determined at the time of installation, but does not need adjusting thereafter.

Lamp Life. The tungsten halogen bulb has a longer life than the nonglare globe in the pendant fixture. However, the more deeply a bulb is dimmed, the more its lamp life is increased. Therefore, the globe can be dimmed more deeply, because it is closer to the tabletop. So, in practice, the globe will give the longer life.

Lamp Color. On the other hand, the color spectrum of the tungsten halogen is wider

and more flattering to a wide range of foods, especially those that are green, like salads.

Invisible Effects. If the frosted globe at 40 watts is selected instead of the tungsten halogen at 100 watts, the diners, the dishes, and the air conditioning system will all be spared some infrared or heat-related problems. The extra energy needed to add those additional downlights may also be conserved.

Fixtures

Beam Shapes. In this instance, manipulating the beam has two objectives: (1) to soften the edges of the beam so that it won't cast harsh shadows, and (2) to cut off the beam at the diameter of the table. Custom perforations encircling the fixture aperture will soften the edge of the beam. The size of the fixture aperture and the fixture's distance from the table determine the beam cut off (Figure C9-6).

Mounting. The fixtures must suspend cleanly from a recessed ceiling track; this allows them to be moved (Figure C9-7). Matte black suspension cords blend into the background so that the fixtures appear to float. Seen together, this grouping of fixtures creates the impression of a more intimate ceiling height.

Costs. *Equipment:* Incandescent fixtures are the least expensive and track mounting provides the least expensive way to wire them. Anthony's fixture requirements are unique, so the fixture selected is a "special," requiring custom manufacture. Note that it is possible to hold such a fixture outside of the construction bidding process entirely, whenever the manufacturer is willing to sell directly to the owner.

Owning/Operating: The most minimal, elementary, but frequently replaced light source to maintain is the screw-based incandescent in a pendant fixture that can be reached from the floor. Ease and consistency of maintenance is one of this restaurant's most outstanding accomplishments. Many beautiful interiors and lighting designs appear in trade journals, but only one out of 50 will appear the same after a year's wear and tear. Anthony's has looked the same for 10 years.

Appearance. The pendant fixture looks like a simple flashlight in chrome. It is intended to convey a modern image in harmony with the silver mirroring of the building's shell.

CONCLUDING THOUGHTS

In the softly blacked-out space, lights suspended from the ceiling catch only the crisp and pristine white table linens and the people seated around them. The contrast sets up perfect relationships of light and color. The food is seen against white china and linen; the faces are seen against a velvet darkness. Seldom has either looked better.

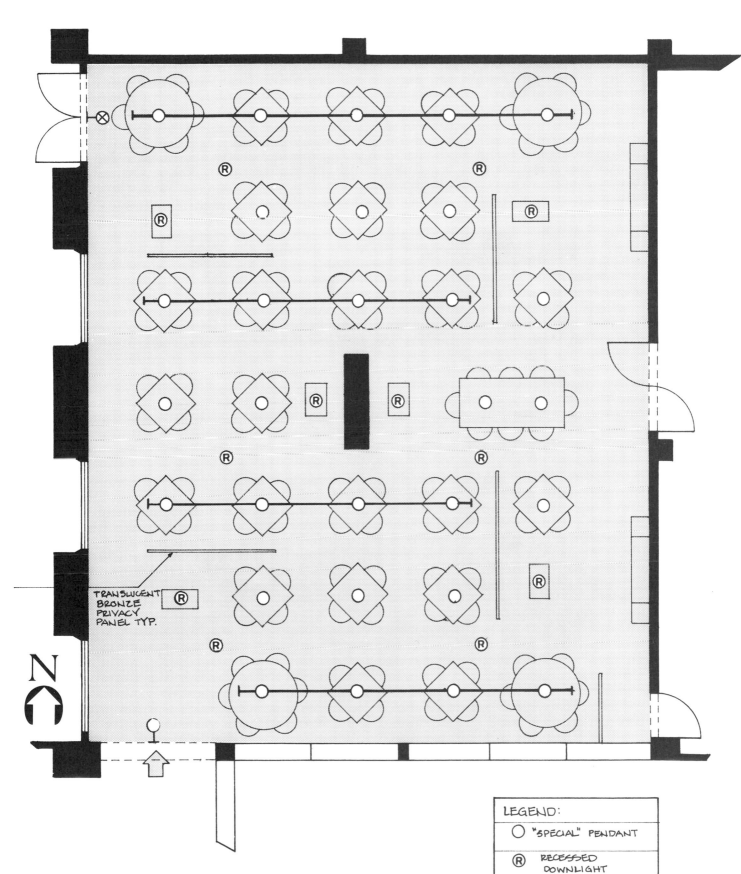

FIGURE C9-7: Reflected Ceiling Plan
Recessed track allows the fixtures to be moved whenever tables are rearranged. *Note:* The transparent bronze panels prevent those movements from being too massive in this floor plan. (Illustration by Reiko Hayashi.)

LEGEND:

○ "SPECIAL" PENDANT

Ⓡ RECESSED DOWNLIGHT

⊢O⊣ TRACK LIGHT

⊢⊗ EXIT LIGHT

SPECIAL LIGHTING NEEDS

Part Three

THE lighting design practices covered in Chapters One through Six are generic. They provide for most lighting-design demands and anticipate most clients' needs. The final three chapters treat special extensions of basic principles and practices: lighting for the aged and infirm, lighting live plants, and light as an art form. Each is a specialized response to the social, aesthetic, and technological demands of our times.

Older people make up the fastest-growing segment of the population. Their housing needs change more—and more rapidly—than at any other time of their lives. An enormous number of people experience and live with infirmities long before reaching old age. To meet the demands of the aged and infirm, design professionals need to provide not only obvious accommodations, such as ramps for wheelchairs, but subtleties such as easily opened window latches for arthritic hands and larger numerals on thermostats that can be read by aging eyes. Chapter Seven outlines some basic points to consider when designing lighting for the aged and infirm.

For city-dwelling clients who crave the green of the country, designers must devise ways to acclimate nature—specifically trees and plants—to city spaces, both indoors and outdoors. Light and lighting is vital to plant growth, and it is important to understand the many facets of this relationship. In lighting interiors with plantings, the designer must anticipate which plant species will survive in which parts of a given room or building. But a designer does not need a certificate in landscape architecture to know that deciduous trees will not live under tinted glass; common sense and an awareness of basic plant needs is enough. Chapter Eight offers some practical approaches for lighting both indoor and outdoor plants.

Light as art is at the frontier of lighting knowledge and is discussed in Chapter Nine. Today's lighting artist is experimenting with perception and illusion. By the end of this century, these "experiments" will have evolved into well-understood principles of psychophysics that can be incorporated into the design of our environments. Designers can then use illusions of light and color to enlarge living spaces, personalize them, and change them at will.

Chapter Seven

LIGHTING FOR THE AGED AND INFIRM

BOTH STATE and federal codes dictate that buildings designated as *barrier free* shall be usable by everyone—including those with disabilities. Under certain circumstances, disabled people can file a complaint to force a building's owner into making the necessary alterations; so the designer who fails to understand the provisions of barrier-free design stands to lose both time and money for the owner.

BARRIER-FREE DESIGN CODES
In some states, barrier-free design regulations affect nearly every type of construction and remodeling except privately funded housing and remodeling projects of less than 50,000 dollars. The provisions usually require that only a percentage of the facilities be accessible, but this percentage varies by type of occupancy and type of construction. For instance, in remodeling projects, the remodeled areas as well as the route to them is subject to barrier-free codes. Public bathrooms, drinking fountains, telephones, exits and alarms, switches, and other hardware are all affected by such codes (Figure 7-1).

Exemptions
Complying with the barrier-free regulations increases construction costs by one percent. Some states allow the local bureau of building inspection to grant an "unreasonable hardship" exemption if "equivalent facilitation" for features like public restrooms and ramps can be provided (Figure 7-2). The only way to avoid equivalent facilitation is through appeal.

Another major exemption often relates to multistory buildings. According to some regulations, even privately funded, multistory buildings must be accessible at the first floor or ground levels. When an elevator or ramp (Figure 7-3) is not available to other levels, those other levels are not required to be barrier-free. In this way, it is presumed that a reasonable portion of the facilities normally sought and used by the public are made available. In some states exemptions do not exist. Be sure to check all the facts with the bureau of building inspection in whose jurisdiction your project is located.

Other than the additional cost, compliance is not difficult. To provide assistance, most states have an association of the physically handicapped. These groups often have computerized lists of products that respond to the needs of the disabled.

THE AGING EYE
For the aging, a significant reduction of visual ability is normal, so lighting that helps compensate for this is crucial. This sight loss can be divided into three areas of concern: (1) presbyopia, (2) filter effects, and (3) changing visual fields (Figure 7-4).

Presbyopia
This is the gradual reduction in the eye's ability to focus on close objects, due to normal changes in the eye's crystalline lens. After age forty, presbyopia causes existing, but heretofore unnoticed, farsightedness to become a problem. In later life, astigmatism also increases. When such changes in vision occur, people use eyeglasses to improve vision, but the feeling persists that more light is needed when reading or doing other detailed or close visual tasks. Such individuals need keyholes and pay phones to have special accent lighting. Luminous switches and wall plates can also be helpful.

As eyesight declines and filter effects join earlier vision changes that involve focusing, distances, steps, doorsills, and pathway obstructions become hazardous. Locations of electrical receptacles should be brought up to current requirements of the National Electrical Code (12 feet o.c. or 3660 mm max) to insure that no electric cords are lying across pathways. Additional light can be designed to warn and guide the elderly. For instance, unidirectional lighting can indicate the approach and height of steps.

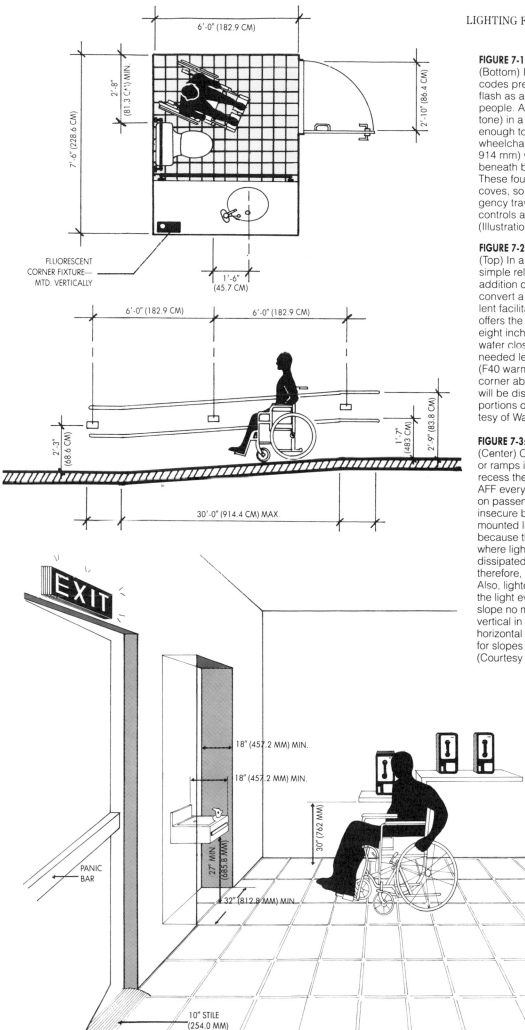

6'-0" (182.9 CM)

2'-8" (81.3 C·) MIN.

7'-6" (228.6 CM)

2'-10" (86.4 CM)

FLUORESCENT
CORNER FIXTURE—
MTD. VERTICALLY

1'-6"
(45.7 CM)

6'-0" (182.9 CM)   6'-0" (182.9 CM)

1'-7" (483 CM)

2'-9" (83.8 CM)

2'-3" (68.6 CM)

30'-0" (914.4 CM) MAX.

EXIT

18" (457.2 MM) MIN.

18" (457.2 MM) MIN.

27" MIN. (685.8 MM)

30" (762 MM)

32" (812.8 MM) MIN.

PANIC
BAR

10" STILE
(254.0 MM)

FIGURE 7-1:   Public Lobbies
(Bottom) In public lobbies where emergency codes prevail, illuminated exit signs must flash as a visual alarm for visually impaired people. At least one public telephone (touch tone) in a public building must be set low enough to be readily accessible to people in wheelchairs. A two- to three-foot (610 mm to 914 mm) wheelchair clearance is required beneath both phones and drinking fountains. These fountains are required to be in alcoves, so as to be out of the path of emergency travel and should be provided with controls accessible to handicapped people. (Illustration by Reiko Hayashi.)

FIGURE 7-2:   Restaurant Men's Room
(Top) In a restaurant remodeling project, the simple relocation of the water closet, the addition of two grab rails, and a new faucet, convert a pre-existing bathroom into "equivalent facilitation." This side entry compartment offers the minimum clearance of two feet, eight inches (813 mm) on one side of the water closet, and the lavatory now has the needed lever control. A lensed fluorescent (F40 warm white) mounted vertically in the corner above the counter assures that light will be distributed throughout the working portions of this pale-colored space. (Courtesy of Watson-Guptill Publications.)

FIGURE 7-3:   Ramps
(Center) One strategy for lighting staircases or ramps is to locate inexpensive fixtures and recess them into the wall (27 inches 686 mm) AFF every six feet. This approach originated on passenger liners where footing was often insecure because of rolling seas. The low-mounted light sources are not glaring and because the fixture is close to the place where light is needed, its light is not uselessly dissipated into the ceiling and wall finishes; therefore, energy is more efficiently used. Also, lighter colors on flooring help to spread the light evenly. Code requires that ramps slope no more than one foot (305 mm) vertical in each twelve foot (4660 mm) horizontal span (1:12). Handrails are required for slopes that exceed 1:15 of any length. (Courtesy of Watson-Guptill Publications.)

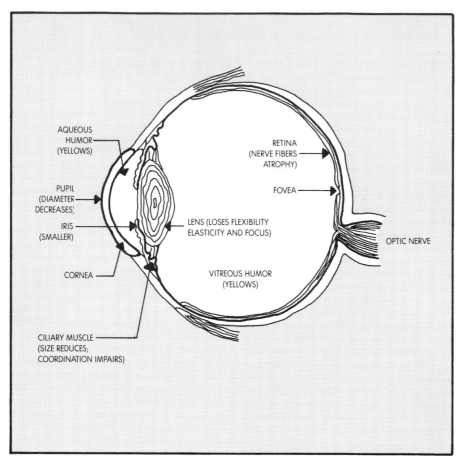

FIGURE 7-4:   The Aging Eye
(Above) The yellowing cornea of the aging eye acts as a color filter; the blue portions of the color spectrum no longer travel as far as the retina and therefore are unseen by the brain. The smaller pupil and iris of the eye admit less light, and in combination with muscle impairment and lens rigidification, cause loss of the eye's focusing capacities. (Adapted from *IES Handbook Reference Volume*, 1984.)

FIGURE 7-5:   A Living Center
(Right) To make room for the chairside electronic marvels that make up a "living center," a table lamp may need to be replaced with a "pin-up" wall fixture equipped with cord and plug. The plug allows the fixture to be rigged into the master switching control by means of an inexpensive module. Lamp shades should be somewhat translucent to reduce the brightness contrast between the shade and the background against which it is seen.

Filter Effects

Five filter effects in the eye are caused by aging. A characteristic yellowish tinge and clouding is frequently experienced as well. When these phenomena occur:

1. Discrimination of hues becomes less accurate

2. The ability to discern or tolerate extremes of light intensity is reduced

3. The aged become sensitive to glare, just at a time when they need more light for visual acuity

4. Night vision becomes a problem

5. Sensitivity to contrast declines

Changes in Visual Field

In old age, both the direction of view and the visual field change considerably. Changes in the skeleton and muscles and the need to look over bifocal eyeglasses cause an individual's body to hunch forward. Such a posture casts the direction of an individual's gaze slightly downward. Also the perception of depth is reduced both in the sense of distance and three-dimensionality; cues to depth are weakened by the filter effects on contrast and the sharpness of edges is blurred. The width of the visual field shrinks as a person normally ages. As an individual's peripheral vision declines, the person is easily disoriented, unaware of objects that are not in direct view.

Design Solutions for Residential Areas

Ambient illumination that changes the light level gradually works best for aging eyes. Glare-free light sources and reflective matte finishes can be used to create such lighting. Because visual impairment is progressive, some experienced designers plan light levels up to 200 footcandles of illumination, but provide dimmers so the individual can adjust his/her own light level as his/her condition changes. Slide dimmers are easier for older fingers, or alternatively, master switching systems with their push buttons may provide such dimming also. Be sure the master control module is not too complicated or the individual buttons too small to distinguish and manipulate.

To minimize falls and spills of a person whose visual field has been altered, clutter can be avoided by designing well lighted and easily reached self-storage accommodations. Suspended lights and other obstructions should be removed. Securely mounted wall fixtures make a good substitute if they are controlled by wall switches or by master switching.

THE AMBULATORY

The ambulatory and the nonambulatory aged and infirm share many disabilities. Rising from a chair is a challenge, so a chairside table that holds a telephone, remote television control, and/or a master switching control minimizes such activity and becomes a "living center." Such a center can enable an aged householder to respond to a variety of situations, such as answering the door by means of an intercom or electrically releasing the door lock (Figure 7-5).

The principal difference between the ambulatory and nonambulatory is in the area of reach. Therefore, the height of switches, outlets, and dials should be in the range common to both—that is, no higher than 4 feet (1220 mm) or lower than 1 foot (305 mm). Familiarity can also be a substitute for sight. Uniform heights in switches and outlets can be a real advantage to the aging. (See Directory in the back of the book for names of manufacturers of switching controls, etc.)

Changing Bulbs
Climbing ladders or even stools to replace a burned out bulb or fuse is too dangerous for the aged (Figure 7-6). To get ten times the life from each lamp bulb, designers often specify fluorescent fixtures where possible and recommend fluorescent adaptors for the remaining incandescent fixtures.

THE NONAMBULATORY
Because both hands are required to roll a wheelchair, it is often difficult for the chairbound to carry things. For this reason, the ambulatory may have one living center that they prefer, but the chairbound person is more likely to have several such living centers. In a residence, the needs of the chairbound vary from room to room.

The Bedroom
Older people spend a steadily increasing part of their lives in bed, so the bedroom becomes the major living center for them (Figure 7-7). The nightstand makes a convenient location for controls. One manufacturer's inexpensive but programmable switching device can be preset to carry out many operations in a 24-hour period. The freedom from remembering to turn entry lights on at dusk, for instance, can be a blessing. For those using this three-way device in a two-story house, the master device can be located and programmed at the upstairs bedside and still have the use of an on/off switch or dimmer near the most frequently used downstairs entry. A wall mounted light with a dimmer on the bedside control is useful for reading prescription labels in the dark. The dimmer is important because certain medications have side effects that can alter vision and additional light will be needed. The final bedroom lighting feature is a low night-light set along the pathway to the bathroom.

The Bathroom
This room is often riddled with glare that can be disturbing to aged and infirm eyes. Matte finishes and light colors for paint, tile, and flooring can help the designer to overcome this by distributing the light evenly around the room. Brightly colored towels will add cheer and are easy to see. The fixtures can cause glare also. One warm white fluorescent tube built into a soffit above the vanity is not glaring, but a small fluorescent PL lamp bulb in the shower and the fluorescent shelf below the mirror could be, if they are not dimmed. The lens-enclosed fluorescent acts as a storage shelf and illuminates the under sides of the face and chin to assist shaving and application of makeup (see Figure 7-8).

The Kitchen
When the cook is an aged person, task lighting becomes much more complex. Remember, the aged eye is slower to see and

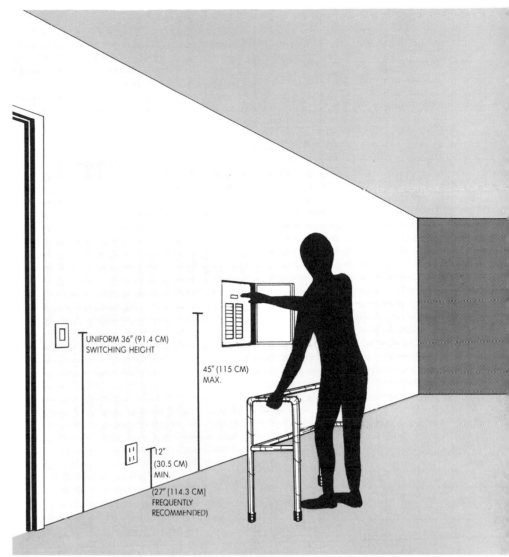

FIGURE 7-6: The Barrier-Free Home
In the Uniform Building Code and in codes published by many offices of the State or Provincial Architect, the following are stipulated: fuseboxes should be in an accessible area for both ambulant and handicapped persons and mounted no higher than 45 inches (1143 mm) AFF, with all circuits clearly labeled. Switches should be pressure or rocker type and mounted 30 inches to 40 inches (762 mm to 1016 mm) AFF, and electrical receptacles (outlets) should be 12 inches to 27 inches (305 mm to 686 mm) AFF. Two out of three wheelchair users prefer 36 inches (914 mm) for switches and 27 inches (686 mm) for outlets. (Illustration by Reiko Hayashi.)

FIGURE 7-7: The Bedroom
Lighting should be adapted to the activities of the invalid. If the chairbound enjoys reading, the lower edge of the lamp shade should be at eye level. The shade should be moderately luminous to avoid excessive brightness contrasts. Shades with an open top allow some light to inter-reflect off the wall, thereby softening brightness contrasts in the immediate area. Bulbs should be the new low-wattage, screw-socket fluorescents positioned low in the shade.

adapt to changing contrasts. Moving from bright counters to darker cupboards can cause visual fatigue and discomfort. Although wood and wood simulations are popular finishes for cabinetry, they are not adequately reflectant. Matte finish, high-reflectancy laminate and tile, matte white paint inside the cabinets are much better choices. Under-cabinet fluorescent lights to illuminate the counters are widely available with their own switches. Overhead, surface-mounted fluorescents (4 feet or 1220 mm) with glare controlling louvers are also available with dimmers or multiple level switching.

Two special lighting needs for the aging cook are one fixture for the stove that is glass-lensed for sanitation and for safety and one fixture above the kitchen table and/or island. The stove fixture should also be gasketed to resist steamy fumes and airborne grease. Such fixtures are mounted vertically or horizontally outside the ventilation hood. Several manufacturers supply these special fluorescents through commercial kitchen dealers and designers.

The other special lighting need is for the kitchen table or island. Because people are prevented from passing underneath, these are good locations for the use of suspended fluorescents. The low mounting brings the tubes closer to the surface where light is needed and where the tubes can easily be changed when they burn out.

Codes that regulate residential lighting energy often require fluorescent light sources in the kitchen, laundry, and bath. Check with your local building inspection department for codes affecting the jurisdiction of a given project (Figure 7-9).

Staircases

In both public and private spaces, the lighting of staircases is a severe problem. Lighting should come from overhead in order to (1) wash the horizontal treads and landings with illumination and (2) emphasize deviations from the horizontal by means of shadowing (Figure 7-10). An additional benefit of locating lights directly overhead of their intended targets is that they are less likely to cause direct glare by protruding into view. Also, if the flight of stairs is long, it is important that the fixtures be indirect or shielded; the classic lighting lawsuit is one brought by an aging person who has fallen and broken a hip on stairs in a public space because "the lights were blinding."

Parking Areas

Lighting these areas is important because to go out, the chairbound driver needs to get from the wheelchair to the driver's seat, lean out to fold up the wheelchair, and put the chair into the back seat. This is a prized skill, but almost impossible to perform without the right light. A garage light should shine into the area outside the driver's door (Figure 7-11).

Too often the "entry" is thought of as the

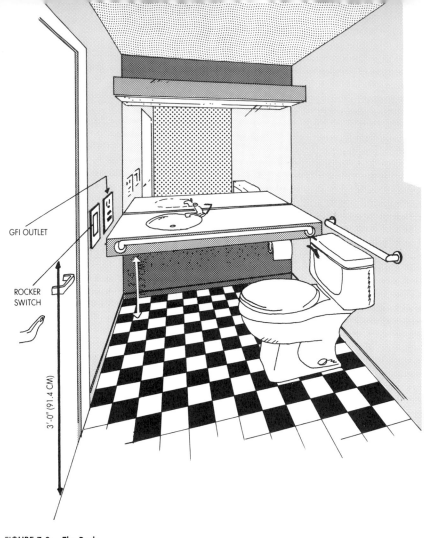

FIGURE 7-8: The Bath
Most codes prohibit electrical fittings near water because of the hazard of electrical shock. However, the same codes may permit these fittings if they are protected by a ground fault interrupter (GFI). The GFI cuts off electrical current so rapidly that only a harmless amount can pass. The GFI device can be in the switch, in the circuit at the fusebox, or in the electrical outlet itself. (Illustration by Reiko Hayashi.)

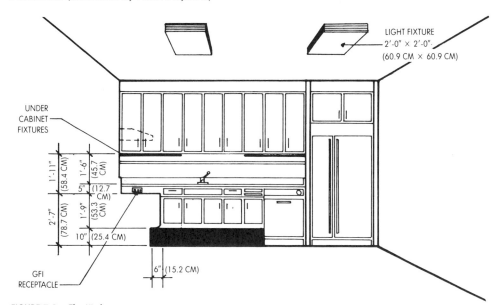

FIGURE 7-9: The Kitchen
Code requires that lighting in the kitchen must be fluorescent. But another reason to use fluorescent lighting is that kitchens for the aged need a lot of light—everywhere. One rule of thumb for kitchen lighting recommends that one watt of F40 fluorescent light per square foot is just about right, but be sure that wall finishes and cabinetry remain reflectant. (Illustration by Reiko Hayashi.)

front door or porch, when the householder actually enters through the garage or back-door. For security, it should be possible to light the route from the driver's seat to the kitchen without getting out of the car. To meet this need, the garage lights and a light at the back door can be rigged into the remote control that opens the garage door, so that these lights turn on when the garage door is opened and turn off when it closes. A second remote controller in the kitchen can turn off the pathway of light upon safe arrival inside.

LOOKING AHEAD

Today any designer who produces an energy-inefficient environment is considered irresponsible. Cannot the same be said for the designer who produces an environment that is insensitive to the special needs of the aging and infirm?

In public spaces, barrier-free design is codified. Beyond the code, however, lie two challenges for the designer. The first is to be creative enough to offer barrier-free features in a subtle and visually harmonious way, so that the person using these features does not feel segregated or labeled by them. The second challenge is to be so in tune with the life process—which creates continually changing individual needs—that the entire design process is permeated with barrier-free logic. For example, a water closet with a toilet mounted at wheelchair height, with the required handrails, will meet code, but if the toilet requires a foot pedal for flushing or the stall can only be locked by a cylinder that must be turned, then barriers have not been completely eliminated.

Designers may begin to incorporate barrier-free planning into residences. Recent advances in medical technology and changes in medical care reimbursements make it desirable for all but the severely handicapped to live at home rather than in an institution. In fact, researchers conclude that the private residential setting reinforces the elderly person's sense of self, and constitutes an emotional support system that fosters a sense of continuity to self, to others, and to nature.[1]

Therefore, it seems likely that the home of the future will contain parents, grandparents, and grandchildren—a three-generation household. Given this trend, plus the increasing costs of construction, today's designer will want to consider barrier-free planning in residences as well as in commercial and public buildings.

CHAPTER NOTES

[1] Ruth Stumpe Brent, "Aging, Environmental Adequacy, and Adaptation," Environmental Design and Research Association Annual Conference, San Luis Obispo, CA, June 1984.

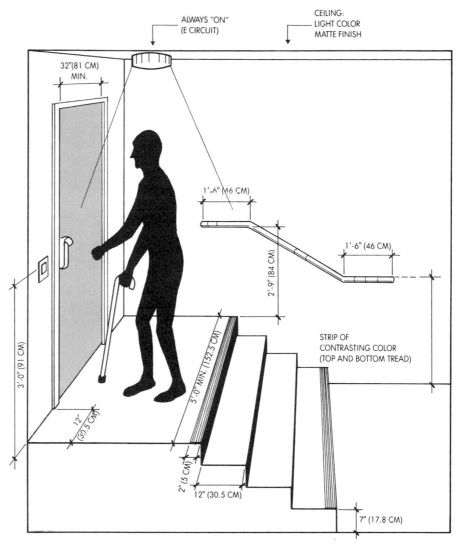

FIGURE 7-10: Staircases
(Above) Steps for those using walkers need to be as much as 12 inches (305 mm) wide. To light them, the light should fall in such a way as to shadow the risers and illuminate the treads. Nosers should be removed. They not only confuse the eye in its attempt to read these shadows, they also cause persons with stiff joints, braces, or artificial legs to catch their toes as they climb. In some code jurisdictions, a 2-inch (51 mm) strip of clearly contrasting color at the upper approach and the bottom tread is also required. If a fall does occur, the top step and landing are the most likely places for one. (Illustration by Reiko Hayashi.)

FIGURE 7-11: The Garage
(Right) The chairbound need a five-foot corridor along the side of an auto in order to get in and out. At the driver's side, lighting is a great benefit to the chairbound driver who stows his or her own wheelchair. Enclosed fluorescents with special "low temperature" ballasts will strike on the coldest days and still offer both infrequent tube replacement and energy conservation. (Illustration by Reiko Hayashi.)

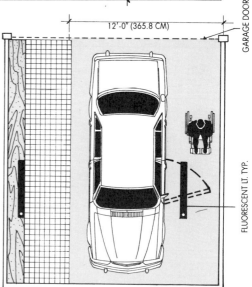

LIGHTING PLANTS— INDOORS AND OUTDOORS

Chapter Eight

FOR PLANTS, light is life. In order to produce plants that are healthy, as well as beautiful, the designer must provide the correct amount of—as well as the most attractive—light. Indoor plants are often lighted in a way that enhances their appearance but jeopardizes their health. Conversely, the lighting that would promote maximum growth for plants often produces cascades of glaring light. Finding the correct lighting balance between these two extremes is the challenge that faces the designer who accessorizes with plants.

INDOORS

For spaces where interior plantings play a predominate role, good design means simulating the light they would receive in their natural setting. In nature, a mixture of beam sunlight, reflected light from the ground nearby, and scattered light from the sky's haze provides seasonal cues upon which the plant's maturation depends. However, indoors, a variety of factors can inhibit plant growth:

Light may come from only one direction.

There are fewer hours of darkness in which the plant can absorb nutrients.

There is usually much less light.

The Need for Light

A plant's need for light will vary over its life span in three areas: color, light intensity, and light duration.

Color. Nature's light blends red, orange, yellow, green, and blue rays. In the sun's spectrum there are also rays of ultraviolet and infrared light that are invisible to humans. Although knowledge on the subject is far from complete, a plant's life schedule seems to depend upon getting the right colors of light at the appropriate time in its growth cycle. For example, cool blue-white and violet light are needed to stimulate the process of photosynthesis, while the warmer end of the color spectrum enables the production of chlorophyll for green parts of the plant's cells. Specific red and far-red rays affect elongation and expansion of various plant parts, notably the formation of flowers and fruit. Sooner or later at least three colors of light are needed during a plant's life to promote healthy growth.

Light Intensity. There seem to be several stages in a plant's adaptation to light. First, there is a level of light at which a plant species will maintain itself but not show a net gain in size or foliage. At the next stage of slightly higher light levels, plants will go through their entire life cycle as seen in Appendix C-3: Light and Light-Related Requirements for Popular Species of Indoor Plants; they will gain in size and reproduce. Finally, at the lowest level, insufficient light produces long, weak stems and leaves and less foliage than normal as the plant stretches toward the light. Even if such a plant is suddenly given adequate light, it may not revive.

Light Duration. The amount and spectrum of available interior daylight must be one of the designer's primary concerns when planning the location and size of interior planters. The direction that the windows face as well as their proximity to the plants is very important because window direction controls the duration as well as the color and intensity of light.

East: During most seasons of the year, the rays of eastern light are blue, green, and yellow. Eastern exposures receive direct morning light only from sunrise to near midday. Although morning light intensity can reach 5,000 to 8,000 footcandles, the room with eastern exposure will be cooler than one with a southern or western exposure, because hot red and infrared rays have scattered into the upper atmosphere to warm the layers of moist morning air. As a consequence, the infrared heat does not reach the building itself to heat it. Most plants prefer such an east orientation, because it is less dehydrating.

South: The seasonal variation of southern light is greater than that on any other side of the building. In the winter, sun streams in at a long, low angle to give plants light and heat in the months when it is most needed. In the summer, the sun spends most of the day overhead; its burning rays radiate on the roof rather than through south windows.

West: Western exposures have the highest average temperatures. Supplemental humidity, good air circulation, and a curtain for light filtration can be of great value to indoor plants from spring through fall months to help survive long days having an overabundance of light.

North: Even on the summer solstice, the longest day of the year, the sun only peeks into a true north window for a few hours. Northern exposures receive the least direct sunlight and the least heat. Northern light may be the most stable in color, heat, and intensity over the course of the day, season, or year. But it will barely provide even maintenance light levels for most plant species. Northern windows offer as little as 200 footcandles on a clear day in midwinter, and that is often with the additional reflections of light off of snow. See Figure 8-1 for a guide to which windows will support which species of plant.

Different Species, Different Light Needs

All of these phenomena involving color, intensity, and duration vary with the botanical species under consideration. Flowering plants require direct light for part of each day or supplemental artificial light if direct daylight is not available. Variegated varieties are to be avoided because white repels light, so maximum photosynthesis is required from the available amount of light and this only occurs in the green parts of plants. Tropical plants are often blessed

with too much light indoors. Their leaves then wilt during the hottest part of the day: they curl downward and develop brown or black burned spots. Alternatively, the foliage may undergo color change and bleach out in an effort to increase reflectivity and reject a higher percentage of assaulting light.

Artificial Light and Plant Growth

Even by manipulating these three qualities of light—intensity, color, and duration—normal interior lighting is never quite right for plant growth. Specialized lighting is required. While artificial lamp bulbs cannot exactly duplicate natural light because their colors and intensities and heat are in different proportions, still certain combinations of artificial light can faithfully induce the natural responses of some varieties of plants.

Plant Growth Processes

Plants will be healthiest if their natural habitat is simulated. In nature, light strongly regulates at least three major plant processes: photosynthesis, phototropism, and photoperiodism.

Photosynthesis. In this process, water and atmospheric carbon dioxide are converted in the catalytic presence of light into carbohydrates which enable growth of new foliage as well as roots, stems, and blooms. In certain indoor species, this photoreaction occurs in relatively low levels of light that may be typical of the season the plant would be a seedling in its native climate. Such growth will not occur equally well when levels of heat and light become too high.

Phototropism. This is the tendency of plants to grow toward their light source. In nature, the sun does the rotating; indoors the designer must compensate. Where the natural light source is a window, plants will bend toward the source, so they may have to be rotated from time to time in order to keep a rounded growth and appearance.

For this reason, with indoor trees, the designer may want to consider pots on wheels. When the lighting is artificial, for most plants the best single location of the electric light source is above the plant. But if all the light is focused onto the upper leaves alone, there is a problem, because these leaves receive all the light and shade the lower leaves. In nature, the lower leaves would receive reflected ground light. Without it, the lower branches of an indoor plant will defoliate. It is therefore best to use light from more than one direction whenever possible; in this case, supplemental indirect light from below.

Photoperiodism. This refers to the fact that all plants are "light-programmed" to their native environment; they perform best in the seasonal rhythms of light and darkness that are found there. For many plants, the length of nights and days is a determining

FIGURE 8-1: Best Plant Placement

☐ PLANTING ZONE

▦ TOO CLOSE UNLESS LIGHT IS FILTERED

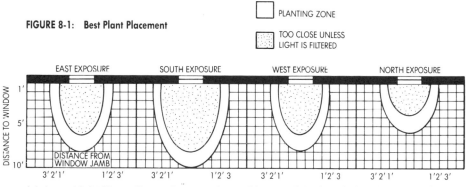

(a) Long-Night Plants: Some plants survive well in more light than their optimum, but few can tolerate less light. Over long periods, below a certain minimum illumination, the plant will use up its stored carbohydrates and die.

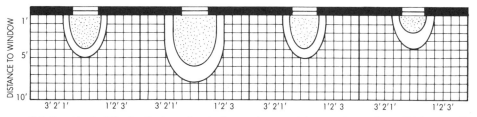

(b) Day-Neutral Plants: Photosynthesis does not occur at temperatures above 85 degrees F; so succulents are among the few plants that can take the four hours of direct sunlight that western windows can provide.

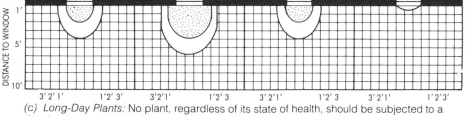

(c) Long-Day Plants: No plant, regardless of its state of health, should be subjected to a drastic change of light without conditioning. If a plant's location is to be changed, it should be done over a period of weeks. (Illustration by Joanne Lim Stinson.)

FIGURE 8-2: Silhouetting
Silhouetting is a lighting technique in which the designer locates an interesting filagree object between the viewer and a lighted vertical surface. In this context, such a vertical surface acts as a background or "negative space." Although the manzanita bough is perfect here, dried materials are not necessary for silhouetting. Because light strikes the plant only indirectly, deterioration is minimal. (Lighting by Jan Moyer, ASID, Luminae; Illustration by Reiko Hayashi; Photograph by Mary E. Nichols.)

FIGURE 8-3: Uplighting
With the technique of uplighting, all the light is cast upwards onto horizontal or diagonal surfaces. Because this lighting effect is not often seen in nature, it is very eye-catching and dramatic. Uplighting is normally used only on trees; in less hardy species, the tree's underleaf—where moisture is stored and nutrients are converted for use—is ill suited to the direct heat produced by this lighting technique. (Lighting by Luminae; Illustration by Reiko Hayashi; Photograph by Julius Shulman.)

FIGURE 8-4: Decorative Fixtures
Using decorative fixtures is a lighting technique that involves delivering light to a space while, at the same time, utilizing as accessories the housings of the lamps. This unusual fixture by Sylvan Designs can be used indoors or outdoors; it is low voltage and encases the transformer in the base where the additional weight lends extra stability. (Lighting by Luminae; Illustration by Reiko Hayashi; Photograph by Mary E. Nichols.)

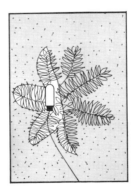

FIGURE 8-5: Backlighting
As a technique, backlighting uses low brightness light sources like cold cathodes and fluorescents to create a field of light behind the translucent plane which the designer wants to feature. Such a technique turns some ferns into luminous sculpture, but because ferns are moisture-loving, too many nights of being backlighted can kill them. (Lighting by Luminae; Illustration by Reiko Hayashi; Photograph by Fran Kellogg Smith.)

FIGURE 8-6: Shadow Play
The technique of shadow play uses objects to interefere with the beam of light to evoke images from nature. For example, the use of cool light for a projection of shadows created by outdoor leaves and branches can bring to mind the image of a moonlit night. As seen here, this technique presents two threats to the health of the plant: (1) the underleaf of most tropical species grown indoors is invariably sensitive to heat, and (2) the normal day-night cycle of the plant is disrupted. (Lighting by Luminae; Illustration by Reiko Hayashi; Photograph by Wen Roberts.)

FIGURE 8-7: Sparkle
Sparkle is a technique used to create sensory stimulation and a sense of celebration or fun. Light sources must be selected that use small bits of high brightness. If the light sources are less than 1/2 watt, their heat (1.7 BTU) can damage only the most tender of new growth. (Lighting by Luminae; Illustration by Reiko Hayashi; Photograph by Mary E. Nichols.)

factor in the time required to reach maturity. Maturity for plants is that stage in the life cycle when reproduction becomes possible. Both flowering and fruiting are stages of plant reproduction. Some plants flower best when the days are long—14 hours or more; still other plants will not form buds unless they receive at least 14 hours of darkness while their buds are setting. Luckily some plants seem not to be as particular as this. (See Appendix C-3: Light and Light-Related Requirements for Popular Species of Indoor Plants. This chart shows which species have a preference.)

Lamp Bulbs for Plant Lighting
Since most colors of fluorescent tubes are rich in foliage-producing blue rays, plants grown primarily for their foliage can subsist on fluorescent light alone. The typical fluorescent tube not only burns more than ten times longer than an incandescent bulb, it also burns cool enough so that the foliage of most plants can touch the tube without injury.

Plants that bloom or fruit, however, require red and far-red rays as well. They must experience sunlight, incandescent light, or light from special fluorescent or high intensity discharge sources if they are to perform well. Because sunlight has both blue, red, and far-red rays, a combination of these rays is best. Ways to achieve this mix are suggested in Table 8-1.

Increasing Light
There are only a few methods of increasing light to a plant:

1. Add more lamp bulbs

2. Move the plants closer to the fixtures

3. Reflect more light to the plant from surrounding surfaces

4. Periodically remove—slowly—the plant to the outdoors for supplemental sunlight

Another way to modify the light level "seen" by the plant is to keep the plant absolutely clean; as much as 80 percent of the available light can be screened away by dust and grime on the foliage.

Reducing Heat
If the designer adds more lamp bulbs to increase light, then heat becomes a concern. Not only can heat desiccate the foliage of a plant, it can also drive away the atmospheric humidity needed by most of the tropical varieties of plants grown indoors.

Incandescent light as the sole source of radiant energy will rarely suffice because it is both too hot and deficient in the blue and ultraviolet portions of the spectrum. There are, however, a couple of ways to reduce the heat of an incandescent lamp bulb: for instance, General Electric's "cool beam" and MR-16 bulbs greatly reduce the amount of heat in the beam by reflecting more than half the heat out the back of the lamp bulb.

TABLE 8-1 ELECTRIC LIGHT SOURCES FOR PLANT GROWTH

LIGHT SOURCE (one each)	DISTANCE	FOOTCANDLES
Gro-Lux Wide Spectrum (Red and UV Additives)	6″	430
	12″	320
F40/Warm White with F40/Cool White	6″	620
	12″	460
F40/Cool White with 30R20 Incandescent	12″	330
160-Watt Wonderlite (Mercury with Supplemental Red)	24″	375
	6′	38
175-Watt Mercury with 250-Watt Tungsten Halogen Flood	4′	641
	6′	285

FIGURE 8-8: Outdoor Lighting
Outdoor lighting is the most creative and dramatic of all areas of lighting design. Here the designer as artist has absolute control of the black canvas provided by the night. (Lighting by Jan Moyer, ASID, Luminae; Photograph by Mary E. Nichols.)

Be sure to use fixtures that are UL-labeled to mate with these bulbs.

A second way to cool the heat in the beam of an incandescent light source is to use an incandescent lamp having krypton-fill gases. This lamp is offered by several manufacturers as a "longer-lived" light source because the krypton gas filling the glass envelope causes the incandescent filament to burn cooler, and therefore, longer. With both of these solutions, however, there is some loss of the red portion of the color spectrum as well. Despite this reduction in the heat of the light beam, do not place these sources too close to the plant or it will burn. One rule of thumb is that if your hand feels warm when held at the foliage closest to the light source, then the plant is too close.

Displaying Plants with Light

There are six primary lighting techniques that can be used effectively to display plants: silhouetting, uplighting, shadow play, decorative fixtures, sparkle, and backlighting. Each one creates unique effects that enhance the appearance of plantings while providing illumination for the interior (see Figures 8-2 through 8-7).

OUTDOORS

The outdoor landscape is lighted chiefly for display. While daylight reveals every detail of the landscape panorama equally, darkness allows lighting to single out landscape features that may have been lost during the day. (See Figure 8-8.) Controlled lighting can emphasize plantings and form them into interesting compositions that can elongate or condense perspective.

Composition

Use the following sequence to compose the landscape with light (Figure 8-9):

1. Discover the most effective as well as the most common viewing points inside the building.

2. Select an object that will dominate the field and help determine the "depth of field."

3. Decide how bright the outside landscape elements must be in order to be brighter than the inside lighting.

The opening to the outdoors acts as the picture frame for the landscape. The farthest brightness from the viewer defines his/her perspective or *depth of field;* the foreground brightnesses nearest the opening are used to catch the viewer's interest. To keep the two from popping unnaturally out of the darkness, some fill light is used to lead the eye through the midground and help it to understand the spatial relationship between the foreground and distance (Figure 8-10).

Safety Concerns

Outdoor landscape lighting is akin to photographic lighting because it is intended for

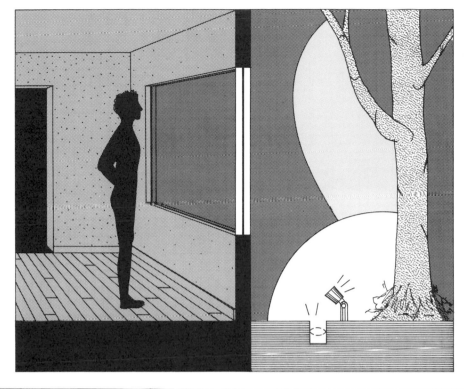

FIGURE 8-9: Balancing Light Levels
The vertical brightness of surfaces inside the room should be lower than those of objects outside, in order to avoid reflective glare on the glass which would obscure the outdoor view at night. In fact, it is very difficult to create high levels of vertical brightness outdoors, because plant materials are seldom reflective. Therefore, the interior level of light must be quite dim in order for the outdoors to seem bright. (Illustration by Reiko Hayashi.)

FIGURE 8-10: Framing the Nightscape
The opening from the interior to the outdoors acts as a picture frame for the landscape and its lighting. (Lighting by Jan Moyer, ASID, Luminae; Photograph by Mary E. Nichols.)

FIGURE 8-11: Lighting Outdoor Steps
If the designer chooses to light the steps from overhead, he/she should take care that the shadow of the walking person does not interefere with the visibility of the steps. (Fixtures © Nightscaping by Loran.)

passive viewing. But there are some areas of the landscape that are used actively at night, such as the driveway, entry, patio, pool, and various sports areas. In areas where people will walk, safety must be a concern. Pedestrians must not be disabled momentarily by glare from uncontrolled light sources and the level of illumination must facilitate safe passage.

Steps. When the designer is lighting steps, the shadow should fall evenly either across the treads or across the risers, so they can easily be identified through their contrasting relationship to one another. Do not broadcast light over steps from the downside, which may destroy the contrast between planes (Figure 8-11).

Pool. A first concern in lighting the pool has to be the safety of children and passersby. With underwater lights on, there is no doubt that all can identify the pool, but the lighted landscape or cityscape reflected on the surface of the pool can only be appreci-

ated when the underwater lights are off. But there are now two kinds of lighting controls that allow safety and beauty.

Dimmers and personnel detectors can be used to make a pool or pond safe for passersby. A dimmer can be useful in allowing a glow from the underwater lights that will identify the presence of the pool while still permitting reflections to be seen on the surface of the water. As an alternative, infrared personnel detectors can cause the underwater lights to electrify only when someone comes near the pool.

Working Procedure for Landscape Lighting

The National Electrical Code and most local and state codes have provisions that are applicable to the installation of outdoor wiring. The local building inspection department will advise the designer and answer questions relating to electrical safety; most communities offer plan review when applying for permits. But the designer needs to remember that the inspector in the field does not regard earlier answers from the inspection department as binding.

In designing the nightscape, landscaping needs are planned first. A preliminary lighting plan is then added, usually as an overlay. For the installation phase, however, the rough electrical wiring goes into the ground at the same time as the plantings. The young transplants are given an opportunity to settle in with as little further disturbance as possible. Later, the fixtures are mounted, wired to the earlier electrical service, and focused.

As the young plants grow from year to year, it becomes an annual spring event to turn on the lights and go into the nightscape to move the stake-mounted fixtures backwards just a foot or so to accommodate the previous year's growth with a larger beam of light.

This issue of permanency versus flexibility is key. Around commercial buildings like banks and medical offices stationary, tamperproof lighting systems are often used, but for residential buildings portable fixtures can be used to achieve a new lighting effect. Portable fixtures can be moved to highlight different plantings in different seasons. This allows an opportunity to check the lamp bulbs and louvers as well as to remove any accumulated leaves and dirt.

Low-Voltage Lighting

Among the outdoor lighting systems, low-voltage ones are the most popular. They are generally considered safer and easier to install than standard voltage systems. They offer more precise and subtle effects and the bulbs operate more efficiently than other low-wattage incandescent light sources, using less electricity to deliver more pleasing outdoor effects. The biggest savings, however, are due to the fact that in most code jurisdictions, low-voltage open-wiring systems can be installed without the

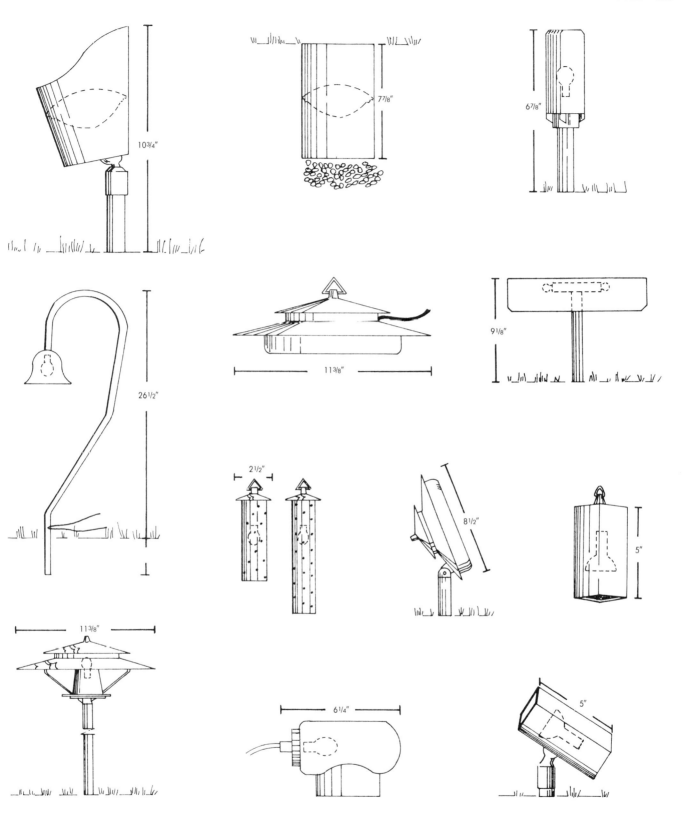

FIGURE 8-12: Low-Voltage Equipment Landscape Lighting
The simplest low-voltage systems have only a few parts: a transformer with a 6-foot cord and plug that is stepping electrical current down from 120 volts to 12 volts, a length of specially insulated conductor cable, several identical fixtures on stakes bearing UL labels for outdoor use, and perhaps, a handful of louvers or special lenses to obscure the beam from view or spread the light. By comparison, most professional designers use a system with a much larger variety of fixture types and fixture finishes to ensure a professional result. Nightscaping by Loran is one of the broader lines of fixturing available to designers and landscapers everywhere. (Designs © Nightscaping by Loran.)

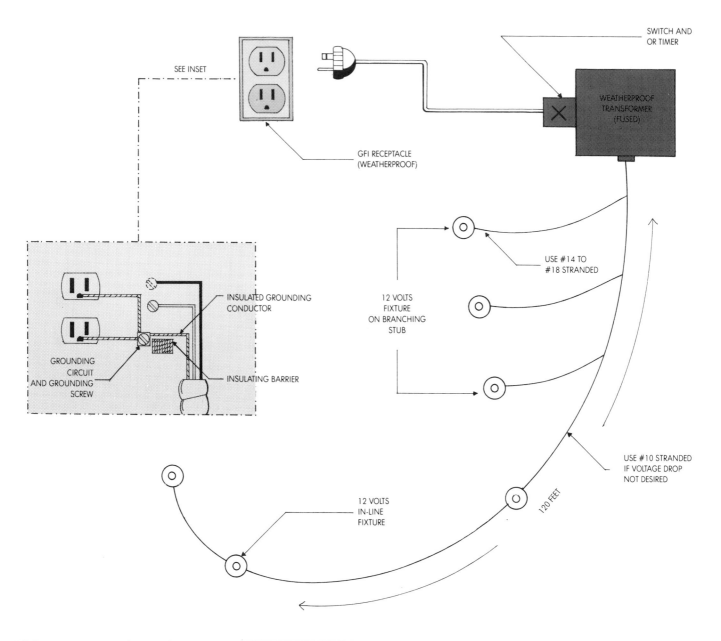

SWITCH AND
OR TIMER

SEE INSET

GFI RECEPTACLE
(WEATHERPROOF)

WEATHERPROOF
TRANSFORMER
(FUSED)

USE #14 TO
#18 STRANDED

12 VOLTS
FIXTURE
ON BRANCHING
STUB

INSULATED GROUNDING
CONDUCTOR

GROUNDING
CIRCUIT
AND GROUNDING
SCREW

INSULATING BARRIER

USE #10 STRANDED
IF VOLTAGE DROP
NOT DESIRED

120 FEET

12 VOLTS
IN-LINE
FIXTURE

FIGURE 8-13: Laying Out the Low-Voltage System
Note: The low-voltage transformer should be mounted at least 12 inches above grade near a weatherproof 120-volt electrical outlet. Specify a transformer of no less than 100 watts (100VA or .1kVA) that has a grounding shield between the primary and secondary windings. This safety feature prevents the more powerful 120 volts from reaching the 12 volt wiring and exploding the low-voltage bulbs. (Illustration by Reiko Hayashi.)

FIGURE 8-14: Concealing Outdoor Wiring
Burying the electric wires is easy. A shovel is thrust about 6 inches into the turf at about a 45-degree angle to open a slit. The wire is tucked in the bottom of the cut and the earth is pressed back into place. The result is no visible wires and no damage to the lawn from digging trenches for 120 volt conduits. There is a special treatment for beds of open earth, however. Here the underground wiring must be protected from spades by placing scrap lumber over the wire as shown. (Courtesy of Lane Publishing Company.)

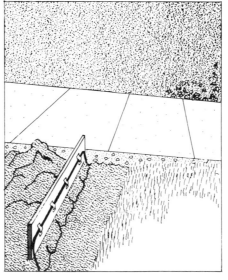

need for conventional electrical conduits, junction boxes, and other components that are required for 120-volt fixtures.

Still another reason for the popularity of low-voltage landscape lighting is its wide-spread availability at all purchasing points in the electrical distribution system. It is available to consumers at the nursery or garden department, to the professional landscaper through his/her wholesaler, and to the professional specifier through any electrical contractor (Figure 8-12).

Lighting Design Procedure
To light a particular area, the greatest cost involves bringing a 120-volt electric current in by means of conduit or piping laid in trenches across the landscape. There are several items to consider when working out the rough plan:

1. How many weatherproof receptacles are present; how many new ones will be

needed? Weatherproof receptacle outlets may be needed in the "damp locations" variety where there is an overhang and in the "wet locations" variety wherever the outlet is exposed to the weather.

2. Approximately how many lights will be needed? The designer must mentally light the object or surface to establish the depth of field first. Then, the designer can work toward the viewing spot.

3. How many transformers will be needed? (Figure 8-13.) Bubble diagramming of a 100-foot radius can be used to corral light fixture locations.

4. Are there trees, eaves, or other overhangs on which equipment can be mounted by the installer?

5. Will timers, dimmers, or other controls be incorporated into the system to minimize maintenance?

6. Is there a master override switch in the building to activate or deactivate the system in an emergency?

Next, if a low-voltage lighting system seems most cost-effective, then the low-voltage wiring is extended from the transformer into the area to be lighted. For fixtures that do not fall along a continuous path of the 100-foot conductor, smaller "branches" of electrical #14 conductor, equally heavily insulated, can be spliced into the main trail of #12 conductor at desired

locations. The smaller branches can be relocated just by unclipping them and clipping them in again at another location along the main trail.

Concealing the Wiring
After the wiring system has been located and the lighting fixtures positioned, the designer must decide if the low-voltage wiring would be better concealed underground. If you know that the fixtures will be moved and adjusted more than once a year, then it is better to leave their conductor branch above grade, if local code permits. However, burying them is not only more attractive, it also moves the wires out of the way so as not to damage passersby or be damaged by children or animals (Figure 8-14).

Controls
The electrical voltage supplied to most homes and offices can vary. This has been especially true since the energy crunch when the load-shedding practices of some utilities increased. For every 5-volt variation in their primary voltage, there is about a half-volt variation at the secondary voltage terminals of a low-voltage transformer. Because low-voltage lamp bulbs are designed to experience only 12 volts, their life, color, and brightness respond radically to any slight change.

For instance, even one volt of secondary reduction (10 volts primary) can extend the life of a 12-volt bulb by 300 percent; the brightness will drop to 75 percent, how-

ever, and the lamp color will become more butter-like. All three effects can be virtues outdoors where subtle lighting effects are prettier. One way to regulate the voltage is to use a special low-voltage dimmer on the primary side of the current to each transformer. There are several new electronic dimmers especially made for low-voltage electrical circuits. By adding the total maximum wattage rating of the transformer(s) to be governed (total Volt-Amps (VA)) and adding in another 20 percent of that total, the maximum capacity needed in a dimmer can be specified.

LOOKING AHEAD
When lighting is skillfully and imaginatively designed, a graceful tree can be easily drawn out of the darkness (Figure 8-15). The lighting designer can become a magician, and with just the faintest wave of the electrical hand, the viewer can be made to see only what is beautiful in nature.

FIGURE 8-15: Landscape Lighting Plan/ Partial Project
The entertainment patio on this Southern California estate is planned for guests who want to enjoy a drink while playing volleyball or watching their teenagers at play. The court is evenly lighted to a very high level for serious players; while the patio is lighted with a mix of uplighted trees and a dappled moonlight effect for serious drinkers. (Illustration by Reiko Hayashi.)

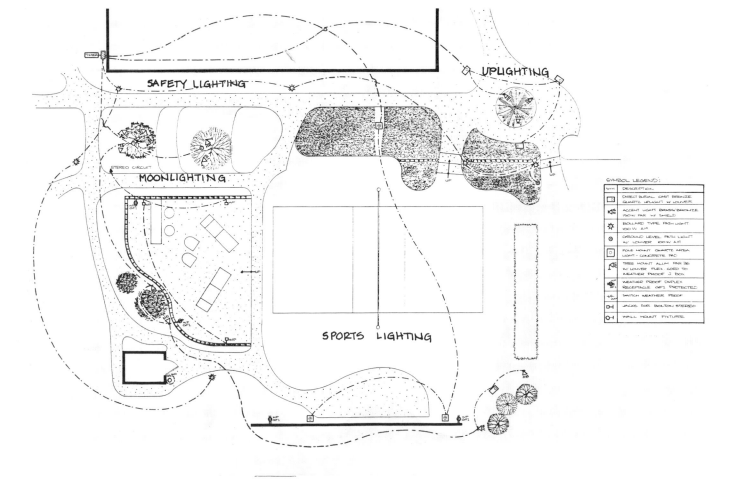

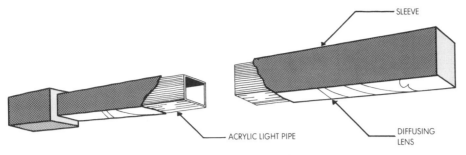

SLEEVE

ACRYLIC LIGHT PIPE

DIFFUSING LENS

FIGURE 9-4:   The Prism Light Guide
(Above) There are practical advantages to using an acrylic light guide: maintenance costs are low; the acrylic material holds its optical properties indefinitely; and since the sleeve forms a dust seal, the system requires no special cleaning. (Courtesy of TIR Systems Ltd.)

FIGURE 9-5:   Luminous Furniture
(Below) Scars or scratches in this luminous furniture diffuse the escaping light. If the depth of the scars becomes increasingly shallow as the scarring moves nearer to the source of the light, the luminosity of etched words or figures will appear more uniform. (Photograph by Mary E. Nichols.)

sible area and the light itself "piped" up to where it is needed.

3. By placing the light source outside of interior spaces, light pipes eliminate the heat load usually placed on air conditioning, thus saving energy.

Acrylic Panels. Etched and frosted acrylic panels are seen everywhere: in restaurants, hotels, lounges, and homes. These panels are like transparent pictures. Frosted words, figures, patterns, and other images can be etched into their clear flat surfaces. Alternatively, the flat sheet itself may be lightly sandblasted all over and the words or figures left clear and transparent. In either case, an acrylic or glass panel will appear luminous in those places where its surface has been broken. But where the surface of the panel is left intact, the light will be unseen as it continues to be imprisoned by principles of internal reflection.

There are at least three reasons why such etched glass or acrylic panels are commissioned:

1. Acrylic is currently fashionable. The revival of art nouveau styles has brought acrylic interpretations of designs originally executed in etched glass.

2. Acrylic creates excellent signs. Light takes on two-dimensional shapes by means of clear acrylic sections contrasted against luminous ones.

3. Acrylic panels are useful as partitions for small spaces. When the panel is mostly clear, it can serve as an acoustic barrier and as a way to block traffic without blocking the view, as well as a way to enlarge an enclosed space. When the partition is mostly frosted, it serves to lend privacy by obscuring the view, to partition a space visually and acoustically, and to prevent passage.

Many techniques used for lighting fibers and light pipes are used for lighting acrylic panels. First, an intense and directional light source is preferable. The location of the light source and the shape of its beam should allow light to enter the interior skin of the panel at an oblique angle. The edge near the light source should be ground and polished to minimize interference of stray particles at this critical juncture in the path of the light. One technique for lighting the acrylic panel is to place the light source in a bay carved out of the panel itself. In this way, light can distribute simultaneously through a wider radius (Figure 9-5). Another technique involves painting or silvering the panel edges that are far from the light source, so as to corral escaping light and force it to continue its course of internal reflection.

KINETIC EFFECTS
When used in interiors, the effects of moving light are mesmerizing and lighthearted.

They are intended to give pleasure and, sometimes, to produce awe. Rainbows slowly encircle the vestibule or atrium of shopping malls or hotels; rainlights shower over the shoulders of merrymakers in discotheques; and, of course, festive spots of light from mirrored balls rotate briskly through ballrooms everywhere. Using light to create certain beam effects like "pools of light" or "rainlight" can be done by anyone. Selecting the right bulb guarantees a predictable result. However, artistry with light goes well beyond the predictable. It includes an element of risk. (What works well in the imagination may not succeed in reality.) At no time is this more apparent than when lighting effects are in motion.

Rainbows

Both diffraction and refraction of light can produce the joyful, moving fragments of a rainbow. Several regionally well-known artists work "in rainbows." They accept architectural commissions in which giant prisms are designed to cast bands of rainbow color through an interior space. Such prisms must be faceted to the specific geometry of the interior and to the sun angles on the site; but the daily, seasonal and climatic changes in nature provide the variety and motion. When the light source is not sunlight, effects can also be generated with electric light sources.

Lumia

Scientifically speaking, light waves underlie the phenomenon of color just as sound waves underlie the experience of music. The similarities between light waves and sound waves have been known for some time. But it is the intuitive response to the combination of music with color, called *lumia,* that is so mysterious and exciting (Figures 9-6, 9-7, and Color Plate 17).

There is a rich tradition for today's visual music that goes back to the 1700s. Over the years, one-of-a-kind instruments with magical names like "the clavilux," "the colortron," and the "celeston" were born. They are actually color organs comprised of combinations of lights controlled by a hand-operated console that creates free-flowing shapes of color. These colored images dance to music. They drift and streak or snap and explode, pulsing with color and then melting into nothingness (Figure 9-8).

Laser Art

During a laser performance, the powerful, collimated beam of laser light moves like a pencil in the night to draw figures in the air with a continuous line. For a few seconds, the retina of the eye holds the completed lines as a bright after-image. In the darkness the after-image combines smoothly with the newer lines as the laser races on. Despite the fact that the images are never all completed at one time, the observer experiences laser performance as a continuous picture. Laser performance holds

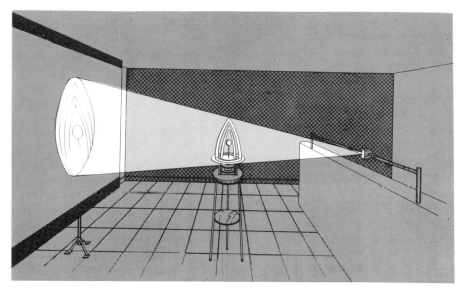

FIGURE 9-6:   Early Lumia
(Above) Spot lights, flood lights, dimmers, prisms, filters, and screens are all examples of fittings used to create lumia. All of these were under the control of an elaborate hand-operated console. (Illustration by Reiko Hayashi.)

FIGURE 9-7:   The Chromaton
(Below) This instrument plays free-flowing shapes of color formed by sculptures like those illustrated in Figure 9-6.

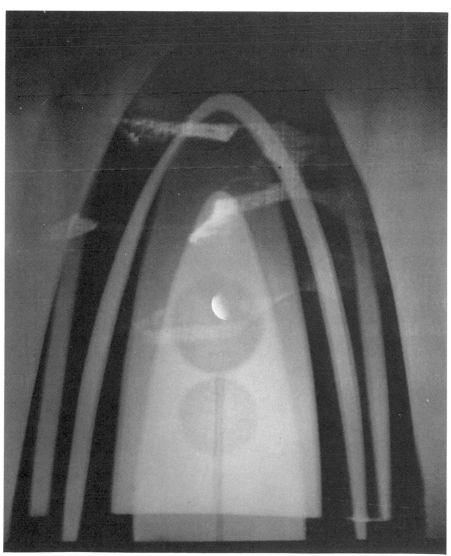

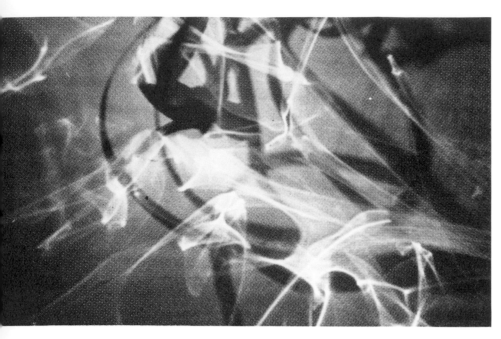

the essence of both theatre and art. When the moment passes, the images are gone—held only in memory.

For the interior designer and the lighting designer, a laser performance provides an opportunity to produce and direct a cast of light beams. However, only a few designers such as Harriet Adams and Tully Weiss of Dallas have taken advantage of this opportunity. Says lighting expert Weiss, ". . . lasers are fascinating in that they can actually restructure some interiors with their colored beams of light. What has been created here . . . are seemingly physical planes or sheets of light in the air."[1] The owner of the interior shown in Color Plate 15, a collector of fine art, changes the 24 preset laser effects as frequently as he changes his collections. In this way, the laser provides a way to make a given space serve multiple purposes—a primary requisite for future habitats.

Laser is an acronym for "light amplification by stimulated emission radiation." There are solid crystal lasers, gas lasers, and semiconductor lasers; but the power of each is similar. It is based on the observation that an excited atom more rapidly and readily gives off photons of light when another photon with the same energy characteristics is present. In effect, the first photon "stimulates" the excited atom to clone a new photon of the same energy, frequency, and phase as the first. Because the emerging photons all travel in the same direction, the beam has very little divergence. For instance, a laser beam directed at the moon left earth with a diameter of 0.197 inches (0.5 cm); it illuminated a circle on the moon that had a diameter of 0.59 inches (1.5 cm).

For the experienced lighting designer or artist, the laser opens a field of visual communication that is as exciting as it is new. It is important to remember that even a low power laser is dangerous. Looking directly into its collimated beam can be even more damaging than staring at the sun.

ILLUSIONS

The third category of light as art consists of illusions created by reflected light. These include holograms, the color aberrations of Dan Flavin, and the disembodied rooms of James Turrell. While these have always been the most magical of lighting effects, only recently have their practical applications been recognized. To escape the boredom and feelings of deprivation inherent in smaller and architecturally simpler interiors, designers can use a surprising number of devices and techniques to create spatial illusions. Such spatial limitations provide challenge and excitement for the future of lighting design. Lighting illusions offer the possibility to enlarge, customize, and change such interior spaces with the flip of a switch.

Figure Illusions: Holography
The first of these illusions is the *holograph*.

FIGURE 9-8: Mobile Color
(Top) A viewer's response to lumia can range from interest in the visual effect to complete immersion in the ambience created by the colors and shapes produced.

**FIGURE 9-9:   *Image of Tutenkamen I,*
by Michael Foster**
(Above) The viewer sees the hologram as if "through a window." The first holograms were recorded and reconstructed with laser light of only one color, but current holograms can be seen in a full spectrum of colors. (Photograph/Hologram by Michael Foster.)

The viewer sees a holograph as if "through a window." All the depth of a scene or figure as well as its height and width are apparent (Figure 9-9). When he/she moves, features that may have been blocked from view by an object are revealed; the new vantage point seems to allow the viewer to "look around" the obstruction. The eye of the viewer refocuses between foreground and background just as it would if it were viewing the real scene. It is as if the scene or figure were actually present. The left eye even sees a view that's slightly different from that of the right eye.

Two procedures are needed in holography: the first is the creation of the *hologram,* a film that records both the amplitude and phases of light that reflect from a scene. The second is a *holograph,* an assembly of mirrors and lenses that create a three-dimensional reconstruction of the scene by using collimated light to retrieve and display the information recorded on the hologram (Figure 9-10). The hologram contains far more information than a phtograph: it indicates not only the pattern of light that plays over the recorded scene, but also the relative directions from which the light comes. However, when the hologram is examined closely, the information on its film seems a chaos of finely grained light and dark regions arrayed across the film's surface. There appears to be no pattern, but in fact 60,000 or more separate lines of visual information must be recorded for each linear inch of the hologram, if it is to be effective.

Although the first holographs were recorded and reconstructed with laser light of only one color, today's successive exposures of three lasers, each with an output of one of the primary colors, has created full color holographic reconstruction. Now a fully colored, three-dimensional image of an object or event can be recorded in all its detail. Even continuous motion can be recorded.

But what practical application does holography have for the lighting designer? One example is that new subterranean habitats like berm buildings could have holographic windows that could show a new landscape each season. For space colonists, the lack of a view would mean the loss of contact with nature and potentially claustrophobia. Futurists believe holograms will serve a purpose here, too—as porthole vistas.

In the future, designers will use light and its effects to reshape spaces, and their tools will be illusions. In fact, a group of artists in California are already working in this perceptualist mode, they include Larry Bell, Robert Irwin, Maria Nordman, and Dewain Valentine. However, the pieces of Dan Flavin and James Turrell best illustrate the intent of this work as a whole.

Color Illusions: Dan Flavin
Artists have always experimented with light and color, but today one artist, Dan

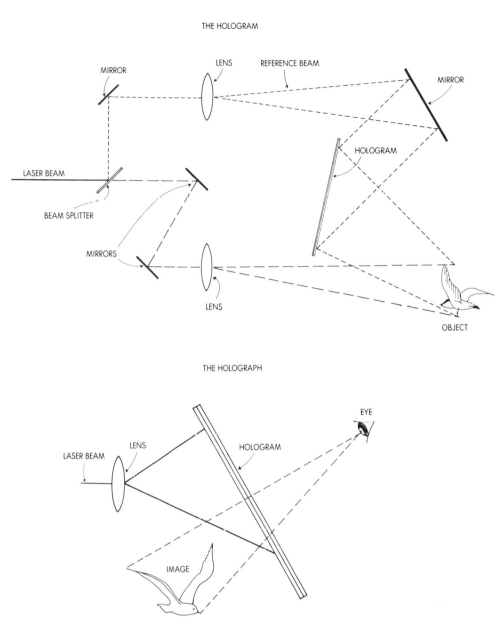

FIGURE 9-10: Holography
In holography, a contained beam of light from a single mode laser is intercepted by a beam-splitter, a half-silvered mirror. This mirror reflects half the light in the beam and allows the other half to pass through. One of the half-beams is reflected again by other mirrors onto the emulsion of a photographic plate. The second half-beam is reflected onto the photographic emulsion too, but it has been reflected from the object to be recorded as well as from a second mirror. The wavelengths of the two half-beams interfere with one another at the location of the photoemulsion. The amplitude of the light striking the object is recorded where the intersecting wavelengths multiply; the phases of the light are recorded wherever there are variations in the interference pattern. (Illustration by Reiko Hayashi.)

FIGURE 9-11:   *Lunette,* **by James Turrell**
A Southern California artist with degrees in art and perceptual psychology, Turrell is interested in "the quality of light inhabiting a space with nothing between you and it." (Lighting/Photograph by James Turrell.)

Flavin, is dealing with this subject in a new, exciting way. One aspect of his work involves the colored after-images that result from confrontations with fluorescent tubes.

In 1969, he began creating a series of corridor spaces that at some point along their length present a barricade made of lighted tubes whose colored light extinguishes everything else in the line of sight (Color Plate 11). Turning away from the colored tubes, a visitor retains the after-image of these lights which mixes with the color perceived on the corridor walls, creating an entirely new, but imaginary, color there. Just as an artist mixes new colors on his/her palette by combining existing oil colors, Flavin mixes his colors with the images of light that remain in the mind's eye of the viewer.

Spatial Illusions: James Turrell

Another contemporary artist utilizing the perception of light and color in occupied space is Jim Turrell. Like the work of Dan Flavin, Turrell's work is site specific and comprised of environments in which the intensity, quality, and angle of light create the appearance, and disappearance, of objects, walls, and even entire rooms (Figure 9-11 and Color Plate 16).

In one such exhibition of his work, first seen in 1983, the visitor, after a short walk along a more and more dimly lighted pathway, enters a large gallery with a high ceiling. On the farthest side of the otherwise empty gallery, an immense black velvet tapestry covers almost the entire wall. The second phase of the visual experience begins when the visitor finally approaches the tapestry to examine it. Depending on the amount of control or decorum of the visitor, it may take some minutes before the viewer finally reaches out to touch the tapestry. But nothing is there! The tapestry is really a hole in the wall.

After an additional lapse of time—as the visitor tries to ascertain how he/she was fooled—the third part of the experience takes place as the viewer starts to suspect the presence of a space or room beyond the hole in the wall. By staring into it, very slowly an entire room becomes visible and is soon clearly present.

In 1983 this constituted the final perception of the sequence. By 1984, beautiful but strange mirages in disembodied colors began to make their way into Turrell's "room beyond." The total elapsed time for the gallery visitor to complete the sequence of experiences is a minimum of 30 minutes for each piece.

How the Illusions Work.

Jim Turrell knows which cues to three-dimensional perception can or cannot be perceived at particular stages of a viewer's progress toward complete *darkness adaptation*—the scientific name for the shift from visual reliance on the cones of the eye that in daylight transmit information to the brain to reliance on the rods of the eye which transmit in darkness. These two transmittors are sensitive to different stimulae: the rods are most sensitive to contrasts of brightness, while the cones are particularly responsive to color contrasts. This shift from cone vision to rod vision is a gradual and lengthy one to complete.

Darkness adaptation happens autonomically in response to the darker and darker spaces through which a visitor to Turrell's environments passes. As the shift occurs, the visitor's depth perception relies on different brightness cues. Among Turrell's recent work, Scelene (1984), experiments with the colors that will be perceived, left behind, or overcome by other colors as darkness adaptation takes place.

A Practical Application. Random interviews with visitors to Turrell's environmental illusions have revealed that each visitor's sequence of experiences with the environment is similar, if not identical. In other words, the physiological patterns of individuals' spatial perceptions can be isolated, specifically stimulated, and then called forth in sequence. Like the behavioral research of the late John Flynn, the art of Jim Turrell points to the day when environments can be designed in which not only the subjective impressions and productive behavior of people can be reliably predicted, but also their perception of the dimensions of the space can be controlled. To paraphrase Flynn: the day is coming when clients will describe how they want a space to appear, to feel, and to cause its occupants to behave—and designers will be able to create exactly such a space.

LOOKING AHEAD

The future of lighting design is being shaped today by the work of researchers such as Sucov and Bernecker who have uncovered the behavioral responses that result from environmental brightnesses. Effective ways to call forth these behavioral responses are being explored in the realm of light-as-art by the talented artists just discussed. The next step will be the discovery of ways to create desired perceptions in order to reshape real environments for large and diverse groups of people. When that knowledge is available, designers will be able to use lighting to do more with less, to make small or crowded spaces comfortable, and to make a single space function as if it were many.

CHAPTER NOTE

¹Tully Weiss, "Luminary in the Lonestar State," *Designers West* 10 (1984): 66.

APPENDIXES

LIGHTING CHARTS

Appendix A

1. STRUCTURAL LIGHTING CHARTS

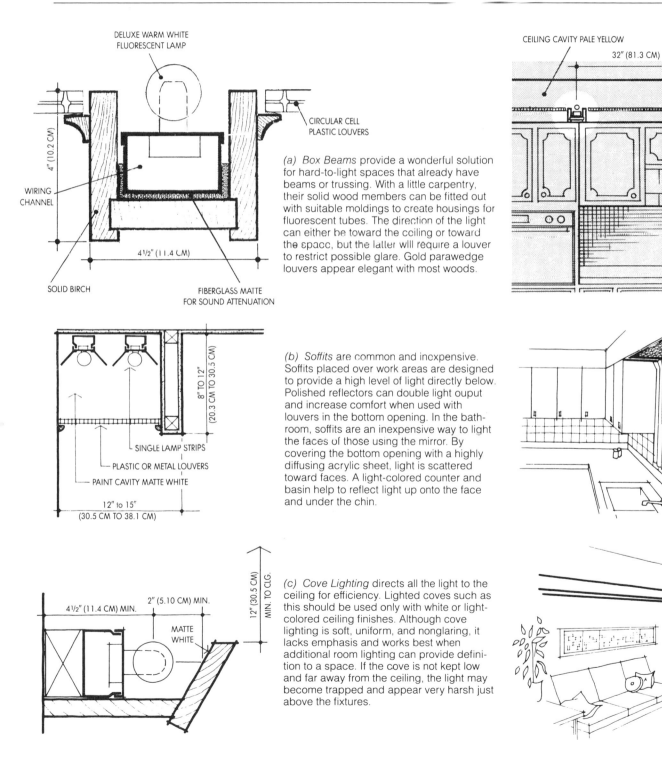

DELUXE WARM WHITE
FLUORESCENT LAMP

CIRCULAR CELL
PLASTIC LOUVERS

4" (10.2 CM)

WIRING
CHANNEL

SOLID BIRCH

4 1/2" (11.4 CM)

FIBERGLASS MATTE
FOR SOUND ATTENUATION

CEILING CAVITY PALE YELLOW

32" (81.3 CM)

10' (25.4 CM)

(a) Box Beams provide a wonderful solution for hard-to-light spaces that already have beams or trussing. With a little carpentry, their solid wood members can be fitted out with suitable moldings to create housings for fluorescent tubes. The direction of the light can either be toward the ceiling or toward the space, but the latter will require a louver to restrict possible glare. Gold parawedge louvers appear elegant with most woods.

8" TO 12"
(20.3 CM TO 30.5 CM)

SINGLE LAMP STRIPS

PLASTIC OR METAL LOUVERS

PAINT CAVITY MATTE WHITE

12" to 15"
(30.5 CM TO 38.1 CM)

(b) Soffits are common and inexpensive. Soffits placed over work areas are designed to provide a high level of light directly below. Polished reflectors can double light ouput and increase comfort when used with louvers in the bottom opening. In the bathroom, soffits are an inexpensive way to light the faces of those using the mirror. By covering the bottom opening with a highly diffusing acrylic sheet, light is scattered toward faces. A light-colored counter and basin help to reflect light up onto the face and under the chin.

12" (30.5 CM)
MIN. TO CLG.

4 1/2" (11.4 CM) MIN.

2" (5.10 CM) MIN.

MATTE
WHITE

(c) Cove Lighting directs all the light to the ceiling for efficiency. Lighted coves such as this should be used only with white or light-colored ceiling finishes. Although cove lighting is soft, uniform, and nonglaring, it lacks emphasis and works best when additional room lighting can provide definition to a space. If the cove is not kept low and far away from the ceiling, the light may become trapped and appear very harsh just above the fixtures.

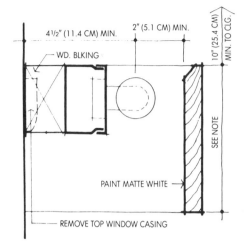

4½" (11.4 CM) MIN.   2" (5.1 CM) MIN.

10' (25.4 CM) MIN. TO CLG.

WD. BLKING

SEE NOTE

PAINT MATTE WHITE

REMOVE TOP WINDOW CASING

(d) Lighted Valances are traditionally used at windows, usually with draperies. They provide uplight which reflects off the ceiling for general room lighting and downlight for drapery accent. When the valance is closer than ten inches to the ceiling, the use of a closed top for it eliminates annoying ceiling brightnesses. Draperies should be hung at the top of their pleats which will cause them to hang flat against the wall, thereby creating the best lighting effect. Faceboards for valances are generally made of wood or metal. Translucent materials such as low-transmittance acrylic may also be used. The dpeth of the faceboard is determined from cross-section sketches that show the probable line of sight of persons who will use the space.

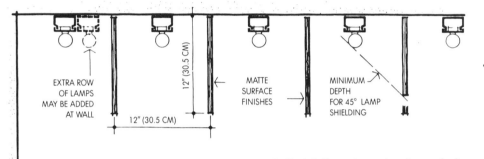

EXTRA ROW OF LAMPS MAY BE ADDED AT WALL

12" (30.5 CM)

12" (30.5 CM)

MATTE SURFACE FINISHES

MINIMUM DEPTH FOR 45° LAMP SHIELDING

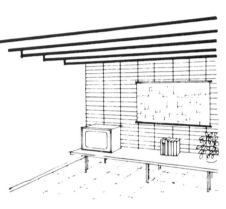

(e) Baffled Ceilings depend on the vertical surfaces of their ceilings to determine their visual effect. They are used mainly in low-ceilinged spaces where attention is focused in a single direction. While the baffles provide lamp concealment in this direction, they are completely exposed lengthwise and become a source of discomfort and glare if viewed in that direction. This can be prevented by adding cross baffles to form a kind of grid or using strip lights that have a simple cross blade louver attachment.

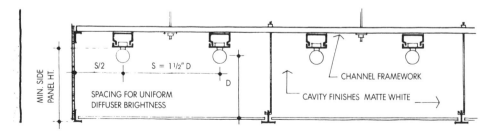

MIN. SIDE PANEL HT.

S/2   S = 1½" D

D

SPACING FOR UNIFORM DIFFUSER BRIGHTNESS

CHANNEL FRAMEWORK

CAVITY FINISHES MATTE WHITE

(f) Floating Ceilings contain a diffuser or louver framework suspended from a ceiling but hanging free of the walls. Such a ceiling not only lights the space, it also puts a high brightness on upper wall areas and visible portions of the ceiling. The use of side panels will prevent disturbing shadows created by the suspension hardware; such panels should stretch from the louver plane to the top of the lamp plane.

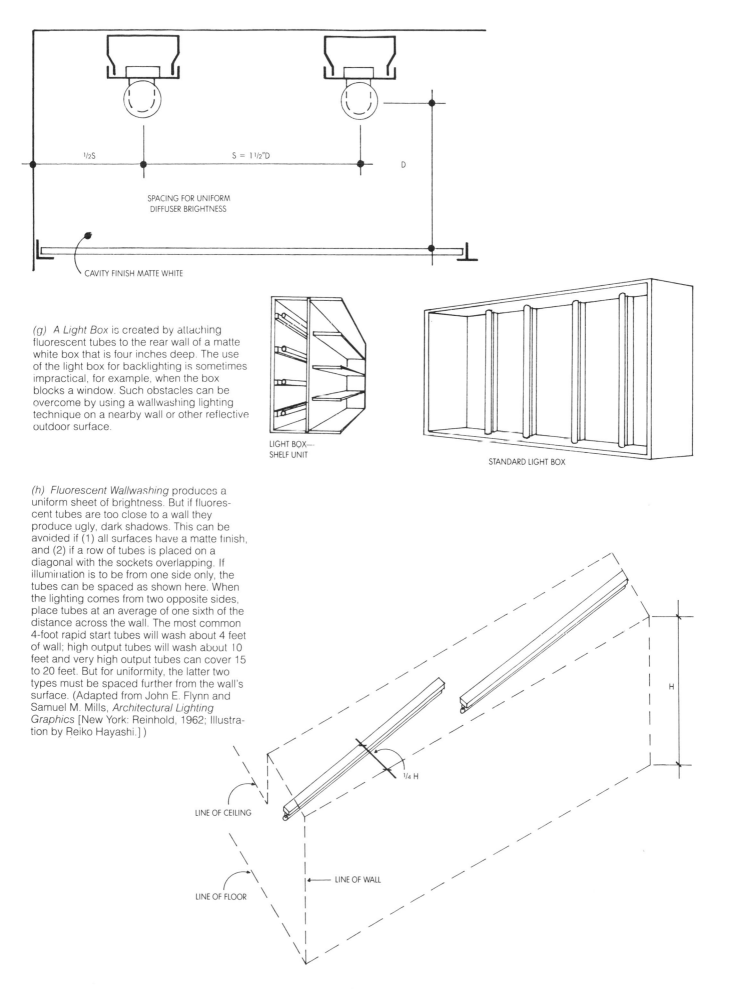

1/2S

S = 1 1/2"D

D

SPACING FOR UNIFORM
DIFFUSER BRIGHTNESS

CAVITY FINISH MATTE WHITE

(g) A *Light Box* is created by attaching
fluorescent tubes to the rear wall of a matte
white box that is four inches deep. The use
of the light box for backlighting is sometimes
impractical, for example, when the box
blocks a window. Such obstacles can be
overcome by using a wallwashing lighting
technique on a nearby wall or other reflective
outdoor surface.

LIGHT BOX—
SHELF UNIT

STANDARD LIGHT BOX

(h) *Fluorescent Wallwashing* produces a
uniform sheet of brightness. But if fluorescent tubes are too close to a wall they
produce ugly, dark shadows. This can be
avoided if (1) all surfaces have a matte finish,
and (2) if a row of tubes is placed on a
diagonal with the sockets overlapping. If
illumination is to be from one side only, the
tubes can be spaced as shown here. When
the lighting comes from two opposite sides,
place tubes at an average of one sixth of the
distance across the wall. The most common
4-foot rapid start tubes will wash about 4 feet
of wall; high output tubes will wash about 10
feet and very high output tubes can cover 15
to 20 feet. But for uniformity, the latter two
types must be spaced further from the wall's
surface. (Adapted from John E. Flynn and
Samuel M. Mills, *Architectural Lighting
Graphics* [New York: Reinhold, 1962; Illustration by Reiko Hayashi.])

H

1/4 H

LINE OF CEILING

LINE OF WALL

LINE OF FLOOR

2. BEAM SPREAD CHARTS

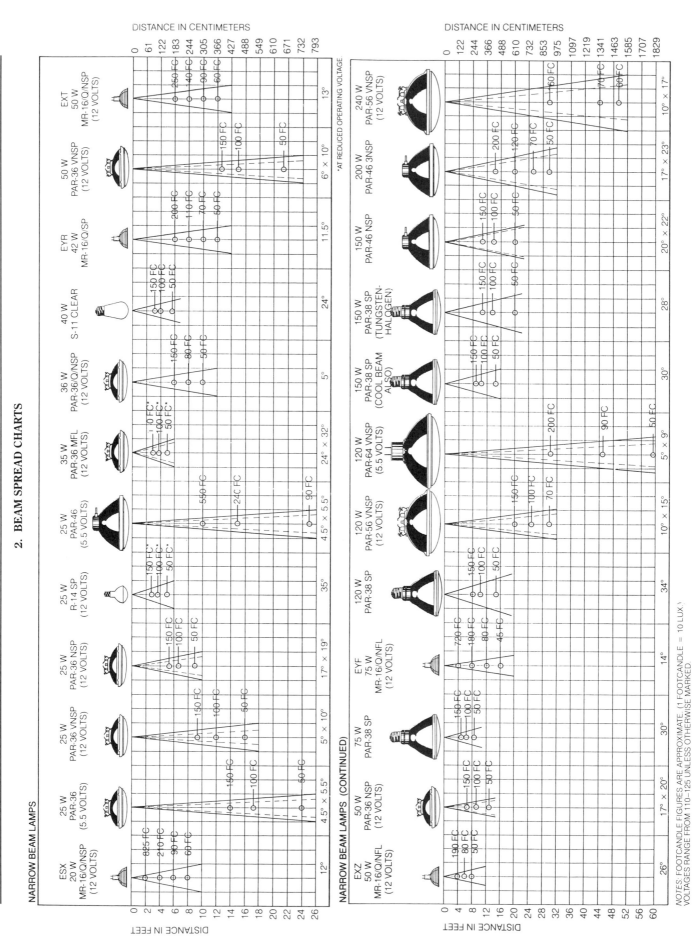

NOTES: FOOTCANDLE FIGURES ARE APPROXIMATE. (1 FOOTCANDLE = 10 LUX.)
VOLTAGES RANGE FROM 110–125 UNLESS OTHERWISE MARKED.

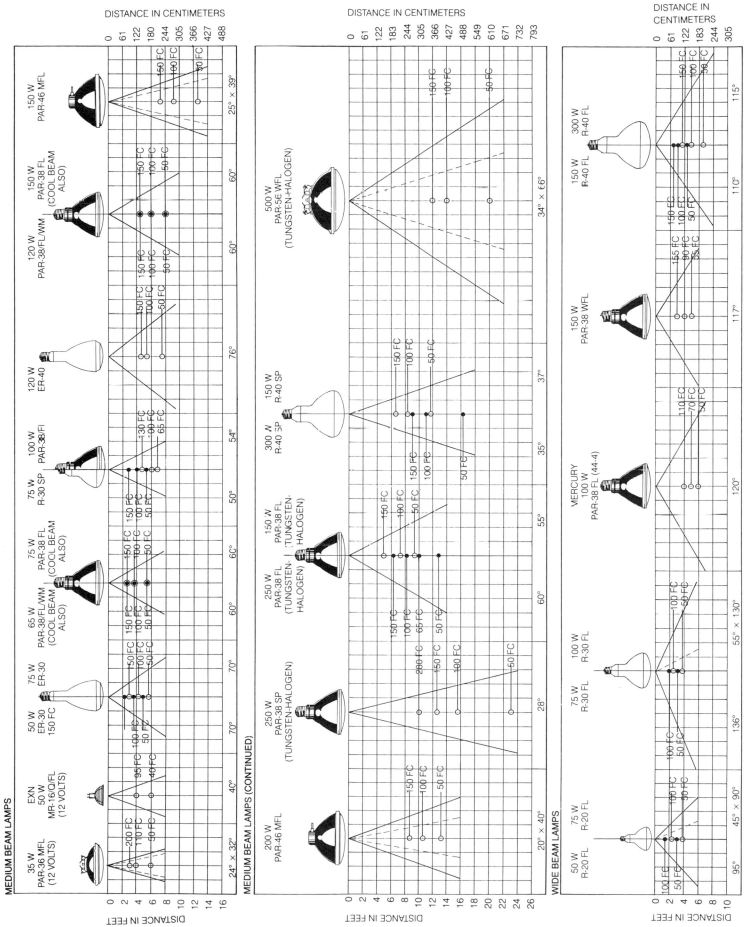

Source: Illustration by Reiko Hayashi, based on research done by David Winfield Willson, IALD, Lightolier, Luminae, and Joanne Lim Stinson.

LIGHTING DOCUMENTS

Appendix B

---

1. SPECIFICATIONS FOR CONSTRUCTION SCHEDULES

Division One
Section 01310

PART I. GENERAL

1.1 *Description*

A. Work Included:
To assist in evaluating progress and to assure adequate planning so that the Work is completed within the number of days allowed in the Contract, prepare and maintain the schedules and reports described in this Section.

B. Related Work:
1. Documents affecting work of this Section include, but are not necessarily limited to, General Conditions, Supplementary Conditions, and Division One of these Specifications.
2. Requirements for progress schedule: General Conditions.
3. Construction period: Form of Agreement.

C. Definitions:
1. "Day," as used throughout the Contract unless otherwise stated, means "calendar day."

1.2 *Quality Assurance*

A. Perform data preparation, analysis, charting, and updating in accordance with standards approved by the designer.

B. Reliance upon the approved schedule:
1. The construction schedule as approved by the designer will be an integral part of the contract and will establish interim completion dates for the various activities under the Contract.
2. Should any activity not be completed within 15 days after the stated date, the Owner shall have the right to require the Contractor to expedite completion of the activity by whatever means the Owner deems appropriate and necessary, without additional compensation to the Contractor.
3. Should any activity be 30 days or more behind the stated date, the Owner shall have the right to perform the activity or have the activity performed by whatever method the Owner deems appropriate.
4. Costs incurred by the Owner and by the Designer in connection with expediting the activity under this Article shall be reimbursed by the Contractor.
5. It is expressly understood and agreed that failure by the Owner to exercise the option either to order the Contractor to expedite an activity or to expedite the activity by other means shall· not be considered to set a precedent for any other activities.

1.3 *Submittals*

A. Comply with pertinent provisions of Section 01340.

B. Construction Schedule: Within 30 calendar days after the Contractor has received the Owner's Notice to Proceed, submit the construction schedule prepared in accordance with Part III of this Section.

C. Periodic Reports: On the first working day of each month following the submittal described in Paragraph 1.3-B above, submit the construction schedule updates as described in Part 3.2 of this Section.

PART II. PRODUCTS

2.1 *Construction Analysis*

A. Graphically show by bar-chart (or a critical path chart) the order and interdependence of all activities necessary to complete the Work, and the sequence in which each activity is to be accomplished, as planned by the contractor and his/her project field superintendent in coordination with all subcontractors.

B. Include, but do not necessarily limit, indicated activities to:
1. Project mobilization.
2. Submittal and approval of Shop Drawings and Samples.
3. Procurement of equipment and critical materials.
4. Fabrication of special materials and equipment and its installation and testing.
5. Final cleanup.
6. Final inspection and testing.
7. All activities by the designer and/or owner that affect progress, required dates for completion, or both, for all and each part of the Work.

PART III. EXECUTION

3.1 *Construction Schedule*

A. As soon as practical after receipt of Notice to Proceed, complete the construction analysis in preliminary form, meet with the designer, review contents of the proposed construction schedule, and make all revisions agreed upon.

B. Submit in accordance with Paragraph 1.3-B above.

3.2 *Periodic Reports*

A. As required under paragraph 1.3-C above, update the approved construction schedule.
1. Indicate "actual progress" in percent completion for each activity.
2. Provide written narrative summary of revisions causing delay in the program and an explanation of corrective actions taken or proposed.

3.3 *Revisions*

A. Make only those revisions to approved construction schedule as are approved in advance by the Designer.

Source: Adapted from Hans W. Meier, *Construction Specifications Handbook,* 2nd ed. (Englewood Cliffs: Prentice, 1978).

2. COMMON CODE PROVISIONS*

1. *Junction box or lighting outlet:* A metal box required to enclose the splice that joins the wiring of the branch circuit to the wiring of a lighting fixture. Junction boxes must be accessible in some jurisdictions.

2. *Receptacle or convenience outlet:* The female receiver for plugs as well as the box in which it is housed. It shall be at least of the duplex type that has two or more plug-in positions except as otherwise specified.

3. *Wall switch:* A switch on the wall, not part of any fixture, that controls one or more receptacles or junction boxes.

4. *Special-purpose outlet:* A receptacle with special female provisions by means of which the wiring system is normally reserved for the exclusive use of a particular piece of equipment or appliance. Clock receptacles that recess into the wall, range outlets that accept only twist-lock male plugs, and bedroom receptacles that accept only three-prong grounded male plugs for room air conditioners are examples.

5. *Fixtures:* Lighting fixtures generate heat; misapplication may cause fires. Many codes require fixtures tested and approved by Underwriters Laboratories and bearing the UL label. There are even UL labels for particular types of environments, such as "weatherproof," "vandalproof," etcetera. Recessed incandescent fixtures must have thermal cut-off switches to prevent overheating that might result from attic insulation packed above them. Fluorescent fixtures for indoor installation must also incorporate thermal protection sufficient to bear the manufacturer's designation as a Class P ballast.**

Electromagnetic radiation from some lamps and control devices like dimmers may cause interference with sensitive electronic equipment that may be nearby, like special band radio transmitters. This interference can be transmitted either by direct radiation or by conduction. Direct radiation is eliminated when codes require that the fixture is metal-enclosed and conduction is reduced when codes require that electrical service is brought in through grounded conduit or shielded cable. Both may be required by codes enforced near broadcasting facilities of various kinds.

Frequently, interior designers select decorative fixtures from foreign countries. Often these imports have *not* been UL-tested and thus require disassembly and rewiring on the project. This is costly and can be avoided by adopting the following language in all specifications: "All fixtures *must* bear UL labels."

6. *Ballasts and transformers:* The hum produced by ballasts and transformers can be particularly distracting in noise-regulated environments such as libraries. Remote ballasting is possible; it usually can be justified in extreme circumstances. Alternatively, codes may require an "A" sound-rated ballast. A "CBM rated" ballast has met ANSI performance standards for both noise and safety ("B" sound-rated or better).

7. *Voltages:* When local voltages are described as 115 and 230 volts, voltage is understood to be nominal and to include, respectively, voltage of 110 to 125 and 220 to 250 to be supplied by the utility. In any location in which the electrical service is furnished at 120/208 volts from a three-phase, four wire system, the local utility should be consulted as to the suitability of particular specifications to local codes.

8. *Low voltage:* It is assumed that low-voltage current is not hazardous except at high amperages. For this reason, many jurisdictions allow low-voltage equipment to be installed without UL labels and allow low-voltage wiring, like doorbell wires, to be run through crawl spaces without enclosing conduit. This determination applies to lighting fixtures of both 12 and 24 volts.

9. *Branch circuit:* This is the portion of a wiring system that extends beyond the final subpanel fuse or circuit breaker protecting the circuit. Most energy codes no longer allow branch circuits to be switched at the subpanel alone.

10. *Loading a branch circuit:* The type of insulation of the electrical wires determines the amount of electrical current that can safely flow. A number 12 copper wire insulated with a type TW insulation will carry 20 amps. A number 12 copper wire insulated with a type MI insulation will carry 30 amps. In assigning lighting fixtures to a switching circuit, it is imperative that the wires not overheat. So, codes require that only 80 percent of the current carrying capacity be assigned. Written assurance of lighting manufacturers of such UL approval should be provided as seen in the following:

(a) 20 amps × 115 volts = 2300 watts "current carrying capacity"

(b) 2300 watts × 80 percent = 1840 watts "derated capacity"

Each unit of a specific fixture requires 100 watts; so only 18 fixtures could be assigned to the switch that controls this branch circuit.

11. *Fusing:* Some designers specify fusing to protect an expensive fixture, or transformer, that may be damaged by the high primary current that can result when a ballast on the same circuit fails or when the utility does not control voltage spiking adequately. A fuse cuts off the passage of current by opening a chasm in the continuity of the wiring before enough high current can pass through to damage the protected item at the far end. The same principle is now required in some jurisdictions for all wiring that is located at or near water locations. To avoid electrocution, a special fuse known as a ground fault interrupter may be required to fuse a circuit that runs a 1200-watt hair dryer which is usually used in front of a sink full of water. (The proper type and rating of the fuse is essential to obtain the protection desired without the nuisance tripping which can occur due to momentary high spiking voltages.)

12. *Usable wall space:* This includes all portions of a wall except the one marked by a door when it is in a normal open position or occupied by a fireplace opening. The minimum usable wall space that requires a receptacle is 3 feet (91.4 cm) in length at the floor line; the maximum usable wall space allowed to have no receptacle is 12 feet (3.66 m) in length.

13. *Work surface:* This includes all areas approximately 30-36 inches (76.2 cm-91.4 cm) above the floor level, exclusive of appliance or sink surfaces, when used in connection with outlet requirement in kitchens or reproduction areas. The minimum frontage of work surface that requires a receptacle is often 1 foot (30.4 cm).

14. *Floor area:* When used as a basis for a requirement for circuits and electrical service, the floor area is computed from the outside dimensions of the building and the number of floors, including unfurnished spaces which are adaptable to future occupancy.

Source: Excerpted from Kenneth L. Gebert, *National Electrical Code Blueprint Reading,* 7th ed. (Alsip: American Technical Publishers, 1977).

* These code references are intended to be representative. Specific code requirements should always be ascertained from those agencies that hold jurisdiction over the geographic location of the project.

** Dimmers have an 80 percent load-carrying capacity much like that of branch circuits.

3. SPECIAL CODE CONDITIONS

A. The National Electrical Code provides specific instructions on when and where special service lighting fixtures are needed. The nature of the environment and its atmosphere often must be known to select the proper one.

    1. Special fixtures are available for certain corrosive atmospheres like sea air.

    2. Explosion-proof, dust-tight, dust-proof, and enclosed-and-gasketed fixtures are available for service where explosive or other dangerous atmospheres exist. (Enclosed-and-gasketed fixtures should be used even for atmospheres with non-explosive dusts and vapors.)

    3. Enclosed fixtures should be used in areas of high humidity.

    4. Waterproof or weatherproof (WP) fixtures should be used for locations where they are mounted without shelter outdoors.

    5. Where there is a possibility that higher than normal temperature conditions may affect an installation, specify a "premium" ballast.

    6. There are also ballasts for cold weather operation.

B. There are often special code provisions regarding noise trespass and light trespass.

    1. When fixtures are located near moving air as in the bathroom ventilation/light combination, the impact of air noise must be considered in multifamily buildings. When these lights are recessed, sound propagation from one room to another through the overhead plenum space can be significant.

    2. Ballasts and transformers produce a humming sound. Generally, the higher the ballast sound rating, the greater the hum. Although manufacturers can provide ballast sound rating information, the noise is not produced by the ballast alone. Many codes reference the installed noise level that will be permitted. Other factors influencing installed noise are: when the ballast is not secured properly to the fixture body; when the fastening of the fixture to its mounting location is not firm; and when the general acoustical characteristics of the space promote reverberation. Often offending noise can be isolated by fastening a heat-resistant pad between the fixture and its mounting.

    3. It is the duty of the manufacturer of lighting fixtures, under product liability law, to protect the public. When a designer specifies a lighting product for a use not intended by the manufacturer, the designer, in effect, incurs a share of the liability, whether the designer is licensed or not.

Source: Excerpted from Kenneth L. Gebert, *National Electrical Code Blueprint Reading,* 7th ed. (Alsip: American Technical Publishers, 1977).

4. SPECIFIC LANGUAGE REGARDING SUBSTITUTED ITEMS

(Lighting in Division Two/Site Work
          Division Eleven/Equipment
          Division Sixteen/Electrical)

2.6   Substitutions

2.6.1   Approval required

2.6.1.1   The Agreement is based on the materials, equipment, and methods described in the Contract Documents.

2.6.1.2   The Designer will consider proposals for substitution of materials, equipment, and methods only when such proposals are accompanied by full and complete technical data and all other information required by Designer to evaluate the proposed substitution.

2.6.1.3   Do not substitute materials, equipment, or methods unless such substitution has been specifically approved for this Work by the Designer.

2.6.2   Equals

2.6.2.1   Where the phrase "or equal" or "or equal as approved by Designer" occurs in the Contract Documents, do not assume that materials, equipment, or methods will be approved by the Designer unless the item has been specifically approved for the Work by the Designer.

2.6.2.2   The decision of the Designer shall be final.

2.6.3   Separate substitution bids: Bidders may, if they wish, submit completely separate bids using materials and methods other than those described in the Contract Documents, provided that all substitutions are clearly identified and described and that the bid in all other respects is in accordance with the provisions of the Contract Documents.

2.6.4   Availability

2.6.4.1   Verify prior to bidding that all specified items will be available in time for installation during orderly and timely progress of the Work.

2.6.4.2   In the event specified items will not be so available, notify the Designer prior to receipt of bids.

2.6.4.3   Costs of delays because of non-availability of specified items, when such delays could have been avoided by the Contractor, will be backcharged as necessary and shall not be borne by the Owner.

Source: Adapted from Hans W. Meier, *Construction Specifications Handbook,* 2nd ed. (Englewood Cliffs: Prentice, 1978) 100.

5. APPLICATION OF ELECTRICAL REQUIREMENTS IN TYPICAL HOUSES*

ALL ROOMS

1. Principal entrance to a room shall offer a switch for the general illumination. (Principal entrances are defined as those commonly used for entrance or exit when going from a lighted to an unlighted condition, or the reverse.)

2. The number of outlets shall be determined by dividing the total linear or square footage by the required distance or area, for example:
Required: one outlet for each 150 square feet
Total square feet of room area = 390
390 divided by 150 = 2.6
Therefore, 3 outlets are required for this room.

EXTERIOR ENTRANCES

1. One or more junction boxes for lighting, wall-switch controlled, shall be located at the front entrance.

2. When a single wall fixture is selected, it should be located on the latch side of the front door.

3. Weatherproof outlets must be located at least 18 inches above grade.

FOYERS

1. A junction box outlet, wall-switch controlled, shall be installed for proper illumination of the entire area.

2. One outlet for each 15 linear feet (457.2 cm) of hallway or for each hall over 25 square feet.

STAIRS

1. Wall or ceiling junction boxes shall be installed to provide adequate illumination on each stair flight. Multiple switch controls at the head and foot of the stairway are arranged so that full illumination may be turned on from either floor.

2. Switches are never to be located so close to steps that a fall might result from a misstep while reaching for a switch.

3. Receptacles are recommended for intermediate stair landings in a large area.

DINING ROOMS

1. There shall be at least one lighting outlet, wall-switch controlled. It is normally located over the probable location of the dining table.

2. Convenience outlets shall be placed so that no point along the floorline in any usable wall space is more than 6 feet from an outlet in that space.

3. Where an open counter is to be built, a split receptacle shall be provided above counter height for the use of portable appliances.

BEDROOMS

1. Good general illumination is particularly essential in the bedroom. Provide outlets that are wall-switch controlled.

2. Outlets shall be placed so that there is a convenience outlet on each side and within 6 feet (182.9 cm) of the center line of each probable individual bed location. Additional receptacles shall be placed so that no point along the floor line in any other usable wall space is more than 6 feet (182.9 cm) from an outlet in that space.

BATHROOMS

1. Lighting both sides of the face when at the mirror is essential. All lighting outlets shall be wall-switch controlled. If the switch is within 6 feet [182.9 cm] (horizontal) of a water location, the switch is required to be ground fault interrupted (GFI).

2. Where an enclosed shower stall is planned, a junction box outlet for a vapor-proof fixture should be installed, controlled by a GFI wall switch outside the door.

3. One GFI receptacle near the mirror, 3 to 5 feet (91.4 cm to 152.4 cm) above the floor. (A receptacle which is a part of a bathroom lighting fixture should not be considered as satisfying this requirement, unless it is rated at 15 amps.)

*These code references are intended to be representative. Specific code requirements should always be discussed with the agencies that hold jurisdiction over the geographic location of the project.

6. SUBMITTALS

Division One
Section 01300

PART ONE—GENERAL

1.1 DESCRIPTION

1.1.1 *Work included:*

1.1.1.1 Wherever possible throughout the Contract Documents, the minimum acceptable quality of workmanship and materials has been defined by manufacturer's name and catalog number, reference to recognized industry and government standards, or description of required attributes and performance.

1.1.1.2 To ensure that the specified products are furnished and installed in accordance with design intent, procedures have been established for advance submittal of design data and for their review by the Designer.

1.1.1.3 Make all submittals required by the Contract Documents, and revise and resubmit as necessary to establish compliance with the specified requirements.

1.1.2 *Related work described elsewhere:* Individual requirements for submittals are described in pertinent other Sections of these Specifications.

1.2 QUALITY ASSURANCE

1.2.1 *Coordination of submittals:* Prior to each submittal, carefully review and coordinate all aspects of each item being submitted and verify that each item and the submittal for it conforms in all respects with the requirements of the Contract Documents. By affixing the Contractor's signature to each submittal, certify that this coordination has been performed.

1.2.2 *Certificates of compliance:*

1.2.2.1 Certify that all materials used in the Work comply with all specified provisions thereof. Certification shall not be construed as relieving the Contractor from furnishing satisfactory materials if, after tests are performed on selected samples, the material is found to not meet specified requirements.

1.2.2.2 Show on each certification the name and location of the Work, name and address of Contractor, quantity and date or dates of shipment or delivery to which the certificate applies, and name of the manufacturing or fabricating company. Certification shall be in the form of letter or company-standard forms containing all required data. Certificates shall be signed by an officer of the manufacturing or fabricating company.

1.2.2.3 In addition to the above information, all laboratory test reports submitted with Certificates of Compliance shall show the date or dates of testing, the specified requirements for which testing was performed, and results of the test or tests.

1.3 SUBMITTALS

1.3.1 *Submittal schedule:* Within 35 days after award of Contract, and before any items are submitted for approval, submit to the Designer two copies of the schedule described in Article 2.1 of this Section.

1.3.2 *Certificates of compliance:* Upon completion of the Work, and as a condition of its acceptance, submit to the Designer all Certificates of Compliance.

1.3.3. *Procedures:* Make submittals in strict accordance with the provisions of this Section.

PART TWO—PRODUCTS

2.1 SUBMITTAL SCHEDULE

2.1.1 *General:* Compile a complete and comprehensive schedule of all submittals anticipated to be made during progress of the Work. Include a list of each type of item for which Contractor's drawings, Shop Drawings, Certificates of Compliance, material samples, guarantees, or other types of submittals are required. Upon approval by the Designer this schedule will become part of the Contract and the Contractor will be required to adhere to the schedule except when specifically otherwise permitted.

2.1.2 *Coordination:* Coordinate the schedule with all necessary subcontractors and materials suppliers to ensure their understanding of the importance of adhering to the approved schedule and their ability to so adhere. Coordinate as required to ensure the grouping of submittals.

2.1.3 *Revisions:* Revise and update the schedule on a monthly basis as necessary to reflect conditions and sequences. Promptly submit revised schedules to the Designer for review and comment.

2.2 SHOP DRAWINGS AND COORDINATION DRAWINGS

2.2.1 *Shop drawings:*

2.2.1.1. Scale and measurements: Make all Shop Drawings accurately to a scale sufficiently large to show all pertinent aspects of the item and its method of connection to the Work.

2.2.1.2 Type of prints required: Submit all Shop Drawings in the form of one sepia transparency of each sheet plus one blue line or black line print of each sheet. Blueprints will not be acceptable.

2.2.1.3 Reproduction of review Shop Drawings: Printing and distribution of review Shop Drawings for the Designer's use will be by the Designer. All review comments of the Designer will be shown on the sepia transparency when it is returned to the Contractor. The Contractor shall make and distribute all copies required for his purposes.

2.3 MANUFACTURERS' LITERATURE

2.3.1 *General:* Where contents of submitted literature from manufacturers includes data not pertinent to the submittal, clearly indicate which portion of the contents is being submitted for review.

2.3.2 *Number of copies required:* Submit the number of copies which are required to be returned plus two copies which will be retained by the Architect.

2.4 SAMPLES

2.4.1 *Accuracy of samples:* Samples shall be of the precise article proposed to be furnished.

2.4.2 *Number of samples required:* Unless otherwise specified, submit all Samples in the quantity which is required to be returned plus one which will be retained by the Designer.

2.4.3 *Reuse of samples:* In situations specifically so approved by the Designer, the Designer's retained Sample may be used in the construction as one of the installed items.

2.5 COLORS AND PATTERNS

Unless the precise color and pattern is specifically described in the Contract Documents, and whenever a choice of color or pattern is available in a specified product, submit accurate color and pattern charts to the Designer for review and selection.

Source: Adapted from Hans W. Meier, *Construction Specifications Handbook,* 2nd ed. (Englewood Cliffs: Prentice, 1978).

7. SAMPLE LIGHTING SPECIFICATIONS

Division 16/Electrical
Section 16520/Luminous Ceilings

PART ONE—GENERAL

16521.1 DESCRIPTION: LUMINOUS CEILINGS

1.1.1 *Work included:* Provide all electrical components as shown on the Drawings and specified herein, complete in place, tested and operating, including but not necessarily limited to
(1) Complete branch circuit wiring for fluorescent system.
(2) Wiring to and connection of junction boxes, lighting fixtures, and wall switches.

1.1.2 *Related work described elsewhere:*
(1) Construction of supporting wood framework, Section 06100.
(2) Painting of plenum, Section 09900.

1.1.3 *Description of the system:*
(1) An array of two lamp surface-mounted fluorescent fixtures.
(2) Custom lensing on wood members suspended below fluorescent tubes.

1.2 QUALITY ASSURANCE

1.2.1 *Standards:*
(1) National Electrical Code, latest edition, as adapted by City of San Francisco
(2) Title 24, State of California Energy Code.

1.2.2 *Qualifications of installers:* For the actual installation and testing of the work in this Section use only trained and licensed wiremen having experience with luminous ceilings and with the manufacturers' recommended methods of installation.

1.3 SUBMITTALS

1.3.1 *General:* Comply with the provisions of Division 1/Section 01300.

1.3.2 *Product data:* Within 30 calendar days after award of the Contract submit:
(1) A complete list of materials proposed to be furnished and installed under this Section.
(2) Manufacturer's specifications and catalog cuts as required to demonstrate compliance with the specified requirements.

1.3.3 *Record drawings:* During the progress of this Work, maintain an accurate record of the installation of all items as per the requirements of Division One/Section 01720.

1.3.4 *Operation and maintenance manuals:* Upon completion of this portion of the Work, and as a condition of its acceptance, compile a Manual in accordance with the provisions of Division One/Section 01350 of the Specifications and deliver one copy each to Owner, Designer, and Lighting Consultant.

1.4 PRODUCT HANDLING

1.4.1 *Protection:* Comply with the provisions of Division One/Section 01600.

1.4.2 *Replacements:* In the event of damage, immediately make all repairs and replacements necessary to the approval of the Designer and at no additional cost to the Owner.

1.5 GUARANTEE

1.6 EXTRA STOCK

1.6.1 *Lamps:* Deliver to the Owner one case of additional fluorescent lamps identical to those lamps installed.

1.7 ALTERNATIVES

PART TWO—PRODUCTS

16522.1 LUMINOUS CEILINGS (custom)

2.1.1 *Fixtures:* Provide two lamp fluorescent fixtures with Rapid Start CBM ballast, having "ladder" configuration with 3'-0" between lamps: Prudential 1452, Globe 142-LG or approved equal.

2.1.2 *Lamps:* Provide Ultralume 4100 F40 Rapid Start fluorescent tubes by Philips-Westinghouse (no equal).

2.6.1 *Approvals:* Comply with the provisions of Division One/Section 01300.

PART THREE—EXECUTION

16523.1 PREPARATION

3.1.1 *Plenum:* Clean plenum and paint matte white (75 percent reflectance required). See also Section 09900 Paint.

3.2 PROCEDURES

3.2.1 *Manufacturers' instructions:* Install lens materials in strict accordance with manufacturers' instructions.

3.2.2 *Special handling:* Virgin opal acrylic lenses require use of white gloves supplied by manufacturer.

16523.3 TOLERANCES

An unobstructed depth of 11" from suspension members to the roof of the plenum is required to allow the lens assembly to be tipped into place. Fixtures obstructing this clearance will be relocated without expense to Owner.

3.4 TESTING

Troublefree operation of lamps, fixtures, and switches should be verified by installers before application for substantial completion.

8. SAMPLE ADDITIONAL WORK CLAUSE*

Additional Work

If at any time after the approval by the Client of final documents, the Client shall require the Consultant to make any changes in the size or scope of the work or require any change in plan, design, or specifications which shall necessitate the preparation by the Consultant of additional sketches, working drawings, or other documents, or the making of any changes in any documents already approved or upon which work shall have been started pursuant to instructions to proceed therewith, the Consultant shall be entitled to just and equitable compensation in regard to fees and expenses.

Source: Excerpted from LeMar Terry and Neil Chassman, Consultants
Lighting Design, Consultation, and Engineering
New York, New York

*This portion of an Agreement is published with the understanding that the authors and publisher are not rendering legal service. If legal advice is required, the services of a competent professional attorney should be sought.

9. SAMPLE WORKSHEET FOR PROJECTING DESIGNERS' HOURS*

PROJECT: The Vatican Pavilion of the Louisiana World Exposition

Time, Fees, and Expenses

I. *Fee schedule*

Our charges per hour are as follows:

V. LeMar Terry, Jr., Senior Consultant and Designer	$ –.00
Neil A. Chassman, Director and Senior Consultant	$ –.00
Associate Designer/Engineer	$ –.00
Detailing and Drafting	$ –.00

We are including all miscellaneous clerical expenses and time, as well as travel time, as company overhead, and are not billing for them.

II. *Breakdown by hours and phases of project***

	TERRY	CHASSMAN	ASSOCIATES	DETAILING/ DRAFTING
A. Basic research on project: analysis, preparation of preliminary lighting design plan, provision of time and cost estimates	14	9	0	0
B. Building design-interior	6	0	0	0
C. Grounds design	8	0	0	0

Source: Excerpted from LeMar Terry and Neil Chassman, Consultants
Lighting Design, Consultation, and Engineering
New York, New York

*This portion of an Agreement is published with the understanding that the authors and publisher are not rendering legal service. If legal advice is required, the services of a competent professional attorney should be sought.
**This is just a section of a worksheet that continued for many pages.

10. SAMPLE AGREEMENT FOR LIGHTING CONSULTING SERVICES†

Agreement made this _____ day of
_____, 19___ between
_____ (hereinafter "Client")
and _____
(hereinafter "Designer")

Recitals*

Client is currently engaged in the *[Here a brief description of Client's project including location]*.

Client wishes to engage the services of Designer to render consultation and advice concerning the lighting and lighting effects to be created on Client's project.

Therefore, the Client hereby engages Designer's services, and in consideration of the mutual promises herein, the parties agree as follows:

Term*

1. This Agreement shall be effective on the date first above written and shall continue in effect until the completion of the lighting installation in Client's *[project-name as above in Recitals]*, or until it has been terminated by either party as provided herein.

Service*

2. *[Here, a detailed description of the services to be rendered by Designer, including the time frame, if any.]*

Use of Associates*

3. To the extent reasonably necessary to enable the Designer to perform the duties required hereunder, Designer shall be authorized to engage the services of any agents, assistants, or associates as Designer may deem proper. The cost of such services shall be billed to Client by Designer at the same rate as Designer's services are so billed hereunder, or at such higher rate as may be first approved by Client.

Fee*

4. An initial, nonrefundable Concept Fee of $_____ shall be payable upon the signing of this Agreement. In addition to the non-refundable Concept Fee, Designer shall be paid $_____ per hour for each hour spent by Designer or Designer's associates in connection with this project. Designer shall further be entitled to reimbursement of out-of-pocket expenses such as telephone charges, postage and delivery charges, reproduction costs, travel costs, etc. Designer will bill Client monthly for fees and costs incurred and the same shall be due and payable upon receipt of the statement. Designer has estimated that Designer's total Consulting Fee for this project will be $_____. While every effort will be made to complete the project for such estimated total Consulting Fee, it should be understood that such estimated fee is not binding on Designer and all services will be billed as provided in this Agreement.

Termination*

5. Either party may terminate this Agreement on _____ days' written notice to the other, mailed first class postage prepaid, as follows:

_____   _____

Client address   Designer address

Relationship of Parties**

6. Designer's relationship with Client under this Agreement is that of advisor and consultant. Neither Designer nor its staff are licensed to practice (nor do they practice) as an architect, engineer, electrical consultant, electrical contractor, or electrician under the ordinances of the State of _____. It shall be the responsibility of Client to see that all construction and electrical installation work is accomplished through duly qualified and, when necessary, properly licensed persons. While Designer, its agents or staff, may from time to time recommend various persons to Client with whom they have worked before, no such individual is an agent of Designer nor is Designer their agent. Designer makes no representation as to the experience, qualifications, or ability of any person not on its staff.

Limitation of Liability**

7. Designer makes no warranty as to the services to be provided under this Agreement and Client hereby waives all warranties, expressed or implied, including any warranty of merchantibility or fitness for a particular use. Client shall hold Designer free and harmless from any obligations, costs, claims or judgments, including attorney's fees, arising from the services to be performed under this Agreement, except when the same have been adjudged by a court of competent jurisdiction to be due to the wilful misconduct of Designer.

The liability of Designer to Client hereunder shall in all events be limited to the amount equal to the total fees paid to Designer by Client for services hereunder and shall not include any consequential damages or contingent liabilities.

Purchasing**

8. No purchasing services shall be provided by Designer. All purchases of lamps, fixtures, controls, circuit components, or other equipment shall be made by Client, the electrical installer, or the interior designer. Designer will advise on its estimate of the best prices and will, on request of Client, enter orders in Client's name for items desired with those contractors, distributors, or manufacturers chosen by Client. Client shall pay supplier directly for all such orders.

Completion**

9. Designer's services shall be deemed completed under this Agreement at such time as Designer so notifies Client in writing. Client shall not use Designer's name, including the name Luminae, in connection with any advertising, publicity, or other public reference to the project without Designer's written consent unless and until Designer has given notice of completion as set forth above.

Arbitration**

10. Any dispute arising under or in connection with this Agreement shall be arbitrated in the City of _____ before the American Arbitration Association pursuant to the rules and regulations of that body then in effect. The arbitrator's decision shall be binding and may be enforced by court of competent jurisdiction. Legal fees and costs incurred by either party hereto shall be paid by the party against whom judgment is made.

Entire Agreement**

11. This Agreement supersedes all other agreements between the parties, whether written or oral, with regard to the subject matter hereof, and constitutes the entire Agreement of the parties.

Assignment**

12. Neither this Agreement nor obligation or duty hereunder may be assigned by Client without the prior written consent of Designer, but subject to the foregoing limitation, it shall insure to the benefit of and be binding on the heirs, executors, administrators, successors, and assigners of the parties hereto.

Governing Law**

13. This Agreement shall be governed by the laws of the State of _____.

Accepted and Agreed to:

_____
Client signature

_____
Designer signature

Source: From Luminae Lighting Consultants, Inc. San Francisco, California

†This Agreement is published with the understanding that the authors and publisher are not rendering legal services. If legal advice is required, the services of a competent professional attorney should be sought.

*Negotiable

**Nonnegotiable

Appendix C

READY REFERENCE

---

1. LINE TYPES AND WEIGHTS

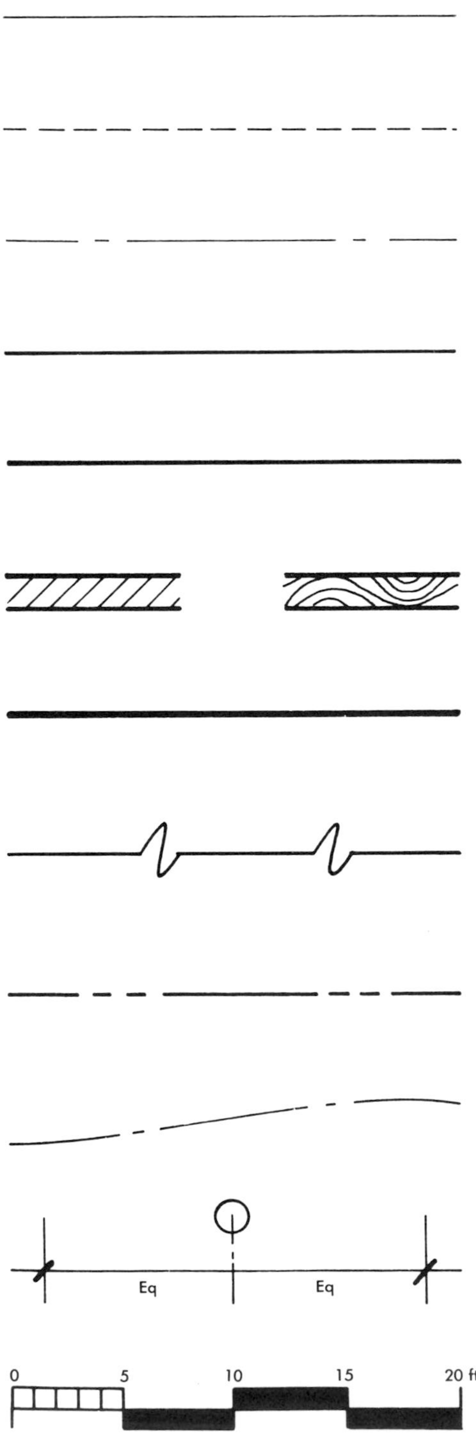

Dimension String

Conceal Line, Above or Below

Center Line and Floor Line

Normal Drawing

Section Outline

Hatching

Cutting Plan, Grade on Elevations

Break-Off Parts of Drawing

Property and Boundary Lines

Switching Intent Lines

Equal Distance Lines

Eq   Eq

0   5   10   15   20 ft

Graphic Scale

Source: Marvin Thomas, *Architectural Working Drawings* (New York: McGraw-Hill, 1978); Illustration by Reiko Hayashi.

2. LIGHTING-RELATED ABBREVIATIONS*

above	ABV	hardware	HDW	permanent	PERM
above finished floor	AFF	heating	HTG	perpendicular	PERP
adjustable	ADJ	heating/ventilating/		piece	PC
air conditioning	A/C	air conditioning	HVAC	plan section	PS
alternate	ALT	height	HT	plaster	PLAS
alternating current	AC	high intensity discharge	HID	plastic	PLS
ampere	AMP or A	high pressure sodium	HPS	plumbing	PBG
approximate	APX	horizontal	HORIZ	plywood	PWD
architect(ural)	ARCH			polyvinyl chloride pipe	PVCP
asbestos	ASB	Illuminating Engineering		prefabricate(d)	PFB
asphalt	ASPH	Society, North America	IESNA	project; projected	PROJ
asymmetrical	ASYM	incandescent	INCAN		
		inch(es)	in	radius; riser	R
below	BLW	include(d); including	INCL	rail(ing)	RL
between	BTW	inside diameter	I.D.	receptacle	RECPT
both ways	B.W.	interior	INT	refer(ence)	REF
bottom	BTM	International Brotherhood		remove	RMV
bracket	BRKT	of Electrical Workers	IBEW	required	REQ
building	BLDG			retaining wall	R/W
		joint	JT	return air	RA
cabinet	CBT	joist	JST	reverse	RVS
ceiling	CLG			revise; revision	REV
center line	C.L.	Kelvin	K	revolutions per minute	RPM
center to center	C-C	kilometer	km	roofing	RFG
centimeter	cm	kilowatt	kW	room	RM
Certified Ballast		kilowatthour	kWh	rough opening	RO
Manufacturer	CBM	light	LT		
clear(ance)	CL	lighting	LTG	schedule	SCH
column	COL	linear foot	L.F.	section	SEC
concrete	CONC	location	LOC	sheet	SHT
conduit	CND	long; length	L	shelf; shelving; shower	SH
continue; continuous	CONT	louver	LVR	skylight	SKL
contract(or)	CONTR	lumens per watt	lpw	soffit	SOF
		lux	lx	space, spacer	SPC
detail	DTL			speaker	SPK
diameter	DIA	manual	MAN	specification(s)	SPEC
dimension	DIM	manufactured	MFD	square	sq
dimmer switch	DIM. or SW DIM.	manufacturer	MFR	square foot	sf
direct current	DC	maximum	MAX	standard	STD
division; divider	DIV	mechanical	MECH	structure; structural	STR
double	DBL	mercury vapor	MV	suspended	SUS
down	DN	metal	MTL	switch	SW
drawing	DWG	meter	m	switchboard	SWBD
		millimeter	mm	symmetry; symmetrical	SYM
each	EA	minimum	MIN	synthetic	SYN
electric(al)	ELEC	mirror	MIR	system	SYS
empty	MT	miscellaneous	MISC		
enclose	ENC	modular	MOD	telephone	TEL
equal	EQ	molding	MLD	television	TV
equipment	EQUIP	motor	MTR	temperature	TEMP
estimate	EST	motor control center	MCC	terminal	TERM
excavate	EXC	mounted	MTD	thick(ness)	THK
except as others indicated	E.O.I.	movable	MOV	threshold	THR
existing	EXIST	mullion	MUL	tongue and groove	T&G
exposed	EXP			top of slab	T/SL
		National Electrical Code	NEC	top of wall	T/W
face of finish	F.O.F.	near side	N.S.	transformer	TRANS
feet or foot	ft	nominal	NOM	typical	TYP
fiberboard	FBD	not in contract	N.I.C.		
finish	FIN	not to scale	NTS	Underwriters	
fixture	FXT	number	no	Laboratories Inc.	UL
flashing	FLG				
flexible	FLX	obsure	OBS	ventilator	VENT
floor	FL	on center(s)	O.C.	vertical	VERT
floor plate	F.PL.	opening	OPG	vertical section	V.S.
fluorescent	FLUOR	opposite	OPP	volt	V
footcandle	fc	outside diameter	O.D.	voltage	volt or V
footing	FTG	overall	OA		
footlambert	fl	overhang	OHG	wallwasher	WW
full size; far side	F.S.	overhead	OH	water heater	WH
furred; furring	FUR			waterproof(ing)	WP
future	FUT	painted	PNT	watt	W
		pair	PR	window	WDO
general contract(or)	G.C.	panel	PNL	wired glass	W.G.
glass; glazing	GL	part; point	PT	with	W/
grab bar	G.B.	particle board	P.BD.	without	W/O
gypsum drywall	GYP	partition	PTN	wood	WD
		pavement	PVMT	wood framing	WF

3. LIGHT AND LIGHT-RELATED REQUIREMENTS FOR POPULAR SPECIES OF INDOOR PLANTS

Common name	Light/footcandles (survival)	(growth)	Hours* of light	Humidity %	Exposure(s)
African violet	100	250	18	45–60	East
Agapanthus	100	250	16	30–40	All but North
Airplane plant	100	250	16	45–60	All
Amaryllis	400	400	16	45–60	All but North
Anthurium	100	125	16	+ 65	East
Aralia, Fatsia	100	200	16	45–60	All but North
Artillery plant	100	250	16	45–60	East and West
Asparagus fern	25	100	16	45–60	All
Azalea	400	400	16	+ 60	East and South
Bamboo	500	4000	16	45–60	West and South
Bird of paradise	500	4000	—	30–45	East and South
Bleeding heart	400	400	16	30–60	All but North
Bromeliads	400	400	16	45–60	West only
Cactus ("Christmas")	100	250	10	45–60	All but North
(others)	500	4000	18	30–45	West and South
Caladium	100	250	16	45–60	All but South
Century plant and	500	4000	18	30–45	West and South
other succulents	500	4000	18	30–45	West and South
Chrysanthemum	400	400	10	30–45	East
Cigar plant	400	400	16	45–60	All but North
Citrus	500	4000	18	30–45	South and West
Coleus	100	250	16	30–60	All but North
Crocus	400	400	16	30–45	East and South
Cyclamen	400	400	16	+ 60	East
Daffodils	400	400	16	30–45	All but North
Dieffenbachia	100	200	16	45–60	East and North
Dracaena	25	100	16	45–60	All but South
Easter lily	400	400	16	30–45	East and South
Elephant ears	400	400	16	45–60	All but North
False aralia (Dizygotheca)	200	250	—	45–60	East and North
Ferns: Boston	100	250	16	45–60	East and North
Fluffy ruffles	25	100	—	45–60	East and North
Maidenhair	50	100 +	—	60 +	East and North
Mother	25	100	—	45–60	East and North
Staghorn	100	250	16	45–60	East and West
Treefern	100	250	16	45–60	All but North
Ficus: creeping	100	250	16	45–60	East and West
Indian laurel (retusa)	100	200	16	45–60	East and West
Rubber plant	50	200	16	30–60	All
Weeping (benjamina)	100	250	16	45–60	All but North
Fittonia	25	100	16	45 +	East and North
Flowering maple	500	4000	16	30–45	East
Fuchsia	400	400	—	45–60	East and West
Gardenia	800	4000	10	45–60	South
Geranium ivy	400 +	500 +	16	30–60	All but North
German ivy	800	4000	10	45–60	All but North
Gloxinia	100	250	16	45–60	East
Grape-hyacinth	400	500 +	16	45–60	All but North
Grape ivy	25	150	16	45–60	All but South

Common name	Light/footcandles (survival)	(growth)	Hours* of light	Humidity %	Exposure(s)
Hawaiian ti	25	100	16	45–60	All
Heavenly bamboo	400	500+	16	45–60	East and South
Ivy (English)	150	150	16	30–60	All but West
Kangaroo	25	100+	16	45–60	East and North
Kaffir lily (Clivia)	400	400	16	30–45	East and South
Lily of the Valley	500	4000	18	30–45	East and West
Moss	25	100	—	45–60	East and North
Mother-in-law tongue	10	75	16	45–60	All
Myrtle	400	400	16	30–45	All but North
Narcissus	400	400	18	30–45	All but North
Nephthytis	50	150	—	30–45	East and North
Orchids: Cattleya	500	4000	10	60+	East
Cymbidium	500	4000	10	30–45	East
Lady Slipper	100	250	—	45+	East
Vanda	400	400	16	45–60	East
Palms: Butterfly	100	175	—	30–45	East
Bamboo	25	125	—	30–45	East
Dwarf date	100	150	—	30–45	East
Kentia (Paradise)	75	100	16	30–45	All
Parlor	10	50	—		East and North
Pepper	400	400	16	45–60	South and North
Philodendron	10	150	16	30–60	All but South
Piggyback plant	25	100	—	45–60	East and West
Pilea (Creeping Charlie)	100	250	16	45–60	All but South
Pittosporum	25	100	16	45–60	All but North
Podocarpus	400	400	16	45–60	East and South
Pothos	25	100	16	45–60	East and North
Schefflera	150	400	16	45–60	All but North
Slipperwort	25	100	—	45–60	East and North
Spanish shawl	400	500	—	45–60	All but North
Star-of-Bethlehem	400	500	16	30–45	All but North
Stephanotis	400	500	—	45–60	East and South
Succulents: Agave	400	500	16	30–45	West and South
Aloe	400	400	16	30–45	West and South
Donkey's tail	400	400	16	30–45	All but North
Echeveria	400	400	—	30–45	All but North
Kalanchoe	400	400	10	30–45	All but North
Poinsettia	400	400	10	30–45	All but North
Temple bells	100	250	—	45–60	East and South
Treevine	100	250	16	45–60	East and South
Tulips	400	400	16	30–45	All but North
Wandering Jew	100	250	16	30–60	East and North
Wax plant	100	250	—	45–60	All but North
Yucca	400	400	16	45–60	All but North
Zebra plant	400	400	16	30–45	East and West

*Hours of light: L—long day plants: 14 or more hours of light produces seasonal flowering. S—short day plants: 14 or more hours of darkness are needed for flower buds to set. DN—day neutral plants: These plants will bloom on a calendar schedule in either 8 or 16 hours of light.

Appendix D DIRECTORY

1. LIGHTING MANUFACTURERS*

Lamp bulbs
Duro Test 17-10 Willow St. Fairlawn, NJ 07410
General Electric Nela Park Cleveland, OH 44112
GTE Sylvania 100 Endicott St. Danvers, MA 01923
Osram Jeanne Drive Newburgh, NY 12550
Philips-Westinghouse One Westinghouse Plaza Bloomfield, NJ 07470
Sunray Lighting 3120 Croddy Way Santa Ana, CA 92704
   (Supplier for specialty, import, antique, and discontinued light bulbs and tubes.)

Architectural fixtures

General
Edison Price Inc. 409 E. 60th St. New York, NY 10022
Elliptipar (Sylvan Shemitz) 145 Orange Ave. West Haven, CT 06516
General Electric 9350 Flair Drive Los Angeles, CA 91734
Kirlin 3401 E. Jefferson Ave. Detroit, MI 48207
Kurt Versen 10 Charles St. Westwood, NJ 07675
R.A. Manning Co. 1810 North Ave. Sheboygan, WI 53081
Marco 6100 S. Wilmington Los Angeles, CA 90001
Prescolite 1251 Doolittle Dr. San Leandro, CA 94577
Rambusch 40 W. 13th St. New York, NY 10011
SPI 7601 Durand Ave. Racine, WI 53405
Trim Trac 1001 NW 159th Dr. Miami, FL 33169

Fluorescent
Alkco 11500 Melrose Ave. Chicago, IL 60131
Columbia Lighting 3808 Sullivan Rd. Spokane, WA 99220
Lithonia Box A Conyers, GA 30207
Peerless 747 Bancroft Way Berkeley, CA 94710
Prudential 1774 E. 21st St. Los Angeles, CA 90058

Low-voltage
(incandescent)
Capri 6430 E. Slauson Los Angeles, CA 90040
Halo 400 Busse Road Elk Grove Village, IL 60007
LSI 150 E. 58th St. New York, NY 10022
Lightolier 346 Claremont Ave. Jersey City, NJ 07305
Litelab Corp. 5200 Venice Blvd. Los Angeles, CA 90019
Lucifer 212 E. Houston St. San Antonio, TX 78205
Neoray 537 Johnson Ave. Brooklyn, NY 11237
Tivoli Industries 1513 E. St. Gertrude St. Santa Ana, CA 92711
Wendlelighting 9068 Culver Blvd. Culver City, CA 90230

Outdoor
Devine Lighting 6645 E. 11th St. Kansas City, MO 64127
Holophane, a division of Johns Manville Montvale, NJ 07645
Hubbell One Electric Way Christiansburg, VA 24073
John Watson 1935 Regal Row Dallas, TX 75235
Kim Lighting 16555 Gale Ave. Industry, CA 91749
Moldcast Interstate 80 at Maple Ave. Pine Brook, NJ 07058
Nightscaping by Loran 4705 E. Colton Ave. Redlands, CA 92373

Accessory equipment

Ballasts
Luminoptics/Advance 12907-H Alcosta Blvd. San Ramon, CA 94583
Universal Ballasts 29 E. 6th St. Paterson, NJ 07509

Louvers
ALP 5458 N. Mason Ave. Chicago, IL 60630
Nova Industries 999 Montegue Ave. San Leandro, CA 94577

Plastics
Rohm & Haas Independence Mall West Philadelphia, PA 19105

Control devices
Automatic Switch Co. Florham Park, NJ 07932
Enertron Inc. 1100 Wicomico St. Baltimore, MD 21230
Infracon/Tishman Research 666 5th Ave. New York, NY 10103
Leviton 59-25 Little Neck Pkwy. Little Neck, NY 11362
Lutron Coopersburg, PA 18036
Novitas 1523-26th St. Santa Monica, CA 90404
Tork One Grove St. Mt. Vernon, NY 10550
Touchplate 16530 Garfield St. Paramount, CA 90723

*Selected list of manufacturers discussed, specifically or generically, in this book.

2. LIGHTING ORGANIZATIONS

American Home Lighting Institute (AHLI)
435 N. Michigan Ave. Chicago, IL 60611
A national association of manufacturers and lighting retailers.

Designers Lighting Forums (DLF)
Information on membership can be found by calling the local IESNA. A loose association of urban chapters of interior designers seeking education on selected lighting topics.

International Association
of Lighting Designers (IALD)
c/o Wheel Gersztof Associates
30 W. 22nd St. New York, NY 10010
The society of lighting consultants in private practice offering services only.

International Association of Lighting
Maintenance Contractors (IALMC)
301 Maple Ave. W. Vienna, VA 22180
An association of service companies specializing in building maintenance, especially lighting.

Illuminating Engineering Society
of North America (IESNA)
345 E. 47th St. New York, NY 10017
A technical organization conducting research and disseminating information on lighting.

Indoor Light Gardening
Society of America (ILGSA)
c/o Mrs. Jas Martin
1316 Warren Rd. Lakewood, OH 44107
A group of individual hobbyists who share information in their bimonthly journal about the growing of plants under electric light sources.

National Association of
Electric Distributors (NAED)
600 Summer St. Stamford, CT 06901
The organization of companies selling lighting and electrical fittings wholesale.

National Electrical Contractors
Association (NECA)
7315 Wisconsin Ave. Bethesda, MD 20814
This organization of electrical subcontractors forms a network of urban chapters that represent the interests of this construction trade—particularly in employment negotiations.

National Electrical
Manufacturers Association (NEMA)
2101 L St. NW Washington, DC 20037
An association of lighting manufacturers that represents a unified response to the electrical testing laboratories and to those who formulate electrical codes and recommendations.

National Fire Protection Association (NFPA)
Batterymarch Park Quincy, MA 02269
The body sponsoring and controlling the advisory National Electrical Code for the protection of life and property.

National Lighting Bureau (NLB)
2101 L St. NW Washington, DC 20037
A not-for-profit educational institute publishing a variety of excellent guides on the conservation, cost benefits, and beneficial uses of lighting for the layperson/reader.

SELECTED BIBLIOGRAPHY

CHAPTER ONE

Bell, L. *The Art of Illumination*. 2nd ed. New York: Franklin Institute, 1912.

Birren, Faber. *Light, Color and Environment*. New York: Van Nostrand Reinhold, 1969.

———, ed. *Itten: The Elements of Color*. New York: Van Nostrand Reinhold, 1970.

Derge, Wana. *Color, Form and Composition*. Berkeley: Wana Derge Art Assoc., 1966.

DeBoer, J. B. and D. Fischer. *Interior Lighting*. 2nd ed. Antwerp: Scholium International, 1981.

Egan, David M. *Concepts in Architectural Lighting*. New York: McGraw-Hill, 1983.

Erhardt, Louis. *Radiation, Light and Illumination*. Camarillo: Camarillo Reproduction Center, 1977.

Evans, Benjamin H. *Daylight in Architecture*. New York: McGraw-Hill, 1981.

Flynn, John E. and Samuel M. Mills. *Architectural Lighting Graphics*. New York: Reinhold, 1962.

Gregory, R. L. *Eye and Brain: The Psychology of Seeing*. 3rd ed. New York: McGraw-Hill, 1979.

Halse, Albert O. *The Use of Color in Interiors*. New York: McGraw-Hill, 1968.

Hopkinson, R. G. and J. D. Kay. *The Lighting of Buildings*. London: Faber & Faber, 1972.

Itten, Johannes. *The Art of Color*. New York: Van Nostrand Reinhold, 1961.

Lam, William M. *Perception and Lighting as Formgivers in Architecture*. New York: McGraw-Hill, 1978.

Langdon, William K. *Moveable Insulation*. Emmaus: Rodale, 1980.

Lynes, J. A. *Developments in Lighting*. Burgess International Ideas, 1. Essex: Applied Science, 1978.

Nuckolls, James L. *Interior Lighting for Environmental Designers*. 2nd ed. New York: John Wiley Interscience, 1983.

Varley, Helen. *Color*. Los Angeles: Knapp, 1980.

Westinghouse Electric Corp. *Lighting Handbook*, rev. ed. Bloomfield: Westinghouse, 1956.

CHAPTER TWO

Arnheim, Rudolf. *Visual Thinking*. Berkeley: U of California P, 1971.

———. *Art and Visual Perception*. Berkeley: U of California P, 1954.

Carrahar, Ronald G. and Jacquiline B. Thurston. *Optical Illusions and the Visual Arts*. New York: Reinhold, 1966.

Clifford, Derek. *Art and Understanding*. Greenwich: New York Graphic Society, 1980.

Erhardt, Louis. *Radiation, Light and Illumination*. Camarillo: Camarillo Reproduction Center, 1977.

Feininger, Andreas. *Light and Lighting in Photography*. New York: Amphoto-Watson-Guptill, 1976.

Gregory, R. L. *Eye and Brain: The Psychology of Seeing*. 3rd ed. New York: McGraw-Hill, 1979.

Kepes, Gregory. *Language of Vision*. Chicago: Paul Theobold, 1969.

Kilpatrick, David. *Light and Lighting*. Kent: Focal, 1984.

Kohler, Walter and Wassile Luckhardt. *Lighting in Architecture*. New York: Reinhold, 1959.

Lam, William M., Albert Beitz, and G. H. Hallenbeck. *An Approach to the Design of the Luminous Environment*. Boston: MIT, 1976

McCandless, Stanley. *A Method of Lighting the Stage*. 4th ed. New York: Theatre Arts Books, 1973.

Nelson, George. *How to See*. Boston: Little, Brown, 1977.

Pelbrow, Richard. *Stage Lighting*. New York: Van Nostrand Reinhold, 1970.

Phillips, Derek. *Lighting in Architectural Design*. London: McGraw-Hill, 1964.

Rhiner, James L. *The Language of Lighting*. Elk Grove Village: McGraw-Edison, 1983.

Rosinski, Richard R. *The Development of Visual Perception*. Santa Monica: Goodyear, 1977.

Stair, J. L. *The Lighting Book*. Chicago: Curtis Lighting Co., 1929.

———. *Sylvania Lighting Handbook for Television, Theatre and Professional Photography*. 4th ed. Danvers: G.T.E. Sylvania Co., 1971.

Williams, Rollo Gillespie. *Lighting for Color and Form*. New York: Pitman, 1954.

CHAPTER THREE

Alcan Building Products. *Aluminum Ceiling Systems*. Warren: Alcan Aluminum Corp., 1981.

Chicago Metallic Corporation. *Concealed Accessible Ceiling Systems Workbook*. Chicago: Chicago Metallic Corporation, 1978.

Clark, David E., ed. *Basic Home Wiring Illustrated*. Menlo Park: Sunset-Lane, 1977.

Columbia Lighting Inc. *Luminaire/Ceiling Interface Information Series*. Spokane: U.S. Industries, Inc., 1982.

Garrett, Wilbur E., ed. *Energy*. Washington, D.C.: National Geographic Society, 1981.

Gebert, Kenneth L. *National Electrical Code Blueprint Reading*. 7th ed. Alsip: American Technical Publishers, 1977.

Hopkinson, R. G. and J. D. Kay. *The Lighting of Buildings*. London: Praeger, 1969.

Illuminating Engineering Society. *Design Criteria for Lighting Interior Living Spaces*. New York: IES, 1969.

Kaufman, John E., ed. *IES Lighting Handbook Application Volume*. New York: IES, 1981.

McLaughlin, Edward D. and James C. Covis. *Electrical Wiring Methods*. Woburn: Hickok Teaching Systems Inc., 1976.

Meier, Alan. *Energy and Buildings/1983 International Daylighting Conference/Technical Proceedings*. Lausanne: Elsevier, 1984.

Meier, Hans W. *Construction Specifications Handbook* 5th ed. Englewood Cliffs: Prentice-Hall, 1981.

National Electrical Contractors Association. *Electrical Contract Documentation*. Bethesda: NECA, 1981.

National Fire Protection Association. *National Electrical Code, 1984 Edition*. Boston: NFPA, 1983.

National Lighting Bureau. *Getting the Most from Your Lighting Dollar*. 2nd ed. Washington, D.C.: NLB, 1982.

Osborn, Richard W., ed. *Tapping the NEC*. Quincy: NFPA, 1982.

Pritchard, D.C. *Lighting*. 2nd ed. London: Longman, 1978.

Schram, Peter J. *The National Electrical Code Handbook*. Quincy: NFPA, 1983.

Sorcar, Prafulla C. *Rapid Lighting Design and Cost Estimating*. New York: McGraw-Hill, 1979.

Stevens, W. R. *Building Physics: Lighting*. Oxford: Pergamon, 1969.

Traister, John E. *Practical Lighting Applications for Building Construction*. New York: Van Nostrand Reinhold, 1982.

CHAPTER FOUR

Allphin, Willard. *Primer of Lamps and Lighting.* 3rd ed. Reading: Addison-Wesley, 1973.

DeBoer, J. B. and D. Fischer. *Interior Lighting.* 2nd ed. Antwerp: Philips Technical Library, 1981.

Erhardt, Louis. *Radiation, Light and Illumination.* Camarillo: Camarillo Reproduction Center, 1977.

Helms, Ronald N. *Illumination Engineering for Energy Efficient Luminous Environments.* Englewood Cliffs: Prentice-Hall, 1980.

Nuckolls, James L. *Interior Lighting Design for Environmental Designers.* New York: John Wiley & Sons, 1976.

Lynes, J. A. *Developments in Lighting-1.* London: Applied Science, 1978.

Westinghouse Electric Corp. *Lighting Handbook,* rev. ed. Bloomfield: Westinghouse, 1971.

CHAPTER FIVE

DeBoer, J. B. and D. Fischer. *Interior Lighting.* 2nd ed. Antwerp: Phillips Technical Library, 1981.

Egan, David M. *Concepts in Architectural Lighting.* New York: McGraw-Hill, 1983.

Flynn, John E. and Samuel M. Mills. *Architectural Lighting Graphics.* New York: Reinhold, 1962.

Helms, Ronald N. *Illumination Engineering for Energy Efficient Luminous Environments.* Englewood Cliffs: Prentice-Hall, 1980.

Illuminating Engineering Society. *Design Criteria for Lighting Interior Living Spaces: A Recommended Practice.* New York: IES, 1973.

Kaufman, John E. *IES Lighting Handbook Reference Volume.* New York: IES, 1981.

Nuckolls, James L. *Interior Lighting for Environmental Designers.* 2nd ed. New York: John Wiley & Sons, 1983.

Rhiner, James L. *The Language of Lighting.* Elk Grove Village: McGraw-Edison, 1983.

Rooney, William R., ed. *Practical Guide to Home Lighting.* New York: Van Nostrand Reinhold, 1980.

Zimmerman, Maureen Williams. *Home Lighting.* Menlo Park: Lane Publishing Company, 1982.

CHAPTER SIX

American Institute of Architects. *Architect's Handbook of Professional Practice.* Washington, D.C.: AIA, 1984.

Erhardt, Louis. *Radiation, Light and Illumination.* Camarillo: Camarillo Reproduction Center, 1977.

Freidmann, Arnold, John Pile, and Forrest Wilson. *Interior Design.* 4th ed. New York: Elsevier, 1984.

Meier, Hans W. *Construction Specifications Handbook.* 2nd ed. Englewood Cliffs: Prentice-Hall, 1978.

Reznikoff, S. C. *Specifications for Commercial Interiors.* New York: Whitney Library of Design-Watston-Guptill, 1979.

Thomas, Marvin L. *Architectural Working Drawings.* New York: McGraw-Hill, 1978.

Wakita, Osamu and Richard Linde. *The Professional Practice of Architectural Detailing.* New York: John Wiley & Sons, 1978.

CHAPTER SEVEN

Duerk, Donna and David Campbell. *The Challenge of Diversity.* Proc. of the EDRA Annual Conference, June, 1984. Madison: Environmental Design Research Association, 1984.

Gregory, R. L. *Eye and Brain: The Psychology of Seeing.* 3rd ed. New York: McGraw-Hill, 1977.

Halse, Albert O. *The Use of Color in Interiors.* New York: McGraw-Hill, 1968.

Harkness, Sarah P. and James N. Groom. *Building Without Barriers for the Disabled.* New York: Whitney Library of Design-Watson-Guptill, 1976.

Illuminating Engineering Society. *Design Criteria for Lighting Interior Living Spaces: A Recommended Practice of the Residence Lighting Committee.* New York: IES, 1969.

Raschko, Bettyann Boetticher. *Housing Interiors for the Disabled and Elderly.* New York: Van Nostrand Reinhold, 1982.

CHAPTER EIGHT

Allphin, Willard. *Primer of Lamps and Lighting.* 3rd ed. Menlo Park: Addison-Wesley, 1973.

Boud, Hohn. *Lighting for Life.* Kent: George Godwin, 1962.

Elbert, George A. *The Indoor Light Gardening Book.* New York: Crown, 1973.

Horne, Bob, ed. *Outdoor Lighting.* Menlo Park: Lane, 1969.

Kaufman, John E., ed. *IES Lighting Handbook Application Volume.* New York: IES, 1981.

Korstad, Peter, ed. *ALCA Guide of Interior Landscaping.* McLean: Associated Landscape Contractors of America, 1982.

McNair, James, ed. *The Facts of Light About Indoor Gardening.* San Francisco: Ortho Book Division, 1975.

Phillips, Derek. *Lighting in Architectural Design.* New York: McGraw-Hill, 1964.

Rhiner, James L. *The Language of Lighting.* Elk Grove Village: McGraw-Edison, 1983.

Stevens, W. R. *Building Physics: Lighting.* London: Pergamon, 1969.

Wilson, William H. W. *How to Design and Install Outdoor Lighting.* San Francisco: Ortho Book Division, 1984.

Westinghouse Electric Corp. *Westinghouse Lighting Handbook,* rev. ed. Bloomfield: Westinghouse, 1981.

CHAPTER NINE

Boud, John. *Lighting for Life.* Kent: George Godwin, 1962.

Jones, Tom Douglas. *The Art of Light and Color.* New York: Van Nostrand Reinhold, 1972.

Kock, Winston E. *Lasers and Holography.* New York: Doubleday, 1969.

Lytel, Allan and Lawrence Buckmaster. *Lasers and Masers.* New York: Bobbs-Merrill, 1972.

Overheim, Daniel R. and David L. Wagner. *Light and Color.* New York: John Wiley & Sons, 1982.

Pownell, Glen. *Lighting Crafts.* Wellington: Seven Seas, 1974.

Williams, Rollo Gillespie. *Lighting for Color and Form.* New York: Pitman, 1954.

Williamson, Samuel J. and Herman Z. Cummins. *Light and Color in Nature and Art.* New York: John Wiley & Sons, 1983.

INDEX

*Numbers in italics refer to material
in illustration captions*

Abbreviations, lighting-related, 215
Absorption of light, *22*
Accent lights, recessed, 68
Accessories, of fixtures, *74-75*
Acoustical ceilings, 44-45
Acoustone ceiling, *44*
Acrylics, 193-94; to filter ultraviolet light, 158; lenses, 76
Activities in space, 22-25; bank, 137; boutique, 148; exhibit installation, 156-57; hotel lobby, 124; open office, 142; recommended light levels for, 22-23; residential dining room, 130; residential entry, 118; restaurant, 168; retirement center, 163-65
Adams, Harriet, 196
Addendum to project manual, 115
Administrative issues, in project manual, 113
Age, and color perception, 20; and vision, 14
Aging process, of eyes, 176-78, *178;* housing needs, *161, 162*
Agreements, 96, 113; between designer and client, 212-13; between designer and subcontractor, 50
Air-handling fixtures, *43*
Alternative lighting layouts, *83*
Ambient light, 23; for aging eyes, 178; general, *83;* open office, *146;* plan drawing, *83;* from portable fixtures, 72; in retirement center, 165, 167; in store, 148; from uplighting, 35
Ambulatory infirm, lighting for, 178-79
Analysis factors, in lighting design, 11-27
Angle of light, 23; for task lighting, 62
Anthony's Restaurant, St. Louis, Mo., 168-73
Appearance of fixtures, 73; bank, 140; boutique, 153; in darkened gallery, 159; low-voltage lighting systems, 133; restaurant, 172; retirement center, 167
Approval drawings, 78-79, 95
Approvals log, *95*
Approvals submittal, 95, *95*
Architecture, silhouetting in, *33*
Art, light as, 35-37, 38, *Plate 10, 104,* 192-99
Artifacts, protection from light damage, 158
Assisted living, 163, *164*
Atmosphere, and daylight colors, *17*
Attached ceilings, 44-46
Autovariac dimmers, 58, *58*

Back door entries, for wheelchairs, 181
Backlighting, 32, *34,* 37, 38; of plants, *184*
Baffled ceilings, *202*
Ballasts, 55-56, 58, 62
The Bank of Tokyo, Ltd., Tokyo, Japan, 134
Banks, downlighting for, 32
Barrier-free buildings, 176, *179*
Baseboard of residential entry, *122*
Bathroom lighting, 163, 179, *180,* 201
Batwing distributions of light, 62, *69,* 147
Beam angles, to avoid glare, 167; bank, 138; boutique, *151;* exhibit installation, 157-58; of hotel lobby, 128; open office, 147; residential dining room, 133; residential entry, 121, *121;* restaurant, 172
Beam of light, characteristics of, 52
Beam play, *30,* 33, 38; fixtures for, 37
Beam shapes, 62; bank, 139; boutique, 153; exhibit installation, 158; fluorescent tubes, 147; hotel lobby, 128; PAR lamps, 133; residential entry, 123; restaurant, 172; retirement center, 167

Beam sunlight, for light pipes, 193
Bedrooms, lighting for the infirm, 179, *179;* bedside lighting, 163
Bell, Larry, 197
Bell, Louis, 8
Bidding, 96; as constraint on lighting design, 50; substitution of fixtures, 73
Black mirrors, windows as, 16, *18*
Body chemistry, and ultraviolet light, 60-61
Boutique ICE, *Plate 12, 106,* 148-53, *150*
Bowersox, Jack L., 160, 163-65
Box beam, 201
Bright surfaces, *Plate 1, 96-97*
Brightness, 14-15, 19-20, *29;* in boutique ICE, *150;* and electrical efficiency, 56, 59; on gray scale, *21;* and human behavior, 8, 15, 23, 28, 199, and reflectance, *Plate 7, 102*
Brightness balances, *24*
Budget, as constraint on light design, 49-51; bank, 138; boutique, 151; exhibit installation, 157; hotel lobby, 128; open office, 145-47; residential dining room, 133; residential entry, 120; restaurant, 170; retirement center, 165-67
Building codes, 89; local, 48. *See also* Code compliance
Building materials, reflectances of, 16
Bulb identification, *55-57*
Bulb replacement, by the aged, 179, *179;* detail drawings, 95
Bulbs: clear glass, 31, *57;* frosted, *57*
Bullet beam PAR lamp, 157-58
Burning position of light source, 52

California: building codes, 150-51; energy code, 145
California First Bank, San Francisco, Ca., 134-41
California School of art, *Plate 16, 110-11*
Canadian Standards Association, 73
Cancer, caused by ultraviolet light, 61
Candlelight, color appearance of, 59
Candlepower distribution curve, 62, *68,* 77
Cash allowance specifications, 113
Catalogs, of fixtures, 76-77, *76;* of large lamp bulbs, *56*
Ceiling height: and lighting plan, *86;* and selection of fixtures, 68
Ceilings, 15, 43-46, *202;* high, fixtures for, 68; sloped, of office space, *144;* with recessed fixtures, *42*
Ceramalux 4 lights, *Plate 3, 99*
Chandelier, installation of, 44
Change orders, 50, *82,* 115
Charter House Retirement Center, Rochester, N. Y., 160-67, *161, 162, 164*
Checklists: code information, 48; drawings conventions, 80; lighting plans drawing, 89
Chemical light sources, 52
Chlorophyll production, light for, 182
Chroma, 20
Chromaton, *195*
Clear glass bulbs, 31, *56*
Clerestory windows, *16,* 158; exhibit installation, 156; retirement center, 160, *163*
Client image, 12; bank, 134; boutique, 148; exhibit installation, 154; hotel lobby, 124; open office, 142; residential entry, 118; residential dining room, 130; restaurant, 168; retirement center, 160
Client motivation, 12-14
Client profile questionnaire, 13
Client vision, 12, 14; bank, 134; boutique, 148; exhibit installation, 154; hotel lobby, 124; open office, 142; residential dining room, 130; residential entry, 118; restaurant, 168, retirement center, 160
Code compliance, 46-49, 89; barrier-free buildings, 176, *179,* 181; bathrooms, *180;* boutique, 150-51; energy-use budgets, 51; exhibit installation, 157; hotel lobby, 127-28;

kitchens for the infirm, *180;* open office, 145; outdoor wiring, 188; private homes, 133; residential entry, 120; restaurant, 170; in San Francisco, 137-38
Cold/warm color contrasts, *Plate 1, 96-97*
Color, 12, 19-22, 28; bank, 137, 139; bathrooms for the infirm, 179; boutique, 148, 153-54; of daylight, 16, *17;* exhibit installation, 156; hotel lobby, 124, 128; incandescent lights, 123; light for plants, 182; open office, 142, 147; and penetration of daylight, 15; perception of, 20; of quartz lights, 158; residential dining room, 130, 133; residential entry, 118; in restaurant, 168, 172; retirement center, 160-62, 167; transmission of, and window glass, *17*
Color constancy, 20
Color contrasts, *Plate 1, 96-97*
Color illusions, 199
Color Key Program, 21
Color reflectancies, 20, *21*
Color rendering of light sources, 58-59
Color response, 20
Color shifting, and light sources, *Plate 4, 100*
Color temperature, 59
Combustion as light source, 52
Commercial project: approvals submittal, *95;* detail drawings, *92;* electrical plan, *91, 92;* multistory lighting plan, *87;* responsibility for electrical plans, 89
Communication of design, 78-115
Communications-related design services, *91*
Complementary color contrasts, *Plate 1, 96-97*
Compositional lighting techniques, 28-39, *29;* boutique, 148-49; hotel lobby, 127; open office, 145; outdoor plant lighting, 186; residential dining room, 130-33; residential entry, 120; restaurant, 170; retirement center, 165
Computer costing of design project, 50
Conditions, general, of agreement, 113
Conflict, legal, precedent in, 95
Constraints in lighting design, 40-51; bank, 137; boutique, 150; exhibit installation, 157; hotel lobby, 127-28; open office, 145; residential dining room, 133; residential entry, 120-23; restaurant, 170-71; retirement center, 165
Construction management, 40
Construction schedules of, 40-41, 206
Construction Specifications Institute (CSI), 113
Consumer-grade dimmers, 58
Conti, Mario, 193
Contract documents, 95, 206-13
Contractor, design contract with, 50
Contractor fixtures, 50
Contrasts: of brightness, 23, 30; of color, 22, 28, *Plate 1, 96-97;* of fixtures to background, 73; of surface textures, *Plate 7, 102,* 130
Control of light level, 19; restaurant, 171-72
Controls of dimmers, 58
Cool beam bulbs, for plant lighting, 185
Cool colors, 20
Copper screening of light sources, 158
Corridors, for light as art, 37
Costs considerations, of daylighting, 19
Costs: bank, 139; boutique, 153; change orders, 115; comparison of, 38; custom fixtures, 134; of electricity, *49;* exhibit installation, 159; hotel lobby, 128, *129;* lighting fixtures, 72-73; lighting systems, 56-57; low-voltage lighting, 133; open office, 147; residential entry, 123; restaurant, 172; retirement center, 167
Cove lighting, *201*
Critical path method (CPM), 40
Crosslighting, 23
CRTs, lighting for, *25. See also* VDT Screens

Crystal Cathedral, Garden Grove, Ca., *33*
CSI Masterformat, 113
Current construction cost, 49-50
Custom fixtures, 43, 73, *132, 134, 135, 136, 137, 139-140, 140, 172;* for energy conservation, *172*

Damage, from light, 16, 59, 154, 158
Dark surfaces, color contrasts, *Plate 1, 96-97*
Darkened areas, fixtures in, 159
Darkness adaptation, 199
Daylight, 12, 14-20; approximation of, 8; borrowed, *163;* colors of, 16, *17,* 59, *Plate 8, 102-3;* penetration of, 15-16, *15;* ultraviolet light in, 158
Daylight fluorescent lights, *Plate 2, 98*
Daylight prediction graph, *146*
Daylighting: bank, 134-37; boutique, 148, *149;* exhibit installation, 154-56, *156;* hotel lobby, 124, *125;* open office, 142-47; residential dining room, 130; residential entry, 118; restaurant, 168; retirement center, 160, *163*
Daylighting circuits, 139
Day-neutral plants, *183*
Decorative fixtures, 37, *37,* 38; for plant lighting, *184;* suspended, 71
Decorative lighting, 35
Deluxe cool white light, *Plate 2, 98*
Deluxe warm white light, *Plate 2, 98*
Descriptive specifications, 113
Detail drawings, 78-80, *85,* 89-95, *92*
Dichroic reflectors, 59
Dimmers, 58, *58,* 157-58; for aging eyes, 178; for outdoor lighting, 191; for underwater lights, 188
Dimming: budget considerations, 128; in hotel lobby, 128, *129;* and lamp life, 57-58, 138; of low-voltage lamps, 121-23; in restaurant, 172
Direct burial uplights, 35
Direct glare, 17-19, 62, *69*
Dirt, and brightness of lamp bulbs, 123
Disabled people, needs of, 176
Display cases: acrylic, 59; glass, lighting of, *157*
Documentation of projects, 95-115, 206-13
Downlights, 32, *34,* 38; in bank, 137; in boutique, 148, *150,* 153; for grazing, 35, *35;* incandescent, 128
Drawings conventions checklist, 80
Drawings of project, 78-95
Duration of light, for plant growth, 182

Earthquake considerations: hung ceilings, 46; suspended fixtures, 71; in San Francisco, Ca., *136,* 137, 140
Eastern exposures, and plant growth, 182-83
Efficiency: of lighting design, 28; of low-voltage highlighting, 30. *See also* Energy conservation
Egress lights, 128, 150-51; Marriott Hotel, *128*
Electric light, *Plates 2, 3, 98-99*
Electrical costs, *49*
Electrical efficiency: 52-55, 56; of low-pressure sodium lamps, *54;* of recessed fixtures, 62
Electrical hazards, of old wiring, 120
Electrical plans, 78-79, 89, *91, 92*
Electrical service, and lighting design, 48
Emergency lighting systems, 48-49
Energy budgets, 50-51, 145, 165
Energy conservation: bank, 138; and brightness, 59; and costs, 50, 56; and daylighting, 19, *19;* hotel lobby, 128; low-voltage highlighting, 30; in museum exhibits, 157; and nonuniform lighting, 27, *29;* open office, 145, *146;* private residences, 133; residential entry, 120; restaurants, 168, 170-71, *172;* retail space, 151; retirement center,

165; selection of fixtures, 50; state codes, 51; and uniform ambient lighting, 23
Energy efficiency: comparative, of lighting techniques, 38; of structural lighting, 72
Enertron light switch, *60*
Entries, 124; Marriott Hotel, *125, 126;* back doors, 181
Environmental influences on light damage, 154
Equals, 43, 113; specification of, 50, 73
Equipment costs, 133; boutique, 153; hotel lobby, 128; open office, 147; residential entry, 123; of restaurant, 172; retirement center, 167
Equivalent facilitation, 176
Erythemal wavelengths, 59-61
Essential functions, 50
Estimates, of lighting design cost, 49-50
Exit signs, 170, *171, 177*
Experimental art, *Plate 16, 110-11*
Experimental lighting concepts, 43
Exposed beam ceilings, 44
Exposed grid trim fixtures, *44*
Extension, contrast of, *Plate 1, 96-97*
Exterior landscape lighting, 130, 133
Eye: human, 14, *14;* old. *See* Old eyes

Fabrics, for backlighting, *34*
Fading, 16, 19, 59, *Plate 5, 100*
Fast-track construction, and design, 127, 128
Fiberoptics, 192-93, *193*
Fibers, resistance to light damage, 16, 19
Figure illusions, 197, *197, 198*
Filter effects, in aging eyes, 178, *178*
Finishes, interior, 8, 22, 58; in bathrooms for the infirm, 179; and brightness, 59; and daylight control, 15, 16, *16;* exhibit installation, 157; in kitchens for the infirm, 180, *180;* in retirement center, 163
Fire sprinkler heads, indication in drawings, *82*
Fire-rated ceilings, 44, 46
Fixture angles, in boutique, *151*
Fixture list, *114*
Fixtures, 62-77; air-handling, *43;* bank, *135, 136,* 139-40; in bathrooms for the infirm, 179; boutique, *150,* 153; commercial market for, 72-73; custom-built plans, *132;* decorative, 37, *37;* decorative, for plant lighting, *184;* designation by type, 89; exhibit installation, 158-59; hotel lobby, 128; incandescent, costs of, 128; in museums, *159;* open office, 147; placement of, 80; recessed, *142;* residential dining room, 133; residential entry, 123; restaurant, 172, *172;* retirement center, 167; for VDT workstation, *147;* for wallwashing, *35*
Flanged trim fixtures, *44*
Flavin, Dan, 196, 197, 199; *Illusions in Color, Plate 11, 105*
Floating ceilings, 202
Flood lights: efficiency of, 157; shielding by louvers, 158
Floor plan of daylighted office, *144*
Florence, Noel, 72
Fluorescent lights, *Plate 2, 98;* ballasts for, 55, *60;* beam shape, 147; boutique, *150,* 152; color of, 59, 153; cost of, 153; dimming of, 57-58; energy efficiency of, 50; for garages, *181;* heat from, 16; in kitchens, 180, *180;* lamp life, 147, 167, 179; low-wattage, screwsocket, 179; for offices, 72, *145, 146,* 147; for plant lighting, 185; wallwashing, 30-31, *203*
Fly screening of light sources, 158
Flynn, John, 22, 25-27, 28, 56
Footlamberts, 20, *21*
Foster, Michael, *Image of Tutenkamen I, 196*
Framing, in lighting composition, 28
Frosted bulbs, *56*
Fugitive colors, 16, *Plate 5, 100*
Furniture: luminous, *194;* and placement of fixtures, *86*

Furniture-integrated lighting, *83*
Fuseboxes, in barrier-free buildings, *179*

Garage, lighting for wheelchairs, *181*
Garden lighting, 186-91
Gaseous-discharge lights, 52, 53, 55-56. *See also* HID lights
Gaslight, 52
Gelman, Marvin, 130
General conditions of agreement, 113
Glare, 16, 165; and fixture selection, 62; in open office, 145; from sparkle, 35
Glass display cases, lighting of, *157*
Glasswall: reflective coating, *156;* sunscreen for, *138*
Gobos, 31
Gray scale, *21*
Grazing light, 32, 35, *35,* 38; in residential entry, 121; and wallcovering, 167
Gro-Lux Wide Spectrum lights, 186
Ground covers, reflectances of, 16
Ground fault interrupters (GFI), *180*
Growth of plants, light for, 182

Hallway lighting, of retirement center, *163*
Halogen gas lights, 53
Hand-held light controller, *61*
Hannon, Phillip M., 154
Hardware of light as art, 192
Harmony, lighting for, 28
Hausermann Furniture Showroom, Los Angeles, Ca., *Plate 11, 105*
Hayashi, Reiko, *La Entrada,* 118-23, 192
Heat: from lighting installation, 95; in open office, 145; in plant lighting, 185-86; from sunlight, 16
Heat loss, from windows, 16
Hendrick, Clyde, 25
HID (high-intensity discharge) lights, 31, 52, 53, 57, 77, *Plate 3, 99, 125,* 128; in bank, 137, 138, 139; in boutique, 152; cost of, 153; energy efficiency of, 50
Highlighting, 30, *30,* 38, *Plate 14, 108;* in boutique, 148, 152; decorative fixtures for, 37
High-pressure mercury lights, ballasts for, 55
High-pressure sodium lights, 36, *Plate 3, 99;* ballasts for, 55
Holograms, 196-97, *197*
Holography, 197, *197*
Home Control System, *60*
Horton, Jules, 134, 137-40
Hotel lobby lighting, 124-29
Hotels, code requirements, 48-49, 127-28
Housing needs, in old age, *161, 162*
Housings for recessed fixtures, 44
Hue, 20; contrasts of, *Plate 1, 96-97*
Human eye, function of, 14, *14*
Humidity, and infrared heat, 59
Hung ceilings. *See* Suspended ceilings
HVAC cross section of daylighted office, *146*

ICE boutique, *Plate 12, 106,* 148-53, *149, 153*
Illuminating Engineering Society of North America (IESNA), 62
Illusions, *170,* 196-99
Incandescent lights, 52, 53, 55, *Plate 2, 98;* bank, 138; bathroom mirror, 163; color of, 123, 153; cost of fixtures, 128, 172; dimming of, 58; energy efficiency of, 50, 56; for grazing, 35; hotel lobby, *126,* 127, 128; lamp life, 57, 158; for plant growth, 185-86; residential entry, 120-21; retirement center, 167; and ultraviolet light, 59; for wallwashing, 30, *35*
Incandescent-fluorescent tubes, *Plate 2, 98*
Indirect fixtures, 35
Indirect glare, 62; from daylighting, 19; in exhibits, 158
Indirect lighting, in dining rooms, 133
Indoor plants, lighting for, 182-86, 216-17
Industrial market for fixtures, 73

Infirm: ambulatory, 178-79; nonambulatory, 179-81
Infracon, 61
Infrared light, 16, 59, 182, 183; heat from, 123, 139, 147, 172; protection of artifacts from, 158
Installation, difficulty of, 38
Installation costs: exhibit installation, 159; incandescent fixtures, 128; low-voltage lighting, 133; open office, 147; residential entry, 123; retirement center, 167
Instructions to bidders, 96
Intensity of light, for plant growth, 182
Interior design, and lighting, 8
Interview with client, initial, 12, 13
Invisible light, 16, 59-61, 128, 133; avoidance of damage from, 123, 154-59
Invitation to tender, 95-96
Irwin, Robert, 197
Ishii, Motoko, Plate 13, 106-7
Itten, Johannes, 22

Junction boxes, 71

Kinetic light effects, 194-96
Kitchens, code compliance, 92; lighting for the infirm, 179-80, 180
Krypton gas lights, 53, 153; for plants, 186

Lakitch, Lili, Drive-In, Plate 10, 104
Lamp bulbs, cleaning of, 123; identification of, 56, 57
Lamp life, 57-58, 128, 179; bank, 138-39; boutique, 152; exhibit installation, 157-58; fluorescent lights, 167; low-voltage lamps, 121-23, 133; open office, 147; recessed fixtures, 62; restaurant, 172
Land, Edwin, 20
Landscape lighting, Plate 3, 99, 186-91
Laser art, Plate 15, 108-9, 195-96
Lath and plaster ceilings, 44
Legal precedent, in contract conflicts, 95
Lenses: acrylic, 76; to protect from ultraviolet light, 59
Liability of designer, 44, 46-48, 73, 89
Life cycle costing, 50, 51; computerized, 57
Life-safety codes, 48
Light: as art, 35-37, 38, Plate 10, 104, 192-99; damage from, 59-154-59; as design medium, 11
Light boxes, 203; for backlighting, 32
Light/dark contrasts, Plate 1, 96-97
Light-level maintenance, and daylighting, 19
Light levels, recommended, by activity, 23
Light-O-Matic ultrasonic motion sensor, 60
Light pipes, 193-94
Light reflectance value (LRV) of color, 23-25
Light sources: for acrylic panels, 194; bank, 138; boutique, 152-53; colors of, 20, 59; exhibit installation, 157-58; for fiberoptics, 192-93; hotel lobby, 128; for light pipes, 193; low-voltage incandescent, 133; open office, 147; for plant lighting, 185-86, 185; and reflectance of color, 25; residential entry, 120-21; restaurant, 171; retirement center, 167; selection of, 52-61; for sparkle, 35; specifications, 43
Light waves, 195
Lighting charts, 201-5
Lighting design: analysis factors, 12-27; components of, 11; composition in, 28, 29; constraints in, 40-51; costs of, 49; philosophies of, 8, 169; preliminary decisions, 37
Lighting documents, 206-13
Lighting fixtures, choice of, 62
Lighting plan, 78-87, 82-83, 86, 87, 89, 92; boutique, 150; residential entry, 123
Lighting Services, Inc., 130
Lighting techniques, comparison of, 38
Liquidated damages, 40
Living center, 178, 178

Local lighting, 23
Location of fixtures, 71
Lockheed Missiles and Space Company, Sunnyvale, Ca., 142-47
Long-day plants, 183
Long-night plants, 183
Longwave light frequencies, 59
Louisiana World Exposition, Vatican Pavilion, New Orleans, La., 154-59
Low ceilings: downlighting, 34; fixtures, 68
Low-pressure lights, 52, 53
Low-pressure sodium lights (LPS), 54, Plate 3, 99; ballasts for, 55
Low-voltage lights, 52, 54, 130; boutique, 152, combined with metal halide HIDs, 153; cost of, 153; dimming of, 58; efficiency of, 50, 157; and highlighting, 30, 30; incandescent, 35, 56, Plate 12, 106, 133; for outdoor use, 188-90, 189; residential dining room, 131; residential entry, 121, 123; transformers, 43, 55
Low-voltage switching, 58, 61
Lumens-per-watt measurement, 56
Lumia, 195, 195, 196
Luminous art, 37, 38
Luminous furniture, 194
Luminous panels, Plate 9, 104
Luminous reflectance, and Munsell values, 20

Maintenance: bank, 140; boutique, 153; of incandescent lights, 128; restaurant, 172; retirement center, 167
Manual of project, 78, See Project manual
Manufacturers, directory of, 218
Markets, in lighting industry, 72-73
Marriott Hotel lobby, Orlando, Fla., 124-29
Martyniuck, Osyp, 25
Masterformat, CSI, for specifications, 113
Men's room, for handicapped, 177
Merchandise, enhancement of, 148-53
Mercury lights, 53, 77, Plate 3, 99; bank, 138, 139; dimming of, 57; for plant growth, 186
Metal ceilings, 46, 47
Metal halide lights, 53, Plate 3, 99; ballasts for, 55; in boutique, 150, 152-53; burning position, 52; combined with low-voltage lights, 153; dimming of, 57
Metalarc C lights, Plate 3, 99
Metamerism, Plate 4, 100
Mood of space, 12, 25-27, 27; boutique, 148; and color, 20; exhibit installation, 157; festive, from sparkle lighting, 35; hotel lobby, 126, 127; residential dining room, 130; residential entry, 118; restaurant, 168; retirement center, 165
Moonlight, color appearance of, 59
Moore, Harriet, Portrait of a Condemned Soul, Plate 14, 108, 118, 119, 120
Morning light, 182-83
Mounting locations, 63, 64-67
Mounting of fixtures: 62, 68-72, 71; bank, 139, 140; boutique, 153; hotel lobby, 128; museums, 159; open office, 147; residential entry, 123; restaurant, 172; retirement center, 167; surface-mounted low-voltage systems, 133; track mounting, 159
Moving lights, 194-96
MR-11 bulbs, 56
MR-16 lights, 56, Plate 12, 106; color of, 153; combined with metal halide HIDs, 150, 153; fixtures for, 151, 152; for plant lighting, 185; residential entry, 121
Multi-vapor II lights, Plate 3, 99
Multilevel fluorescent ballasts, 58
Multistory buildings: barrier-free regulations, 176; lighting plan drawings, 87
Munsell Color System, 20
Museums, light fixtures in, 159
Music, visual, 195

Neon lights, 192; in boutique, 150, 150; sculp-

ture, Plate 10, 104
Night, and solar lighting, 16-19
Nightlighting: hotel lobby entry, 126, 127; restaurant, 169
Nightscapes, 187, 188
Noise pollution, 44-46
Nonambulatory infirm, 178, 179-81
Nonfire-rated ceilings, 46, 47
Nontask activities, lighting for, 23-25
Nonvisual components of work tasks, 22
Nordman, Maria, 197
Northern exposures, 183
Northwestern National Life Insurance building, Minneapolis, Minn., Plate 13, 106-7
Obata, Guy, 168; design philosophy, 169
Occupancy scheduling, and daylighting, 19
Office furniture, lighted, 72
Offices: daylighting of, 142-47; emergency lighting systems, 49
Old eyes, 14, 176-78, 178; color perception, 20; lighting requirements, 160, 176-81; uniform ambient lighting for, 23
Operating costs: boutique, 153; exhibition installation, 159; hotel lobby, 128; lamp life, 57; of low-voltage lighting, 133; open office, 147; residential entry, 123; restaurant, 172; retirement center, 167
Optical characteristics of light sources, 52
Optimum-angle lighting, 23, 24
Organizations, lighting-related, 218
Orientation of windows, 12; and plant growth, 182-83
Ott, John, 61
Outdoor lighting, seen from indoors, 187
Outdoor plants, lighting of, 186-91, 186
Outdoor stairs, 167
Overhead fixtures, and glare, 62

Pan fixtures, in residential dining room, 132
Panels, acrylic, 194
PAR lamps, 123, 133, 157
PAR-36 auto headlights, 133
Parking areas, lighting of, 180-81
Passive solar design, 19
Pendant fixtures. See Suspended fixtures
Penetration of daylight, 14-15, 15
Perception of color, 20
Performance standard specifications, 113
Personnel detectors, 19, 58, 59, 60, 61; for underwater lights, 188
Phases of design, 79
Philosophies of lighting design, 8
Photobiology, 59-61
Photocells, 58; in daylighted workstation, 145
Photodegradation, 59, 154. See also Invisible light
Photometric profile of light fixture, 62
Photoperiodism, 183-85
Photosensors, for light-level maintenance, 19
Photosynthesis, 183; light for, 182; temperatures for, 183
Phototropism, 183
Physiology of color, 20
Plan views: bank, 137, 139; exhibit installation, 156; hotel lobby, 126; residential entry, 120; retirement center, 164, 162
Planning perception chart, 39
Plantings to control daylight penetration, 15
Plants, indoor: light requirements, 216-17; lighting for, 182-91
Plenum, 43, 43; in suspended grid ceilings, 46; in exhibit installation, 157
Point light sources, 52, 54, 56
Pools, lighting of, 188
Portable lighting fixtures, 72; decorative, 37; for landscape lighting, 188
Portable workstations, 72
Presbyopia, 176
Primary colors, contrasts of hue, Plate 1, 96-97
Primary electrical service, 48

Primary focus, in lighting composition, 28
Prism light pipes, 193-94, *194*
Privacy, and solar lighting, 16
Probable cost projection, and lighting design estimate, 50
Product data, 95
Productivity, increasing of, 134-41
Programmable switches, 179
Project drawings, 78-95
Project management, team relationships in, *41*
Project manuals, 78, 95-115; addendum to, 115; changes in, 115
Projection bulbs, 56; color appearance of, 59
Properties of light sources, 53
Proprietary specifications, 113
Psychology: of lighting, 25-27; of color contrasts, 20-22
Public lobbies, exist signs, *177*

Quartz lights: color of, 59, 158; efficiency of, 157; lamp life, 157

R20 incandescent lamps, in, residential entry, 121, 123
Rainbow lights, 195
Ramps, for the disabled, 163-65, *177*
Recessed fixtures, *42, 44,* 68, 76; in attached ceilings, 44; of bank project, *140;* exhibit installation, 157; residential dining room, *132*
Reduction of costs, of lighting design, 50
Reference standard specifications, 113
Reflectance characteristics, 23, 28-30, *Plate 7, 102;* for beam play, 31; of building materials, 16; and grazing, *35*
Reflected ceiling plan drawings, 80, *80, 82, 84;* modified, *84;* hotel lobby, *129*
Reflected light, *22;* color of, *20*
Reflective coating of glasswall, to control daylight, *156*
Regressed trim fixtures, *44*
Residential project: detail drawings, *85;* electrical plan, *92;* lighting plan, *86;* reflected ceiling plan, *84;* responsibility for electrical plans, 89
Resistance dimmers, 58, *58*
Response to color, 20
Restaurant lighting, 168-73; uplighting, 35
Retirement center lighting design, 160-67

Safety considerations: bank, 140; boutique, 150-51; exhibit installation, 157; hotel lobby, 128; of lighting fixtures, 73-76; open office, 145; in outdoor lighting, 186-87; in private residences, 133; residential entry, 120; restaurant, 170; retirement center, 165
Samples, 95
San Francisco, Ca., building code, 137-38
Saturation of color, *Plate 1, 96-97*
Scale of construction, 43
Schedule constraints, 40, 133; bank, 137; boutique, 151-52; exhibit installation, 157; hotel lobby, 127; open office, 147; restaurant, 171; retirement center, 165
Screening of light sources, 158
Sculpture, lighting of, 121
Secondary electrical service, 48
Secondary focus, in lighting composition, 28
Secondary light sources, bright surfaces as, *Plate 1, 96-97*
Selkowitz, Steven, 142
Shading, from sunlight, 15, *15*
Shadow play, 31, *32,* 38; decorative fixtures for, 37; plant lighting, *185*
Shanus, Michael D., 145
Sheetrock ceilings, 44, 46
Shemitz, Sylvan, 72, 147
Shop drawings, 95
Shortwave light frequencies, 59
Sight line sketch of boutique project, *149*
Silhouetting, 31, *33,* 38; decorative fixtures for, 37; of indoor plants, *184*

Silver screening of light sources, 158
Simultaneous color contrasts, *Plate 1, 96-97*
Sky, clear blue, color appearance of, 59
Skylights, of daylighted office space, *144*
Small site lighting controls, 19
Small space, lighting design, *Plate 6, 101*
Socialization, in retirement center, 163
Sodium lights, 53, *Plate 3, 99;* dimming of, 57
Soffits, *201*
Solar geometry, 15, *15*
Solar heat, of daylighted office, 145, *146*
Solid state dimmers, 58
Southern exposures, and plant growth, 183
Sparkle, 35, *36,* 38; decorative fixtures for, 37; plant lighting, *185*
Spatial illusion, 196, 199
Specification grade dimmers, 58
Specifications, *63,* 78, 95, 113; from catalogs, 77; and ceiling type, 43-44; and construction schedules, 40; and costs, 73; for large-scale projects, 43; substitutions, 73; for track lighting, 72
Specifier market for fixtures, 73
Spectral Distribution Chart, 22, 59
Spectrum profiles, *Plates 2, 3, 98-99*
Spencer, Terry, 25
Spread lenses, 157
Stairs, lighting for, 176, *177,* 180, 188, *188;* retirement center, *167;* for walker use, *181*
Stores: brightness in, 30; downlighting for, 32; lighting project, *Plate 12, 106,* 148-53
Structural lighting, 32, 38, 72; charts, *201*
Styletone mercury lights, *Plate 3, 99*
Suberythemal wavelengths, 59-61
Substitutions for specified fixtures, 72-73, 96
Subtractive color theory, *21*
Succulents, *183*
Sucov, E. W., 25
Suitability of fixture, *63*
Summer sunlight, color of, *Plate 8, 102-3*
Sunlight, 182-83; damage to fabrics, 16
Supplementary conditions of agreement, 113
Surface brightness, and human behavior, 8
Surface-mounted fixtures, 68, 123; and attached ceilings, 44; low-voltage systems, 133
Surfaces, 28, 30; for beam play, 31; contrast of, *Plate 7, 102,* 130
Suspended ceilings, *44,* 46
Suspended fixtures, 71; earthquake safety, 140; in hotel lobbies, 128; in kitchens for the infirm, 180; restaurant, 172
Switches: height of, 178; height in barrier-free buildings, *179;* programmable, 179

Task angles, in bank, 139
Task lighting, 22-23, *25,* 72, 77; bank, *136,* 137, 138; fixtures for, 37, 62; open office, 145, 147; plan drawing, *83;* retirement center, 165
Taylor, L. H., 25
T-bar ceilings, *47*
Team relationships in project management, *41*
Telephones, accessible to wheelchairs, *177*
Temperature Kelvin measurements of color, 58, 59
Terry, LeMar, 130, 157-59, *158*
Textiles, protection from light damage, 158, *158*
Texture, 28, 30; and grazing light, 35; and reflectance of color, 23-25
Thermal losses, from windows, 16
Time constraints on lighting design, 43
Time switches, 19, 58, *60*
Tinted glass, 16, *17,* 19, 145
Total internal reflection, 192, *193;* in acrylics, 193
Track-mounted lighting, 71-72, 159; for acoustical ceilings, 46; cost of, 172; exhibit installation, 157; residential entry, 121
Traffic patterns, 23-25; bank, 137; boutique,

148; exhibit installation,. 157; hotel lobby, 124-27; residential dining room, 130; residential entry, 118; restaurant, 168; retirement center, 163
Transformers, *54;* for track-mounted fixtures, 159
Translucent materials, backlighted, 32, *34*
Trees, uplighting of, *184*
Tropical plants, light needs, 183
Tungsten filament lights, 53, 59
Tungsten halogen lights, 52, 172; dimming of, 58; for plant growth, 186
Turrell, James, 196, 197, 199; *AMBA, Plate 16, 110-11; Lunette, 198*
Types of fixtures, indication of, 89

UF-3 acrylic, 59
Ultralume fluorescent bulbs, 59, *Plate 2, 98*
Ultraviolet light, 16, 59, 139; and body chemistry, 61; protection of artifacts from, 158
Underwater lights, 188
Underwriters Laboratories (UL), 73; installation inspection, 46
Uniform ambient lighting, 8, 23
Union labels, necessary in San Francisco, Ca., 138
Unit Power Density (UPD), 23
Unity, lighting for, 28
Uplighting, 35, *36,* 38; bank, *138, 140;* of plants, *184*
Use of space. See Activities in space

Valances, lighted, *202*
Valentine, Dewain, 197
Value, of color, 20
Value engineering, 50
Variegated foliage, light needs, 183
Vatican Pavilion, Louisiana World Exposition, New Orleans, La., 154-59
VDT screens: glare from, 19; lighting of, *25, 147;* visual tasks required, 142, *145*
Vision, human, 14, *14*
Visual Comfort Probability (VCP), *69*
Visual field, changes in old age, 178
Visual tasks, 22; of VDT users, 142, *145*

Wall-bracketed fixtures, 68-69; for the aged, 178; uplights, 35
Wallcovering, and grazing light, 167
Walls, tall, uplighting for, 35
Wallwashing, 27, 30-31, *30, 35,* 38, *76,* 121, 203; and ceiling type, 43; low-pressure sodium lights for, *Plate 3, 99;* specifications for, 50
Warm colors, 20; contrasts, *Plate 1, 96-97*
Weatherproof receptacles, 191
Weiss, Tully, 196; *Private Laserium, Plate 15, 108-9*
Western exposures, and plant growth, 183
Wheelchairs, accommodations for, *177, 179,* 180-81, *181*
Wilfred, Thomas, Lumia: A Study from "The Firebirds," *Plate 17, 112*
Willson, David Winfield, 130-33
Window coverings, and energy conservation, 19
Window glass, and color transmission, *17*
Window wall, reflective coating to control daylight, *156*
Windows: as black mirrors, 16, *18;* configurations, and penetration of daylight, 15-16, *16;* heat loss from, 16; shading of, 145; tall, 16, wide, 16
Winter sunlight, color of, *Plate 8, 102-3*
Wiring: old, hazards of, 120; outdoor, building codes, 188; concealment of, *190,* 191
Working samples of light sources, 59
Workstations, *143,* 147, *147;* portable, 72